ROMANTIC LEGENDS OF SAKYA BUDDHA

ROMANTIC LEGENDS OF SAKYA BUDDHA

BY

SAMUEL BEAL

GYAN

ISBN : 978-81-212-1806-1(HB)

First Published, 1875

Published, 2018

Published by

Gyan Publishing House
5, Ansari Road
Daryaganj, New Delhi-110002
Phone: 011-47034999, 9811692060
www.gyanbooks.com
E-mail: books@gyanbooks.com

Printed at: G. Print Process, Delhi.

TO

JAMES FERGUSSON, Esq., F.R.S., D.C.L., etc.

Dear Mr. Fergusson,

When I first discovered in the India Office Library a Chinese copy of the following work, I purposed to publish an entire translation of it. Being unable to carry out this purpose, I still desired to publish it in as complete a form as possible. But even here fresh difficulties arose, nor should I have been able to produce the following abbreviated translation, had it not been for your generous and liberal support. I gladly avail myself, therefore, of your permission to inscribe to you the work, such as it is, in grateful acknowledgment of your assistance, and in the hope that it may still be of service in supplementing (to some extent, at least) your own labours in the field of Buddhist Archæology.

INTRODUCTION.

THIS work is a translation of the Chinese version of the "Abhinishkramana Sûtra",[1] done into that language by Djnanakuta, a Buddhist priest from North India, who resided in China during the Tsui dynasty, *i. e.*, about the end of the sixth century, A.D.

It would seem from a consideration of the title of the seventeenth chapter, "Leaving the palace for a religious life", that originally the story of the "Abhinishkramana"[2] was simply that of Buddha's flight from his palace to become an ascetic. Afterwards, the same title was applied to the complete legend (as in the present work), which includes his previous and subsequent history.

A very valuable date, later than which we cannot place the origin of the story, may be derived from the colophon at the end of the last chapter of the book. It is there stated that the "Abhinishkramana Sûtra" is called by the school of the Dharmaguptas *Fo-pen-hing-king;* by the Sarvastivadas it is called *Ta-chwang-*

---

1 Wassilief (*Bouddhisme*, § 114).

2 Burnouf, *Lotus*, p. 333, has an instructive note on this word. The expression used in the Chinese perfectly confirms his criticism; *Shi-kung chuh-kia*, "leaving the palace to become a recluse", is the title of the chapter in question.

yen (great magnificence, *i.e.*, "Lalita Vistara"); by the Mahâsañghikas it is called *Ta-sse, i. e.*, Mahavastu.[1]

We know from the "Chinese Encyclopædia", *Kai-yuen-shi-kiau-mu-lu,* that the *Fo-pen-hing* was translated into Chinese from Sanscrit, by a priest called Chu-fa-lan, so early as the eleventh year of the reign of Wing-ping *(Ming-ti),* of the Han dynasty, *i. e.*, 69 or 70 A.D. We may, therefore, safely suppose that the original work was in circulation in India for some time previous to this date.

It must be borne in mind, however, that several translations of the "Legend of Buddha" are quoted under the name *Fo-pen-hing.*[2] The first, which we have already alluded to, the original of which was lost so early as the beginning of the Tang dynasty, was in five chapters (*kiouen*). There is allusion to another translation (*Kai-yuen-shi-kiau-mu-lu,* vol. i, cap. i, fol. $\frac{36}{2}$), bearing the same name but in *one* chapter, now lost. Again, it is stated (vol. ii, chap. xiii, fol. $\frac{20}{2}$, and vol. iii, chap. xx, fol. $\frac{32}{2}$, *op. cit.*) that a work called *Fo-*

---

[1] The Chinese title of this book is given by Wassalief (*Bouddhisme,* § 114), as "da cine", in the German edition (*Der Buddhismus,* § 114) as "ta-king", in either case I suppose there is a mistake of transcription, as the title is plainly "ta-sse", the "great thing or compilation". That this is really the equivalent of "Mahavastu" is evident, not only because "vastu" is the literal rendering of "sse", *thing*—but also from the remarks of Bournouf (*Introd. to Ind. Bud.*, p. 452). The latter writer speaks of the Mahavastu, as "volumineux recueil de légendes relatives à la vie religieuse de Çakya," a description which agrees completely with the character of the work here translated.

[2] Amongst others, the work here translated is constantly referred to in the "Fa-yuen-chu-lin" (*e. gr., Yuen,* 8th fol. $\frac{31}{2}$) and in the "Commentary of *Wong-Puh*", as the *Fo-pen-hing.*

sho-hing-tsan-king-fu," in five chapters, composed originally by Asvagosha, and translated into Chinese by Dharmalatsin, an Indian priest of the Northern Liang dynasty (502-555 A.D.), is also called by many writers *Fo-pen-hing.* Again (vol. ii, chap. xiii, fol. $\frac{21}{1}$, *op. cit.*), it is said that a work called *Fo-pen-hing-king,* in seven chapters, was translated by a Shaman of Liang-Chau (called *Ratnamegha,* chap. xx, fol. $\frac{32}{2}$, *op. cit.*), of the Sung dynasty (420-477 A.D.) The writer then adds that this last-named translation is sometimes called *Fo-pen-hing-tsan-king.* The Chinese word *tsan* is generally used to denote the class of Buddhist works known in Sanscrit as Udanas, *i. e.,* works composed in laudatory verses.[1]

These statements are in agreement with the opinion of the learned translator of the "Lalita Vistara", from the Thibetan. In his opinion, that work was finally adjusted in its present form at the last council held under Kanishka,[2] four hundred years after the death of Buddha. "This would give it an antiquity of two thousand years," he adds,[3] although the original treatise must be attributed to an earlier date.

The inscriptions found on Buddhist ruins, recently

---

1 This copy of the *Fo-pen-hing,* is probably another translation of the one originally composed by Asvagosha *in verse.* The date of Asvagosha is uncertain; we know that he was contemporary with Nagarjuna, who is generally placed 400 years after Buddha; we shall not be wrong, therefore, if we suppose him to have lived somewhere during the first century B.C.

2 The date of Kanishka is the great desideratum in the History of Northern Buddhism.

3 "Histoire du Bouddha Sakya-Mouni," by Mme. Mary Summers, Index, *sub voc.,* "Lalita Vistara."

discovered in India, confirm this hypothesis. Many of the stories related in the following pages are found sculptured at Sanchi, and some, as I believe, at Bharhut. If the date of these topes is to be placed between Asoka (about 300 B.C.) and the first century of the Christian era, it will be seen that the Records of the Books and of the stone Sculptures are in agreement.

The author of "Three Lectures on Buddhism" states, however, "that nearly all the legends which claim to refer to events many centuries before Christ, cannot be proved to have been in circulation earlier than the 5th or 6th century A.D."[1] The legends to which this writer refers are these, "the pre-existence of Buddha in heaven—his birth of a virgin—salutation by angels—recognition by Asita (Simeon)—presentation in the Temple—baptism by fire and water—disputation with the doctors—temptation in the wilderness—life passed in preaching and working miracles—transfiguration on the mount — descent into hell — ascension into heaven," etc. Some of these events I do not find named in any Chinese work within my reach. But others are undoubtedly commonly referred to. The previous existence of Bodhisatwa in heaven—his miraculous incarnation — the songs of the Suddhvasa Devas (angels) at his birth—the events of his early childhood—his temptation in the desert—and his life of continual labour and travel—these points of agreement with the Gospel narrative naturally arouse curiosity and require examination.[2]

---

1 Three Lectures on Buddhism, by the Rev. E. Eitel. Lec. i, p. 5.
2 They have ever done so. The Franciscan monk Plano Car-

If we could prove that they were unknown in the East for some centuries *after* Christ, the explanation would be easy. But all the evidence we have goes to prove the contrary. Nor can we dismiss this consideration in the way a late writer has done (Bastian, "*Weltauffassung der Buddhisten*", p. 18), by saying that all these legends or stories (*erzälungen*), wherever found, are equally worthless, that they are, in fact, "exploded myths".

How then may we explain the matter? It would be better at once to say that in our present state of knowledge there is no complete explanation to offer. We must wait until dates are finally and certainly fixed.[1]

We cannot doubt, however, that there was a large mixture of Eastern tradition, and perhaps Eastern teaching, running through Jewish literature at the time of Christ's birth, and it is not unlikely that a certain amount of Hebrew folk-lore had found its way to the East. It will be enough for the present to denote this

---

pini reports that "the Cathayans have an Old and New Testament of their own, and Lives of the Fathers, and religious recluses, and buildings used for churches," etc. (*Yule's Cathay*). Compare also what Andrew Corsalis says in his letter to Duke Lorenzo de' Medici (do. cxli, *n.*) In a Chinese work on the "Art of War" (under the heading *Fa-lan-ki*—gun), it is particularly mentioned that the Portuguese on their first visit to Canton from Malacca, spent the greater portion of their time in reading Buddhist books. [For other allusions, *vide Yule, op. cit., passim,* and other writers down to Huc and Gabet.]

[1] It would be a natural inference that many of the events in the legend of Buddha were borrowed from the Apocryphal Gospels (compare *e. gr.*, the "Gospel of the infancy", cap. xx; "Our Lord learning his alphabet", with the account given in chap. xi, of this volume), if we were quite certain that these Apocryphal Gospels had not borrowed from it.

intercommunication of thought, without entering further into minute comparisons.[1]

It would be out of place in a work like this to enter into questions which seem to present such little difficulty to the numerous writers on Buddhism, who, in their lectures and articles, tell us that it teaches atheism, annihilation, and the non-existence of soul. These statements are more easily made than proved. It would be better, at least, if they were not so frequently repeated in the face of contrary statements made by those well able to judge respecting the matter.[2]

I have called this work a "Romantic Legend", because, as is well known, the first romances were merely metrical histories. There can be no doubt that the present work contains as a woof (so to speak), some of the earliest verses (Gâthas) in which the History of Buddha was sung, long before the work itself was penned. These

---

[1] Readers will observe several coincidences in the following pages beyond those already referred to. The most singular of these is the aim of Buddha to establish a "Religious Kingdom" (Dharmachakra), *i. e.*, "a Kingdom of Heaven." We are told again (Lightfoot, *Exercit. Talmud*, sub cap. ix, v. 2, St. John's Gospel) that the Jews believed in the pre-existence of souls, and a modified form of the metempsychosis. The singular agreement between the Buddhist "Metta," and the "Charity" of the New Testament has called forth a remark from Mr. Alwis that the coincidence is "very remarkable" (*Pali Translations*, part i, p. 16). The account given by St. Peter (Ep. ii, cap. 3) of the earth once destroyed by water, and about to be destroyed by fire, is in agreement with the Buddhist story (*vide Catena, sub voc.*, Kalpa); many other parallellisms might be pointed out.

[2] Compare for instance the remarks of the priest Migettuwatte, in the Buddhist controversy held at Pantura, August 26th, 1873, respecting the existence of "individual soul." Many of the writers on "Buddhism" place such implicit faith in the statements of M. Bart. St. Hilaire as to adopt his clever epigrams as facts, without enquiry.

verses, even in the Chinese, are frequently so confused (like the Greek chorus) as to defy exact analysis. They were evidently composed in another dialect. Just as "the Romance language was first employed to signify the Roman language, as spoken in European provinces," so these Gâthas were evidently composed in different Prakrit forms (during a period of disintegration) before the more modern type of Sanscrit was fixed by the Rules of Panini, and the popular epics of the Mahâbharata and the Ramâyana.

The interest of the book will be found to result, not from any critical studies (which I would fain have attempted), found herein, but from the stories which throw light on contemporaneous architectural works in India.[1] One or two of these stories occur in the Panchatantra. With respect to others, they are at least amusing, and lend an interest to the subject (from their very *naiveté*), if not of any scientific value.

I am responsible for most of the restorations of proper names from the Chinese. I cannot doubt that many of these are defective and some incorrect. But no one who has attempted such a task as the conversion of obscure phonetic symbols, like the Chinese

[1] An interesting identification is derived from p. 302 in the present work, from which we see that fig. 2, pl. xxxi, *Tree and Serpent Worship*, relates to Buddha, when a fierce storm inundated the region of Uravilva. It is plain, from the trees being half immersed, that the occasion is a sudden inundation; the square or oblong dry spot in front, is where Buddha had been sitting; the boat in front is that in which he suddenly appears; and the fig-tree and throne on the right, fix the locality as in the neighbourhood of Uravilva. It is satisfactory to be able to explain this scene, which has hitherto baffled the curiosity of those interested in the subject.

sounds found in this book, into intelligible language, will be severe in criticising these mistakes.

I hope, however, that the errors are not of so grave a character as to mislead the student. I have carefully compared all the available authorities with my own restorations, and where I could find guidance or information, I have willingly and thankfully adopted it.

It only remains for me to express my great acknowledgments to Dr. Rost, the Librarian of the India Office, for his invariable kindness in encouraging these studies, but particularly for securing for me temporary employment in his department, through which I was able to find and use the Chinese work here translated.

THE

ROMANTIC HISTORY OF BUDDHA.[1]

THE Legend opens with an account of Mâudgalyâyana's[2] visit to the city of Râjagriha, to beg his daily alms. Being early, he transports himself by his spiritual power from earth to heaven.[3] In heaven he hears strange tidings respecting the difficulty of meeting with a Buddha. On his part, he instructs the occupants of the heaven he visited in the mysteries of the law, and again descends to earth.

CHAPTER I.

THE first part of the first section, termed "Fah-sin-kung-yang-pin," *i. e.*, "exciting a disposition to nourish and cherish (religious principles)."

Djnãnakûta,[4] a Shaman (of the) Brahman (caste and) a native of

---

1 The original title is "Fu-pen-hing-tsi-king," which Wassiljew (p. 114, "Buddhismus") translates "Biography of Sâkyamuni and his Companions."

2 In the original the name of this disciple of Buddha is always rendered Muh-kin-lin, which should be restored to Mugalan, showing (as it would seem) that the Chinese version was made from Prakrit.

3 In the original, "the pure abodes," *i. e.*, the Heaven known as that of the Suddhavâsa kayikas, who occupy the third tier of the Rupaloka.

4 I have restored the original "Tche-na-kiu-to," to Djñanakûta

the country of Gandhâra,[1] of North India, reverently adores (the name of) Vairôchana[2] Buddha, the infinitely wise.[3]

Thus have I heard; on a certain occasion, Bhagavat (the Blessed one, *i. e.*, Buddha) was residing in the city of Râjagriha, within the Kalanda venuvana,[4] with a congregation of the great Bhikshus, five hundred in all. At this time Tathâgata was established in the condition of a Buddha, free for ever from the possibility of sorrow and pain, and was therefore named Djina[5]—possessed of all wisdom—versed in the practice of it—perfectly acquainted with it; firmly grounded in the ways of Heaven (heavenly conduct) and in the ways of purity and holiness—possessed of independent being,[6]—like all the lords of the world (Buddhas)—ready to accommodate himself to all possible circumstances. Thus gifted, he was dwelling amongst the four orders of his disciples, Bhikshus, Bhikshuṇîs, Upâsakas, and Upâsikâs, by whom he was religiously venerated and honoured exceedingly: and besides these

---

(mass or heap of wisdom) from Julien's "Méthode," No. 119, where there is a similar restoration of Djnãnabhadra. The *tika* in the Chinese original explains the name by the rendering "virtuous mind or thought" (tih-chi).

[1] For an account of Gandhâra, as a most flourishing seat of Buddhism, *vide* Jul. iii, 307. It corresponds with Cabul and neighbouring district.

[2] Vairôchana, rendered into Chinese as *pien-chao, i. e.*, universal brilliancy. This agrees very well with its derivation from *ruch*, to shine, with the preposition *vi*, denoting dispersion (and so agreeing with Ch. *pien*). In vindication of a translation I have already given of this title ("Catena of Buddh. Scp.," p. 373), as equivalent to "the Omnipresent," I will add here, that the Chinese explanation in the "Fa-kai-lih-tu" (*Kieuen-hia-che-hia*, p. 12), is "present in every place" (*pien-yih-tsai-chu*).

[3] Literally "ocean of wisdom,"—compare "Dalai Lama."

[4] A garden of bamboos, near Râjagriha.

[5] The Vanquisher.

[6] In the Chinese "tseu-tsai," which is the general rendering of the Sanscrit *Isvara* , but Jul. "Méthode," p. 79, explains the term by the Sanscrit *Prabhu, i. e.*, master or lord. On the other hand, the term is of very frequent occurrence in later Buddhist books, as equal to *Swayambhu*, or the Pali *Sayan bhu* (not communicated by others). Mr. Hodgson seems to favour the idea that the Nepalese expression *Nirlipt*, is only another rendering of the same phrase. ("Collected Essays," p. 105.)

there were various kings, ministers, and nobles; with Brahmans, Shamans, and heretical teachers — all desirous to provide him with food and drink, clothing and bedding and necessary medicines, the four requirements (allowed to every Bôdhisatwa).

At this time, the honourable Mogalan at early dawn, having arranged his robes, and holding his begging dish in his hands, entered the city of Râjagriha, desiring to go his round to ask for food (go a-begging). Then Mogalan standing alone, thought thus: "I am somewhat early this morning for begging, let me then first visit the Suddhavâsa Devas." Having thought thus with himself, just as a champion (Malla or Litchavi) stretches out or draws in his arm or his neck, so from Râjagriha did he transport his body invisibly to the heaven of the Suddhavâsa Devas, and there stand awhile in a fixed position.

At this time an innumerable number of the Devas of this Heaven having observed Mogalan thus present in their midst, were filled with joy, and each one addressing his neighbour, said, "we ought all of us now to go to worship the venerable Mogalan." Having spoken thus together, they repaired to the place where Mogalan was, and paid reverence to his feet, and then stood apart.[1] They then addressed him thus: "Venerable Mogalan! seldom does this occur! seldom indeed!

"Oh! venerable Mogalan, how hard is it to see or to encounter in the world one who is known as Buddha, the world honoured,[2] Tathâgata, Araható sammá sambhuddassa![3] one who through countless Kalpas has been diligently practising all the necessary conduct for attaining this condition, even as the Gâtha[4] says:

"'Through myriads of Kalpas
Diligently seeking the way of Bôdhi,

---

[1] Yih-mien, corresponding to "ekamantam"—on one side, *i. e.*, either in front, or the right or left hand.

[2] This title of Buddha, so far as I know, is not found in the southern school. It is restored by Julien to *Lôkadjyêshtha*. It corresponds in a remarkable manner with the Greek phrase "Anaxandrōn" ("Juventus Mundi," chap. vi).

[3] For an explanation of these words, *vide* Spence Hardy, M.B., p. 359.

[4] These Gâthas occur throughout the work we are translating, and probably represent the old memorial verses, by which a know-

After the lapse of such a period
The Heavenly treasure appears with men!
The one difficult person to see in the world,
Is simply this Buddha—world honoured name!'"

At this time the venerable Mâha Mogalan hearing this Gâtha from the mouth of the Suddhavâsa Devas, his entire frame trembled with awe, and the hairs on his body stood on end; then he reflected thus: "Seldom! seldom indeed beyond expression! and difficult, is it to see or encounter one who is called Buddha, etc.; difficult to meet with such an one who appears but once through countless ages!"

At this time the venerable Mâha Mogalan, for the sake of those Devas, and in their abode, delivered innumerable profound and mysterious expositions of the Law—made clear countless religious truths—set forth to their very bottom endless difficulties of the deepest meaning, so that all these Devas were filled with joy, and derived the greatest benefit from the instruction thus delivered. Having thus explained the law in its various relations, the venerable Mogalan forthwith descended again to Jambudwîpa, just as a champion lets his arm drop down after exercise. So he returned to Râjagriha, and forthwith proceeded in an orderly manner to beg his food from door to door, and then returned to his own place of rest. Having finished his necessary meal, he bound up his begging dish in his garment, and having washed his feet, straightway proceeded to the place where Buddha was, and having arrived there, after religiously venerating the foot of Buddha, he took a seat on one side. After being thus seated, he turned towards Buddha and spoke as follows, with respect to the places he had visited: "World-honoured! this morning I have been to Râjagriha to perform my duty of begging alms; and having by the way gone to the Suddhavâsa Heavens, the Devas there spoke to me thus: 'It is difficult to see, difficult to meet with Tathâgata,[1] honoured by the world, amongst men.'" Having said so much he

---

ledge and history of Buddhism was perpetuated before the discovery of the art of writing. *Vide* Max Müller's "Chips," vol. i, p. 300. [The explanation given by Babu Rajendralal is fully borne out by the character of the Gâthas in the present work.]

[1] The expression Tathâgata is so well known, that it needs no

continued his address thus: "World-honoured! this communication, so wonderful to hear, having been finished, I felt truly in a strait how to understand what was said, viz., that only once in the midst of countless Kalpas does a Buddha appear!"

At this time Buddha addressed Mogalan and said: "Mogalan! the Devas of the Suddhavâsa Heavens have little knowledge and imperfect perception — they may by their limited wisdom know something of the affairs of a myriad kalpas[1] or so; but Mogalan! I can remember the virtuous principles which were adopted by countless, infinite Buddhas as the groundwork of their future supremacy. Mogalan! I remember when in former days I was a Chakravarti Râja,[2] that I met with thirty tens of myriads of Buddhas, all of them named by the same name, which was Sâkya Tathâgata, all of whom were attended by disciples (hearers), many and honourable, who provided for their masters the four necessary requirements, that is to say, clothes, meat and drink, bed furniture, and medicinal preparations. But from none of them did I receive an intimation that I should become a Buddha, etc. Mogalan! I remember in bygone ages when I was a Chakravarti Râja, that I met with eighty myriads of Buddhas, all called Dipañkara, whose disciples, etc.

"Mogalan! I remember in bygone ages, when I was a Chakravarti Râja meeting with thirty myriads of Buddhas, all called Pushya,[3] etc.

"Mogalan! I remember in bygone ages meeting with nine myriads of Buddhas, all called Kâsyapa, etc. [and so with sixty thousand called Dipaprabhâsa,[4] etc.[5]] At length I remember that Mâitreya, for the first time, conceived the purpose of arriving at the condition of a Buddha; he was then a Chakravarti Râja, called Vâirôchana.

---

explanation—it seems to correspond very closely to the phrase rendered from the Greek, "he who should come."

[1] A Kalpa, a sæculum or αἰών of somewhat indefinite length.

[2] A Chakravarti Râja, *i.e.*, a universal monarch. One who governs a *Sakwala*, or entire world (*vide* "Journal Asiatique," tome ii, No. 4).

[3] *Vide* Jul. "Méthode," 30.

[4] Teng-ming.

[5] I have not considered it worth while to enumerate these purely fictitious personages.

"Mogalan! this Vâirôchana preceded me by more than forty kalpas, after which I also began to aspire to the condition of a Buddha."

BUDDHA now proceeds to mention in detail the different names of his predecessors. This corresponds to the list found in the "Buddhawanso," as the succeeding section does to the "Râjawanso" (*vide J. R. A. S. B.*, 1838. 926 *ss.*)

§ 2. At this time the world-honoured one was residing at Srâvastî, in the Jetavana Vihâra, possessed of the same supereminent qualities as we have before briefly mentioned. Then Buddha, having finished his meal, during seven days lost himself in contemplation,[1] and recalled to his memory the history of all the Buddhas of bygone ages.

At this time, Ananda,[2] after the seven days had elapsed, went to the place where Buddha was, and after adoring his feet, stood on one side, and addressed Buddha thus, "World-honoured! seldom indeed (do we meet with) Tathâgata! his body so pure, and his presence so full of dignity and beauty as now I behold, and still more beautiful and ever more so! World-honoured one! with such boundless faculties for perfect abstraction as you possess, tell me, what are the memories that engage you in Samâdhi, and what the rules and marks of it?"

At this time the world-honoured addressed Ananda, and said: "It is even as you say, Ananda! Tathâgata, if he enters Samâdhi, remembers through bygone ages all the Buddhas who have appeared, and obtained perfect wisdom and spiritual capacities, and in this condition he can remain either a kalpa or any portion of one, reflecting on the character of hundreds of thousands

---

[1] Samâdhi, a condition of ecstacy, in which the mind or soul is freed from all restraint, and enjoys perfect communion with the "other world."

[2] Ananda, the chief of Buddha's disciples, now becomes the interlocutor.

of myriads of Buddhas; for the wisdom of Tathâgata is boundless! And because Tathâgata is possessed of all this wisdom, he has therefore arrived at that shore.[1] Ananda! Tathâgata having finished his meal, passes away for any period of time and meditates upon the affairs that have occurred in other ages, without let or hindrance. What then! Tathâgata practices with ease the Samâdhi, called 'of all the Buddhas,' and passes over to that shore; and this of all the Samâdhis is the most excellent."

Buddha addressed Ananda, "Ananda! I remember in previous ages, endless kalpas ago, there was a Buddha in the world called Indraketu Tathâgata, etc., who saved countless creatures, and was strong to exercise love for their sakes, and by the power of his compassion for all flesh, gave them rest and peace. He was of great personal dignity, and was surrounded by a holy retinue of disciples. Ananda! he had five thousand myriad of followers, all fully arrived at the condition of arhats; the years of his life were five thousand years. This Indraketu Tathâgata predicted that a certain Bôdhisatwa should afterwards appear as a Buddha, and be called Uttaraketu Tathâgata; he in his turn predicted the arrival of a Buddha called Gunaketu; he predicted Prîtiketu; he predicted Dasaketu."[2]

[This first kiouen of the Fu-pen-hing-tsi-king, contains 5235 words, and the cost of carving these words was 2.617 taels (1 tael =6s. 8d.) Ch. Ed.]

CHAPTER II.

THE second part of the first section "exciting a heart ready to nourish and cherish the cause of religion."

"ANANDA! Samantabhadra predicted the advent of a Buddha named Chandra Tathâgata; he predicted Pundara; he predicted Vimala; and so on for twenty-six generations.

---

1 "That shore," an expression for Nirvâna—a condition of perfect release.

2 And so on through sixty-four generations of Buddhas, down to Samantabhadra.

"Ananda, all these Tathâgatas down to the last, each in his turn, received the promise of future perfection, and each of them, I, in my own person, attended and cherished."

At this time the world-honoured one proceeded to recite the following gâthas:

"All these various Tathâgatas,
Sâkya the great Teacher
Using the pure and holy eyes of Buddha[1]
Beholds, without any exception.
Thus the wisdom of Tathâgata
Is inconceivable; the way of Buddha
Neither Devas, nor men,
Are able to understand.
If there be a wise man
Who desires to seek after true wisdom,
Let him read over the names of these Buddhas,
And not long hence he will attain it."

At this time, Ananda addressed Buddha, and said, "World-honoured! that which I have now heard proceed from the golden lips of Buddha, I will hold fast in my memory and not let slip, viz., that which relates to the incomparable and infinite wisdom of all the Buddhas, which has no bounds or limits. World-honoured! Tathâgata truly knows the character of this wisdom; is it not so?"

At this time, the world-honoured addressed Ananda, and said, "the wisdom of Tathâgata is perfectly and thoroughly possessed (by me). My knowledge is that which has no limits or impediment; Tathâgata, as he desires to make the boundaries (of his wisdom) large or narrow, or as he wishes to reflect on the wisdom of all the Buddhas in large or small proportions, is perfectly able to do so according to his wish."

At this time, Ananda addressed Buddha, "World-honoured! like as the Honourable Aniruddha,[2] with his pure and heavenly

---

[1] Buddha acknowledges no teacher, or inspiration of a God; he is "samanta chakkhu," *i.e.*, his eye surveys all the boundaries of knowledge, and he clearly perceives at a glance all truth. (Gogerley).

[2] Aniruddha, one of the Sâkya princes and a disciple of Buddha. Super-eminent for his power of "Divine Sight."

eyes, exceeding the power of men's sight, is able to see a chiliocosm of worlds—(so is the sight of Buddha)—but Tathâgata says, my power of perception is boundless,—pray explain to me the meaning of this."

Buddha, on this, remained silent: and so he continued after the question had been thrice uttered, but then he opened his mouth and answered thus! "Never, Ananda, never should you attempt to compare the wisdom of Tathâgata with that of one of his followers. For let me tell you, at this moment, I, with my pure and heavenly eyes, exceeding the power of human sight, can behold all the Bodhisatwas of all the Buddhakshetras,[1] numerous as the sands of the Ganges, belonging to the Eastern regions of space, and trace the virtuous principles which actuated them first of all to aim at the attainment of Supreme Wisdom. I can see all those Bôdhisatwas who have received the prediction of their future perfection, and those who are now advancing in the way to this end. I can see countless others who, having pursued a consistent course of pure conduct in the presence of all the Buddhas, are now incarnatod from the Tusita[2] Heavens in their mothers' wombs. I can see others who are born (tan-yuh) from their mothers' sides; others I can see growing up as youths; others, living within their palace walls, indulging themselves in sensual pleasures; others finally rejecting the thought of becoming Chakravarti Râjas, and quitting their homes as hermits, to practice the attainment of wisdom; others I can see conquering the four sorts of Satanic attacks they are subjected to; others, under the Bôdhi tree, aiming at Anuttara Samyak Sambôdhi; others emancipated and filled with joy! others, I can see, seated in a becoming manner, considering the distinction of two ways (of proceeding)[3]; others, I can see, turning the wheel of the law[4]; others, I can see, for the sake of all creatures, giving up their life, and preparing to enter the perfect condition of Nirvâna. Again, I can see others who, after they have entered Nirvâna, have left the true law to abide, and the law of Images,[5] for longer or shorter

---

[1] *I. e.*, the innumerable worlds of space.

[2] The joyous heavens in which all the Bôdhisatwas (beings about to become Buddhas) are born, prior to their last incarnation.

[3] *I. e.*, whether to preach the law or refrain from doing so.

[4] This expression will be considered under a future section.

[5] For a full explanation of these periods, *vide* "Lotus," p. 365.

periods. Thus, Ananda, can I see the countless Bodhisatwas of the Eastern region of space, and the various stages and histories of the Buddhas. And as with the Eastern, so with the Southern; Western, and other quarters of space.

[The second kiouen contains 6481 words, and cost 3.24 taels.]

CHAPTER III.

Exciting to religious sentiment.

At this time, Ananda arose from his seat, and, baring his right shoulder, &c., addressed Buddha thus:—"World-honoured! Tathâgata in ages past, by religious service to the various Buddhas, sought to attain perfection; by whose aid and instrumentality was it, that Buddha, sowing the seeds of virtue for the sake of future ages, thus aimed at Bôdhi?"

Buddha replied, "Ananda! listen and examine my words! For your sake, I will recount the names of those Buddhas, and the places where those seeds of virtue were sown. Ananda! I remember in ages gone by, there was a Buddha born in the world, called Dipañkara Tathâgata, &c., and by his side I laid the foundation of a virtuous life for the future perfection of Buddha.

Again, there was a Buddha who appeared in the world, called Anuttara; after him, Padmottara; after him, Atyushagami [and so on for five generations]; after him, Vipasyi; after him, Sikhi and Vishaman; after these, Kakutsanda and Kanakamuni, and Kâsyapa. Moreover, I have practiced every virtuous principle by the side of Maitreya Bôdhisatwa, for the benefit of future ages. And so the Gâtha says,

'This eminently virtuous Buddha,
Sâkya muni Tathâgata,
Removing lust, arriving at Rest;
Has sedulously prepared himself for coming.'"

At this time, Ananda asked Buddha this question—"In all these cases what means did Tathâgata employ for the purposes aforesaid?" On this, Buddha addressed Ananda, and said, "Ananda! I remember when Dipañkara Buddha was born into the world, that countless multitudes of people were spreading their priceless garments in the way for him to walk upon; they covered the earth with them completely. Seeing this, and having on me only a deer-skin doublet, I took this off to spread on the ground. Then all the people, in anger, took my poor garment from the place where it lay, and dragged it away, and flung it on one side; whilst I, in grief, thought, 'Alas for me! Will not the world-honoured Dipañkara pity my case and think of me in my distress?' No sooner had I thought thus, than Buddha, knowing my heart, took pity on me. Accordingly, by his Divine power, he caused a portion of the road to appear as if it were covered with mud,[1] on which those men, in astonishment looked at one another, but not one of them entered the muddy place to help Dipañkara across. Then I, after some thought, spread out my skin garment on the muddy spot, and undoing my hair, covered the garment with my hair, so that Buddha might cross over in perfect comfort, as on a bridge. And then I prayed that I might in future ages become a Buddha, even as Dipañkara, possessed of the same miraculous power, and worshipped alike by gods and men; and then I vowed that if Dipañkara did not give me a prediction of becoming Buddha, I would not rise from out the mud. Then the earth quaked six times, and Dipañkara predicted that I should be born as Sâkya Muni[2].

"Ananda! observe well my words, they are not equivocal words! for as Dipañkara Buddha gave me this distinct assurance and instructed me, so, relying on the merit of my long preparation for this dignity I have now arrived at the condition of Anutara Samyak Sambôdhi."

At this time the world-honoured one uttered this Gâtha, and said,

"Though the heavens were to fall to earth,
And the great world be swallowed up and pass away:
Tho' Mount Sumeru were to crack to pieces,
And the great ocean be dried up,
Yet, Ananda! be assured
The words of the Buddha are true."

The world-honoured having pronounced this Gâtha, he again

---

1 This fable is alluded to in Julien, ii, 97, and also by Bigandet, "Legend of the Burmese Buddha," p. 400.

2 *Vide* this fable fully translated, J. R. A. S., Feb. 1873.

addressed Ananda and said "Ananda! I remember in years gone by there was a Tâthâgata born, whose name was Sarvâbhibu (Tsing-yeh-tsai); on one occasion I scattered some golden flowers before this Buddha, and uttered this vow: 'may I in years to come obtain a body endowed with all the distinguishing marks and properties of this world-honoured Tathâgata.' Then that Buddha knowing the thoughts of my heart immediately smiled gently,[1] on which his disciples respectfully inquired the reason of his doing so, whereupon that Buddha addressed them thus: 'Bhikshus! do you see this man scattering upon me (or before me) these golden flowers? To which they replied in the affirmative, on which he continued, this man, after a Kalpa has gone by, shall become a Buddha, and his name shall be Sâkya-muni Tathâgata. On that occasion, Ananda, although I received this positive assurance, I ceased not in my earnest endeavours to obtain the requisite merit for arriving thus at perfection, and so I was born in countless worlds in the Brahma heavens, and as a Chakravarttin monarch, and on one occasion I was born as a king called Sadarsana. The very streets, and gates, and towers of my capital city were all ornamented with the purest gold, and so the gardens, fountains, tanks, etc., were all ornamented, and this in consequence of my merit in giving the golden flowers, and shortly afterwards I attained the perfection of a Buddha, and turned the pure and incomparable wheel of the law.

"Ananda, I remember in ages gone by, there was a Tathâgata called Padmottara, and in whose honour I scattered silver flowers and made a similar vow, and from whom I received a similar prediction, in consequence of which, among other births I was born as a king called Mahâsadarsana, in a city called Kusina, all of silver (as before). Ananda! from the remotest period till now it has always been the case, that at the time of the birth of Bôdhisatwa, he should without assistance walk seven paces to the East, the West, the North, and South. Ananda! at the time of the birth of Pad-

---

[1] This notice of the smile of Buddha, illustrates the reference to the same token in many mediæval legends, such as, *e. g.*, that of Edward the Confessor when he saw the Seven Sleepers of Ephesus; also when he smiled during the celebration of the Holy Sacrament, seeing the King of Denmark drowning as he fell from his boat, etc. (*Vide* Carter's "Specimens of Ancient Sculpture," p. 17.)

mottara Buddha, when his feet touched the ground in each place as he walked to the North, South, East, and West there sprang up a Lotus for his feet to rest on, and hence his name, for it came to pass that countless thousands and myriads of Devas, Nagas, Yakshas, Gandharvas, Asuras, Mahoragas, men and not men, (Kinnaras), at one time cried out with a loud voice in every place 'this great Bôdhuatwa's name shall be Padmottara,' and because of this he was so named by men.

"Ananda! I remember in years gone by there was a Buddha born called Atyushagami, etc., in whose honour I offered a handful of golden millet, and in consequence he predicted that after a thousand Kalpas I should become a Buddha called Sâkya Muni (as before). Ananda! Atyushagami Tathâgata, when he wished to go to a town or village to beg his food, would proceed with footsteps six cubits from the ground, and so with a loud voice the supernatural beings, before named, cried out 'his name is Atyushagami (going very high),' etc. Ananda! I remember in years gone by there was another Buddha, on whom I conferred a house as a charitable offering, and invited the priests and Bhikshus to come to it. In consequence of this I received a prediction that I should be born after five hundred Kalpas as Sâkya Muni (as before); in one of my subsequent births I was born as a Chakravarti Râja called Sudarsana, on which occasion Sâkra sent Visvakarman to build me a house,[1] after which I obtained perfection (as before).

"Ananda! I remember in years gone by there was a Buddha born called Sâkya Muni, etc., his name the same as mine, and his father and mother in name and life the same as mine. I offered to this Tathâgata a Kusumana flower (The Kâsyapiya school says he offered 'a handful of gold,') on which I received a prediction that after one hundred Kalpas, etc. And so finally by fully keeping the Bôdhi pakckika Dharma,[2] I obtained perfection. Ananda! I remember in years gone by there was a Buddha born called Tishya Tathâgata, etc., before whom I scattered a handful of powdered

---

[1] Literally a hole or sty dug out of the earth, ornamented with different precious things.

[2] That is, the thirty-seven conditions necessary for those to possess who are to become Buddhas. (*Vide* "Eitel Handbook," *sub voc.*)

sandal wood, and so received the prediction that after ninety-five Kalpas, etc. Ananda! I remember in years gone by there was a Buddha born called Pushya Tathâgata, etc., and whilst this Buddha was residing in a Pansal,[1] I was so overjoyed by beholding him that for seven days and seven nights with raised palms interlaced together, and standing on one foot, I repeated this Gâtha of praise, 'Above heaven, below heaven, there is no one like Buddha. In every region of the universe there is none to be compared with him. I have seen an end of all perfection in the world, but no such being as Buddha have I seen!' Ananda! after thus applauding that Buddha, and having vowed as before, then that Buddha predicted that after ninety-four Kalpas I should attain perfection and be called Sâkya Muni. Ananda! after this prediction I relaxed no effort, but after various births as a Chakravarti Râja, and as Brahma, etc., having attained incomparable skill in dialectical discussions, and the interpretation of the Sacred Books I obtained perfection.

"Ananda! I remember in ages gone by there was a Buddha born, called Chun-li (true reason.) [The Kâsyapîyas call him Kin-yih-tsai-li (Satyadarsi).] I offered all sorts of flowers to him, and obtained a positive prediction to the same effect (after ninety-three Kalpas).

"Ananda! I remember in years gone by there was a Buddha born called Vipasyi, to whom I offered a handful of pulse, and obtained a positive prediction (ninety-one Kalpas), after which I was born as a Chakravarti called Agrajanman (teng-sing), possessed of the four quarters of the world, and afterwards obtained the half seat of Sâkra and occupied it, and then reached perfection. Ananda! I remember in ages gone by that there was a Buddha born called Sikhi, to him I offered a priceless robe, as well as to his followers, praying as before, from whom I received a positive prediction that after thirty-one Kalpas I should attain perfection, after which passing through every kind of birth I was possessed of the most beautiful garments of Kasi wool, etc., and then reached perfection.

"Ananda! I remember a Buddha called Viswabhû, to whom I made offerings of the richest food, and obtained a positive assu-

---

[1] That is a "leafy hut" or a cell covered with leaves.

rance (thirty Kalpas). Ananda! I remember a Buddha called Kakusanda, and another called Kanakamuni, and another called Kâsyapa. So I remember through endless ages gone by, by the side of Mâitreya Bôdhisatwa making these religious offerings to countless Buddhas, with a view to obtain for myself the perfection I now enjoy.

"And now to recount; I remember one hundred asañkheyas of Kalpas ago, a Buddha called[1] Dipankara, etc., a hundred tens of myriads of Kalpas ago, a Buddha called Sarvabhibhû;[2] five hundred Kalpas ago a Buddha called Atyushagami[3] (doubtful); one hundred Kalpas ago a Buddha called Sakyamuni;[4] ninety-four Kalpas ago a Buddha called Pushya;[5] ninety-three Kalpas ago a Buddha called Satyadarsi;[6] ninety-one Kalpas ago a Buddha called Vipasyi;[7] thirty-one Kalpas ago a Buddha called Sikhi,[8] and in the middle of the same Kalpa a Buddha called Devasruta,[9] and in the present Bhadra Kalpa[10] Kakutasanda,[11] Kanakamuni,[12] Kasyapa, and myself.[13] Ananda! Dipañkara's life numbered eighty-four thousand myriad lakhs of years. [This is according to the Mâhîsâsakas. The Kâsyapîyas say that Dipañkara lived one Kalpa.] Sarvabhibhû lived eighty thousand lakhs of years. [The Mahîsâsakas say so, but the Kâsyapîyas say one Kalpa.] Padmottara Buddha lived eighty thousand years. Atyushagami seventy thousand years; Sakyamuni eighty thousand years; Tishya Buddha sixty thousand years; Pushya Buddha fifty thousand years; Satyadarsi Buddha forty thousand years; Vipasyi Buddha eighty thousand years; Devasruta Buddha sixty thousand years; Kakusanda forty thousand years; Kanakamuni thirty thousand years; Kâsyapa twenty thousand years; myself eighty years. And so the Gatha says:

"'There are Buddhas who by their spiritual power
Remain in the world to receive homage from men,
And also others their object attained,
Having finished their course, who enter Nervâna.'

---

[1] Brahman. [2] Kshatriya. [3] Brahman.
[4] Kshatriya. [5] Brahman. [6] Kshatriya.
[7] Brahman. [8] Kshatriya. [9] Kshatriya.
[10] Brahman. [11] Kshatriya. [12] Brahman.
[13] Kshatriya.

"Ananda! Dipañkara had 250 myriad lakhs of disciples; after his death, the true law endured 70,000 years; Sarvabhibhû had 14,000 disciples; the true law endured but for a short time; Padmottara had 70,000 disciples; the true law endured 100,000 years; Atyushagami had 60,000 disciples; the true law lasted 71,000 years; Sakyamuni had 1250 disciples; the true law 500 years; the law of images 500 years; Tishya 60,000 lakhs of disciples; the true law 20,000 years; Pushya, countless lakhs of disciples. Satyadarsi had 32,000 lakhs of nahutas of disciples; but the true law lasted but for a short time after his death. Vipasyi held three great assemblies. The true law lasted 20,000 years. Devasruta had two great assemblies; the law lasted 50,000 years. Kakusanda had 40,000 disciples; the true law lasted 500 years. Kanakamuni had 300 myriad disciples, and the true law lasted 29 days. Kâsyapa had 20,000 disciples, and endured 7 days. I, Ananda! have 1250 disciples; my true law will last 500 years, and the law of images 500 years. And now I will briefly recite a Udâna verse—

"'I have spoken of the gifts, and the number of years,
The various names, and the years of their lives;
The various assemblies of the disciples,
The endurance of the true law, and the law of images,
And how all these various Tathâgatas
Entered Nirvâna after dwelling in the world.
The great lion of the tribe of Sâkya
Having said all this, has finished his task.'"

CHAPTER III.

Containing a list of kings (Mahârâjawanso) belonging to the present kalpa (Bhâdra kalpa).

On one occasion Buddha was residing at Râjagriha, in the Kalanda venu vana, with his great disciples, five hundred in all. At this time the world-honoured one, in conformity with the laws of all the Buddhas, etc., addressed the Bhikshus thus: "Listen and weigh well my words all ye Bhikshus."

Then they replied, "gladly and with a believing heart do we attend."

Then Buddha continued, "When the earth was first firmly established, at that time there was an eminent and wealthy Chakravarti called Sammata (chung-tsah-chih). Having firmly established (order), then the whole body of sentient creatures addressed him thus: "Our Lord and Master should now exercise his authority in punishing the wicked and rewarding the good. He ought to divide the lands and distribute to each of us a part for cultivation, and we will pay back to our Lord a portion of the fruits." And he acted accordingly. [Hence he was called "Tai-chung-ping-tang," *i. e.*, equal agreement of all creatures. He was also called KING, and because he looked after the division and protection of the land, he was called Kshatriya Râja.]

Thus things were settled in the first period, and men governed and ruled according to law. Afterwards Sammata[1] Raja had a son called Chun-shih, a Chakravarti, possessed of the seven insignia; in his days the earth was perfectly level, without precipices or valleys, and the fruits of the earth flourished abundantly; there was no crime and no punishment, etc. Among his thousand sons the chief was "i-fi" (Manôrama ?) also called "tsz-yung." He also was a Chakravarti; his chief son was called "chi-che" (the wise one), so called because he received instruction (lit. received rules); he also was a Chakravarti. His son was Agrajanman (head-born), his son Mahâ-Sâgara, and so on down to Mahâ-Prâtapa.

[This fourth Kiouen contains 6490 words, and cost 3.245 taels.]

CHAPTER IV.

BHIKSHUS! that Mahâ-Pratâpa had a son called Manôbhirâma, [and so on for eleven generations down to Sudarsana, Mahâ Sudarsana, Meru, Mahâ Meru]. Bhikshus! Mahâ Meru's descendants were a hundred and one little Chakravartins, who lived at Pattana Poura (Patna ?). The last of that race was Sinhayana, his descendants were sixty-one, all little Chakravartins, who lived at

[1] Ta-chung-so-lai-che-wang.

Benares; the last of these was Narîyana, his sons and grandsons were fifty-six little Chakravartins, who reigned at Ayôdhyâ; the last of this race was Yen-in-Sang (Pratâpajati ?), his descendants were one thousand little Chakravartins, who lived at Kapilaya. The last of these was Brahmadatta, and his descendants fifty-six, who lived at Hastinapoura, the last of these was Hastipa; his descendants, twenty-five who lived at Takshasila; the last of these was Gupta; his descendants, one thousand two hundred, lived at Syâna (?); the last "able to destroy" had ninety descendants, who all lived at Kanyakubja; the last of these had two thousand five hundred descendants, who lived at Champa; the last of his descendants was called Nagadeva; his descendants, twenty-five in number, lived at Rajagriha; the last of these had twenty-five descendants, who lived at Kusinagara. [I omit other names.] Bhikshus! you must know that these little Chakravarti monarchs were all possessed of such merit, that they received the reward of it in their various births in the world, and the excellency of their dominion over men and the great earth.

Bhikshus! I will now proceed to detail the names of the different kings who descended from U-Wang (Fish-King),[1] who reigned at Mithila; he had a son called Chun-Sang (true born), the merit of his ancestors being well exhausted, he was the last of this royal line, and men began to talk about his want of merit and degradation. As the poorest, most pitiable, they also called him O-keuh (Okaka?), and this became his common name; his last descendant was called Ta-man-tso (Mahâkusa?), who having no son, thought thus with himself, "all my predecessors, when they saw the first white hair appear, were in the habit of resigning their kingdom, and after a charitable bequest to the priesthood, they shaved their heads, and became ascetics; and now I have no son, whom then shall I select to succeed me? who is there of my race of sufficient dignity and renown, seeing that I am cut off from the line of kings? Again he thought, "If I do not become an ascetic then I shall lose all connection with the line of holy men who have preceded me." Having reflected thus, Ta-man-tso immediately gave over the kingdom to his great ministers, and surrounded by a vast multitude of followers he left the city and shaved his head, and put on the

---

[1] Makhadeva (Turnour).

robes of a hermit. Having done so, and religiously observed the precepts of morality, and persevered in all the practices of religious meditation, he finally obtained the five supernatural powers and became a Rishi; the years of his life having been extended to a great length, his hairs were white, his flesh withered, and his shoulders bent, unable even with his staff to go far. At this time his disciples, anxious to go here and there for the purpose of begging food, took some soft pliable grass, and having lined a basket therewith they put the Royal Rishi in it, and hung him up from a branch of a tree, for fear the snakes or wild beasts should come and hurt him in their absence. So then they all went their ways, to beg their food. After they had gone it so happened that a huntsman on his tour penetrated so far as these desert mountains; at a distance he perceived the Royal Rishi (hanging in his basket from the tree), and supposing him to be a great white bird he immediately shot him dead. At this time, the Rishi having then been shot, two drops of blood issuing from the wound fell down on the earth below, and then he died; just at this time his disciples having begged their food came back again to the spot, and beheld their old master just expiring, and the two drops of blood on the ground. Then letting down the basket from the tree, and raising a mound of earth, having collected wood they burnt the body of the king, and collecting his bones raised a tower over them, and then offered every kind of perfumed wood and sweet scented flowers before it, in honour of his memory. Meanwhile, on the spot where these two drops of blood fell, there immediately sprang up shoots of the sweet sugar cane, which gradually increased in size and height, till at last, ripened by the heat of the sun, both of the canes burst asunder, and from one there came out a boy and from the other a girl, very beautiful, and quite incomparable for grace. Then the disciples of the Rishi, remembering that their royal master in his life-time had no sons, regarded these two children as his legitimate offspring, they nourished and protected them, and acquainted all the late king's ministers of the extraordinary circumstance of their birth. On hearing it the said ministers were greatly rejoiced, and going to the forest they respectfully conducted the two children back to the palace of their royal father, and had them properly instructed by the Brahmans. Then when they came to consult with the astrologers as to their names, the reply made was this "the first, born by the heat of the sun's rays on the sugar cane, shall be called Sujata (well born); he shall also be called "born of the sugar cane" (Ikshwaku virûdaka), or because of the sun's rays having begotten him, his name shall be Sun-born (Suryavansa). Then the ministers immediately made Ikshwaku king, and Subhadrâ (the name given to the girl), the first of his queens.

Now it so happened that the second wife of the king being extremely lovely had four sons, but Subhadrâ had only one, whose name was "long lived" (Janta), very graceful, and of incomparable beauty, but his size and appearance of strength give no promise of his being king (literally, the bone-sign was not favourable to his being king).[1] Then Subhadrâ, his mother, thought thus within herself, "the children of Ikshwaku are four, viz., Torch-face (ulka mukha), etc., and these are lusty and strong, but my son, and the only one I have, although very beautiful, is not so able-bodied as they, nor so fit for the place of king, by what device then can I contrive to get this my son elected to the kingly office?"

Again she thought "the king when he visits me overflows with passionate love; what then? I will deck myself out in the choicest attire, prepare my body according to the most approved method, by washing, perfuming and painting. I will adorn my hair with the loveliest flowers, and by every wile and device in my power I will enflame the heart of Ikshwaku to inordinate love, and then, if I succeed in so doing, when we are together in secret, I will ask him to comply with my desire." Having reflected thus, and adorned her person, as she intended, with the greatest care, she came forthwith to the presence of the king. The king, seeing his wife coming, was inflamed with excessive love towards her, which she perceived, and was glad to find her plan so successful. Then when the two were reposing together, the wife said "Great king! be it known to you that I should wish to ask a favour, if the king will grant it me." The king replied, "Great queen! whatever you ask I will give without grudge, with much joy." The queen again said, with great earnestness, "Great monarch! without a rival (tsz-tsai), if you consent to give me what I ask, then there must be no change or repentance on your part; if you

[1] No doubt it refers to strength of bones, *i. e.*, manly vigour.

change then I will ask nothing." The king replied, "If I change then let my head burst into seven parts." Then the queen said, "Great king! would that you would expel from the country those four sons of yours, Torch-face and the others, and let my son Janta succeed you on the throne!" Then Ikshwaku Râja replied at once and said, my four sons have done nothing worthy of exile; if you can show me any wrong they have done within my dominions, then they shall not stop here, but shall be expelled at once." The queen answered, "Your majesty has sworn that if you repent or recall your promise then your head shall split into seven pieces." Then the king promised to do what she had requested, and at early morn on the following day called for his four sons and said, "My sons, you have my permission to go where you please, you cannot dwell any longer within my dominions." Then the youths, with bent knees and clasped hands, desired to know what wrong they had done, or what law they had broken, or what fault they had committed, that they should be thus suddenly exiled and driven from the country." Then the king said, "I know, my sons, that you are innocent! it is not my doing or wish to expel you thus, but it is the wish of Subhadrâ, the queen. She asked me to grant her her desire, and I cannot recall my promise, and her request was that you should be banished."

[The mother of the four youths now comes to the king and asks if it be true that her sons are to be banished. The king tells her it is true. Then the concubines, the ministers, soldiers, artificers, and men of all professions, come and desire permission to go into exile with the four princes, their sisters also, and all connected with them, on which the king gives his permission for them all to go.]

Being thus banished, the exiles proceeding northward, arrived at the Himatala mountains, where abiding for a short time, they crossed the Bhâghîrathî river and ascended the Snowy mountains above the river, and there abode for a long while. The four princes dwelling there, in the mountain heights, supported themselves by hunting, feeding on the game they shot. Then gradually going forwards, they arrived at a valley on the southern slopes of the mountains, broad and level, without any precipices or hillocks; the lands fertile, and with no brambles or weeds, and very free from stones and grit. Nothing but the most beautiful forest trees grew there—the Sâla tree, the Talas tree, the Nyagrôdha tree, the Udambara tree, the Kalila tree (kaliya ?), and others; all intertwining their branches, and so making an agreeable shade. Moreover, there was a great variety of flowers there, as *e. gr.*, the Atimukta flower, the Jambu flower, the Asoka flower, the Patra flower, the Palasa flower, the Kuranya flower, the Kubitara flower, the Danara Karaka flower, the Muchilinda flower, the Sumana flower, and so on.

Some of these flowers were just opening and some falling—some in the bud and some burst from the bud; again there was every variety of fruit tree—such as the Amrapala, the Jambu, the Lingusa, the Panava, the Tinduka, the Amraka, and so on; some ripening, others ripe, others passing off. Besides this there were great numbers of wild animals there—the Stag, the water Buffalo, the white Elephant, the Lion, and so on. Again there were many varieties of birds—such as the Parrot, the Peacock, the Kalabiñgka, the mountain Pheasant, the white Pheasant, and so on. Again there was every variety of pleasant lake, with flowers floating thereon—the Utpala, the Padma, the Kumuda, and so on; and on the banks of the lakes every kind of flower growing, overhanging the water—the water perfectly pure and bright, neither deep nor shallow; and on the four sides, among the trees that surround the lakes, every kind of amphibious animal—Turtles, Tortoises, etc., and every kind of aquatic bird, Ducks, Geese, etc.

Now in the midst of this delightful vale, there was an old Rishi living called Kapila. When, therefore, the princes beheld the spot, they said one to another, "Here is a place where we can found a city and establish our rule." Then it came to pass that the princes abiding here, remembered the injunction of the king their father, that in case they married not to marry wives except belonging to their own tribe, and rather than do so, to take their sisters and make them their wives; and so at first they desired to do, but on second thoughts they feared to pollute their race by such intermarriages.

At this time, the Suryavansa Ikshwaku King summoned to his presence a great Brahman, a distinguished teacher (kwo sse), and spake thus to him: "Great Brahman! where now are my four sons dwelling?" He replied, "Mahârâja! your sons, with their sisters, etc., having gone to the Northern region, and settled there, have become the parents of beautiful children.

Then Ikshwaku, because he loved the princes, his heart filled with joy, said "Those princes are able to found a kingdom, and govern it well." Hence the name Sâkya (able), and because they lived under tents made from branches of trees, they are also called Sikya.[1] And because they lived in the place where Kapila had resided, their town was called Kapilavastu.

Now after three of the sons had died, the survivor reigned alone in Kapilavastu, and governed the people. He had a son called Kuru, he had a son called Gokuru, he had a son called lion-jaw (Sinhahanu), he had four sons, the first called Sudhôdana, the second Suklôdana, the third Tulodana, the fourth Amritôdana, and one daughter called sweet-dew-taste (Amrita).

Sinhahanu's eldest son, Sudhôdana, succeeded his father at Kapilavastu. Now at this time, not far from Kapilavastu, there was a city called Tien-pi (Devadaho),[2] in which was settled a member of the Sâkya family, a rich householder, whose name was Su(pra) Buddha, abounding in wealth—his house like that of Vaisravana of the Northern region. This nobleman had eight daughters, the first called Manasâ [or, it may be "Mâyâ"], the eighth was called Mahâprajâpatî.

This Mahâprajâpati was the youngest of all the daughters, and when she was born all the Brahman astrologers said, "This girl, if she has a son, will be the mother of a Chakravartin." So gradually they grew up, and became marriageable. Then Sudhôdana desired to have Mahâprajâpatî in marriage; but the king, Supra Buddha, refused until the seven elder sisters were married, on which Sudhôdana promised to provide for them all. Then Sudhôdana taking the eldest and youngest himself, and giving two to each of his brothers, the king retired to his Palace with the two, and lived according to the rules of all the kings who reign over the four quarters.

---

[1] *Vide* Fă Hian, p. 83. [2] The same as Koli.

CHAPTER V.

The ascent and sojourn (of Bôdhisatwa) in the Tusita Heaven.

§1. At this time, Bôdhisatwa Mahâsatwa, from being a faithful and obedient follower of Kâsyapa Buddha, at the time of his death, was straightway born in the Tusita Heaven, at which time all the Devas of that heaven gave him the name of Prabhâpâla,[1] and on this account he is so named. Then all the Devas announced the title by which he was known to the worlds above Tusita, and the sound thereof reached even to the Akanishta[2] Heaven. Then the Devas also sang together, and said, "Prabhâpâla Bôdhisatwa has come to be born in this Tusita Heaven." The sound of this strain was heard in the Trâyastriñshas[3] Heaven, and in the Heaven of the four kings,[4] and it reached even to the abodes of the Asuras[5]; so that each one of them addressed the other in these words, "Prabhâpâla Bôdhisatwa has gone up to be born in the Tusita Heaven." So, from the lowest abode of these Asuras, to the highest Heavens of the Akanishta, there flocked (innumerable beings) to the Tusita Heaven, to the abode of Prabhâpâla Bodhisatwa, to hear the law from his mouth.

Now the years of the life of the Tusita Devas is 4000 years, These years having past, then the five indications of change appear, that is to say, the chaplet on the head begins to fade; the armpits exude perspiration; the garments become less beautiful; the body loses its splendour; there is a restlessness on the chair or throne. And so it came to pass, when the Tusita Devas observed these signs affecting Prabhâpâla, they uttered a loud cry, and said, "alas! alack-a-day!" and speaking between themselves, they said, "Oh! misery! misery! Prabhâpâla will not be with us much longer! he

---

[1] Hou-ming, *vide* Jul. ii, 358. But there is some confusion in Julien's translation. According to the "Lalita Vistara," Bodhisatwa's name was Swetaketu.

[2] The highest of the Rupa (*i. e.*, material) heavens.

[3] That is, the Heaven of Sâkra, on the top of Sumeru.

[4] That is, the four kings who keep watch over the earth. Their abodes were placed half way up Mount Sumeru.

[5] The demons, or Titans, who live below the earth.

is leaving our Heaven! his spiritual qualifications are departing—what can we do to keep him here?" And so the sound of this lamentation reached upwards to the Sudarsana Heavens, and the Akanishta Heavens, and was repeated in every place, "Alas! alas! by the five indications, it is plain that Prabhâpâla will soon descend from the Tusita Heaven;" and the news reached down even to the Asura râja's palace; and the cries of lamentation were heard in every place, "Alas! alas! he will soon descend!"

At this time, the Devas of the Superior Heavens again descended to Tusita, whilst the Devas of the Inferior Heavens ascended and assembled together in one place; so also the Nâgas, the Yakshas, Gandharvas, Asuras, Kinnaras, Garudas, Mahoragas, Kumbhandas, and so on, came flocking upwards to the Tusita Heavens, and there assembled in one place; and then they all began to say one to another, "We now see for ourselves that this Prâbhapâla is about to descend to Earth." [The five indications are apparent for twelve years before the departure of the Deva, Ch. Ed.]. At this time, the Suddhâvâsa[1] Devas said amongst themselves, "We have seen previously the expected Buddha descend from the Tusita Heaven, to be born in the world." Then all this innumerable multitude of Devas, beholding, by the infallible signs, that Bôdhisatwa was about to descend to be born in Jambudwîpa, together uttered this cry, calling to the people who inhabit the earth, "Ye mortals! adorn your earth! for Bôdhisatwa, the great Mahâsatwa, not long hence shall descend from Tusita to be born amongst you! make ready and prepare! Buddha is about to descend and to be born!"

Now, at this time, there were dwelling in Jambudwîpa, five hundred Pratyeka[2] Buddhas, in the midst of a forest, practising their religious exercises; these five hundred Pratyeka Buddhas, having heard this cry, immediately rose up into the air and went together to Benares; having arrived there, they began to exhibit their supernatural powers: causing their bodies to ascend into space, and emit all sorts of brilliant appearances; and then

---

[1] The period of the life of these Devas being so long, they had seen previous Bôdhisatwas descend to be incarnated on earth.

[2] The Pratyeka Buddhas correspond very much in character to the old rishis or genii. They cannot teach the law for the benefit of others, but they can exhibit miraculous proofs of their dignity (principally by flying through the air).

having uttered a Gâtha, one after the other, they ended their term of days and entered Nirvâna.

So then, at this time, Prabhâpâla Bôdhisatwa, observing all this vast assembly of Devas, etc., his heart unaffected by any fear or inordinate emotion, spake as follows, "Respectable ones! I would have you know, each one of you, that I plainly see by these indications of my person, that I shall shortly descend from Tusita, and be born amongst men." Then Brahma, Sâkra, and so on, answering, said, "Venerable Prabhâpâla! as you see these indications, it is necessary that you should shortly descend and be born in the world; but, doubtless, you remember your former words and prayers, (that this might really be your destiny)!" Then all those countless Devas, having heard these words, the very hairs of their bodies became erect, and their hearts were filled with great fear and reverence; so they clasped their hands, and fell down before Prâbhapâla and adored him. Then Prâbhapâla replied, "Doubtless it is even so; the destiny which was certainly foretold, is now about to be accomplished! ye, therefore, should reflect on the character of impermanency! you should consider the character of the sad destiny that may await some of you in the future! Consider well the impure character of all bodily forms; that by the lusts of the flesh, and the desires of the natural heart, there is no escape from the bonds of continual birth and death. Now, as ye stand here with your fingers clasped in adoration, behold this body of mine, which I have not yet been able to cast off; and now I am about to quit it for ever! weep not then, nor lament for me!" Then all these Devas replied, "Venerable Prabhâpâla! oh! would that in your infinite love you would not depart hence to be born."

[Kiouen V contains 6978 words, and cost 3.489 taels.]

CHAPTER VI.

On the ascent and sojourn of Bôdhisatwa in Tusita.

§2. At this time, in the midst of the Devas of the Tusita Heaven, there was one called Gold Mass[1] who for many years had, over and

---

[1] Kin-t'hwân. This Deva is not mentioned by name in the "Lalita Vistara."

over again, gone down to Jambudwîpa. Prabhâpâla knowing this, addressed him thus: "Devaputra, you have often gone down to Jambudwîpa; doubtless, therefore, you know the cities, towns, and villages, and the various lineages of their kings; and in what family Bôdhisatwa, for his one birth more, ought to be born."

The Devaputra answered, "Venerable! I know them well, and if you permit me, I will recount them to you." Prâbhapâla replied, "Well! do so!" Then he spoke thus, "This great Chiliocosm has one sacred place called the 'Bodhimandala,'[1] situated in a country called 'Magadha,' in Jambudwîpa; here, from all time, the kings have arrived at perfect illumination. Prâbhapâla! in the midst of this district, is a river called 'Ganges'; on the southern bank of that river, is an eminence where dwells an old Rishi; the name of the place is 'Vâjra,' or otherwise, 'Pandava-Vaihara (Vipoura) kudaka-parvata, [or, it may be, 'the solitary-peak[2]-mount.' called 'Pandava Vaihâra (Vibhara) kuta']. This peak is surrounded by mountains, which encircl it and keep it in, as a string of pearls. In the middle of this (peak), is a little village called 'Mountain-abundance;[3] and not far from the mount is a large city called 'Râjagriha.' In this city, there was, formerly, a certain royal Rishi called 'Udapali.' He had, without interruption, descended from the Kshatriya caste (royal caste). He had a son called 'Bahuka'; and from that time till now, those who have reigned in that city have all descended from this Rishi in regular succession. If Prabhâpâla is to be born in Jambudwîpa, it would become him to be born as the son of the king of that city."

Prâbhapâla answered the Deva, and said, "Although this be so, yet the pedigree is not a pure one; and the city is a frontier one, and the country hilly, and broken with valleys; the ground stony and covered with weeds, etc.; wherefore you may select another place where a Kshatriya family resides."

---

1 The Bôdhimanda is the area around the Bôdhi tree, under which the Bôdhisatwas arrive at supreme wisdom.

2 Is this the same as "the small rocky hill standing by itself?" (Fa-hien, cap. xxviii).

3 Those Chinese compounds which I am unable to restore, I merely translate.

Golden-mass again remarked, "Prabhâpâla! in the Kasi country there is a city called 'Varanâsi'[1]; the râja Rishi called 'Shen-kwong'[2]; you may, perhaps, think this family worthy of you!" To which, Prabhâpâla replied, "This may be so; but there are four heretical schools there, so that you had better look elsewhere."

Then the Deva observed again, "Prabhâpâla! in Kôsala, in the city of Savatti, there is a king called 'Griya'(?); the people numerous, and the king powerful; will it please you to be born there?"

"No!" said Prâbhapâla, "for the kings of Kôsala have descended from Matañgas,[3] both on the mother's and father's side, of impure birth; and in former days they were of small repute, without any personal courage or nobleness of heart; the country comparatively poor, although there are the seven precious substances there; yet they are in no abundance. Therefore, I cannot be born there!"

Then he said again, "In the Vadsa country, the city Kausambi, there is a king called 'thousand excellences' (tsien-shing); his son, called 'pih-shing' (hundred excellences). That king has elephants, horses, the seven gems, and armies (the four sorts of military force) in abundance; will it please you to be born there?" To which Prabhâpâla replied, "Although what you say may be true; yet the mother of the king of Vadsa was born of a strange parent, and therefore the son is not of pure descent; you must look elsewhere."

Golden-mass said again, "This Vâjora country has a city called Vâisali,[4] rich in every kind of produce; the people in peace and contentment; the country enriched and beautiful as a heavenly mansion; the king called 'Druma râja'[5]; his son without the least stain on his scutcheon; the king's treasuries full of gems, and gold and silver; perhaps you will be born there."

---

[1] This of course is Benares.

[2] Virtuous—lustre.

[3] Matãngas, *i. e.*, pariahs. Compare these and subsequent passages with the "Lalita Vistara" (Foucaux's translation, p. 24).

[4] An old town on the Gandak River, a little to the north of Patna.

[5] Tree-king.

To which Prabhâpâla replied, "This may be so; but the disposition of the people of that country is hard and self-willed; each one of them says 'I am king!'. 'Sufficient in myself!' and so they are haughty and disobliging. Again, they are without proper reverence for high or low; arrogant and self-sufficient; you must look elsewhere, therefore [the king, moreover, is not influenced by just considerations in the administration of justice, saying, 'This is law,' and 'this is not law']."

Golden-mass then said, "In the Mâvanti country, the city called 'Ujjayani[1]; the king called 'bright lamp' (Pradyôta?); his son called 'Purna'; the king's personal strength very great: able to subdue all those around him; here may Bôdhisatwa be born?"

Prabhâpâla replied, "All this may be so; but the king of that country is governed or restrained by no fixed law, and believes not in the certain result of actions, good or bad, in a future state; you must, therefore, look elsewhere."

Then he observed, "Mathura,[2] the capital city of Jambudwîpa, has a great king, called 'Subahu'; will it suit Prabhâpâla to be born in this family?"

To which Bôdhisatwa replied, "That king is a heretic; how then can an expectant Buddha be born there?"

Once more he rejoined, "This city of the white elephant (Hastinapoura); the kings belonging to the Pandavas, of the greatest strength and beauty; unrivalled in the world; able to subdue all hostile armies; perhaps you are agreeable to be born there!"

To which Prabhâpâla replied, "This may be so; but the race of the Pandavas, pure as it may be, is yet of confused and indefinite origin; hence we find the eldest son of that king (*i.e.*, of Pandu), called 'Yudistira,' spoken of as the son of Dharma, a Brahma Deva; the second son, called Bhîmasena, is spoken of as the son of the wind-spirit (Vâyu) Râja; the third son, called 'Arjuna,' is spoken of as the son of Sakra; again, there are two sons born of different mothers; one Nakula, the other, Sahadeva; these two are said to be the sons of Asuna (Asvin), the Deva of the stars. For this reason, I cannot be born there."

---

1 Oujein.

2 In the province of Agra (L. V.)

Then the Deva continued, "Prabhâpâla! the city of Mithila, in Jambudwîpa, is governed by a king of the Mithila family, called 'Sumitra;' he possesses abundance of elephants, horses, chariots, oxen, sheep, and all kinds of property of this sort; together with countless wealth, gold, silver, gems, pearls, and so on. That king, Sumitra, is devoted to the practice and study of the true law; will you, therefore, be born there?"

Prabhâpâla replied, "What you have said may be so; Sumitra Raja may possess all this wealth, and be devoted to religion; yet he is old and decrepit, and no longer able to attend to the business of his government; moreover, he has already a large family of sons. For these reasons, I cannot be born there."

Golden-mass continued, "Prabhâpâla! besides these kings of the middle country, there are other kings of the frontier country, who hold heretical views; for instance, there is the island of Pindu, in which there is a kingdom governed by a king of the Brahman race; he resides on the top of Pindu, and is called 'Moon-branch'; pure in descent, both on his father's and mother's side; particular in his religious devotions to all the gods (Devas); perfectly versed in the knowledge of the four Vedas. Will you, venerable one, be born in that family?"

To whom Prabhâpâla replied, "It may be so; but when I am born, I desire to be born in the Kshatriya caste, and not in that of the Brahmans. So pray look elsewhere."

The Deva replied, "I have now named every kingdom I can think of in Jambudwîpa; every town, village, and the race of all the kings of the Kshatriya race; and now I am overcome with so much sorrow, in consequence of my failure to find a family worthy of you as a son, that my memory fails me as to any other name, and my mouth cannot further declare the character of these families."

Prabhâpâla replied, "It is as you say; you are yet at fault in finding me a pure Kshatriya family, worthy of me as a son!"

The Deva replied, "I, looking carefully and anxiously for a place worthy of you when born, suddenly find I have forgotten one Kshatriya family."

Prabhâpâla replied, "What is the name thereof?"

The Deva continued: "An ancient family, descended in direct line from successive Chakravarti Râjas, related to Ikshwaku, in the far distance of antiquity; they live at Kapilavastu, of the race of the Sâkyas; the king's name Suddhôdana, son of Sinhahanu, celebrated among men and Devas; perhaps you will condescend to be born in that family."

Prâbhapâla replied, "It is well—well! you have well selected this family from the rest. I remember belonging to this family, and I am willing to be born in it as you suggest. Devaputra! it has ever been the rule that the expectant Buddha, when born, must appear in a family possessing sixty marks[1] of excellence, what, then, are these sixty signs of excellence? 1.—All the holy ones (Buddhas) regard that family with complacency. 2.—That family must practise no wickedness. 3.—The origin of that family must be perfectly pure. 4.—The descent of that family, in every line, must be faultless. 5.—The maternal descent must be without flaw or interruption. 6.—It must, from its origin, have been in the royal line. 7.—All the kings throughout the line, by descent, must have had deep religious principles (deeply-sown, virtuous principles—roots). 8.—The origin of that family must always have been made a subject of commendation by the various Buddhas (saints). 9.—The members of that family must possess great personal dignity. 10.—The women of that family must be famed for their beauty. 11.—The young men must be famous for their wisdom. 12.—The disposition of the members of that family must be agreeable and amiable. 13.—Not given to songs or plays. 14.—They must be fearless. 15.—Not weak or delicate. 16.—Well gifted with intellectual power. 17.—Given to handy work. 18.—Afraid of committing sin. 19.—Not mixed up in trade, or eager in getting wealth. 20.—Faithful in friendships. 21.—Not given to kill either beasts or reptiles, or anything that has life. 22.—The names of that family chosen with discretion. 23.—Able to practice self-denial. 24.—Not easily led by others. 25.—Not fickle or changeable. 26.—Not doubtful or sceptical. 27.—Not led by fear to follow others. 28.—Adverse to slaughter. 29.—No remorse for sin. 30.—Successful in obtaining charity (?). 31.—Liberal in charity. 32.—Invincible. 33.—Regular in religious conduct, and willing to comply with all the rules. 34.—Fond of relieving others.

---

[1] The "Lalita Vistara" makes the number of signs, sixty-four (*Vide in loc.* L. V. 27).

35.—Exact in determining the rules of reward and punishment. 36.—Strong and vigorous. 37.—Pious to Rishis and saints. 38.—Reverent to spiritual powers. 39.—Pious to Devas. 40.—Respectful to wives. 41.—No family jealousies. 42.—Well known through the ten regions. 43.—The most distinguished by all families. 44.—Ancestors, holy men. 45.—The most conspicuous amongst such holy men. 46.—Constantly connected with Chakravarti Ràjas. 47.—Associated with men of the highest dignity. 48.—Surrounded by very large retinues. 49.—Their family associations not to be broken. 50.—Their family associations superior to all others. 51.—Reverent to mothers. 52.—Obedient to fathers. 53.—Pious to Shamans. 54.—Pious to Brahmans. 55.—Plenteous in grain. 56.—Rich in possessions. 57.—Abounding in cattle, slaves, elephants, horses, oxen, sheep, etc. 58.—Not exacting on others. 59.—Not deficient in any worldly possessions. 60.—The race perfectly pure through every generation from its very origin."

"Devaputra! all expectant Buddhas, when they become incarnated in their mother's wombs, must be born of mothers possessing the thirty-two superior signs of female excellency; and what are these? 1.—She is of perfect virtue, or grace. 2—Her limbs perfect. 3.—Her gait perfect. 4.—Her place of delivery well known (?). 5.—Her going abroad at the time of expecting labour. 6.—Her connections perfectly pure. 7.—Her appearance beautiful. 8.—Her name propitious. 9.—Her figure well proportioned. 10.—Not yet had a child. 11.—Of great religious merit. 12.—Fond of pleasant recreations. 13.—Her heart always virtuously submissive. 14.—Without evil thoughts. 15.—Her body, mouth, and mind, pure. 16.—Her heart fearless. 17.—Recollective. 18.—Extremely handy in female pursuits. 19.—Her heart without guile. 20.—No quarrelsome disposition. 21.—No envy. 22.—No anger. 23.—No hatred. 24.—No roughness. 25.—No levity. 26.—Her body with every propitious mark. 27.—Great patience. 28.—Great modesty. 29.—Hating sensuality, anger, and doubt. 30.—Without the faults of women. 31.—Obedient to her husband. 32.—Possessed of all grace and virtue from the time of her birth."

Such is the character of the mother of an expectant Buddha; the time of Bôdhisatwa's incarnation is, when the constellation

Kwei[1] is in conjunction with the sun. Before his conception, his mother must have undertaken the eight fasts (is this, fasted for eight days?), and after that the conception takes place.

Again Prabhâpâla spoke thus: "I now am about to assume a body (Shan yeou); not for the sake of gaining wealth, or enjoying the pleasures of sense; but I am about to descend and be born among men (take this 'one-birth'), simply to give peace and rest to all flesh; and to remove all sorrow and grief from the world."

At this time, in the midst of the assembly, there was a Deva who spake thus to another: "Our Bôdhisatwa Prabhâpâla is about to descend to be born amongst men! he is about to leave our heavenly abode. When he is gone, how shall we, any longer, be joyous or glad in this place?" Then the other replied, "How indeed? how indeed! what can we do then to obtain the privilege of going down into the world to see the place where our illustrious Bôdhisatwa shall be born?" A third Deva said, "Oh! I wish my years in this heaven were passed that I might be born there with him!" A fourth Deva said, "Let not your hearts be sad! Our great Bôdhisatwa is indeed about to be born amongst men, having completed his years as a Deva in this heaven; but how much more certainly will he come back to us again." Then another Deva called out and said, "Prabhâpâla! venerable one! you are now going down to be born in the world of men. Oh! great sir![2] forget us not! forget us not!" At this time, Prabhâpâla Bôdhisatwa replied to these Devas thus: "Let not sorrow and grief affect you thus! for I have already told you that all things are impermanent as the plantain-stalk; without any true foundation; like a thing borrowed which must be returned; like the lightning flash (or, a flash of light), a phantom, a bubble; so are all things which exist around you."

Then Prabhâpâla Bôdhisatwa again addressed the Devas, and said, "There is a cause for all the partings and separations that take place in every form of being, and this cause is 'birth and death!' Be not grieved on my account! Through ages past I have prepared for myself a destiny (Kama), which secures me now from long continuance in the world. Soon shall I obtain final

---

1 Corresponding to four stars in cancer (γ, δ, η, θ).
2 Mahâpurusha?

release. Through ages past have I acquired the merit to be derived from 'Buddha,' 'the Law,' 'the Church.'[1] I have ever prepared my heart for the possession of supreme wisdom, and now, having obtained the result of my constant vows and prayers, I am about to consummate all in the acquisition of it. You should rejoice, therefore, and not be sad."

Then all those Devas having heard these words said amongst themselves, "Look Devas! look well at this Prabhâpâla Bôdhisatwa Mahâsatwa, for soon he will descend to earth and be born amongst men," and then they raised their voices and said, "the Venerable Prabhâpâla, the exalted one, shall soon be born as a man. Soon! soon shall all the beauty and the glory of this heaven disappear, and all the happiness of its inhabitants. What services shall we have to render? What religious homage to pay, when the venerable one departs to be born in the shape of perishable man!"

Then Prabhâpâla rejoined—"Again I repeat in your ears the truth of the doctrine—all things are perishable—Let this be bound and fixed in your memories, forget it not for a moment, and now I go down to earth to be born, to arrive at the goal of Anuttara Samyak Sambôdhi, to preach the incomparable truth. You on your parts should each pray to be born in the world likewise, and so obtain deliverance from all sorrow, and arrive at perfect Rest." Now there was a certain palace in the Tusita Heaven called "Exalted Standard," equal in length and breadth, *i.e.* sixty Yojanas each way. In this palace, from time to time, Bôdhisatwa was in the habit of preaching the law for the advantage of the Tusita Devas. So on this occasion, having repaired to this abode and taken his seat, he began to speak to all the Devas of the Tusita Heaven, and said "Ye Devas! assemble here and listen! not long hence this body of mine shall descend amongst men, and be born in the world; let me now therefore on your account recite in succession the names of the various modes of salvation (fă mun), as a means to your conversion, now for the last time I name these particulars to you, and impress them on your memory, that you, on your part hearing them may derive joy and peace from their recital.

[1] The three objects of reliance, or refuge, for the Buddhists.
[2] Utchadhvaja. "Lal. Vist." p. 37.

Then all the Devas of this Tusita Heaven, having heard these words, assembled together in that heavenly palace to listen to what Prabhâpâla had to say.

Then Prabhâpâla, sitting on his Lion throne, surrounded by an incalculable number of Devas, and honoured by every kind of external homage, spake thus, "Devas, before the once-born Bôdhisatwa descends to earth to be incarnated he desires on your account to recite the one hundred and eight methods of salvation, listen therefore and weigh my words whilst I recite these methods to you."

At this time Prabhâpâla Bôdhisatwa, having delivered these one hundred and eight gates of the law,[1] impressed upon his auditors that they should diligently keep them in their momories, and not let them slip.

[Kiouen VI contains 6177 words, and cost 3·09 Taels.]

CHAPTER VII.

The descent into the Royal Palace.

At this time Prabhâpâla Bôdhisatwa, the Winter being now passed, and the opening month of Spring arrived, when all the flowers and the trees put out their sweets, the vernal air soft and serene, neither too cold or hot, the young grass and other verdure freshly come forth, brightly shining on every side. At the time of the junction of the constellation Kwei (with the sun), having repeated the necessary portions of the law (as before given), in the hearing of all the Devas, causing their hearts to be filled with joy and ravishment, having by his excellent discourse led them to discard all thought and things so transient in their nature, as are subject to life and old age, and disease and death, and to seek after the brighter state of being, at this time (I say) Prabhâ-

---

[1] These hundred and eight gates of the law are given by M. Foucaux, "Lal. Vist." pp. 46-7. The Chinese list agrees almost entirely with his.

pâla Bôdhisatwa Mahâsatwa about now to descend and to be born, his heart at rest, without excitement, with no anxiety or confusion of thought, again spake thus to the assembled Devas, "Know well! and consider, ye Devas all, that this is my very last and final birth." Then Bôdhisatwa, his mind immovably fixed, descended from Tusita, as other Devas had done, the years of their sojourn in Tusita being come to an end.

At this time, when Bôdhisatwa was about to descend, and in a spiritual manner enter the womb of Queen Mâya;[1] then that Mâya on that very night addressed Suddhôdana Râja, and said, "Mahârâja! I wish from the present night to undertake the eight special rules of self discipline, to wit, not to kill anything that lives; not to defraud any one; to have no sexual pleasures; not to lie; not to prevaricate; not to calumniate; to have no irreligious conversation; and, moreover, to pray that I may not covet, or be angry, or hold foolish doubts, so as to avoid all heretical teaching, and adopt all that is true and right. I now bind myself to observe these rules, and I desire to produce in myself a loving heart towards all living creatures." Then Suddhôdana Râja replied to Mâya thus, "As your heart desires! act as you wish. I will even give up my kingdom rather than that you should not so act, if you desire it, according to the Gâtha,

"'The Râja beholding the Mother of Bôdhisatwa
Respectfully rose from his seat before her,
Regarding her as his Mother or elder Sister,
His heart wholly free from any thought of sensual desire.'"

Then Prabhâpâla Bôdhisatwa, with a fixed heart and perfectly self-possessed, descended from Tusita to sojourn on earth, and entered on the right side[2] of Queen Mâya, wife of Suddhôdana Râja, and there rested in perfect quiet.

Then Devas and men, Mara[3] and Brahma, Shamans and Brah-

---

[1] Mâya, the wife of Suddhôdana Râja. The "incarnation scene" is frequently met with in Buddhist sculptures. *Vide* (amongst others) Pl xxxiii, "Tree and Serpent Worship."

[2] He is generally represented as descending in the shape of a white elephant. The *tikas*, however, explain this as indicating "Power and Wisdom."

[3] Mâra, the author of evil. Sometimes called the "King of

mans, beheld a wonderful light, which shone through the entire world, and lit up the gloom of the external mountain depth, where eternal darkness reigns. Then every creature beholding this light began to speak to his fellow thus, "What does this sudden appearance amongst us portend?" Then the great earth quaked six times, and all the mountains of the great Sakwala shook; the seas roared, and the rivers turned backwards in their course, whilst all forests, trees, flowers, and every kind of herb, exuded their rich nourishment, and shed it on the ground; and so even down to the bottommost Hell of Avitchi,[1] there was a feeling of joy instead of misery.[2] [*The light shone in the darkness, to show that hereafter Bôdhisatwa would arrive at perfect enlightenment. and by the preaching of the four truths, illuminate the darkness and ignorance of men's minds. The mountains shook and the seas roared, etc., to indicate that hereafter Buddha, having arrived at perfect wisdom, should shake the powers of evil which afflict the world, and draw men to the true Nirvâna; the rivers flowed backwards to indicate that hereafter Buddha should cause the natural tide of events, the perpetual flow of life and death to be reversed, and men to find deliverance,* and so with the other indications.] Bôdhisatwa having then descended into the womb of Mâya the Queen, she in the midst of her sleep had a dream to this effect, "she thought she saw a six tusked white elephant, his head coloured like a ruby (or red pearl), etc., descend thro' space and enter her right side." In the morning the queen addressed her husband Suddhôdana thus, "Mahârâja, be it known to you that last night I had the following dream, it appeared to me that a white elephant entered my right side, and gave me such joy as I never had before! From this time forth I will no more partake of any sensual pleasure, and I pray you find out some interpreter of dreams who will tell me what this wonderful vision of mine may portend." Then Suddhôdana called to the women who were waiting outside, and bade them go in haste

---

Death," at other times the "God of the World of Pleasure" (Kamaloka).

[1] Avitchi, the no-interval hell—the bottomless pit.

[2] These explanations are part of the original text, introduced without any comment. They are probably of a later date than the thread of the narrative. When they occur they will be printed in italic letters.

and tell Mahânamaputra, his prime minister, to summon at once to his presence the eight Brahmas who excelled in interpreting dreams, to wit, Yajñabhadanta, Visakabhadanta, Ishwarabhadanta, Pindubhadanta, Brahmabhadanta, these five, and with them the three sons of old Kâsyapa. The messengers then addressed the king, "we dare not disobey the Mahârâja's commands." Then these messengers in obedience to the king's commands went forth to the palace gates, and cried with a loud voice before the gates, "Who is there on guard?" Then there was before the gate a certain guard, Rojana by name, who answered the messenger belonging to the interior (*i. e.* the harem), "I am here." Then the messenger said "Mahârâja has given orders to summon to his presence the eight Brahmans, interpreters of dreams, by name [as before]. Then Rojana, went forthwith to the presence of Mahanamaputra, the prime minister, who having heard his words, immediately summoned the eight Brahmans aforesaid, and soon both Mahanamaputra and they together entered within the royal palace. Then Suddhôdana Râja addressed the interpreters of dreams, and said, "Last night the Queen had this extraordinary dream [relating it], what is the interpretation of it?"

Then the Brahmans, having heard the king's words, perfectly understanding all portents, and able to interpret all dreams, replied, "Mahârâja! listen and hear the meaning of this dream, according to the explanation given by the old Rishis, and in the books of divine wisdom; thus it is written in the following Gâthas:—

"'If a mother in her dream, behold
The Sun Deva enter her right side;
That mother shall bear a son
Who shall become a Chakravarti Râja.
If she sees in her dream
The Moon Deva enter her right side,
That son, borne of that mother,
Shall be, of all kings, the chief.
If the mother, in her dream, behold
A white elephant enter her right side,
That mother, when she bears a son,
Shall bear one chief of all the world (Buddha);
Able to profit all flesh;

Equally poised between preference and dislike;
Able to save and deliver the world and men
From the deep sea of misery and grief.'"

Then the Brahmans addressed Suddhôdana, and said, "Mahârâja! the dream of the queen is a very propitious one. Your Majesty ought now to have a very special regard for the queen; for the child born of her will certainly be a holy child, and in after time arrive at perfect wisdom; his name spread far and wide." At this time, Suddhôdana Râja, having heard the words of the Brahmans, the interpreters of dreams, his heart was filled with exultation and joy not to be surpassed. He placed before them meats and drinks of the most exquisite character; delicacies and fruits of the choicest flavour; and conferred every kind of present: bidding them enjoy themselves as they list! moreover, he added gifts of money and precious stones, and after the propitious interpretation, he distributed food, drink, clothing, flowers, unguents, cattle, horses, chariots, and every kind of gift, among the people of Kapilavastu, beyond the four gates, and also in the streets, passages and lanes of the city; giving to each just what was most requisite or most desired; and all with a view to conduce to the prosperity of Bôdhisatwa.

Now, at this time, there was a certain Rishi called Asita, thoroughly grounded in all the wisdom of the various heretical sects, and who, by putting away the love of pleasure (by self-denial, discarding the five desires), had arrived at great spiritual power; possessed of the five miraculous qualities (irdhipàda), he was able, at will, to go to the thirty-three heavens, and enter at his pleasure the assemblies of the Devas. This Rishi dwelt very much at a place in South India, called "Tchapati," in a village called "Ganganadi"; not far from there, was a shady thicket called "increasing-length" (dirghavardana?). Now, at this time, it happened that the Rishi was living in this grove, practising himself in acquiring the supernatural wisdom of the Genii; whilst all the people of Magadha said of him that he was a Rahat, and greatly reverenced him.

Then, having acquired the knowledge he sought, this Rishi was imparting the secret to others, when a certain youth of the village afore-named, called "Narada,"[1] of tender age, being scarcely eight

---

[1] Naradatta, *vide* "Lalit. Vist." 103.

years old, was brought by his mother to Asita, with the request that he would adopt him as one of his disciples; on which the youth made every sort of religious offering to the Rishi; and after Asita had accepted and used them, he paid him ceaseless worship. Now, it so happened, that Asita was, on one occasion, sitting in the Tsang-chang grove, practising the severest austerities, and day and night controlling his mind to fixed contemplation, and the boy, Narada, was sitting on one side by himself, behind his master, employed in brushing away, and removing, all noxious creatures from coming near the Rishi. This was just at the time when Bôdhisatwa descended from Tusita and entered into the right side of his mother; on which occasion, there was a supernatural light spread every-where, and the earth quaked again. Asita perceiving these miraculous events (adbhuta .dharma), was greatly awe-stricken, and the very hairs on his person stood erect; and he thought with himself, "what mean these miraculous portents?" Thinking thus for a little time in silence, his thoughts perfectly fixed in firm composure, then suddenly his mind conceived unutterable joy, and he cried out and said, "A great saint, inconceivably holy, is to be born in the world; now Mahâpudgala Bôdhisatwa is descending from Tusita, and about to enter the right side of his mother, and receive birth (incarnation)." Having said this, he ceased.

Then again there was a certain Deva called "Fleet-goer," who, with rapid flight, went down to all the hells, and cried out with a loud voice, "All ye wretched ones! understand now that Bôdhisatwa is incarnated; quickly, then, pray ye and vow with all your might, that ye may be born on earth." Then the wretched inmates, having heard this cry, as many of them as in ages gone by had acquired any merit, but for some consequent act of sin had been born in hell,—these, I say, regarding one another, saw plainly their appearance changing, and their bodies becoming bright and beautiful; and so their minds received great joy; and when they heard the voices of Fleet-goer and all the angels singing on earth, they were delivered from hell; and such as had acquired previous merit were born on earth, in the immediate neighbourhood of Kapilavastu.

Again, at the time of Buddha's conception, Sâkra Deva, and the four Maharajas, to wit, Dhritarashtra Râja, Virûdhaka Râja,

Virupaksha, and Vaisravana Râja, addressing one another, said, "Sirs! surely, now that Bôdhisatwa has gone down to earth to be born, we ought to keep guard and watch lest any of those noxious beings called 'Kinnaras' should molest or hurt him, or depute others to do so. For it is right that we Devas should guard the illustrious person of Bôdhisatwa, and not leave the task to men." [*There are four chief occasions on which this special protection is required,—at the conception, the time of gestation, the birth, and the arrival at supreme wisdom. There are also several special circumstances that distinguish the conception, gestation, and birth of Bôdhisatwa. He always remains on the right side of his mother, without movement; such movement, from right to left, giving constant pain and anxiety to the mother. But Bôdhisatwa remains ever at rest, whether the mother rise, or sit, or sleep; this is one peculiarity (ardbhuta dharma). So also nothing impure takes place, either during the gestation, or at the birth, of a Bôdhisatwa; this is another peculiarity. So also the mother of a Bôdhisatwa suffers no pain, but rather is sensible of great delight during the period and at the birth. She consents to no nuptial intercourse. She practises all the laws of purity. She suffers no extremities of heat or cold. He is formed perfectly when he enters the womb; there is no change from embryo to Arbuda (from stage to stage of development). All demons who torment either man or woman, flee from the face of the mother of a Bôdhisatwa. All diseased persons are cured by the touch of the right hand of the queen Mâya, or, if they cannot secure an opportunity of being touched, then a shrub, or a leaf, or a blade of grass which Mâya has held in her right hand, given or sent to the sick person, will infallibly heal the disease. Such are the wonderful circumstances connected with the gestation and birth of Bôdhisatwa.*]

The Birth beneath the Tree.

Part I.

At this time, the holy mother Mâya, having just completed ten months since her conception of Bôdhisatwa, felt the time of birth approaching. Then the father of the queen Mâya, Supra Buddha,

Grihapati (chang-che) by name, sent certain messengers to the king Suddhôdana, at Kapilavastu, [*the Mahâsanghikas say his name is Supra Bôdha*], who presented to the Mahârâja this request from the queen's father, "As I am informed my daughter, Mâya, the queen of your majesty, is now with child, and already far advanced in pregnancy, and, as I fear that when the child is born, my daughter will be short lived, I have thought it right to ask you to permit my daughter Mâya to come back to me and rest in my house; and I have prepared for her reception the Lumbini garden, and every proper amusement. Let not the king be displeased at this request, for immediately the confinement is over, I will send my daughter back to her home with you."

Then Suddhôdana Râja, having heard the words of the messengers of Supra Buddha, immediately issued orders to have all the road between Kapilavastu and Dewadaho [*vide* "Lalit. Vist.," p. 413, M.B., 136] made level, and freed from all weeds, pebbles, filth, and obstacles of all kinds; and to have the ground swept and sprinkled with scented water, and all kinds of flowers to be scattered along it; and he ordered, moreover, the queen Mâya, to be ornamented with every kind of precious stone, and her person decorated with the choicest flowers and unguents; and thus accompanied by music, dancing women and guards, and with special attendants going before to announce her approach, she set forth on her journey. So it was the queen Mâya, mounted on a white elephant, pursued her way, the Devas having caused a perfectly beautiful gem-adorned covering to appear on the elephant's back for her to sit upon. And so, thus seated, she arrived at last at her father's house in the city of Devadaho; and as she approached, surrounded by the vast retinue of warriors, elephants, horses, and chariots provided by Suddhôdana Râja, then forth from Devadaho came Supra Buddha and all his ministers and nobles to meet and welcome her approach.[1] At length, in the second month of spring, on the eighth day, the constellation Kwei being now in conjunction, the king, accompanied by his daughter Mâya, went forth towards the garden Lumbini, anxious to see the beauties of the

---

[1] The text here proceeds to explain that the Lumbini garden was so called after the name of the wife of the chief minister of Supra Buddha.

earth. Having arrived at the garden, the queen Mâya stepped down from her chariot, adorned as we have before described, surrounded by dancing women, etc.; and so passed from spot to spot, and from tree to tree in the garden, admiring and looking at all! Now, in the garden, there was one particular tree called a Palasa, perfectly strait from top to bottom, and its branches spread out in perfect regularity, its leaves variegated as the plumage of a peacock's head, soft as Kalinda cloth, the scent of its flowers of most exquisite odour. Delighted at the sight, Mâya rested awhile to admire it, and gradually approached under the shade of the tree; then that tree, by the mysterious power of Bôdhisatwa, bent down its branches, and, forthwith, the queen with her right hand took hold of one; just as in the air, there appears a beautifully tinted rainbow stretching athwart heaven; so did she take hold of that curving branch of the Palasa tree and look up into heaven's expanse. Thus, standing on the ground, and holding the branch as we have described, with clasped hands and bended knee, the heavenly women who surrounded the queen, addressed her thus:—

"The queen now brings forth the child,
Able to divide the wheel of life and death
In heaven and earth, no teacher
Can equal him;
Able to deliver both Devas
And men from every kind of sorrow.
Let not the queen be distressed,
We are here to support her!"

At this time, Bôdhisatwa perceiving his mother, Mâya, standing thus with the branch in her hand, then with conscious mind arose from his seat and was born.

Bôdhisatwa being thus delivered from the right side of his mother, a marvellous light spread around, and forthwith all the Devas and men, Mâra, Brahma, Shamans, and Brahmans, perceiving this miraculous light said amongst themselves:—"What means this wonderful portent." [*Now this miraculous light is one of the signs of Buddha's future conquest over the powers of darkness and sin.*] Thus was Bôdhisatwa born.

Now at the time of Bôdhisatwa's birth, Sâkra, with a beautifully fine Kasika garment, advanced and wrapped the body of the child in it, whilst the four Mahârâjas, taking the child, wrapped thus in his swaddling clothes, brought him and showed him to his mother, and uttered these words, "Now may men rejoice; the royal mother has brought forth a son; the Devas may be glad, much more may men!"

When Bôdhisatwa was thus born, he said, "Now then I have arrived at my last birth; no more shall I enter into the womb to be born; now shall I accomplish the end of my being, and become Buddha." [*This refers to the utterance of Bôdhisatwa when he had arrived at complete enlightenment. "Now I have finished my births; I have completed my course; I have done all that I had to do; there is no further form of life for me to assume."*]

[The seventh Kiouen contains 6790 words, and cost 3.395 Taels.]

CHAPTER VIII.

Birth beneath the Tree.

Part II.

Bodhisatwa having thus been born without any assistance or support, he forthwith walked seven steps towards each quarter of the horizon; and as he walked, at each step, there sprang from the earth beneath his feet a lotus flower; and as he looked steadfastly in each direction his mouth uttered these words; first looking to the east, he said, in no childish accents, but according to the very words of the Gâtha, plainly pronounced, "In all the world I am the very chief; from this day forth my births are finished." [*Now this about his walking without assistance, and so forth, is an adbhuta dharma, to signify that when Buddha arrived at perfect enlightenment, he attained also the seven Bôdhyanga (vide Eitel, sub voce). His looking to the four quarters signifies his obtaining the four fearless rules; whilst the words he uttered refer to the universal reverence paid to him by Devas and men after his enlightenment, and also to those memorable words he then spoke, "Oh! housebuilder," etc.*] Bôdhisatwa having been born, the attendants looked everywhere for water; hurriedly they ran in every direction, but found none; when lo! before the very face of the mother there suddenly appeared two beautiful tanks, one of cold, the other of hot water which she mixed as most agreeable to herself, and used. And so again from the midst of space, there fell two streamlets of water, cold and hot, with which the body of Bôdhisatwa was washed. [*These again are adbhuta dharmas, pointing to the power of Samâdhi and Vipasina to remove all sorrow and desire, whilst the spontaneous appearance of the water refers to the natural consequence of these habits of mind to procure all that is desirable for their possession.*] Then all the Devas brought a golden seat for Bôdhisatwa to occupy, which done, he refreshed and washed his body with the grateful streams of water. [*This refers to the beautiful Lotus throne on which Buddha sat, after his enlightenment.*] [*The light, again, which appeared at his birth, refers to the excellency of his doctrine (wheel of the law).*] [*Again, when it is said that this miraculous light obscured even the sun, it refers to the superiority of Buddha's eminence as a teacher, and the honour he received from all the Shamans, etc.*] [*Again, what is said about the trees and the flowers bursting into life at the time of Bôdhisatwa's birth, refers to the faith which those were able to arrive at who heard the first teaching of the sage. Again, what is said about the Devas holding over the new-born babe an umbrella, large as a chariot wheel, with a golden handle, refers to the calm and passionless method in which Buddha, having arrived at supreme wisdom, obtained complete release from all the sorrows and afflictions incident to the state of "birth and death."*][1]

At this time, there was a great minister of state (koue sse) whose family name was Basita, and his private name Mahâṇama. He, in company with various other ministers and Brahmans, went together to visit the Lumbini garden. Having arrived there, and standing without the gates, at that time Basita addressed the ministers and said, "Do you perceive how the great earth is rock-

---

1 The text then continues to relate the miraculous events that took place at the time of the birth; the Devas singing together and scattering flowers, a soft rain falling, etc. I omit these notices.

ing as a ship borne over the waves? And see how the sun and moon are darkened and deprived of their light; just as the stars of the night in appearance! And see how all the trees are blossoming as if the season had come—and hark! whilst the heavens are serene and calm—listen! there is the roll of thunder! and though there be no clouds, yet the soft rain is falling; so beautifully fertilising in its qualities! and the air is moved by a gentle and cool breeze coming from the eight quarters—and hark to the sound of that voice of Brahma so sweetly melodious in the air, and all the Devas chanting their hymns and praises! whilst the flowers and sweet unguents rain down through the void!"

Then a minister answered Mahanama and said, "These things are so! yet it is nothing extraordinary; it is the nature of things (earth) to produce such results!" Another said, "No doubt these things are very wonderful and not to be accounted for." Thus they deliberated together on the point. All at once, from the garden, there came tripping along a woman who came forth from Lumbini and stood outside the very gate where Basita and the Brahmans were in consultation; on seeing whom, she was greatly rejoiced, and could not contain herself for very gladness of heart; and so she cried out, "Oh! ye sons of Sâkya! hurry away as fast as possible to Mahârâja." Then the ministers replied, seeing her high spirits, "And what news shall we give him when we see him; what does your manner signify—is it good tidings or bad?" To whom she replied, "Oh! Sâkyas! it is wonderfully good news!" "What is it then," they said; "come! let us know." Then she continued, "The queen has borne a son! oh! so beautiful and such a lovely child! a child without peer on earth! and the Devas are scattering flowers about him, and there is a heavenly light diffused round his person." The great ministers having heard these words, their hearts were filled with joy, and they could not contain themselves for gladness of heart!

At this time, the great minister Basita loosed from his neck the string of precious stones that he wore, and gave it to the woman, because of the news she brought; but having done so, again he thought, "This woman, perhaps, is a favourite of the king, and his majesty seeing her so beautifully adorned, will naturally inquire and find out where these pearls were obtained, and so it will cause trouble." So he took back the gems and desired that whatever merit would have attached to the gift, that this might redound to the woman's benefit.[1]

Then dismissing the other Brahmans to go to the king and tell the joyful news, he himself began to question the woman straitly as to the character of the event which had happened. To whom the woman replied, "Great minister! pray listen to me well; the circumstances attending the birth of the child were very wonderful! for our queen, Mâya, standing upright on the ground, the child came forth of her right side; there was no rent in her bosom, or side, or loins! when the child came forth, from the air there fell beautiful garments, soft as the stuff of Kasi, sent by the Devas! these the Devas wrapped round the body of the babe, and holding him before his mother, they said, "All joy be to you, queen Mâya! rejoice and be glad! for this child you have borne is holy!" Then the child, having come forth from his mother's side, said these words, "No further births have I to endure! this is my very last body! now shall I attain to the condition of Buddha!" then, without aid, standing on the ground, he walked seven steps, whilst Lotus flowers sprang up beneath his feet, and faced each quarter; and whilst looking to the east, in perfectly rounded accents, unlike the words of a child, he said, "Amongst all creatures I am the most excellent; for I am about to destroy and extirpate the roots of sorrow caused by the universal evil of birth and death." Then there came forth from mid-air two streams of water hot and cold, respectively, to refresh and cleanse the child's body as he stood there on the ground; and again there was brought to him a golden seat on which to repose whilst he was washed. Then such brightness shone around, eclipsing the very sun and moon, and all the Devas brought a white umbrella with an entire gold handle, it was large as a chariot wheel, with which to shelter him, and they held great chamaras in their hands waving them over the child's head! whilst in the air, there was the sound of beautiful music, but no instruments; and there was the voice of people singing hymns of praise in every direction; and flowers beautifully scented fell down in profusion, and though the sun was shining fiercely, yet they withered not, nor dried!"

Then Mahânama, the great minister, having heard this descrip-

[1] An exquisite example of state-craft.

tion, immediately reflected, "wonderful! wonderful! doubtless a great teacher has been born into the world in the midst of this wicked age! Now then will I myself go to Suddhôdana Râja, and acquaint him with these wonderful circumstances."

Then the great minister, taking his swiftest horses, and yoking them to a beautiful chariot, drove, fleet as the wind, from the gate of Lumbini straight to Kapilavastu, and without waiting to see the king, he sounded aloud the drum of joy,[1] until his very strength was exhausted. Now, at this time, Suddhôdana Râja was sitting on his royal throne, settling with his ministers some important affairs of state, surrounded by attendants on every side; suddenly hearing the sound of the joy-drum, the king, in surprise, inquired of his minister, "Who is it so abruptly dares to make this noise in front of the gate of one of the Ikshwaku family? exhausting all his strength in beating the drum of joy!" Then the guard in front of the gate replied, and said to the king, "Mahârâja! your majesty's minister, Basita, surnamed Mahânama is approaching in a four-horsed chariot, swift as the wind, from the direction of Lumbini; and now he is getting down from his chariot, and, with all his might, beating the drum of joy belonging to the Mahârâja, and without any further words, he demands straightway to see the king." The Suddhôdana replied thus to his ministers, "What can be the good news which Basita Mahânama has to tell that he comes so hurriedly to my presence?" The ministers replied, "Let him be summoned to your majesty's presence." So then Mahânama, coming before the king, cried out with a loud voice, "May the king be ever victorious! may the king be ever honoured." Having said this, he paused to regain his strength. Meantime, Suddhôdana, having heard these words, addressed Mahanama, and said, "Mahânama! great minister of the Sákyas! tell me why you thus come without preface into our presence, your strength exhausted with beating the drum of joy!" Then the great minister, Mahânama, replied, "Oh king! your majesty's queen, the queen of the ruler of the city of Devadaho and Lumbini, having gone forth into the midst of that garden, has brought forth a son, beautiful as gold in colour, heralded into the world by a supernatural light, and provided with a cradle by the Devas!"

---

[1] The drum of joy, *i. e.*, the drum or gong hung in front of the palace, which was sounded when there was good tidings brought.

Then Suddhôdana Râja pressed on Mahânama to give him all particulars as to the portents that attended the birth, and the time of their appearance, on which the great minister related, as before, what he had himself seen and heard. Then Suddhodana replied, "You are, indeed, the bearer of good tidings; tell me what recompense can I give? what return can I make for the news you bring?" After some delay, he replied, "Oh! grant me the privilege of attending constantly on the Prince Royal!" To whom Suddhôdana replied, "be it so, as you wish."

Then forthwith Mahânama, surrounded by ministers and officers, proceeded to Lumbini to conduct the Prince Royal to the city of Kapilavastu. On the way thither, Suddhôdana Râja thus addressed Mahânama, and the great ministers, and said, "I scarcely know, great ministers, whether to be glad or sorry about these tidings of the miracles attending the birth of the child." To whom Mahânama replied, "it is certainly an occasion for great joy, Mahârâja, and not for sorrow; for is it possible that your majesty has not heard that these circumstances ever attend the birth of heaven descended mortals; as, for instance, in the case of the Brahman called Dashthaka, who was born from a flower, and after his birth, without any human instruction whatever, but entirely self-instructed, was able thoroughly to explain the four Vedas. And have you not heard, O king, of that wonderful birth in the old times, of a king from the head of his father (agrajanman), and who, after being so born, gradually grew up from a little boy to be a mighty king who ruled the four empires of the world. Or has your majesty not heard of a king in the old days, called Vîka (?) (or, Vaska), who was born from the hand of his father, without any mother; or has your majesty not heard of that king born in old times from his father's stomach, called Rupa; or of that one called Katspa born from his father's arm; or, is it possible your majesty does not recollect the origin of your own house and family in days gone by when Ikshwaku was born from the sugar cane? All these were born in a manner quite incomprehensible to us, even as the Prince, your son, is born." To whom Suddhôdana replied, "Yes! very true, Mahänama! but all these whom you have named were of great personal dignity and renown; but in this case, it is not so plain that such is the case!" To whom Mahanama answered with great joy, "Be it known to you, Mahârâja, that this prince will far exceed all those in the particulars you have mentioned." "But what proofs have you of this superiority," said Suddhôdana, "Your minister, Mahârâja, has compared the various signs which attended the births of those before-named with the signs at the nativity of the Royal Prince, and finds the latter far more excellent and noteworthy." To whom the king replied again, "Let there be no trifling in this matter; for a father is naturally anxious for his son to excel others in quickness and knowledge, in conduct and decorum, in judgment and resolute application; when this is so he rejoices naturally."

And so, halting at length, they came to Lumbini. Having arrived at the outer gate of the garden, they immediately dispatched a messenger to the Queen to congratulate her on the auspicious event of the birth and its attending circumstances, and to express the king's desire to see the child. To which the queen made reply, "Go! tell the king he may enter the garden!" Then a woman in attendance, seeing the king in the garden, took the child in her arms, and approaching the king, said, "The royal babe salutes his father." To whom the king answered, "Not so! first of all send him to the Brahman ministers in attendance and afterwards let him see me!" Then the nurse forthwith took Bôdhisatwa to the place where the Brahmans were. At this time, the chief minister (Kwo sse), and the Brahmans, having looked at the child, addressed Suddhôdana in the following terms of congratulation, "All honoured be the King, and prosperous for evermore! even as we see that this babe will prosper! even so may the king and all the Sâkya race increase and ever flourish. Mahârâja! this child will certainly, and of necessity, become a holy Chakravartin monarch!"

At this time, queen Mâya, the mother of Bôdhisatwa, beholding Suddhodana and the ministers, her face glowing with joy, immediately inquired of the king in these words, "Mahârâja! recite to me I pray you the distinguishing signs of one who is to become a Chakravartin monarch! tell me, I pray you, what these are that my heart may also rejoice!" Then Suddhôdana Râja desired the Brahman ministers to explain and point out the distinctive signs of a Chakravartin monarch. To whom they replied as follows,

---

1 The nature of the Chakravarti monarch has been exhaustively discussed by M. Senart, in the "Journal Asiatique," Aug. and Sept. 1873.

speaking both to the king and queen, "Listen then, O king, and discriminate whilst we recite the various signs of an universal monarch, derived from all the ancient Shasters: A Chakravartin monarch is possessed of such personal virtue, that he can fly through the air for the purpose of carrying on his government of the people; if there is a drought any where, he can cause the rain to descend; at his birth all discord and enmity amongst men cease, and there is universal joy and fellow-feeling amongst all people. A universal monarch is always possessed of seven precious insignia, viz., a golden discus, a magic jewel, an elephant, a horse, a fair wife, a treasurer, a warlike minister (or, a general). These are called the seven insignia (sapta Ratnani); the life of a Chakravartin is very long, and his death a quiet, painless one; his body beautiful beyond human comparison; universally beloved and reverenced by his people, even as one loves an only son, whilst he cares for and cherishes his people more than one would cherish a naked and perishing child."[1]

Then Suddhodana thought with himself thus, "And now what means of conveyance have I for my son in returning to the city." No sooner had he thought thus than the skilful Visvakarman caused a precious palanquin to appear of itself; so perfect that no human art could have made it so, and there were none to be compared with it.

Then Suddhodana took immediate steps to have the road prepared, the streets of Kapilvastu adorned, and all the singing men and women of the place summoned to accompany the Prince on his return. Besides these, he ordered all the conjurers, and athletes; the pearl-players (ball-players?), the water-spouters, the masqueraders, and all such, to attend the *cortége*. Then these all came to the spot, accompanied by vaulters, tumblers, ball-players (?), drum-players, stilt-walkers, pole-climbers, walkers on their hands (head down, feet up), turners round and round like a wheel, tight-rope dancers, spear-twisters (?), sword-kickers, and so forth; every kind of such light and laughable exhibition, with musical accompaniments. Then the four guardians of the world (Chatur Mahârâjas), changing their appearance, assumed the garb of Brahmans, of youthful age and distinguished beauty, and themselves took charge of

---

[1] The narrative then proceeds to speak of the birth of previous "Universal Monarchs."

the Palanquin of Bodhisatwa. And at same time Sâkra Devarâja, changed his appearance into that of a young Brahman of remarkable beauty, with his hair bound with the usual spiral twist, and his body clothed with yellow garments; in his left hand he carried a golden water pitcher, and in his right a beautiful gem-adorned staff; and so furnished, he went before the face of Bodhisatwa, and as he proceeded he exhorted all those whom he met in these terms, "My friends! prepare the way, clear the road! for now the most excellent of mortals is about to enter the city!"

At this time, Brahma Râja and the Devas of the Rupa heavens, joined together in this old strain of laudation,—

"In heaven above, in earth beneath, there is no such being as Buddha.

"In all the regions of space, through all the worlds, there is none such.

"I have looked through and examined every form of life amongst men,

"And I find there is none to be compared with him called the All-wise (Buddha)."

At this time, not far from Kapilavastu, there was a Deva temple, the Deva's name being "Tsang Chang" (Dirghâvardana?), at whose shrine the Sâkyas paid unwonted honours; then Suddhôdana forthwith took the infant in his arms to this temple and addressed his ministers in these words, "Now my child may pay worship to this Deva." Then his mother (or, nurse), took the child to pay the customary honours, at which time a certain Deva, called "Abhaya" (wou wei), took the image of the Deva in the temple, and made it come down and bow before Bôdhisatwa with closed hands and prostrate head, and addressed the nurse thus, "This Prince of mortals is not called on to worship, but is deserving of all worship; let me adore him, for to whom he bows down, instant destruction would follow."

[Kiouen VIII contains 6550 words and cost 3.275 taels to print.]

CHAPTER IX.

Return from the Garden to Kapilavastu.

§1. At this time there were five hundred Sâkya princes (ministers) who, in readiness for the return of Bôdhisatwa to the city, had prepared five hundred Viharas (pure abodes) for him to rest. So it came to pass as he entered the city that each of these Sâkyas stood before the door of his own abode, and with joyful heart and clasped hands paid reverence to him and said, "Oh! thou God among Gods! I pray thee enter this my pure abode! Oh! thou captain of the ship! enter this my pure abode! Oh! thou golden bodied, purest among creatures, enter this my pure abode! Bestower of universal joy, enter this my pure abode! Renowned in every place, enter this my pure abode! Incomparable for virtue! enter this my pure abode!"

Then Suddhôdana Râja, for the sake of those five hundred relatives, through consideration for them, caused Bôdhisatwa to enter each dwelling in succession whilst he prepared for him his own peculiar abode.

Now, on the day of his birth there were five hundred Sâkya princes born, of whom Bôdhisatwa himself was by far the most illustrious; there were five hundred Sâkya princesses born, of whom Yasôdharâ was chief; there were five hundred children born of the concubines of Suddhôdana, of whom Tchandaka was chief; there were five hundred children born of the slaves of Suddhôdana, who became personal servants of the Royal prince; there were five hundred foals born of the white mares belonging to the Royal stud, of which Kantaka was chief; and so also five hundred white elephants appeared of themselves, and went round the city of Kapilavastu; five hundred lovely gardens, with fountains, tanks, &c., appeared on each side of the city; five hundred merchant-men with gold, silver, and precious stones, arrived at the city; moreover, they had (or, there were) five hundred superb umbrellas, and five hundred golden dishes filled with different sorts of grain (as tribute), sent from five hundred different princes; on the delivery of which the bearers spoke thus: "Accept these things, O King! which we offer in respect for the Prince now born." At the same time came five hundred Brahmans and great Kshatriya nobles, each one accompanied by his wife, to offer their congratulations to Suddhôdana Râja.

Then, Suddhôdana seeing that all these things were perfectly accomplished, thought thus with himself, "What name shall I give my new-born child?"—and then he reflected, "since on the day of his birth all things were so perfectly accomplished, therefore, I will name him Sheng-li (Sarvârthassiddha[1]) (perfect prosperity)." Then Suddhôdana opened his treasury, and took a hundred lakhs of gold to offer to his child as he gave him the name, according to the words of the Gâtha:—

"Thus within the King's palace
All things were entirely prosperous,
Therefore, the young child's name
Shall be this—Sarvârthassiddha."

Casting the Horoscope.

§ 2. THEN Suddhôdana Râja issued his commands that all the astrologers and fortune-tellers should at once repair to the Palace to examine the child and cast his horoscope; and on their arrival he bade them look well to every sign, whether good or bad, and draw a true conclusion as to the child's destiny. On hearing this, the Brahmans, &c., with earnest purpose examined well the child's appearance, and comparing what they saw with all that was explained in their Sacred Books, they finally drew their conclusions, and thus addressed the King, "Mahârâja! what great fortune is yours! And why? Because of the great dignity of this child,—he is indeed born a king of all that lives! For know, Oh! King, that his body is marked by the thirty-two infallible signs of greatness. And of persons so marked there are two sorts—if they be Secular, then they are all universal monarchs (Chakravartins); but if Religious, then they become perfectly illuminated (all-wise), and are destined to be perfect Tathâgatas."

Then Suddhôdana further addressed the astrologers, and said, "What are the signs and the particular places of the signs, concerning which you speak?"

---

[1] This is generally contracted into Siddhârtha.

The astrologers replied, "The thirty-two signs of every great man are these following:—first of all, the sole of the foot is perfectly flat and level, all of it equally plump and full. 2. Underneath both feet are the thousand ray'd circles, beautiful and distinctly visible. 3. The Prince's fingers are tapering and long. 4. The heel of the foot round and smooth. 5. The instep high. 6. The fingers with round pliable joints. 7. The fingers and toes severally connected with a fine net-like membrane. 8. The shoulders (?) round as the King of the Stags. 9. Without stooping the hands reach to the knees. 10. That which ought to be concealed is concealed. 11. Every hair of the skin separate. 12. The hair of the body properly arranged. 13. The skin soft and smooth as the cotton of the Talas palm. 14. The hair the colour of gold. 15. The body itself cool and pure. 16. The mouth shaped perfectly within. 17. The cheek-bones like those of the King of Lions. 18. Both the legs large and broad. 19. The body above and below perfectly proportioned as the Nyagrôdha tree. 20. The seven places,[1] full and round. 21. Possessed of forty teeth. 22. All the teeth even, and close together. 23. The teeth without discoloration or tendency to decay. 24. The four canine teeth [ya-(nga)] white and pure. 25. The body pure, and of a golden yellow colour. 26. The voice soft as that of Brahma. 27. The tongue wide and long, pliable, and red. 28. Possessed of delicate taste. 29. The eyes blue. 30. The eyebrow constantly moving[2] like that of the King of the oxen. 31. Between the eyebrows a white circle of soft and pliable hair. 32. An excrescence of the top of the head.

"Mahârâja! these are the thirty-two superior signs. Whoever is marked with these will become either a Chakravartin or a perfect Buddha."

The King, having heard this explanation, his heart was filled with joy; he exulted greatly, and rejoiced.

Now at the time of the birth of Bôdhisatwa in Lumbini, when the supernatural light appeared and the earth shook, then the Rishis and the Devas, who dwelt on earth, exclaimed with great

---

1 The French version of the Lalita Vistara gives "protuberances."

2 There is some confusion in the Chinese, and this rendering is doubtful.

joy, "This day Buddha is born, for the good of men, to dispel the darkness of their ignorance," &c. Then the four heavenly kings took up the strain, and said, "Now because Bôdhisatwa is born to give joy and bring peace to the world, therefore is there this brightness." Then the Gods of the thirty-three Heavens took up the burthen of the strain, and the Yama Devas, and the Tusita Devas; and so forth, through all the Heavens of the Kama, Rupa and Arupa worlds, even up to the Akanishta Heavens, all the Devas joined in this song and said, "To-day Bôdhisatwa is born on earth to give joy and peace to men and Devas, to shed light in the dark places, and to give sight to the blind."

Now at this time there was a Rishi, called Asita[1], dwelling at peace above the thirty-three Heavens, who, observing this demonstration of joy among the Devas, asked them and said, "Excellent Devas! tell me why ye are thus singing, and waving your garments and caps for joy;"—to whom they replied, "Is it possible, that you have not heard that in the city of Kapilavastu, just below the Snowy Mountains has been born a child of perfect beauty, &c., distinguished by the thirty-two great signs, and by the eighty lesser ones, destined to attained Supreme wisdom and to turn the wheel of the Divine Law, and to bring perfect deliverance from sorrow, life and death, to men and Devas?"

Asita, having heard these things, immediately accepting them as true, descended from the Heaven in which he was staying to the Tsang-chang grove where he usually dwelt on earth.[2] Then taking with him his attendant Narada he passed through the air, and alighted not far from Kapilavastu. Standing there he thought thus with himself: "I will enter this city on foot, without any miraculous exhibition of my power as a Rishi."

Entering the city, therefore, he passed through the crowded streets, and arrived at the palace gates; meanwhile, the people stood looking on in wonder, some before their doors, others at their windows, others leaning over the balustrades, others on the tops of

---

[1] The story that follows and related by Asita, is in the "Southern Records," referred to a *tápaso* (ascetic) called Kaladewalo. *Vide* Turnour's "Pali Buddhistical Annals," R. A. S. B., 1838, p. 801.

[2] Here the description and locality of this grove are given, almost in the same words as in the previous account.

their houses, all fixed in their attention on the proceedings of the Rishi; and they said one to another, "When this Rishi entered the city on a previous occasion, he exhibited his miraculous power, and proceeded through the air to the Palace; but now he walks pace by pace. Why is it he does so?" Meanwhile, Asita, standing before the palace gates, addressed the Warder thus: "Go! tell the King I am here."

On hearing the message, the King, rising from his seat, ordered the Warder to conduct the Rishi to his presence without delay. Being seated, the King paid him reverence, and said, "I respectfully pay homage to your Reverence;" to whom Asita replied with the following salutation (chant): "Eternal peace to your Majesty." Then the King addressed the Rishi thus: "What is the occasion of your coming, O Rishi? is it some lack of garments or food or other necessary? If so, permit me to supply all that you require." To whom Asita replied, "No such trivial matter as this, O King! has brought me here to-day; but I have come from very far to see the child just born to your Majesty. I trust that your Majesty, of your great kindness, will let me see the babe." [Accordingly, Asita and Narada proceed to the apartment where the child lay.]

Then Mâya, taking the child in her arms, with her hand gently raised, attempted to make him bow his head in reverence towards the feet of Asita. But the child by his spiritual power turned himself round in his mother's arms, and presented his feet towards the Rishi. On which the King, taking the babe, made the same attempt three successive times, with the same result.

Now when Asita came to look at the child, a brightness like that of the Sun shone from his body, and illuminated the great earth, and his perfectly beautiful and graceful body sparkled like gold; his head like a precious covering, his nose straight, his shoulders round, his limbs perfectly proportioned.

Then Asita rose from his seat and addressed the King: "O King! make not the child bow his head to me! but let me rather worship his feet!" And again he recited this hymn of praise: "O rare event! Oh! seldom seen! A great Being has been born! —a very great being has been born! The tidings I heard in Heaven are indeed true, respecting this beautiful babe!"

Then Asita, unbaring his right shoulder and bending his right knee to the ground, took the child in his arms, and, returning to his seat, rested on his knees.[1]

Then the Queen said, "Venerable one! surely you will let the babe reverence you by saluting your feet!" To whom the Rishi replied, "Say not so, O Queen; for, on the contrary, both I and Devas and men should rather worship Him!"

Then the King taking costly jewels and precious substances, presented them to Asita, who, on his part, pouring water on the King's hands, received the gifts; but having done so, he at once presented them to the babe as an offering. Then Suddhôdana addressed him and said, "O great Rishi! I offered these things to you, as a tribute of reverence! I beseech you, keep them yourself!" To whom the Rishi answered, "Your Majesty gave them to me! I in my turn gave them to this most excellent child." Suddhôdana said, "Because I know the excellency of your merit, O Rishi! I presented these things to you." "But because I perceive the superiority of this child's excellency, I in my turn present them to him." To which Suddhôdana replied, "I fail to understand you, O Rishi!" To whom Asita replied, "Know, O King! that with the deepest reverence of body and mind, I take refuge in and submit to this child." Then Suddhôdana said, "What are the reasons for your so doing? I pray you expain yourself."

To whom the Rishi answered, "Listen, then, Mahârâja, and I will narrate from beginning to end the circumstances of the case. Know then that I was some time ago dwelling in the Trâyastriñshas heavens. When lo! I saw all the Devas around me rejoicing and dancing for joy, waving their jewelled caps and their garments in the air. On inquiring the reason of this demonstration they said, 'Know you not that this day is born in the world, in the Northern region just under the Himâlaya Mountains in the city of the Sâkyas, called Kapilavastu, of a Father Suddhôdana, and a Mother Mâya, a very beautiful child, perfect in every respect; endowed with the thirty-two superior signs, and the eighty inferior ones; and destined to become completely illuminated, and to preach the perfect Law. Doubtless this child by his Divine wisdom is com-

---

1 *Vide* Speirs' "Ancient India," page 248, for a picture of this scene from Cave of Ajunta.

pletely acquainted with all events, past and future, and will therefore be able to preach the Law, even for our sakes, and determine how we and all sentient creatures may escape the entanglements of sorrow and pain.' On hearing this, O King! I came hither to see for myself this beautiful child!"

[A long conversation then follows between Suddhôdana and Asita, during which the latter speaks of the impossibility of the child ever becoming a Chakravartin, as the astrologers predicted, and as evidence points out eighty personal signs on his body.] [These signs refer to the colour of the nails, the shape of the knees, the mode of movement, the scent of the body, and so on.[1]]

[Kiouen IX contains 6150 words and cost 3.075 taels].

CHAPTER X.

"MAHARAJA, if, in addition to the thirty-two superior signs, there be also present on the person these eighty inferior ones, know for a certainty that the possessor of these will become a perfect Buddha, and preach the Law." Asita, having spoken thus to the King, began to revolve in his mind at what age the Prince would arrive at complete emancipation, and so considering, he perceived by the powers of his intuition that it would be when he was thirty-five years of age, that then he would be completely inspired, and begin to preach the Law for the good of men. And then Asita, seeing plainly that he would not be alive when this took place, began to weep, and exclaimed in his grief—"Alas! woe is me!"—whilst the

---

[1] One of these signs is this. "The hair curly, and turning to the right in imitation of the figure 卐." From this it seems that the figure in question, viz., of *the Swastika*, is the symbol of the sun's apparent movement, from left to right. (For a very curious instance of this ancient practice of turning sun-ways, *vide* Joyce, "Irish Names of Places," Second Edition, p. 29.)

Another sign is "the fleshy projection at the top of the cranium like a mountain," and again "the top of his head so sublimely high that no man can trace it;" but the Chinese edition adds—"These three signs are wanting in the original." For an account of these signs *vide* M. B., 367 ss.

tears coursed down his cheeks; and then the King and the Queen, the great Ministers, and all the Sâkyas wept with him. Then the King, whilst the tears filled his eyes and flowed down his cheeks, sorrowfully inquired of the Rishi, "Oh! Asita! were not all things carefully attended to? Did I not fulfil my duty on the birth of this my child? Were not the signs and portents propitious that now you weep and lament thus? Tell me, oh, Rishi! why you are thus afflicted?" Then Asita replied, seeing the King's grief, as follows: "Be not cast down or sorrowful, oh, King! for in truth I see no unpropitious circumstance whatever connected with the birth of the child; but, on the contrary, every sign and circumstance is in the highest degree favourable; but because I perceive that owing to my age I shall not be privileged to listen to the declaration of the Law, which at the appointed time he shall proclaim to the world; on this account I weep!" And then for the sake of the King he repeated the following Gâtha:—

"By grief and regret am I completely overpowered,
Not to meet Him when he shall have attained Supreme wisdom!
Not to hear the words of Him thus born miraculously!
What loss—what damage—is mine!
Alas! I am old, and stricken in years;
My time of departure is close at hand;—
Reflecting on this strange meeting at his birth
I rejoice and yet I am sad!
Mahârâja! greatly shall this redound to the glory of thy race!
What happiness from the birth of this child shall ensue!
The misery—the wretchedness of men, shall disappear;
And at his bidding peace and joy shall everywhere flourish."

"Mahârâja! This is the reason why I weep, because of the thousands who shall find deliverance from this sorrow, and who shall be delivered from the consequences of their errors and sins, and arrive at perfect wisdom through the preaching of this your child, and that I shall not be found amongst these. But it is as the udambara flower which appears only once in myriads of myriads of years, so with the Buddhas, and that I should witness the birth of this child, the future Buddha, and not benefit by his teaching; this is why I weep, &c,"

[Then Asita begs Suddhôdana to explain all the circumstances of the birth (which have already been related). Suddhôdana having first respectfully offered to the Rishi twenty suits of raiment, only one of which Asita accepts, complies with the request.] And so Asita, having heard from the Father of the child an account of these miraculous occurrences was filled with joy, and, rising from his seat, began to withdraw from the Palace; step by step he advanced to the door; holding Narada by the right hand he took him by the left shoulder and flew away through the air, bearing his body along with him, and finally alighted at the village of Avanti, in South India. Then Asita addressed Narada as follows: "Be it known to you, my child, that a Buddha has come forth, and been born in the world; you ought, therefore, to become a disciple and practise the purity of a Brahmachari, so as to obtain after a period the inestimable benefit of so doing, and secure for yourself Rest and Peace.

Then again Asita reflected as to the place where Siddhârtha should obtain final illumination, and where he should begin to preach, and he perceived that the first would take place in Magadha and the second at Benares. Then Asita further reflected that he would impress the question of Buddha's birth on the mind of Narada in this way, he would take him to Benares and prepare a Vihâra for him to rest in, and thrice every day and thrice every night repeat in his hearing the tidings of Buddha's birth, and urge him to become his follower, and so secure rest to himself.

And so he did; and after thus living to a good old age he died full of years. But Narada, overpowered by worldly vanity, on account of the great fame which he had acquired as the disciple of Asita, was unable to attain to the knowledge of the three previous gems, or to say this is Buddha, this is Dharma, this is Sângha.

Then Suddhôdana, hearing of Asita's death, spake thus to all the counsellors of his empire, "Know ye my fears that the words of Asita will surely be accomplished, and this child will assuredly attain to supreme wisdom. Assist me then, great ministers, and let us endeavour to prevent this result by such expedients and precautions as are advisable for the purpose." To whom the ministers replied: "Doubt not, Mahârâja! but that our words will be accomplished, and that your son will become a Chakravartin. But at any rate, to prevent the possibility of any misadventure, let the king use such expedients as are necessary, and multiply around the young prince as he grows up every worldly allurement, and so gradually draw him to love his home and family pleasures so that he shall have no desire to stray to the hills and desert places or to practice austerities and become a hermit." Then Suddhôdana, although his heart was filled with apprehensions that the words of Asita would yet be accomplished, nevertheless resolved to follow the advice of his ministers and use every expedient to avert it. He, therefore, summoned all the Sâkya princes and warned them not to say a word to the young Prince when he grew up about the prediction of Asita, and then he called his ministers, and ordered them to release all prisoners throughout his empire, and to liberate every beast and creature that was bound. Moreover, he requested them to summon all the Brahmans throughout the kingdom, to receive from him offerings and gifts, so that in every temple and at every altar there might be held religious services on behalf of the child's future welfare.

Then the ministers convoked the Brahmans, according to the king's command, from the four regions, 32,000 in all, who entering the Palace of Suddhôdana, each received the appointed offerings during seven days, with a view to secure for the young prince the merit of such unbounded charity, as the Gâtha says—

"The heart of Suddhôdana filled with joy
Desired to secure for the prince great merit.
He ordered, therefore, his assembled ministers
To loose every captive in his empire,
And then arriving suddenly at his right mind,
He desired above all things to act according to the Law,
So assembling the 100,000 milch kine,
With golden-tipped horns and silvered hoofs,
Young in years and of brilliant colour,
Each with her calf behind her;
Her skin glossy, rich in milk,
At each squeeze of the hand yielding a pint;
And preparing, moreover, endless rare and costly jewels,
Gold, silver, grain and all such presents,
For the sake of securing good fortune to the prince
These all he presented to the assembled Brahmans."

[Kiouen X contains 6,090 words and cost 3,045 taels.]

CHAPTER XI.

The selection of a foster-mother (wife's sister).

1. THE Prince Royal now being seven days old, his mother the Queen Mâya, being unable to regain her strength or recover the joy she experienced whilst the child dwelt in her womb, gradually succumbed to her weakness and died.

[*But some of the old Masters say that this is a universal rule with the mothers of all Buddhas, that they should thus die on the seventh day after the birth of their child. For how could they bear to see their babes become Ascetics? Whilst others say, that seeing all the wonderful miracles attending the birth of their child, they die of joy.*]

Mâya, having thus finished her earthly course, was translated at once to the Trâyastrinshas heavens, where she was surrounded on every hand by countless Devas who attended her, and whence from time to time she descended to earth to comfort Suddhôdana, and assure him that her joy was now equal to that she experienced during the period of her gestation, and that he should on no account grieve for her, and added this Gâtha—

"Freed from all partialities,
Persevering without interruption,
Ever thinking aright
Without confusion from first to last.
His appearance pure as gold,
His faculties perfectly under control,
My son can declare the Law,
And is worthy of all honour."

Mâya having uttered this Gâtha disappeared, returning to her celestial abode. Suddhôdana, after this vision, immediately assembled all the Sâkyas and addressed them thus: "Now that this babe has lost his mother, who is there we may select to take her place, and act as a foster mother to the child?" Then 500 recently married Sâkya females replied: "I! I! am able to take charge of the babe." To whom they replied: "All ye are too young, Mahâprajâpati alone is fit for this charge, and so they all agreed to elect Mahâprajapati for the purpose. Then Suddhôdana committed the child to her charge, and allotted to her thirty-two waiting women—eight to nurse the child, eight to wash him, eight to feed him, eight to amuse him.

[Now Suddhôdana Râja had two sons, viz., Siddhârtha and Nando; Suklôdana had two sons, Nandaka and Batrika; Amritôdana had two sons, Aniruddha and Mahânama; the sister of Suddhôdana, called Amritachittra, had one son called Tishya.]

At this time Mahâprajâpati, the royal prince's foster-mother, spake thus to the King—"As your Majesty commands, my care over the child shall be most constant." Thus she sedulously attended him without intermission, as the sun tends on the moon during the first portion of each month, till the moon arrives at its fulness. So the child gradually waxed and increased in strength; as the shoot of the Nyagrôdha tree gradually increases in size, well-planted in the earth, till itself becomes a great tree, thus did the child day by day increase, and lacked nothing, as the Gâtha says—

" The five kinds of grain, and wealth and jewels,
Gold, silver, and all kinds of raiment,
Both made and not made.
These things were all self-supplied in abundance.
The child causing his loving mother
Always to abound in most nutritious milk,
So that even supposing it were not sufficient (naturally),
It became more than enough (thro' his influence)."

Thus the King and his empire enjoyed complete peace and prosperity. Neither plague nor famine or other evil came nigh the people, and in every place the love of religion (the Law) increased and flourished as in the old times, when truth and justice were universally prevalent.

The Presentation of Gifts.

§ 2. Now at this time Suddhôdana Râja, at the period when the Asterism Chin (the last of the twenty-eight constellations) was passing, and the asterism Koh (α and ζ in Virgo) coming on, caused every kind of costly ornament to be made, viz., bracelets for the arms and wrists, for the legs and ancles, necklets composed of every species of precious stone, and cinctures, turbans and coronals; in addition to these, there were five hundred Sâkyas related to the Prince Royal, each one of whom had made other ornaments similar to the above, and having so made them brought them to Suddhôdana Râja, and spake as follows: "Sadhu! Great Râja! would that your Majesty would permit us during seven days and seven nights to ornament the person of the Royal Prince with these costly decorations which we have made; and so not cause us to have laboured in vain!" Then Suddhôdana Râja, on the morning (of the junction) of the asterism Kwei (Pushya), accompanied by the chief minister Udâyana [*Father of the Bikshu Udayi*[1]] and five hundred other Brahmans, all chanting the strain, "This is indeed a lucky time," went with the child to the garden Vimalayûha, from the earliest time ever regarded as a sacred place.

Within this garden were assembled countless multitudes of people, men and women, young and old, desirous to see the face of the infant child. Moreover, as they went through Kapilavastu, they ordered chariots full of every sort of gift, to precede the Royal Prince, and the charioteer to cry out as he went, "Every one who wants these things may now have them for asking." Again they ordered every kind of music to accompany and go before him, whilst countless women, with every kind of ornament upon their person, occupied the tops of the balconies and towers, the windows and the open vestibules, holding flowers in their hands, desirous to behold the Royal Prince, and to scatter the flowers on his person. Moreover, there were crowds of women on each side of the road accompanying the procession with fans to fan his body, and with brushes to clear the road from impediments; whilst all the Sâkyas joined round Suddhôdana Râja, and formed a regular procession. Then Mahâprajâpati, with the child on her knee, rode in the precious chariot, and proceeded to the garden.

---

[1] *Vide* "Manual of Buddhism," p. 199. No doubt Udayi, who is so frequently spoken of in this work, is the same as the Káludáyi of Turnour (R.A,S.B., 1838, p. 801); but he must not be confounded with Láludáyi (*i.e.*, Udáyi, the simpleton) of the Somadatta-Jâtaka (Fausböll, "Five Jâtakas," p. 31).

At this time the chief minister, the Father of Udâyi, with the five hundred other Brahmans, began in endless laudatory phrases to congratulate the prince, whilst they attached the costly ornaments they had brought to his person. Having done this, the glory of the prince's body eclipsed the glory of these gems, so that their brightness was not seen, and they all appeared dark and black, even as a drop of ink, utterly lustreless—just as if we were to compare the brightness of the priceless gold, called Jambunada, with that of ashes—so all the gems on his person were lost as the glow-worm's spark in the light of day.

Then those men, seeing this wonderful miracle (ardbhûtadharma), began to recite the following words: "How strange! how rare! how strange! how seldom seen!"—whilst all for joy, and with many smiles, waved their garments, and clapped their hands with delight.

Now within this garden there was a certain Guardian Spirit called Vimala, who, on this occasion, mounted into space and without being seen began to chant these lays;

"Though this great and wide earth
With all its cities, towns and hamlets,
Its mountains, rivers, and forests,
Were all composed of Jambunada gold;
Yet one ray of glory from a pore of Buddhâ's body,
So full of splendour is it,
Would eclipse all that gold, and make it appear as a drop of ink.
In comparison with the fullness of true religious merit
The brightness of gems is as nothing.
A man possessed of the distinctive signs,
The result of superior excellence,
Needs not the adornment of precious stones."

Having uttered these words, the Spirit immediately caused innumerable flowers to descend from space, and rest upon the person of the child, after which he returned to his own abode.

The Prince enters School.

§ 3. AND now Suddhôdana Râja, remembering that the young prince was eight years of age, summoned all his ministers and great officers of state, and addressed them as follows: "Illustrious ministers! I am now in a state of uncertainty as to the most learned man, and most deeply versed in the exposition of the various Shasters whom I may appoint to instruct the prince."

Then the various ministers replied to the King as follows: "Mahârâja! know that Visvamitra is the most perfectly acquainted with all the Shasters, and in every respect the most suited to become teacher of the prince, in all and every kind of scholarlike erudition."

Then Suddhôdana despatched messengers to Visvamitra to speak to him thus—"Will you, oh, learned Sir! undertake to instruct the Prince Royal in the various branches of polite learning and the usual manual accomplishments?"

Then Visvamitra replied—"I am ready to obey the Râja's commands." Then the king was glad at heart, and forthwith selected by divination a fortunate day, when a propitious constellation was in the ascendant, and summoned all the old men of the Sâkya race to perform such ceremonies as were necessary for the occasion, and then, surrounded by five hundred of the Sâkya youths and countless others, male and female, he sent the young prince to the Hall of Learning. Then Visvamitra, beholding the exceeding dignity of the prince's bearing, unable to control himself, arose from his seat, and instantly fell prostrate at the feet of the child and adored him. Afterwards, rising up, he looked towards each of the four quarters, and reddened with shame. Whilst Visvamitra was thus abashed at his conduct, there came from the Tusita heavens a certain Deva called Suddhavara,[1] accompanied by countless other Devas, appointed to watch over the young prince, and, without appearing to the sight of any, he chanted this song:—

"Whatever arts there are in the world,
Whatever Sûtras and Shasters

1 [Sing-mian. The "Lalit. Vist." gives Subhanga, p. 120].

This (child) is thoroughly acquainted with all,
And is able to teach them to others.

* * * * * *

The Deva, having finished this hymn, showered down on the prince every sort of flower, and returned to his abode.

And now Suddhôdana Râja, having bestowed gifts on the Brahmans and having delivered the young prince into the care of his nurses and of Visvamitra, returned to his Palace.

Meanwhile, the royal prince first entering on his course of study, taking some most excellent slabs of sandal-wood, known as Gôsîrshachandana[1], to use as writing boards, adorned with the choicest jewels, and the outside (or, the back) sprinkled with the most delicious perfume; taking these, he came and stood before Visvamitra Acharya, and spake thus: "My Master! (Acharya). In what writing will you instruct me? shall it be in the writing of the Brahma Devas (or, of Brahma Deva), or the Kia-lu-sih-cha (Kharôsti) language [*this word signifies "the lips of an ass"*], or in the writing used by Pushkara Rishi [*this signifies the "Lotus flower"*] or the Akara writing [*this signifies member-divisions* (is it Añgara?)], or the Mangala language [*this word signifies "lucky"*], or the Yava language [*this word "yava" has no recognised signification*], or the language called Ni [*this signifies the language of the great Tsin country, i.e., China*], or the writing called Anguli [*this word signifies "fingers"*], or the writing known as that of the Yananikas [*this word signifies "chariot riders"*], or the writing called Sakava [*this word signifies a "cow" or "heifer"*], or the writing called Pravani [*this means "leaf of a tree"*], or the writing called Parusha [*this signifies "a bad word"*], or the language of the Davida country (for Dravida?) [*this means "Southern India"*], or the language of the Pitachas [*this word means "to raise a corpse"*], or the language of the Dakshinavatas [*this means "to turn to the right"*], or the language of the Tirthi [*this means "naked men"*], or the language of Uka (for "ugra"?), [*this word signifies "bright" or "solemn" glare*], or the Sankya

---

[1] Ox-head sandal-wood, so called from its colour—a fiery red; it is a question worth considering, whether Alexander's horse, Bucephalus, was not so named from its color, and not from its shape, as Arrian seems to think.

language [*this signifies the art of "numbers"*], or the language called Adamourdha [*this signifies to "cover" or "repeat"*], or the language called Anouroma, or the language called Vyadashra [*this signifies "confused"*], the language called Darada [*name of a mountain*], the language called "Sikyani" [*no meaning*], the language called "Kousa" [*this signifies a "bridle"*], or the language of Tchina [*i.e., of the "great Tsui"* (or China)], or the language called Mana [*i.e., a measure equal to a "pint"*], the Madhyachari writing [*the letters of the "middle"*], or the language called "Vitsati" [*i.e., a man*], or the writing called Pushpa [*a "flower"*], the language called Deva [*a God*], or Naga [*a dragon*], or Yaksha [*no signification*], or Gandharva [*a Deva of music*], or Asura [*no wine drinker*], or Garuda [*golden-winged bird*], or Kinnara [*neither man*], or Mahôraga [*a great dragon*], or Meigachaka [*the sound of all beasts*], or Kakaruda [*sound of birds*], or Bhâumi Devas [*earth gods*], or Antarikshadevas [*Devas of space*], or Uttakuru [*the northern region*], or the language of Purvavideha [*eastern continent*], or of Utchepa [*that which is raised*], or of Nikchepa [*that which is rejected*], or of Sâgara [*the sea*], or of Vajra [*diamond*], or of Lekhaprakileka [*gone after*], or Vikhita [*fragments of food*], Aniboutta [*not yet existing*][1], or Sastravartta or Kannavartta [*revolving numbers*], Utkchepavartta [*raised and revolving*], Nikchepavartta [*rejected, revolving*], Padalik(hita) [*foot*], Dvikuttarapadna [*union of two sounds in one word*], Yavaddasatara [*ten sounds*], Madhyaharini [*middle flowing*], Rishiyastapatpata [*the sufferings of all the Rishis*], Dharanipakchari [*seeing the earth*], Gayanaprekchini [*beholding space*], Sarvasatanisanta [*all medicinal plants*], Sarsanyagrahani [*united wisdom*], Sasruta [*all sounds*]."

The young prince, having recited these different languages, again addressed Visvamitra, saying, "Of all these different styles of writing which does my master design to teach me?"

To which Visvamitra, with a smiling face, without any personal feeling of envy or shame, replied in these Gâthas :—

"This child of rare and excellent wisdom,
Following the customary rules of the world,

---

[1] This is the general explanation of the *Adbhutadharma* section of the sacred (Buddhist) Books.

Himself, altho' acquainted with all the Shasters,
Has deigned to enter my school.
And now he has thoroughly recited from beginning to end
The names of different writing, of which I never heard,
Surely this is the Instructor of Devas and men,
Who condescends to seek for a master!"

At this time, five hundred noblemen entered the college with the royal prince, and began to learn the sounds of the different letters, on which occasion, the Prince, in virtue of his Supreme wisdom, gave forth the sound of each letter in the following excellent manner:—

1. In sounding the letter "A," pronounce it as in the sound of the word "anitya."

2. In sounding the letter "I", pronounce it as in the word "indriya."

3. In sounding the letter "U", pronounce it as in the word "upagata" (?).

4. In sounding the letter "ri", pronounce it as in the word "riddhi."

5. In sounding the letter "O", pronounce it as in the word "ogha" (?).

6. In sounding the letter "ka", pronounce it as in the word "karma,"

7. In sound the letter "kha", pronounce it as in the word "khanda."

8. In sounding the letter "ga", pronounce it as in the word "gata" (?).[1]

At this time Suddhôdana Râja, again assembling all his ministers of state for consultation, spake to them thus: "My Lords and Ministers!—Which of you can tell me of a skilful teacher of the military arts and the science of war, whom I may appoint to instruct Siddârtha, my son?"

Then all the ministers respectfully answered the king and said, "Mahârâja! the son of Supra Buddha, Kshantedeva by name, is thoroughly competent to teach the Prince all the martial accomplishments of which you speak."

To whom Suddhôdana replied, with great joy, "Go summon

[1] [And so on, for all the letters (there are thirty-eight)]. Compare the "*Lalita Vistara,*" p. 124 n.

this Kshantedeva to my presence;" on whose arrival the Râja spoke thus: "Kshantadeva! I hear that you are able to instruct my son Siddârtha in all martial accomplishments,—is this the case, or not?" Then forthwith Kshantadeva addressed the king and said, "Your servant is able and willing to do so." "If so," replied the king, "you have now the opportunity—do so."

On this occasion Suddhôdana appointed a garden for his son's accommodation, in which he might practice all the athletic and martial accomplishments. (This garden was called Kan-kü, diligent labour).

Then the prince, entering the garden with five hundred Sâkya youths, engaged himself in every delightful recreation. At this time Kshantedeva, bringing forth the different martial and athletic instruments, began to attempt to instruct the Royal Prince. But, on his part, the prince requested his teacher to devote himself to the other Sâkyas; "As for me," he said, "I will be my own instructor;" on which Kshantadeva applied himself to perfect the five hundred young Sâkya noblemen in all the arts of his calling —riding the elephant, archery, chariot racing, and so on.

This being accomplished and the youths having acquired skill in all these arts; then Siddârtha also replied, "It is well, I am self-taught" (and in the same way with respect to other things). On which, the teacher, Kshantedeva, uttered this Gâtha:—

"Though young in point of years,
Yet without using any great effort,
How easily he explains and asks learned questions,
In a moment he sees through every thing.
After a few days' study,
He surpasses those who have devoted years to it,
Perfect in all manly arts
He excels all those who enter with him into competition."

[Kiouen XI has 5615 letters, and cost 2·807 Taels.]

CHAPTER XII.

On the excursion for observation.

§ 1. Now the Royal Prince, up to the time of his eighth year, grew up in the royal palace without any attention to study; but from his eighth year till his twelfth year he was trained under the care of Visvamitra and Kshantedeva, as we have related.

But now, having completed twelve years and being perfectly acquainted with all the customary modes of enjoyment, as men speak, such as hunting, riding and driving here and there, according to the desire of the eye or for the gratification of the mind; such being the case, it came to pass on one occasion that he was visiting the Kan-ku garden, and whilst there amused himself by wandering in different directions, shooting with his bow and arrow at whatever he pleased; and so he separated himself from the other Sâkya youths who were also in the several gardens enjoying themselves in the same way.

Just at this time it happened that a flock of wild geese, flying through the air, passed over the garden, on which the young man, Devadatta,[1] pointing his bow, shot one of them through the wing, and left his arrow fixed in the feathers; whilst the bird fell to the ground at some distance off in the middle of the garden.

The Prince Royal, seeing the bird thus transfixed with the arrow, and fallen to the ground, took it with both his hands, and sitting down, with his knees crossed, he rested it in his lap, and with his own soft and glossy hand, smooth and pliable as the leaf of the plaintain, his left hand holding it, with his right hand he drew forth the arrow, and anointed the wound with oil and honey.

At this time Devadatta, the young prince, sent certain messengers to the Prince Royal, who spoke to him thus—"Devadatta has shot a goose which has fallen down in your garden, send it to him without delay."

Then the Prince Royal answered the messengers and said, "If the bird were dead, it would be only right I should return it forthwith to you; but if it is not dead you have no title to it."

---

[1] Devadatta is generally called the cousin of Siddârtha. According to Spence Hardy, he was his brother-in-law. M. B., p. 61.

Then Devadatta sent again to the Prince Royal, and the message was this: "Whether the bird be living or dead it is mine; my skill it was that shot it, and brought it down, on what ground do you delay to send it me?" To which the Prince Royal answered, "The reason why I have taken possession of the bird is this, to signify that in time to come, when I have arrived at the condition of perfection to which I tend, I shall thus receive and protect all living creatures; but if still you say that this bird belongs not to me, then go and summon all the wise and ancient men of the Sâkya tribe, and let them decide the question on its merits!"

At this time there was a certain Deva belonging to the Suddhavasa heaven, who assumed the appearance of an old man and entered the assembly of the Sâkyas, where they had come together, and spoke thus: "He who nourishes and cherishes is by right the keeper and owner; he who shoots and destroys is by his own act the loser and the disperser."[1]

At this time all the ancient men of the Sâkyas at once confirmed the words of the would-be clansman and said, "Verily, verily, it is as this venerable one says, with respect to the difference between Devadatta and the Royal Prince."

The Story of the Ploughing Match.

§ 2. Now at another time it happened that Suddhôdana Râja assembled all the Sâkya princes, and took with him the Prince Royal to go to see a ploughing-match (or field cultivation or sowing). Then in the enclosed space were assembled the half-stripped men, each labouring hard in the ploughing contest, driving the oxen and urging them on if they lagged in their speed, and from time to time goading them to their work. And now, when the Sun increased in his strength, and the sweat ran down both from men and oxen, then for a few moments they ceased from their labours. In the meantime, various insects came forth from

---

[1] The principle of this decision is not unlike that recorded of Solomon.

the ground, and flocks of birds, in the interval of the ploughing exercises, came down in multitudes and devoured them.

The Royal Prince, seeing the tired oxen, their necks bleeding from the goad, and the men toiling beneath the midday sun, and the birds devouring the hapless insects, his heart was filled with grief, as a man would feel who saw his own household bound in fetters, and, being thus affected with sorrow on behalf of the whole family of sentient creatures, he dismounted from his horse Kantaka, and, having done so, he walked about in deep reflection, thinking about the misery attaching to the various forms of life, and as he meditated, he exclaimed, "Alas! alas! how full of misery is human life. What unhappiness there is in birth and death, old age and disease, and in the midst of all this wretchedness to know of no means of escape or deliverance! But why do men seek for no release? Why do they not strive after rest from toil? Why do they not contend earnestly for that wisdom which alone can lead them to escape from the miseries incident to life and death? Oh! where may I find a quiet spot for meditation—to cast over these causes of sorrow in my mind?"

Then Suddhôdana, having watched the ploughing-match, accompanied by all the Sâkyas, returned to the garden.

Then the Royal Prince, wandering about and looking from place to place for a convenient spot for rest, suddenly saw a secluded space under a Jambu Tree where he could sit in quiet, and then he addressed his attendants on each side, and bade them disperse themselves in other directions," for I," said he, "desire to be alone for a short period."

Then, gradually approaching the tree, he sat down beneath its shade with his legs crossed, and began to think upon the subject of the sorrows and pain belonging to every form of life. And then, through the power of the love and pity which these reflections produced in his heart, he was wrapt into a state of unconscious ecstacy: and, finally, by separating his thoughts from every kind of impure or worldly taint, he reached the first condition of Dhyâna.[1]

At this time there happened to be five Rishis flying, by means

---

[1] This incident seems to be the subject of Fig. 1, Pl. xxv., "Tree and Serpent Worship."

of their spiritual powers, through the air, possessed of great energies, and thoroughly versed in the Shasters and Vedas. They were going from the south towards the north, and when they arrived just over the Jambu tree in the garden aforesaid, wishing to go onwards, suddenly they found themselves arrested in their course. Then they said one to another, "How is it that we, who have in former times found no difficulty in flying through space and reaching even beyond Sumeru to the Palace of Vaisravana and even to the city of Arkavanta[1], and beyond that even to the abode of the Yakshas, yet now find our flight impeded in passing over this tree? By what influence is it that to-day we have lost our spiritual power?"

Then the Rishis, looking downwards, beheld the prince underneath the tree, sitting with his legs crossed, his whole person so bright with glory that they could with difficulty behold him. Then these Rishis began to consider—"Who can this be?" "Is it Brahma, Lord of the world?—or is it Krishna Deva, Lord of the Kama Loka?—or is it Sâkra?—or is it Vaisravana, the Lord of the Treasuries?—or is it Chandradeva?—or is it Sûrya Deva? —or is it some Chakravartin Râja?—or is it possible that this is the person of a Buddha born into the world?"

At this time the Guardian Deva of the wood addressed the Rishis as follows: "Great Rishis all! this is not Brahma Deva, Lord of the World; or Krishna, Lord of the Kama Heavens; or Sâkra or Vaisravana, Lord of the Treasuries; or Chandra Deva or Sûrya Deva; but this is the Prince Royal, called Siddhârtha, born of Suddhôdana Râja, belonging to the Sâkya race. The glory which proceeds from one pore of his body is greater by sixteen times than all the glory proceeding from the bodies of all those forenamed Devas! And on this account your spiritual power of flight failed you as soon as you came above this tree!"

The Rishis, having heard the words of this guardian spirit, forthwith descended from the air, and, standing before the prince, they uttered the following verses of commendation one by one.

The first Rishi said:

"The world destroyed by the fire of sorrow

---

[1] Ho-lo-kia-pan-to.

This one is able to provide a lake of water[1] for escape,
This excellent Law once possessed (or revealed)
Is able to destroy all the sources of sorrow."

The second said:

"In the midst of the ignorance and darkness of the world
There is one who can produce such brightness as this!
Once possessed of His most excellent Law,
The darkness is dispersed—the world is illumined."

The third said:

"In the midst of the vast bog and wilderness of sorrow
This great means of conveyance can carry us thro' all,
Once possessed of this most excellent Law,
Then we can pass over the three worlds without difficulty."

The fourth said:

"From all the bonds and shackles of worldly sorrows
There is some contrivance able to give good deliverance;
So this most excellent Law
Can deliver men from all the bonds and shackles of life."

The fifth said:

"Whatever miseries of life or death are in the world,
This great Physician is able to cure all;
And so the most excellent Law
Is a perfect remedy for all the sorrows of birth and death."

Thus the Rishis, having saluted the prince with these verses, they bowed down at his feet, and three times proceeded to circumambulate the place, and then flying away again they went on their way through the air.

Now at this time Suddhôdana, having for a moment lost sight of the prince, was very much alarmed, and asking a man who passed by, he said, "Have you any knowledge as to which way my son the Royal Prince has gone? [*These two former sentences are repeated in the Sanscrit original. Ch. Ed.*] He has just now suddenly disappeared."

Forthwith the king sent his ministers in every direction to seek for the prince, wherever he might be. Then one of the ministers unexpectedly saw him sitting beneath the Jambu tree in the

---

[1] Literally—"the water of the Lake of the Law."

shade, lost in meditation and wrapped away in ecstasy. Moreover, he saw that the shadows of the other trees had turned. but the shadow of the Jambu tree alone remained, overshadowing the form of the prince. Then the minister, beholding this miraculous circumstance, was filled with exultation and joy, and going away on foot, he summoned the king to the spot, and said—

"The son of the Mahârâja is now dwelling
Beneath the shade of the Jambu tree, wonderfully seated,
With his legs crossed, lost in meditation and ecstasy,
The brilliancy of his person like the brightness of the Sun or Moon,
This in truth is the great Master,
From whom the shadow of the tree turns not away.
Oh! would that the king himself would come and see,
And say what means this wonderful appearance of the prince;
So bright his body that he resembles Mahâ Brahma,
Or Sâkra Deva, god of Trayastriñshas,
So wonderful the brilliancy of his spiritual splendour
That it lights up with glory all that wood!"

Suddhôdana Raja, having heard this intelligence, immediately went to the spot beneath the Jambu tree, and there he beheld his son sitting cross-legged beneath the tree, just as in the darkest night a burning mountain belching forth fire from its summit is visible, or as suddenly from the black clouds the bright moon emerges, or as a lamp shines in a dark room. Then the Râja, having witnessed the sight, was filled with awe, the hairs on his body were ruffled and stood erect, whilst he bowed down at the feet of his son and, filled with inexpressible joy, exclaimed, "Sadhu! Sadhu! my son has indeed great personal merit." And then he added these verses—

"As the flaming top of a mountain in the night,
Or as the full autumn moon in the midst of darkness,
So beholding my son as he sits in meditation,
Every hair of my body is imperceptibly moved."

Then the king again bowed at his son's feet, and added this Gâtha—

"I now bend this body of mine
Before the thousand radiated excellent foot,

Now for the first time since his birth
Beholding unexpectedly the Prince lost in meditation."

At this time there were some little children engaged in play, dragging along a rabbit trap (?), and passing the place where the king was, they were making a noise and laughing, on which one of the Ministers reproved them and said, "You children! hold your tongues, and make no noise!" On which they replied, "And why may we not make a noise and play?" On which the minister replied in a verse—

"The sun, though it is past noon,
Cannot draw its shadow beyond this tree,
And so the exceeding brightness,
Unequalled in the world,
Of this one who sits in meditation beneath the tree
Unmoved and unaffected as Sumeru,
Siddhârtha the prince royal! from the depth of his heart
Causes the shadow not to depart."

On the Betrothal of the Prince.

[*Lit. pushing—art—contention—marriage.*]

§ 3. And now the Prince, growing up by degrees, reached his nineteenth year. And when at this age, his father Suddhôdana Râja caused three Palaces to be constructed for him, each of them for a different season of the year. The first a warm palace, calculated for the winter; the second a cool palace, for the summer; the third fit for the spring and autumn. These palaces were severally surrounded by gardens, in which were tanks and pleasant streams of water, and every kind of delightful flower to please the senses.

Moreover, the king appointed a great number of skilful and distinguished personal attendants to wait on his son. Some to rub his person, others to smooth it, and others to anoint and bathe him. There were hairdressers, looking-glass holders, etc., etc., besides some to perfume his garments, others to keep the Bezoar (new hwang); others to keep the hair chaplets; others again were in charge of his wardrobe, every garment in which was made of Kasika material. [*Whereas his Royal Father only wore Kasika on the outside, his under garments being made of every miscellaneous stuff.*]

Moreover, the prince was surrounded by servants both male and female, brought up on the purest food. The Prince himself partook only of the daintiest fare, and every sort of luscious fruit. Thus every day and every night brought him some fresh joy and pleasant diversion, protected by a beautiful white umbrella during the day, and sleeping under the finest gauze canopies by night.

Now at this time Suddhôdana Râja, having watched his son gradually growing up to manhood, once more recalled the words of the Rishi Asita to his memory, and in consequence he summoned the great ministers of the Sâkya race to an assembly, and spake thus to them: "Do you not remember at the time of the birth of the Royal Prince that the assembled Brahmans and Asita all bare record when they calculated the babe's horoscope, that if he remained a prince he would be a Chakravartin, but if he became a recluse, he would be a supreme Buddha. Now then, my Ministers, tell me by what contrivance I can prevent the Prince leaving his home and assuming a religious life?"

Then the Sâkyas answered and said, "You ought, O King! to construct another Palace for the Prince, and let there be prepared there every accommodation for voluptuous pleasures, with women and hand-maidens; so the prince will give up the idea of leaving his home and becoming a recluse; as the Gâtha says:—

"The record of Asita
Certain and unchangeable,
The Sâkyas exhort (the king) to build a palace,
Expecting to prevent (the prince) from leaving his home."

Then Suddhôdana Râja said again, "Sâkyas! which of all the daughters of our race is fit to be the wife of the Prince Siddârtha?

At this time five hundred of the Sâkyas exclaimed, "My daughter! my daughter, is fit!" [*The two previous sentences in the Sanscrit original are repeated several times. The present is a digest. Ch. Ed.*]

Then Suddhôdana Râja began to think with himself thus: "If

I do not go to the Prince Royal and consult with him about taking a wife, then I shall but provoke him to disobey and thwart my design; and again, if I do go to him and consult, then I fear he will take the subject deeply to heart, and in the end not fall in with my views. What then shall I do? what expedient shall I adopt? I will do this; I will cause every sort of precious ornament to be made, and, when complete, I will offer them to the prince with the request that he will distribute them among the females of his tribe, and then, having trusty persons in watch, I will request them to look well and observe the prince's countenance, and on whichever of the ladies he looks with tenderness, her will I select, and propose to him for a wife."

Accordingly the king ordered every kind of jewelled ornament, and delightful trifle (un lung), to be made of silver and gold; and then he sent messengers throughout Kapilavastu to proclaim as follows: "After seven days the Prince Royal desires all the ladies of the Sâkya race to assemble at the court, and after receiving them he purposes to distribute among them every kind of precious ornament and delightful toy. Let all the ladies, therefore, come, as they are bidden, to the palace gate!"[1]

Then six days passed, and on the seventh the Prince Royal, first going forth, arrived in front of the gate of the palace, and advancing towards his cushioned throne, he sat down. Thereupon the ladies, decorated with every sort of precious jewel, began to assemble in numbers before the palace, desiring to see the prince, and still more anxious to receive from him the jewels and precious toys he had promised to bestow upon them.

The prince, seeing the ladies coming, took the jewels he had by him, and the ornaments which had been made, and began to bestow them as he proposed; whilst the ladies, because of the grace and beauty of the prince's demeanour, could not look him straight in the face; but each one simply passing by and bowing the head in profound obeisance, took her gift and departed. And now, when all the gifts were exhausted, at the very last, there came a certain damsel of the family of Basita, of the Sâkya tribe, whose name was Yasôdharâ, the daughter of Mahanama, the great minister of state, surrounded on every side by a circle of personal attendants, to see

[1] Swayambarâ, *Speir*, "*Anc. Ind.*," p. 126.

the Prince Royal. With an easy gait, and her eyes fixed before her, she advanced towards the prince, as one who had known him in old time, and, without any timidity, addressed him thus—"Your Royal Highness! what gift or costly ornament have you for me?" The prince forthwith replied, "You have come too late, the presents are all distributed." To whom she replied again, "And what have I done that you should not have reserved one for me?" To whom the prince said, "I do not refuse to give you one, but why did you not come in time." Now, on the prince's finger there was a very costly signet-ring worth a hundred thousand (pieces of gold). Taking this from his finger, he offered it to Yasôdharâ. Yasôdharâ rejoined, "Your Highness! I can remain here by your side, perhaps you may have something else to give." On this the prince replied, "You can take my necklace of pearls if you please;"—to whom she rejoined, "It would be a pity for me to do that, and so deprive the prince of that which so much becomes him." Saying which, she departed in no very amiable temper.

The Story of Yasôdharâ.

§ 4. [1] At this time the world-honoured one, having arrived at complete enlightenment, was addressed by the venerable Udâyi as follows: "How was it when you were still residing in your father's royal palace, and you offered to Yasôdharâ the priceless jewels and ornaments that adorned your person, you were unable to cause her any gratification?"

On this Buddha answered Udâyi as follows: "Listen! and weigh my words. It was not only on this occasion that Yasôdharâ was discontented with the gifts I offered her, but from old time, because of an offence she had taken through successive ages, she has never been pleased with me." On which Udâyi said,

[1] Here we have the first of the frequent episodes (Avadânas) which occur in this history. It is a story of Yasôdharâ in a previous birth. In all these stories the supposition is made that Buddha has arrived at complete inspiration or enlightenment before he enters on the narrative, and so is able to reveal all that occurred in time past.

"Oh! would that the world-honoured Buddha would recount this history to me."

At this time Buddha addressed the venerable Udâyi and said, "I remember in ages gone by, there was in the country of Kasi, and in the city of Benares, a certain king who was an unbeliever. That king had a son who, for some trivial fault, was banished by his father from the kingdom. As he wandered along, he came to a certain Devâlaya, and having there contracted a marriage[1] with a woman he stopped in the place, and lived with her. Now, after a time it so happened that, all their food being exhausted, this king's son went out to hunt to try to get something to eat. It so chanced that on that day he shot a large sort of lizard, and having skinned it, he cut up the flesh, and put it in a pot of water to boil. When it was nearly cooked, the water in the pot having boiled away, the king's son said to his wife, 'This flesh is hardly done yet, will you run and get some more water?" She immediately consented, and went to fetch it. In the meanwhile, her husband, overcome with hunger and not having patience to wait, began to eat the flesh that was in the pot, and at last finished it all, without leaving a morsel. Just as he had finished, his wife came back with the water, and, seeing the pot empty, she asked her husband 'Where has the flesh gone?' He immediately prevaricated, and said, 'Do you know, just after you left, the lizard came to life again, got out of the pot and ran away.' But his wife would not believe that the half-cooked lizard had really so suddenly come to life again and got away; for she said, 'How is it possible?' and so she thought to herself, 'the fact is, this man of mine has eaten it all up, and now he is mocking me by telling me this story about the animal running away.' So she took offence, and was always in a poor temper.

"Now, after the lapse of a few years, it came to pass that the king, the father of the prince, died; at which time all the ministers sent for the young prince, and immediately anointed him king. On this the king, having ascended the throne, caused every kind of precious jewel, costly ornament, and splendid robe, to be brought to him, and these he forthwith presented to his wife, the queen.

---

[1] It must be understood that in all these stories many expressions are rendered into *polite* English.

Notwithstanding this, although so liberally and ungrudgingly provided, her face revealed not the slightest pleasure or happiness; but she remained gloomy as before. On this the king addressed her and said, 'How is it, notwithstanding the priceless gifts I have bestowed on you, that you still remain so gloomy and so sad? You are just as unhappy now as you were before?' Then the queen forthwith replied in the following Gâtha,—

"Most noble monarch! listen!
In years gone by, when you went to hunt,
Taking your arrows and your knife,
You trapped and killed a certain lizard.
You skinned it and put it on to boil,
You sent me to fetch more water for the pot;
You ate the flesh, and did not leave a morsel;
You mocked me and said it had run away.'

And now, Udâyi! you should know, that at this time, the king was myself—the queen was Yasôdharâ, and by this one transgression in those days long gone by, I entailed on myself this perpetual result, that no gift of mine or precious offering can ever cause joy to Yasôdharâ."

The Competition.

§ 5. Then those messengers whom Suddhôdana had appointed to observe secretly the conduct of the Prince Royal, having with great care watched the glances of his eyes as he was confronted with each of the maidens or spoke to them—having observed all this with great attention, immediately sought the presence of the king, and addressed him thus—"Mahârâja! there happened to come to the reception, amongst others, a daughter of the chief minister, Mahânama, who, after saying a few words to the prince, stood by him for some short time, and in a smiling way conversed with him. We observed how their eyes met, and what secret glances there were, and we doubt not about the meaning of these interchanges of look!"

Then the King, having heard this report of the secret messengers, began to think whether the prince really intended to show preference for this maiden. At length, having selected a lucky day, he sent a certain Brahman, the Lord of the Empire, to the house of that Sâkya Prince, Mahânama, to deliver this message—"I understand your highness has a daughter; let her, I pray you, contract a marriage with my son, the Prince Royal." Then Mahânama replied, "Our Sâkya rules are these—if a man excel all others in martial exercises, then he is crowned victor, and carries off the prize of the fairest maiden; but if he fail, then no such prize can be his. I fear the Prince Royal has been brought up delicately, and has learned none of the arts and practices of chivalry, either in tilting, or wrestling or boxing; but how can I wed my child to one so utterly void of skill in these arts, as I fear the prince to be?"

The messenger, viz., the Lord of the Council, having heard this, returned forthwith to Suddhôdana and reported it. The Râja, on hearing the message, was afflicted with chagrin, for his thoughts were these—"These words of Mahânama, I fear, are true words;" and so he sat silent and still, lost in thought and cast down by his reflections. The Prince Royal, observing this, respectfully approached his father's presence, and three times in succession inquired the cause of the Râja's grief. His father at first told him he had far better not inquire; but on the question being repeated three times, he told the prince precisely how the matter stood.

The prince, having learned the truth, spake thus to his father—"Let your majesty issue a proclamation that I am ready to compete with all comers, in the arts and exercises of war; or, is it not your will that I should so compete?" The king, hearing these words, was much rejoiced, and could not overcome his feelings of exultation, and turning to his son he asked him earnestly—"And are you, my son, prepared to carry out this project, and compete, as you say, against all comers in the arts and exercises of war?" The prince replied, "Listen to me, Mahârâja! I am quite prepared and able! only let the Sâkya youths be assembled, and I will challenge them all in the arts, and every feat of strength and skill!" Then the king ordered it to be proclaimed throughout the city of Kapilavastu, in every one of the principal thoroughfares and at the head of every street, that at the expiration of six days, and on the seventh, the Prince Siddârtha would go forth to the place of tournament and contend in the arena, against all comers! Then on the seventh day all the Sâkya youths, belonging to the five hundred families, with Siddârtha at their head, having assembled together, went forth from the city and proceeded to the place of tournament.

At this time the great Minister, Mahânama, having caused his daughter Yasôdharâ to be adorned with every choice ornament (placed her in a conspicuous place), and made this proclamation respecting the victor—"Whoever the victor may be in this contest of skill and of arms, he shall carry off this my daughter as his prize."

Then Suddhôdana and all the old Sâkya lords arrived at the jousting place, and with them countless crowds of young men and women, belonging to the ordinary population, desirous to see the prince and the Sâkya youths contest for the prize. And first they determined to compete in the art of writing, and they appointed Visvamitra to be umpire, to decide both as to the quickest and neatest and best writer among them. At this time Visvamitra, knowing already the prince's eminent skill in every kind of writing and his incomparable talents, smiled gently to himself, and repeated this Gâtha:—

"Amongst men, or in heaven above,
Amongst Gandharvas, Asuras, or Garudas,
Whatever writing or books there be,
The Prince is able thoroughly to understand them.
Neither I, nor any of you,
Know even the names of these different writings,
Although I am appointed here to judge and decide,
Yet I certainly know that he will entirely surpass you."

Then those Sâkya youths proceeded in a body and addressed Suddhôdana Râja thus—"We have found out that the prince, your majesty's son, is far superior to us in writing; but now let there be an examination in the art of figures, that we may know who is best in this."

Now, there was in the assembly a very eminent master of arithmetic, called Ardjuna—the most skilful of all professors of the art. Him the Sâkya youths requested to act as umpire, saying, "Your honour will please decide as to which of us excels in the art of calculation and arithmetic."

Then the prince proposed a sum to one of the young Sâkyas. The youth copied it down, but was unable to do it, and so with two of them and three; till at last all the five hundred copied it down, but could not solve it. Then the prince invited them to propose a calculation for him to make, on which one of the Sâkyas cried out, "I will give you a sum you cannot do;" but he failed; [and so two, up to the whole five hundred]. Then Ardjuna, in astonishment and delight, uttered this Gâtha:—

"Well done! a victory this to be ever kept in mind!
Clearly answering every proposed calculation without error!
The five hundred Sâkya youths challenged him to the trial;
But though all together they made the trial—'twas vain!
Oh! what depth of wisdom and memory is here!
What power of calculation and what quickness!
Surely we have found a master of figures
Able even to count the drops of the ocean!
Be silent, then, all ye Sâkyas—and hold your peace!
To contend with an one like this, ye are unable!
He who has exhibited such rare talents
Ought only to be allowed to contend with myself!"

At this time all the Sâkyas, conceiving great reverence in their hearts for the young prince, rose up at once from their seats, and, with joined hands, did him homage and exclaimed, "Siddârtha! O mighty prince! yours is the victory! verily, yours is the undoubted victory!"

And then they addressed Suddhôdana and said, "Wonderful! wonderful good fortune is yours, Mahârâja! in possessing such a son! gifted with such merit, such wisdom, such aptitude of speech, so sweet, so soft, so perfect in every word of his mouth!"

Then Suddhôdana, filled with joy and satisfaction, turned to the prince with a smile and said, "Well done! but are you able, do you think, to compete with Ardjuna, the master of figures, in proposing some rare problem or expedient, in solution of questions of this sort?" The prince replied, "Mahârâja! I am able to do so." The king answered, "If you are able to do so! now is your time." Then Ardjuna, the master of figures, asked the prince the following question, "Respectable prince! are you able to recite the numeration of figures above a lakh?"

The prince replied, "I am able." Then Ardjuna, the master of figures, replied, "If so, let me hear you!"

Then the prince began, "One hundred hundred thousand is called a koti [*i.e., a thousand myriad,* (*Ch. ed.*)], a hundred kotis is called an Ayuta [*i.e., ten lakhs* (*Ch. ed.*)], a hundred Ayutas is called a Niyuta, a hundred Niyutas is called a Prayuta, a hundred Prayutas is called a Kañgkara, a hundred Kañgkaras is called a Vivara, a hundred Vivaras is called an Akshobya, a hundred Akshobyas is called a Vivasa, a hundred Vivasas is called an Utsañga, a hundred Utsañgas is called a Bahuna, a hundred Bahunas is called a Nâgabala, a hundred Nâgabalas is called a Titibala, a hundred Titibalas is called a Vyavasthânaprajña(pa)ti, a hundred of these is called a Hetuhila (and so on in the centenary scale, as follows): a Kalapôta, a Hetvindrata, a Samantalambha, a Gannaganti, a Nimaradjya, a Madabala, an Agamada, a Sarvabala, a Visandjñâpati, a Sarvasandjñâ, a Vibûtagama, a Parikshaya; if this numeration is used it is done by pounds, ounces, grains, etc. contained in Mount Sumeru (when ground to powder). Above this is an enumeration called Dhavadjaganimana; above this there is another enumeration called Savâni; above this is another called Iñgga; above this another called Karôshtavata; above this another called Sarvanikchepa, by aid of this numeration one proceeds according to the sands of one Ganges, or two, and so on. Above this, again, is an enumeration called Agasava; in this one proceeds according to the sands of myriads of kotis of Ganges Rivers. There is an enumeration above this called Paramânu pravesa."

At this time Ardjuna, the master of figures, addressed the prince and said, "And as to the enumeration which depends on the number of minute atoms of dust as a basis, are you able to explain this also? If so, be pleased to do so."

The prince replied, "Listen, then, to what I am about to tell you. Seven grains of these minute atoms of dust make one mote (such as one sees in a sunbeam), seven motes make one hare-grain (such as a hare raises in running?), seven hare grains make one sheep-grain, seven sheep-grains make one ox-grain, seven of these make a nit, seven of these a flea grain, seven of these a mustard-seed grain, seven of these a grain of barley, seven of these a finger-joint, seven finger-joints make half a foot (cubit), two of these a foot, two of these a forearm, four of these a bow, five bows a halbard, twenty halbard lengths make what is called a breath (*sih, i.e.,* as far as one can walk with one inspiration of the breath), eighty of these make a krôsa, eight krôsas make a yôjana. Now, then, who in all this assembly can tell me how many minute grains of dust there are in one yojana?"

Then Ardjuna, the master of figures, replying to the prince, said, "Most illustrious sir! I indeed feel this question beyond my knowledge—I am in utter confusion of mind, how much more others, who are comparatively ignorant. Nevertheless, I pray you answer the question yourself—how many minute grains of dust *are* there in a yojana?"

[Kiouen XII contains 6,782 words, and cost 3.391 taelsto print.]

CHAPTER XIII.

The competition in martial exercises (*continued*).

§1. (The prince, having answered the previous question, the narrative proceeds).

Then Ardjuna, the master of figures, and all the Sâkya youths were highly delighted and exulted with great joy. They took off their costly garments and jewels to present to the prince, and addressed him in these laudatory stanzas. "Well done! well done! thou art indeed pre-eminent amongst us in the knowledge of figures, O prince! as well as in the art of writing. Incomparable is thy skill and thy knowledge." And then they added again, "We acknowledge thy victory in these matters, let us now compete in martial exercises!"

At this time, there was amongst the assembled Sâkyas one great minister whose name was Sahadeva, him they appointed umpire.

Then Ananda began the joust, having placed at the distance of two krosas an iron drum as a target. Devadetta placed one at four krosas distance; whilst Nando (Sundarananda) placed one six krosas off. The great minister Mahânama, of the Basita family, placed one eight krôsas off. Then Siddârtha placed a target, hard as diamond, ten krôsas off. Forthwith Ananda began, and hit his target in the midst, but could not go beyond, and so with Devadatta and the others. Then Siddârtha, the prince, having taken his stand, and received the bow handed to him, desired first of all to try its strength, and so bent it with his hand till it broke. "Is there no one," he then said, "in the city, who has a bow fit for me to use?" Then Suddhôdana Râja was greatly rejoiced, and replied, "There is;" whereupon the prince inquired, "Mâharâja, tell me, where?" To whom the Râja answered, "Your grandfather, called Sinhahanu, had a bow which now is kept in a temple of the Devas, and is ever honoured by offerings of incense and flowers; but all the Sâkyas in the city cannot string that bow, much less draw it when strung." Then the prince desired his father to send for the bow at once, and bring it to him. Then when it was brought each of the Sâkya princes attempted to string it, but in vain, not even Mahânama with all his strength.

Then it was handed to the Royal Prince, who without even rising from his seat, and with no show of great exertion, having taken the bow in his left hand, took the string in his right and with his finger in a moment he strung it and thrummed the string, the sound of which filled the city of Kapilavastu, and filled the hearts of the people with fear as they inquired, "What sound is that?"

Then certain persons told them, "It is Siddârtha, the prince, who has just strung the bow of his grandfather Sinhahanu, on which account his father has bestowed upon him every sort of gift."

Then the prince, taking the arrow in his right hand and fixing it, drew back the string of the bow home to his breast, shot his arrow beyond each of the targets till it came to the one ten krosas distance, which it penetrated through, and then disappeared in the far distance.

Then the assembled Devas sang in space—

"Thus the most victorious and virtuous on earth,
(Hereafter) seated on the throne of the Buddhas of old,
He whom all the people and families of Magadha
Now behold the conqueror with the arrow and bow;
Having perfected the six Paramiṭas by the force of his wisdom,
Shall overcome all his opponents and his enemies,
Mara, Sorrow and Death, etc. etc.

The Devas, having uttered these stanzas, showered down on the prince every kind of beautiful flower, and so disappeared. Meanwhile, the Lord of Heaven, Sâkra, seizing the arrow, which the prince had shot as it passed through space, took it to the thirty-three heavens, wherefore in that heaven this day was constituted a fortunate one, and all the Devas, assembled in mass, paid reverence to it by scattering flowers and incense; and even to this time the day of the Arrow Festival is observed amongst them.

Then the Sâkya youths exclaimed, ' The Prince Siddârtha has conquered all comers in this matter of distance. Now let us compete in shooting for the purpose of penetration." [1] Now not far off, there was a succession of seven Talas trees close together; through these trees they were accustomed to shoot, some of their arrows going through one or two or three of the trees. The prince taking an arrow, sent it entirely through the whole of the seven, and the arrow entered the earth at some distance beyond, and broke into a hundred bits. Then they placed the figure of an iron boar between the trees, and the prince shot his arrow right through the seven, and where his arrow entered the ground beyond the seventh, it penetrated down to the very bottom of the earth (yellow fountain), and there sprung up through the hole it made a spring of water, which is called to this day the " Arrow Well."

Then they placed seven iron jars of water at equal distances, and fastened lighted tow on the top of their arrow; they shot some through one and some through two, without extinguishing the flame; but the prince shot through the seven, and his arrow then set on fire a grove of Sala trees beyond the seventh. Then the Sâkya youths allowed themselves conquered also in this exercise.

They then agreed to compete with the sword, as to who could strike the heaviest blow. Then one of them cut through one Talas tree, another through two, but the prince cut through seven, and so clean was his cut that the trees fell not until the Devas raised a fierce wind, which caused the trees to fall to the ground. Then the Sâkyas, who thought that the prince had not even cut through one tree, were convinced of his prowess and skill. (And so the contest continues, in riding, wrestling, and boxing.)

---

[1] These various feats of skill and strength are to be found among the sculptures of Boro Buddor, copies of which have been recently published by the Dutch Government.

At length Siddârtha, the prince, having achieved the victory in every contest greatly rejoiced the heart of his father Suddhôdana, he exulted with delight which he could no longer repress. He therefore ordered his own white elephant to be harnessed with every sort of costly housing, and to be brought to the place of tournament for the prince to return to Kapilavastu.

The elephant, accordingly, was being brought forth from the city, when it so happened that Devadatta was just entering the gate (through which it was proceeding). Seeing it, he asked somebody, "Where is this elephant going?" Whose reply was this—"The elephant is going to fetch Siddârtha, who is about to return to the city on its back."

Then Devadatta, filled with envy on account of the prince's victories in all the martial exercises, stepped in front of the elephant, and, seizing his trunk with his left hand, with his right hand struck him one blow on the head and felled him to the ground, and then hurling him round three times, he deprived him of life.

Thus the elephant lay in front of the gate, so that the inhabitants of the city could not enter or depart from it.

Devadatta had scarcely departed when another Sâkya youth, called Nanda, approached, who, wishing to enter the city gate, was unable to do so on account of the carcase of the elephant lying in the way. So he inquired of the people, "Who did such a deed as this?" They replied, "None other than Devadatta, who, taking the elephant's trunk in his left hand, felled him to the ground with one blow of his right."

Then Nanda, considering the great strength of Devadatta, was astonished, yet, thought he, the carcase of the creature is in the way of the people who want to leave or enter the city, so he seized the elephant's tail with his right hand, and dragged him some seven paces behind the gateway.

A little while after the Prince Royal himself approached, about to enter the same gate of the city, and observing the elephant lying as it was left by Nanda, he inquired of the passers by, "Who killed this elephant?" to which they replied, "Devadatta, with one blow, killed him." Then the prince said, "It was an unseemly thing to do." Then again he inquired, "And who dragged him away from the gate?" The crowd replied, "It was Nanda, the youth, who seized his tail with his right hand, and dragged him to the spot where he is." The prince on this said, "It was a right thing, and a seemly thing to do."

And then the prince considered with himself, "Notwithstanding this exhibition of strength on the part of these two Sâkya youths; yet the carcase of the elephant may cause a nuisance, lying here so close to the city." Thus thinking, he took the elephant with his left hand, and raising it with his right hand, he hurled it through the air beyond the seven gates and the seven ditches of the city, more than a krôsa's distance. Then the elephant, falling on the ground, caused a deep indent, which up to the present time is called the Elephant-ditch.

Then the assembled multitude exclaimed, "Wonderful! wonderful! what a strange and surpassing miracle is this;" and then they added the following stanzas:

"Devadatta indeed killed the elephant,
And Nanda dragged it seven paces from the gate,
The prince with his hand hurled it thro' the air,
And thus formed the deep ditch without the city."

At this time the great minister Mahânama, seeing the prowess and skill of the prince, repenting him of his former rash words, exclaimed, "(I said), 'The prince is unskilful in martial exercises, and brought up softly within the palace, how then can I betroth to him my daughter?' But now I have witnessed his skill, and I pray him to accept my child in wedlock."

At this time the prince, selecting a fortunate day, sent every kind of present of jewels and costly ornament to Yasôdharâ, whilst she, attended by five hundred dancing women, came to the Palace of the prince, entering which they retired to the inner apartments, and there indulged themselves in every species of nuptial delight, as the Gâtha says,—

"Yasôdharâ, the daughter of the great Minister,
Whose fame was known in every land,
Selecting a fortunate day for her marriage,
Approached and entered within the royal precincts,
And afforded the Prince every sort of pleasure.

. . . .

Even as Kusika, the Lord of Heaven,
Enjoys the company of Sasi his Queen."

The Story of the Nobleman who became a Needle-maker.

§ 2. At this time the world-honoured one, having arrived at complete enlightenment, was addressed by Udayi as follows:—"World-honoured! Tathâgata! how was it in days gone by when you first gained the company of Yasôdharâ, not induced by her high extraction or family renown—or riches, or even by her beauty—but by superiority in competition with your rivals?" To which Buddha replied, "Listen! Udâyi! and I will tell you—weigh well my words! It was not only on this occasion that I thus gained possession of Yasôdharâ in marriage; but it was so from very remote time. I remember, for instance, in ages gone by, beyond computation, that there was a certain cunning workman in metals, living in Benares, who had a daughter very beautiful to look at, and her body perfectly formed, her eyes large and even, so that there were few in the world equal to her! She was loved by many! It so happened that at this time there was a nobleman of Benares who had a son, who also was extremely personable and attractive. And on a certain occasion this youth caught sight of the girl, before named, as she was looking out of a window in the tower of the dwelling where lived her father. No sooner had he seen her than there was produced in his breast an ardent love. Thinking of nothing but his love, he returned homewards to his parents' abode, and there addressing his father and his mother he said,

"In the house of So-and-So, a worker in metal, I have seen a girl, the daughter of the artizan, whom I love with all my heart, and desire to possess as my wife.' Then his parents replied to him thus: 'You must not, by any means, take this girl, the child of a mechanic, or defile the threshold of our door with her presence; if you want a wife, choose one from the family of a minister of state, or of a nobleman, or at least of a respectable householder.' Then the youth replied, 'It is no use my looking elsewhere for a wife, I desire none other but this child of the worker in metals; if I do not possess her I will put an end to my life, for it benefits me not to live without her.' On this the parents of the youth, fearing he would put an end to himself, went forthwith to the house of the iron worker and spake thus—'Your daughter may contract a marriage with our son.' But the iron-worker said, 'I cannot permit my daughter to marry any one who is not skilful in working metals.' Then the father and the mother said, 'Respectable Sir! what possible use would it be for your daughter to marry such a man—one who could never afford to give her either comforts or clothes and scarce food enough?' The iron-worker said, 'I know all that, yet I seek a fellow-craftsman for my daughter, and to none else will I give her.'

"The father and the mother, having understood this, went straightway and told their son just what the man had said. Then the youth, being resolved to possess the girl, went and provided himself with the tools fit for a worker in metals, and applied himself thoroughly to master the craft. He soon contrived to learn how to make needles, and having manufactured a good many, he began to rub them to a great degree of fineness, and with oil and polishing made them beautifully bright and clean. Then making a needle-case of a joint of bamboo, he went straightway to the abode of the iron-worker, and approaching the street, standing at the head of the road, he began to chant this song—

"'Made of the smoothest, purest iron,
Shining bright and polished well,
The work of deftest iron-worker,
Who'll buy my needles!'

"At this time the daughter of that iron-worker was sitting at the window in the tower, and hearing the nobleman's son singing his ditty, she replied to him in the following song:—

"'Oh my! how mad the man must be!
You cannot have the least reflection;
To come thus to the iron-master's house,
And shout, "Who'll buy my needles?"'

"Then the nobleman's son again sang a verse in reply to the maiden,—

"'Most fair and lovely maid!
Indeed I am not mad or rash!
My talent is that of a skilful handicraftsman,
Who knows quite well to make superior needles;
Your father, if he only saw

The beauty and the finish of my work,
Would give your hand to me in marriage,
And with yourself confer upon me boundless wealth!'

"Then the girl ran down and told her father and mother the purport of the words she had heard, and said, 'Oh! my dear parents! there is a man outside our door who has just spoken as I have told you, and sang it in a loud voice, about his needles.' Then the old people immediately called out to the nobleman's son to approach and come indoors, and then they asked him and said, 'Well, Sir! and is it true that you are able to make beautiful needles?' He replied, 'I am able.' The old man then added, 'Let me see some of your ware, that I may have an idea of your skill.' Then the noble youth took out of his bamboo cane a needle to show him. The old man, having examined it, replied, 'Respectable youth! you are skilful in making needles; you drill the holes well.' Then the noble youth answered—'This needle is nothing! I have others in my case far superior to this;' on which he took another out of his bamboo case and showed it to the old man. Having examined it, he again began to praise the workmanship and said, 'Very well made and drilled indeed!' Then the youth said, 'Oh! this is nothing, I have others better than that.' So he took out a third and showed to the old man, who, having looked at it, cried out—'Beautifully made! beautifully drilled indeed!' Then the youth said, 'Oh! I have better needles than that;' on which he took out another and showed him. The old man, having examined it, exclaimed, 'You are indeed a clever craftsman, you are able to make beautiful needles;'—and so again and again till the sixth needle, on seeing which the old man said, 'This excels anything I ever saw. Oh! it is very fine work indeed!' Then the youth, taking that needle in his hand, placed it gently in a vessel of water, and lo! it floated on the surface. Seeing this, the old man cried out—'Wonderful! never have I seen such a thing;' and, being filled with delight, he turned to the nobleman's son and said—

"'Never before have I heard or seen such a thing!
Such needles were never yet made;
Now my heart is glad indeed—
You may take my daughter, I give her to you!'"

Then Buddha addressed Udâyi and said, "You must know, Udâyi, that at that time I was the nobleman's son, the girl was Yasôdharâ, and that I took her then to wife, not on account of her distinguished family and not on account of her excessive beauty, but I took her only as a witness of my skilful handiwork—even so now I take her as a proof of my skill (in other matters)."

The Choice of Gôtamî.

§ 3. AT this time then of all the Sâkya princes, the three who excelled in the arts and martial exercises were Siddârtha first, then Nanda, and then Devadatta. Now it happened that just at this time there was a certain noblemen in Kapilavastu, a chief minister of the family of Dandi, whose name was Pani. He was very rich in every kind of property, both in cattle and grain, money and slaves, with jewels and precious gems of every sort in vast abundance, so that there was nothing for his heart to desire more, and his palace was like that of Vaisravana.

He had an only daughter called Gôtamî; she was very beautiful, and unequalled for grace. Not too tall or too short, not too stout or too thin, not too white or too dark. She was young and in the prime of her beauty. Then Suddhôdana, hearing of her fame, having selected a favourable day, sent a messenger, a Brahman, to the house of the minister Pani, who spake thus—"I hear you have a daughter called Gôtamî, we ask you to give her to the Prince Siddârtha in marriage." At the same time, the father of Nanda sent a similar message on behalf of his son, and so also Devadatta, having heard that Suddhôdana was seeking Gôtamî for Siddârtha, sent a message to Dandi, and said, "I require you to give me your daughter in marriage, if you do not I will bring great loss to you." Then Dandi was in much distress of mind, and he reflected thus—"These three powerful families have sons unequalled in skill and prowess, and I have only one daughter, and they each demand her in marriage; so that if I give her to Siddârtha, I make the others my mortal foes, and so likewise if I give her to Nanda or Devadatta—I know not what to do." Being thus exceedingly perplexed, he became pensive and sad and could do nothing but sit still and think over the matter, trying to contrive some expedient by which to escape from the dilemma.

Then Gôtamî, seeing her father thus silent and sad as he sat still, came to his presence and said, "Honoured father! why are you so sorrowful and pensive as you sit here in silence?" To this her father replied, "Dear Gôtamî! ask me not, nor inquire further—these matters are not for you to know." Yet she asked him a second time, and notwithstanding a similar reply, she pressed him a third time to tell her the reason of his grief. Even then he refused to tell her; but when a fourth time she said, "Dear father, you ought to let me know the cause of all this, nor try to conceal it from me;"—then he answered her and said, "Dear Gôtamî! since you insist upon it, listen to my words and weigh them well! You must know then that Suddhôdana Râja has sent to me demanding you in marriage for the Prince Siddârtha; but at the same time both Nanda and Devadatta are making similar overtures, and threaten me with their anger if I do not consent, and therefore, because I do not know how to adjust this matter so as to avoid trouble, I am in perplexity and sit here in grief. Then Gôtamî answered her father and said, "Dear father! don't be distressed! I will arrange this matter myself. I will give my father no further trouble than to ask for a man to follow my directions and make my intention known, and then I will select the husband of my choice."

At this time Dandapani, having attended to Gôtamî's directions, immediately sent to the Râja, and begged him to proclaim throughout the city of Kapilavastu that after seven days, Gôtamî, the Sâkya princess, would select a husband; "Whatever youths therefore desire to obtain her hand let them, after six days, assemble together (at the Palace) for her to choose one of their number." Then after six days all the Sâkya youths, with Siddârtha at their head, were assembled at the Palace gate. Then Suddhôdana, taking with him all the old and reverend Sâkya ministers, and surrounded by countless multitudes of men and women, came all together to the place of assembly. Then Siddârtha with the Sâkya youths around him, waited to see on whom the choice of Gôtamî would fall. At this time the maiden Gôtamî, the six days having expired, very early on the morning of the seventh, arose, and bathing her person she proceeded to decorate herself with the choicest jewels and the most costly robes; around her head she wore a chaplet of the loveliest flowers, and, surrounded by a suite of maidens and accompanied by her mother, she proceeded to the place of assembly. Gradually she drew near, and having come she entered the Palace.

Meantime the Sâkya youths, of whom Nanda and Devadatta were foremost, had in the early morn anointed themselves with every kind of unguent and perfume, and decorated their persons with gems and costly robes, all except Siddârtha, who had taken no pains to ornament his person, and was dressed in his usual attire, simply wearing his earrings, and having three small golden flowers in his hair as ornaments. Then Gôtamî, accompanied by her mother, entered the assembly, and her mother spoke to her thus—"Whom will you select of all these as a husband?" Then Gôtamî, looking on one after the other till she had observed the whole of the five hundred youths, answered her mother thus—"Dear mother! it seems to me that all these youths are very much decorated with ornaments. As to their persons they appear to me more like women than men. I, indeed, as a woman, cannot think of selecting one of these as a husband, for I cannot suppose that any youth possessing manly qualities, fit for a woman to respect in a husband, would dress himself out as these have. But I observe that Siddârtha, the Prince, is not so bedizened with jewels about his person, there is no love of false appearances in his presence, I do not think that he is of the effeminate disposition that these are—my heart is well affected to him. I will take Siddârtha as the husband of my choice." Then Gôtamî in her right hand holding a beautiful wreath of Sumana flowers (jasmin), advancing past all the youths in succession went straight up to Siddârtha, and having reached him she stopped, and then taking the jasmin wreath, having fastened it around the neck of Siddârtha, she gently put her arm upon the back of his head and said, "Siddârtha! my Prince! I take you to be my lord and my husband!" Then Siddârtha replied, "So let it be—so let it be, even as you say." At this time Siddârtha in return took a jasmin wreath and fastened it round the neck of the maiden Gôtamî, and spoke thus—"I take you to be my wife; you are now my own wife."

Then Suddhôdana Râja, seeing this wonderful course of events, was greatly rejoiced, and his heart danced with delight, so that he could not conceal or overcome it, and all the people present, who had witnessed the proceeding, were pleased with the happy result, and shouted at the top of their voices; they danced and sang, and again they cried, "Hurrah! hurrah!" They struck up the music and waved their garments and their caps in the air. But the Sâkya youths were greatly cast down and dejected; they hung their heads in shame and disappointment, and each in stealth slipped away in every direction, and returned to their homes.

Meantime, Siddârtha causing the choicest gems which he possessed, and every jewelled ornament to be brought forth, presented them to Gôtamî with which to adorn still more her person, and then, surrounded by five hundred dancing girls, she proceeded towards the palace of the prince her husband, and entering into the inner apartments she partook of the joys of wedded life.

[Kiouen XIII contains 6726 words, and was printed at a cost of 3.363 taels.]

CHAPTER XIV.

Story of Gôtamî.

§1. It came to pass in aftertime, when the world-honoured one had arrived at complete enlightenment, that Udâyi asked him the following question—"What were the previous relations between yourself and Gôtamî that led to her selecting you as her husband from amongst all the Sâkya princes?" To whom Buddha replied, "Listen, Udâyi, and weigh my words well. It was not only on this occasion that Gôtamî rejected the proffered addresses of others and exhibited a preference for me; but I remember in ages gone by that in the Himalaya region there were assembled together every kind of beast, each of whom wandered here and there seeking food according to its taste and preference. At this time amongst those beasts there was a very beautifully marked tigress, unrivalled for grace of form and strength, her skin sleek and shining. All the male beasts were on this account enamoured of her, and wished to possess her as their own, one saying, 'Come with me,' and another 'Come with me.' So at last the beasts said one to another, 'Let us not quarrel over this matter, but let the lovely tigress herself decide whom she will select for herself, and let him be her husband.' Now at this time I was king of these beasts. So, first of all came the buffalo king, and advancing to the tigress he said, 'Amongst men my very droppings are used, to make the purest and sweetest incense! For this reason, oh! beautiful tigress, you ought to select me to be your husband.' Then the tigress replied to the buffalo king and said, 'Above the back of your neck I observe a high projection, fit for a yoke to rest upon by which you may draw a chariot or other vehicle—how can I select you, possessing such an objectionable form, or desire to have you as my lord and husband?' Then came a large white elephant towards the tigress and addressed her thus—'I am the great elephant-king of these snowy mountains—in all warfare I am used as one that invariably secures victory. Such vast strength do I possess, you cannot refuse to select me as a husband.'

"Then the tigress replied, 'But you, if you come near to or hear the roar of the lion king, are filled with fear and trembling and take to instant flight, you give proofs of abject terror and confusion as you go, how then can I take you to be my husband?'

"At this time, in the midst of those beasts, the lion king of the herd came forward towards the tigress and spake thus—'Look well and examine my proportions and my form; see how in the fore part I am large and powerfully made, whilst in the flank I am graceful and sleek. I dwell in the midst of the mountains, and pass my life without restraint, and I am able to protect and feel for other creatures, I am lord of all the beasts, there are none who would dare to compete with me, whoever sees my form or hears the sound of my roar takes at once to instant flight; I am not able to speak further about my prodigious strength or my majestic and graceful form; but I ask you, dear tigress, as you know all this, to select me and take me as your husband.' Then the tigress replied to the lion and said, 'Your strength is very great, and your spirit high and noble, your body and entire mien are in the highest degree graceful; now, then, I have selected you as my husband, and I desire to honour and respect you henceforth as I ought to do.'

"Now at this time I was the king of these beasts, and this beautiful tigress was Gôtamî that now is, the other beasts were the five hundred Sâkya princes, and as the tigress then selected me after my address, so in the present life Gôtamî selected me as a husband in preference to all the Sâkyas."

Life in the Palace.

§2. At this time Suddhôdana Râja established three separate palaces for the accommodation of the Prince. In the first palace there were appointed a certain number of women to attend upon him during the first portion of the night; in the second palace (or apartment of the palace) others were appointed for the middle of the night; and in the third, for the after part of the night. Yasôdharâ was queen of the first, surrounded by twenty thousand attendants. Manôdara [*this means "thought-hold"*] was queen of the second. [*There are some Doctors of the Law who say that the attendants on Manôdara only knew her name, but never saw her presence.*] Over the third palace Gôtamî[1] was queen. All the women who waited on the Prince were together six myriads. [*Others say ten myriads.*] In each apartment two myriads, all of them Sâkya-born, and besides these eight myriads of others who were not Sâkya-born.

Moreover, Suddhôdana, in recollection of what Asita had predicted, caused a vast hall to be constructed, with a half-subdued light, like that of the Autumn Sun when it is clouded over, in which matters might be only half observed as it were, and adapted for secret pleasures at any time; and all the approaches and passages connected with this he ordered to be constructed in a manner to conceal no dirt or refuse of any sort, lest the Prince, perceiving such things, should at any time be disgusted. Moreover, within the Palace he organised a performance of music of many thousand instruments; amongst which were the following:—A thousand flat-lutes of twenty-three strings (hong-hau), a thousand harpsichords (ku-chang), a thousand five-stringed guitars (in), a thousand small drums, a thousand dulcimers with thirteen cords (chuk), a thou-

[1] There is much confusion in the different books about the wives of Buddha. In the present work there are three names given, viz.—Yasôdharâ, Manôdara, and Gôtamî. In the *Lalita Vistara* the names are Yasôdharâ, daughter of Dandapani; Mrigadjâ (born of a Gazelle) and Utpalavarna (*Lal. Vist.*, p. 152, n.). The Chinese memoir, at the end of the Shan-men-yih-tung, gives three names, viz., Kieou-i (this corresponds to Gôtamî); Yasô(dharâ), the mother of Rahûla; Lou-ye, which is generally restored to Mrigadàva. Burnouf (*Introd.*, p. 278), quoting from Ksoma, makes

sand large lutes (kàm), a thousand viols (pí pa), a thousand soft drums (sai ku), a thousand large drums, a thousand fifes (tik), a thousand organ-like instruments (shang), a thousand copper cymbals, a thousand pandean pipes (sin), a thousand dulcimers (pat chuk), a thousand bamboo flutes with seven holes (chí), a thousand conch trumpets (lo). All these musical instruments, producing different sounds, were played and accompanied by singing, and regulated by movements of the hand by day and night, within the royal apartments of the Prince's Palace, without interruption—resembling in sound the uncertain and deep muttering that comes forth from a great cloud.[1]

Thus then the Prince passed his time in the midst of a hundred thousand most beautiful and accomplished women, enjoying every species of delight and receiving every service and attention at their hands, whilst they, adorned with every kind of ornament of gold, silver, and precious stones, etc., conspired to amuse and gratify him with music and dancing, even as Sâkra participates in every sort of pleasure at the hands of his attendants, sometimes chatting with one in words of soft dalliance, glancing at one another, smiling at one another, embracing one another, sighing, ogling, looking at one another with head inclined, indulging in every kind of soft caress, etc. Thus! thus did the Prince pass his time with the beautiful women of his harem, and receive every possible pleasure, without leaving his palace.

Meanwhile Suddhôdana Râja, in recollection of the prediction of Asita, endeavoured, as the Prince grew in years, to remove from him

---

the three wives to be Yasôdharâ, Gopâ, and Utpalavarna; but in the *Lalita Vistara* (p. 96, n.) it is said that Yasôdharâ and Gopâ are often confounded. Eitel, on the other hand, says (*sub. voce, Gautamî*) that Kieou-i is the same as Mahâprajapati. Remusat (*Fo-koue-ki*, p. 70,) speaks of Kieou-i as the wife of Buddha, and the mother of Rahûla; but again, Klaproth (*Fo-koue-ki*, p. 204) makes Kieou-i the same as Katchânâ, evidently guided by Turnour, who makes Buddha speak of his wife as Buddhakachanâ, *i.e*, Yasôdharâ (R.A.S.B., 1838, p. 816). In any case I do not think Kieou-i can be restored to Gopâ, it must be either Gôtamî, or Kumarî; the former is the more probable.

[1] This passage is well illustrated by Plate lxxiii., Fig. 1, *Tree and Serpent Worship;* the scene of that plate can be no other than the appearance of Udayi in the Zenana, to exhort the women to renewed blandishments (*vide infra*).

all acquaintance with suffering or other evil association, and surround him with subjects that might cause him to turn his mind to other pursuits than those of a religious life, and for this reason he restrained him within the precincts of the palace; even as the Gâtha says,—

"Mahârâja, because the Prince was increasing in years,
And because he was mindful of the words of Asita,
Removed from him all knowledge of sorrow or crime,
And constantly consulted with his wise minister (how to effect his purpose)."

The Fear of Bimbasâra.

§ 3. In this manner for ten years the Prince lived within the palace of his father the Râja, nor once removed without.

Now at this time, in the Southern country of Magadha, there was a king whose family name was Sanrâni,[1] and his own name Bimbasâra, who, being fearful of some enemy arising who might overturn his kingdom, frequently assembled his principal ministers to hold discussion with them on this subject. Being so assembled on one occasion, he addressed them thus—"Do you, my ministers, make diligent inquiry and search throughout the kingdom, and see if there be anyone therein capable of overcoming me (in personal strength), and so able to deprive me of my regal power; and if so, see to it that he is prevented from doing so." The ministers accordingly went forth and dispatched two messengers to go through the dominions of the Râja, and have a care to the directions of the king. These two men accordingly, having heard the directions, proceeded throughout the limits of the kingdom and its borders in order, and when about to return homewards there was a man came to them and said, "Away to the North, there is a very high precipitous mountain belonging to the Himalăya range; underneath the wooded belt of that mountain there is a separate tribe of people called the Sâkyas; belonging to this race is a

---

[1] Shen-lin-ni, doubtless for Srenika, *Foucaux*, 96, n.; or *Srenya*, *vide* 229, n. 2.

youth newly born, the first-begotten of his mother, whose appearance is very beautiful, and the most distinguished both of that territory and of that family, in every respect most admirable and in every particular perfect. His body possesses the thirty-two signs of a great man and the eighty inferior signs. On the day of his birth the Brahmans calculated his horoscope, and this was the result, that in view of the marks above named on his body, if he remained in secular life he would became a Chakravartin, and rule over the four continents, possessed of all the insignia of a universal monarch; if he became a recluse that he would be a Budda Tathâgata Arahato Sammasambuddha, and possessed of the ten names peculiar to so great a Saint, etc." At this time those two messengers returned immediately to Bimbasâra Râja, and narrated what they had heard just in the same words, and exhorted him at once to raise an army and destroy the child, lest he should overturn the empire of the King.[1] Then Bimbasâra, the King of Mâgadha, replied at once, "Respectable Sirs! speak not in this way; for if, as you say, this youth is to become a Holy Chakravarti Râja and to wield a Righteous sceptre, then it becomes me to reverence and obey him, in consideration of his spiritual power and dignity, and so we shall obtain peace and joy under his rule. If he becomes a Buddha, his love and compassion leading him to deliver and save all flesh—then we ought to listen to his teaching and become disciples. So that looking at each or either of these beneficent results, it is quite unnecessary to excite in myself any desire to destroy such a Being."

The Gates around the Palace.

§ 4. At this time Suddhôdana Râja caused a wall to be constructed around the palace which the Prince Royal occupied, which wall had only one gate to it; this gate (or wall) was named, "Ye-

---

[1] Here is another of the singular coincidences of the narrative with the Gospel History. The Thibetan books, moreover, tell us that Bimbasâra had, after a long conflict with the King of Anga, been obliged to pay a general tax to mark his subjection to the latter. (*Ass. Trans.*, xx, p. 47.)

shan" (desert—beast); behind the gates were barricades constructed, which required five hundred men to open and remove, and when the gate itself was rolled back on its hinges the sound thereof could be heard for a distance of half a yôjana. Moreover, in the immediate garden-precinct of the palace he constructed a gate with a bolt and bar that required three hundred men to move, and when the gate was opened the sound thereof could be heard at a distance of a krôsa; and then, again, in the very palace itself he constructed a similar gate that required two hundred men to open, and the sound whereof could be heard at a distance of half a krôsa. These three gates were guarded within and without with guards armed with morion and glaive, spear and bow, and triple-pointed halberd (and other warlike weapons), to keep strictly the approaches to the palace. Such great preparations and precautions did the King take, lest his son should leave the allurements of his home and wander away to the wild mountain solitudes.

The voice from Space exhorting him to flee.

§5. At this time dwelling in space there was a Devaputra called T'so-Ping (make-pitcher). This Deva, having watched the Prince Royal for ten years dwelling in the palace and enjoying every sensual pleasure, began to consider and think thus—" This Prabhâpâla Bôdhisatwa Mahâsatwa too long a time is indulging himself with worldly pleasures, dwelling in his palace and partaking of the five enjoyments of sense. We must not permit these lusts to cloud and besot him, his mind and senses to be darkened and deluded;—quickly! quick! flies the time. Prabhâpâla must be taught now to recognise the just limits of such things, and that he ought at once to let them go and leave his house (*i.e.*, become a recluse). If I do not take some preparatory step in this direction, and incite him to flee from these things, it will be too late. I will now, therefore, recite some verses in praise of such a proceeding, and so urge and strengthen him to action." On this Deva Putra T'so-Ping, in the middle of the night, recited these verses—

" A man whose own body is bound with fetters, who yet
Desires to release others from their bonds,

Is like a blind man who undertakes to lead the blind.
But having one's own body free, and then to free others,
Is like a man who has eyes, undertaking to lead others.
Thou virtuous one! Your years are now complete,
It is time now to give up your home, and to accomplish your vows, etc."

T'so-Ping, having uttered these Gâthas in the regions of space for the purpose of exciting spiritual reflection, and stirring up the prince to cultivate the virtuous and meritorious principles which were lying dormant in him, moreover caused the songs of the women of the harem, instead of fostering lustful desires, rather to encourage thoughts of Nirvâna, and increase the prince's faith in it. And at the same time, of their own accord, the following verses were produced in exquisite tones:—

"The things of the world are transitory
Just as the flash from the cloud;
Honour'd one! the time is come.
It becomes you to leave your house and home!
All the things of sense (sanscara) are impermanent,
Like the potter's earthen vessel!
As a thing borrowed for a moment's use,
As a wall made of dry earth heaped up,
Ere long to be cast down and destroyed.
Yea! as a heap of dust in summer-time,
Or as the sands on either bank of a river
Whose very existence implies impermanence;
Or as the light which is produced by a lamp
When produced quickly returns to nothingness;
Or as the restless and inconstant breeze
Which suddenly changes, and is never fixed
Without any semblance of constancy or endurance.
As the inside of the plantain fruit (or tree)
Shadowy as a madman's reflections;
Or as the empty fist which deceives a child,
So all things which exist (sanscara),
And all that is produced in the sequence of cause and effect,
And every individual substance
Is the mere figment of the ignorant,

Just as the silken thread
Is produced from the distaff;
Or as a seed sown produces a sprout,
Remove the seed and there will be no sprout—
So all relationships removed there is no knowledge (perfect idea)."

At this time within the palace, when the ladies of the harem began to play upon the instruments of music, such sounds as the above, being in fact pious utterances of religion, proceeded from the instruments; all of them with a view to cause the prince to quit the world and prepare his heart for Supreme Wisdom.

The Excursions without the Palace.

§ 6. Now it came to pass that the Devaputra T'so Ping desiring to draw the prince out of his palace and to bring before him in the garden certain sights which might induce him to quit the fascinations of his present life,—to effect this, he caused the songs of the ladies who surrounded the prince to convey this suggestion to him. The sounds seemed to him to be of this sort—"Let the Holy One listen! the grounds of the garden are lovely! adorned with choicest flowers and trees and fruits. There are birds of every kind whose notes are delightful to the senses."

The prince, hearing these utterances, resolved to proceed forth, and thereupon he summoned his charioteer, and addressed him thus—"My good charioteer! draw forth and prepare for me at once a choice and fitting chariot, as I wish to ride out and inspect the lovely grounds of the surrounding gardens."

The charioteer, so instructed, replied, "I will attend, my lord, to your commands."

Forthwith he sent the intelligence to Suddhôdana, and made this communication—"Mahârâja! be it known to you that the Royal Prince desires now to go forth into the garden grounds to inspect the beautiful earth."

Then Suddhôdana caused to be proclaimed throughout Kapilavastu that all persons within and without the city should thoroughly cleanse, sweep, and water the streets and the precincts, so that not a stone, or a potsherd, or any pollution whatever should lie in the way; but that every place should be adorned and made delightfully smooth—that the choicest perfumes should be sprinkled on the ground, with flowers, etc.; moreover, that lamps should be hung up and down the streets, and that at the head of all the cross-roads vessels full of water should be placed; moreover, that flowers should be hung up and flags, etc., on the trees; that they should be, moreover, ornamented with jewels and choice stones of every description. That, from all the trellis-worked lattices, bells should be hung, made of silver and ornamented with jewels, which as the wind sighed might send forth a pleasing sound. Moreover, that images of Suryadeva and Chandradeva, decorated with every ornament, should be placed, together with figures of the other Devas, between the lattice rails; and also flags, chamaras, etc., placed in the immediate neighbourhood of these figures.

In agreement with these commands the city of Kapilavastu was forthwith decorated as above, until it bore the appearance of the fairy city of the Gandharvas.

Moreover, the King commanded the garden to be swept and garnished in the same way. The trees of the garden, moreover, which had male names were decorated with ornaments worn by men, whilst those that had female names were decorated with ornaments worn by women.

Moreover, the King ordered it to be proclaimed throughout Kapilavastu by the sound of the drum and bell (gong)—"All ye people! remove from every part of the city and the highways whatever can remind the Prince of old age, disease, or death; let no blind man, or deaf or impotent person, be seen anywhere; let nothing of an unlucky or sinister character anywhere meet the eye of the Royal Prince!"

Forthwith, the charioteer prepared a delightful chariot, and harnessed thereto a team of horses beautifully decorated, having done which he proceeded to the presence of the Royal Prince and announced that all things were ready for the tour of inspection through the gardens.

Then the prince arose from his seat, and proceeded to the place where the chariot was awaiting him, and having ascended it, he assumed the attitude and look becoming his exalted position, and proceeded forthwith through the eastern gate of the city wall, desiring to visit the gardens without the city precincts to examine the beautiful trees and flowers.

At this time the Devaputra T'so-Ping caused to appear before the eyes of the prince, in one of the streets, the body of an old decrepid man, his skin shrivelled up, his head bald, his teeth gone, and his body bent down with age and infirmity; he carried a staff in his hand to support his tottering limbs, whilst, as he proceeded, he gasped with pain, and the breath from his mouth sounded, as it came, like the raspings of a saw.

Thus he stood right across the way of the prince as he advanced in the chariot. Seeing him, Siddârtha inquired of his charioteer "What human form is this, so miserable and so shocking to behold, the like of which I have never before seen?"—even as the Gâtha says—

"Illustrious coachman! listen to me at once!—
What man is this I see before my eyes,
His body bent and crooked, his head bald and bare,
Is it his birth that made him thus—or his age?"

Then the coachman replied, influenced by the spiritual power of the Devaputra T'so-Ping, "Great Prince! this man is what is called 'old.'"

The prince again inquired, "And what is the sense of this term 'old,' as it is used in the world?"

The coachman answered, "Old age implies the loss of all bodily power, the decay of the vital functions, and the gradual destruction of the mind and memory. This poor man before you is just such an one! At any moment he may die—his life is uncertain from morning till night; for these reasons I speak of him as old and approaching his end." Just as the Gâtha says—

"This name of old age implies sorrow and pain,
Gone all the pleasures of sense and the joys of wedded life,
The senses blunted, the memory lost,
The limbs and joints in tremor all, disobedient to the will."

Then the Prince Royal, having heard these verses, asked his chariot driver again, "Is this man only one of the sort, by himself, or is this Law an universal one applying to all alike?"

To which he replied, "Reverend and holy youth! know thou that this man is not a solitary instance of the character of age;

but that this is the common lot of all that lives—all that is born must come to this if life is preserved."

The prince then asked, "And my body!—must I also become old as this object before me?"

The coachman answered, "Even so! even so! Holy Prince! the rich and the poor alike are destined for this! everything that lives must share in this common lot!" The prince replied, "If this be so, and even I must soon become worn out and decayed as this old man, I cannot think of proceeding further towards the gardens whither we were going to sport and laugh. Turn your horses homewards, let us return to the palace! it were better for me to pass my time in thinking how to contrive to escape, or at least to palliate this evil of 'age'!" At this time the charioteer, replying to the prince, spake thus—"According to your command, O Prince! I desire to act;" and forthwith, turning the chariot, he proceeded towards the city. Then the prince, having entered his palace, sat down upon his throne, and gave way to thoughts of this character—"So then I too must become old!—the laws of old age being universal, how may I escape and deliver my body and soul from such calamity?"

Then Suddhôdana inquired of the charioteer—"My worthy coachman! tell me whether the objects observed by the prince, as he went to the garden, were all agreeable and pleasant?" To whom he replied, "Mahârâja! be it known to you that the prince, when arrived halfway to the garden was unwilling to proceed further, and commanded me to turn his chariot homewards;"—on which the king at once inquired the cause of this, and the charioteer added, "For scarcely had we got halfway, when there appeared in the middle of the road an old man bent double with age, his personal appearance wretched in the extreme; and as soon as the prince beheld this form he did not wish to go further; but desired me to return to the palace, where he now is lost in meditation and serious thought;" on this the king exclaimed, "Wonderful! wonderful, indeed! This is precisely what Asita the soothsayer predicted, warning me not to let the prince leave his home, lest he should behold that which would induce him to become a recluse!"

Then the King resolved to increase within the palace of the prince the means of indulgence and objects of desire, with a view to prevent him from longing to leave the society of his female companions for the outer world: and this is what the Gatha says—

"Within the palace every source of pleasure and joy,
Yet the prince desired to go forth—and lo! the old man!
Returning within his palace grieved and distressed!
Alas! he cried, that I cannot escape this lot!
The King, his father, having heard thereof,
His heart fearing lest his son should become a recluse,
More than doubled the sources of pleasure in the palace,
Hoping thereby to induce him to become a King."

So the prince dwelt still in his palace, and indulged himself in all carnal pleasures—having as yet only this one subject of doubt or cause of distress.

[This book contains 7,269 words and cost 3.67 taels.]

CHAPTER XV.

The Dreams of King Suddhôdana.

§1. Now it came to pass that the Devaputra T'so-Ping, still desiring to cause the prince to arrive at a resolution to become a religious recluse, by the exercise of his spiritual power, on that very night caused Suddhôdana Râja to dream seven different dreams. And they were of this sort;—as soon as Suddhôdana had retired to his couch and fallen asleep, he dreamt that he saw a great imperial banner like that of Indra, around which were gathered innumerable crowds of people, who, lifting it and holding it up, proceeded to carry it through Kapilavastu, and finally went from the city by the Eastern gate.

The second dream was on this wise, he saw the prince riding in a royal chariot drawn by great elephants, and so driving he passed through the Southern gate of the city.

The third dream was that he saw the prince seated in a four-horsed chariot, very magnificent, and thus proceed through the Western gate of the city.

The fourth dream was that he saw a magnificently jewelled discus fly through the air and proceed through the Northern gate of the city.

The fifth dream was that he saw the prince sitting in the middle of the four great highways of Kapilavastu, and holding in his hand a large mace smote therewith a large drum.

The sixth dream was that he saw in the midst of Kapilavastu a high tower, on the top of which the Royal Prince was seated, and as he sat he scattered towards the four quarters of heaven countless jewels of every kind, which were gathered by the innumerable concourse of living creatures who came together for the purpose.

The seventh dream was that he beheld outside the city of Kapilavastu, not very far off, six men who raised their voices and wailed greatly and wept, whilst with their hands they plucked out the hair of their heads, and flung it by handfuls on the ground.[1]

At this time Suddhôdana, awaking from his sleep, and recalling the visions he had seen was greatly troubled, so that the very hair on his body stood erect, and his limbs trembled on account of the strange doubts that filled his mind.

Then he forthwith summoned to his side within his palace all the great ministers of his Council, and exhorted them in these words—"Most honourable Sirs! be it known to you that during the present night I have seen in my dreams strange and portentous visions—there were seven distinct dreams which I will now recite (he recites the dreams): I pray you, honourable Sirs! let not these dreams escape your memories, but in the morning when I am seated in my palace, and surrounded by my attendants, let them be brought to my mind (that they may be interpreted)."

The ministers of the council having heard this charge laid upon them, replied, "It shall be even as your majesty commands."

At morning light the King, seated in the midst of his attendants, had the dreams again recited to him according to his directions. After which he issued his commands to all the Brahmáns, interpreters of dreams, within his kingdom, in these terms —"All ye men of wisdom explain for me by interpretation the meaning

---

[1] It will be noticed that according to the *Lalita Vistara* the king has only one dream.

of the dreams I have dreamt in my sleep; now the dreams are these [as before]."

Then all the wise Brahmans, interpreters of dreams, having understood the desire of the King, began to consider each one in his own heart, what the meaning of these visions could be; till at last they addressed the King and said, "Mahârâja! be it known to you that we never before have heard such dreams as these, and we cannot interpret their meaning!"

On this Suddhôdana was very troubled in his heart, and he thought thus with himself—"If, after all, the Prince my son does not become a Chakravarti Râja, it cannot but be that the very dignity of Chakravarti Râja comes to an end in the world! my heart within me is exceedingly distressed, who is there can satisfy these doubts of mine?"

At this time T'so-Ping, the Devaputra, being present in the inner palace of Suddhôdana Râja, and perceiving the sorrow and distress of the King, after observing his condition, suddenly disappeared from the interior, and assumed the appearance of a Brahman with his hair dressed in the usual manner and the customary cap on his head, his appearance dignified and self-possessed, arrayed in the skin of the black deer, and under this form he stood at the gate of the King's palace and cried out in the following words—"I am able fully to interpret the dreams of Suddhôdana Râja, and with certainty to satisfy all his doubts."

Then the gate warders, hearing these words of the Brahman, hastened to the presence of the King, and prostrating themselves before him addressed him in these words—"Mahârâja! be it known to you there stands at the palace gate a Brahman who with his mouth announces his ability to interpret your dreams."

Then Suddhôdana Râja immediately ordered him to be brought to his presence, and when he had arrived he joyfully addressed him, "Is it true, oh wise Brahman! that you can interpret my dreams? if so, be it known that my dreams were of this sort. It was but yesternight, in the middle of the hours of sleep, I saw these seven visions [here he recites his dreams as before]. And now my heart is troubled exceedingly, not knowing whether the interpretation of these visions is good or evil. But do thou, oh wise Brahman! tell me, one by one, the meaning of my dreams!"

Having spoken thus, the King remained silent, anxiously expecting to hear the interpretations.

Then T'so-Ping Devaputra forthwith replied to the King and said, "Mahârâja! be it known unto you that the first dream, in which you saw the vast multitude surrounding the Banner of Indra, and carrying it forth from the city gate, signifies that the prince, your son, will soon give up his present condition, and, surrounded by innumerable Devas, proceed from the city and become a recluse. This is the interpretation of your first dream.

"Again, when the Mahârâja dreamt that he saw the prince riding in a chariot drawn by ten mighty elephants, proceeding from the South gate of the city, this signifies that the prince, having left his home, will forthwith attain to the knowledge of all things (Sarvadjña or Sarvasandjña) and the ten powers of mind (Dasabalas). This is the interpretation of the second dream.

"Again, when your Majesty dreamt that you saw the Royal Prince driving in a four-horsed chariot, and proceeding through the West gate of the city; this signifies that the prince having left his home and attained the perfect knowledge before-named, he shall likewise arrive at the condition of perfect fearlessness.[1]

"Again, when your Majesty dreamt that you beheld a richly-jewelled discus proceed through the North gate of the city, this signified that the prince, having left his home and attained perfect enlightenment, would turn the precious wheel of the perfect Law for the good of gods and men. This is the interpretation of the fourth dream.

"Again, when the King saw in his dreams the prince sitting in the midst of the four highways of Kapilavastu beating a mighty drum with a mace held in his hand; this signified that the prince having attained to the condition of Bôdhi, and begun to turn the wheel of the Law, that the sound of his preaching should extend through the Highest Heavens (the Heavens of Brahma) even as the sound of the drum is heard through the inferior worlds.[2] This is the interpretation of the fifth dream.

"Again, when your Majesty dreamt that you saw in Kapilavastu

---

[1] The four intrepidities, Vaisaradyas, *vide Lotus*, p. 346. This is the interpretation of the third dream.

[2] This dream corresponds to the Avadâna, translated by Stas. Julien, "Le Roi et le grand tambour," *Les Avadânas*, vol. i, p. 1.

a high tower, and the prince seated on the top scattering precious gems towards the four quarters of heaven, whilst countless multitudes of creatures were gathered together collecting these precious gifts; this signifies that the prince, having arrived at perfect wisdom, will scatter the precious gems of the Good Law in every direction for the sake of Devas and men and the eight classes of creatures. This is the interpretation of the sixth dream.

"Again, when your Majesty beheld the six men outside the city Kapilavastu weeping and lamenting and tearing their hair; this signifies the misery and distress of the six heretical teachers whom the prince after his enlightenment shall discomfit and expose; to wit, Pourna Kasyapa, Mavakaragosaputra, Adjnitasa Kimbala, Parbata Katyayana, Sanjipayatijitaputra, and Nirganthajatiputra. This is the interpretation of the seventh dream."

Thus T'so-Ping, the Devaputra, having explained the dreams of Suddhôdana Râja, he further addressed him and said, "Mahârâja! your heart should be filled with joy and not with grief; for in truth these dreams are of the most felicitous character, compose your heart then, and let there be no more anxiety or distress." Thus speaking, he suddenly disappeared, and was no more seen.

Then the King, having heard these words, resolved to increase yet more the enticements to sensual indulgence in the palace of the prince; hoping thus to prevent his going forth to see the world.

And so the prince still remained in the indulgence of his animal passions, without any reflection.

Seeing the Sick Man on the Road.

§ 2. Now, then, the Devaputra, T'so-Ping, again began to bethink himself thus—"This Prabhâpâla Bôdhisatwa Mahâsatwa is still living within his palace indulging himself in mere animal enjoyment, giving rein to his passions, whilst the world is perishing! I must arouse him by some spiritual manifestation." Having thus reflected; he caused the prince, whilst sitting within the palace, suddenly to conceive a desire to make another tour of inspection through the gardens without (the city).

Then the prince summoned his coachman again to his side and said, "My worthy coachman! I wish to take another drive without the city towards the gardens for the purpose of seeing the trees and the flowers."

The coachman replied, "Even so, my lord! as you say!" Then having received his instructions, he forthwith sent the intelligence to Suddhôdana Râja, who issued similar instructions throughout the city for the decoration and cleansing of the streets and highways, and the ornamentation of the trees of the garden.

Then the coachman, having prepared a magnificent chariot, approached the prince and said, "The chariot is even now ready, and awaiting your orders." Then the prince, mounting into the chariot, took his seat with the dignity and appearance of a king, and proceeded through the South gate of the city, and slowly advanced towards the gardens without.

At this time T'so-Ping Devaputra caused to appear in the way, just before the prince, a sick and pain-worn man, with cramped limbs and swollen belly, giving evidence of agonising suffering, pale and miserable, scarcely able to draw his breath, every now and then lying down in the dirt through exhaustion: till at last, unable to rise through weakness, he exclaimed with much difficulty in suppliant tones—"Oh! I humbly intreat you, raise me up to sit upon the road."

Then the prince, seeing this wretched object and hearing his intreaty, immediately addressed his coachman and said, "Who or what is this unhappy being? his breath like the steaming of a caldron, his body emaciated and wan, his skin yellow as parchment, and as he goes groaning and sighing 'Ah me! what pain!' and again, 'Alas! alas! pity, master! pity!' Indeed I cannot bear to hear such misery, I will go to raise him up."

Then the Devaputra, T'so-Ping, inspired the coachman to answer thus—"Holy youth! listen to me; this is a sick man."

Then the prince rejoined, "And what does that signify?"

The coachman replied and said, "Sacred Prince! this man's body is unsound and deprived of all vital power and grace; his limbs cramped and helpless; sighing for death; without refuge or protection; father and mother both forgotten—no one to sympathise with him; in this plight, daily looking for death, he still endures his misery, without help, without remedy! For this reason, O Prince! he is called a sick man!" And so the Gâtha says—

"The Prince asked the coachman and said,
'What man is this enduring such pain?'
The coachman replied to the prince—
'The four elements ill-adjusted, therefore sickness is produced.'"

Again the prince inquired, "Is this sickness confined to the case before us, or is it common to men generally?" To which the coachman replied, "It is not restricted to this man alone, but gods and men alike are unable to avoid this misery." "And must I too some day be sick?" asked the prince; "alas! if this be so, what fear, what anxiety?" And again he said, "If this really be so, O charioteer! then I feel in no temper to go to the gardens to enjoy the beauty of the trees and flowers; turn again, turn again to the palace." The coachman replied, "I will do as your highness commands." Then the prince, having returned to the palace, sat pensively and sadly reflecting on the truth he had heard, that he also must some day be reduced by sickness to the condition of the man he had seen.

Then Suddhôdana Râja inquired of the coachman whether the prince had enjoyed his visit to the gardens or not. On which the charioteer explained the circumstance which had occurred, to the sorrow and grief of the King, who recalled the words of Asita, and in consequence he resolved to increase even more the inducements to pleasure within the palace of the prince, even as the Gâthas say—

"The Prince Royal, for a long time dwelling within his palace,
After a time desired to go forth to the gardens to enjoy
himself.
In the way he saw a sick man, lean and worn,
Which caused him to loathe the thought of pleasure.
Sitting still he reflected on this misery of sickness—
What joy can I have, seeing I cannot escape this?—
Dissatisfied with the pleasures of sense,
Though possessed of the most lavish means of enjoyment.
Such happiness and incomparable felicity did he inherit
From his former good deeds and virtuous conduct,"

Thus, then, the prince lived within his palace still absorbed, night and day, in the pursuit of sensuous pleasures.

Beholding the Corpse.

§ 3. AND still again T'so-Ping, the Devaputra, reflected within himself as he beheld the prince thus engaged in self-indulgence and pleasure—"How can I best stir up this Prabhâpâla Bôdhisatwa, to leave these foolish pleasures and become a Recluse." And so he again caused the prince to long to go forth from his palace, and visit the gardens beyond the city. Whereupon the prince, calling his charioteer, addressed him as before, who on his part forthwith reported the matter to Suddhôdana Râja. Then the same preparations and precautions having been adopted, the prince went forth. Then the Devaputra caused to appear before the prince as he rode onwards, a corpse lying on a bier in the road. Then he saw the people lift up the bier and carry it along, some were spreading over it every kind of coloured grass (?), whilst on the right and left were weeping women, tearing their hair and beating their breasts with grief; others striking their heads across either arm; others throwing dust on their heads; others wailing and lamenting and weeping drops fast as rain, such sad and bitter cries as could seldom be heard!

The prince, witnessing this scene, his heart was overwhelmed with sorrow, and turning to his coachman he asked him, "Respectable coachman! who is this lying thus on his bed, covered with strangely-coloured garments, his head wrapped up, and surrounded by people lamenting and weeping as he is carried onwards?"—in the words of the Gâtha—

"The gracefully-formed and ruddy prince
Asked his respectable coachman, 'Who is this
Lying upon the bed borne on the four sides by men,
And surrounded by friends weeping and lamenting?' "

Then T'so-Ping Devaputra by his supernatural power caused the coachman to answer thus—"Most holy prince! this is called a dead body (or a corpse laid out)." "And what is a dead body?" inquired the prince. To which the coachman answered, "Great prince! this person has now done with life; he has no further beauty of appearance, or desire; he is one with the stones and the wood, just as the dead wall or a fallen leaf; no more shall he see father or mother, brother or sister or other relative; and therefore it is called 'a dead body;'" as the Gâtha says—

"Without thought or mind, or any sense,
Inert as a log or a stone, the dead body lies,
All its friends surrounding it and calling lamentably on his name,
About to be separated for aye from the object of their love."

Then the prince again inquired, "Must I, dear coachman, also die?" To whom he said, "Most holy prince! your sacred body must also come to this and die; for neither Devas or men can avoid this inevitable fate." Even as the Gâtha says—

"This is the final destiny of all flesh—
Gods and men, rich and poor alike, must die,
Whether their present condition be good or bad,
All creatures at the appointed time meet the like fate."

Then the prince replied, "If this be really so, and this body of mine must die and become like this, then what have I to do with pleasure, or why should I go to the garden to find enjoyment? Turn again, O coachman! turn again your chariot! and take me back to my palace that I may meditate on what you have said." Then the prince entered his palace again, and sat silently down and pondered on death and the impermanency of all things.

Now just as the prince was entering his palace gate, it so happened that outside there was standing a certain mad astrologer who, looking with a sort of wild expression on the prince, first at his face and then down over his body, cried out—"All ye folks! listen to what I have to say and attend! Within seven days from the present time this prince shall have possession of the seven gems which attend the person of a Chakravarti."

Then Suddhôdana Râja asked the coachman [as before]; on hearing the reply he was deeply grieved, and continued to urge on the prince every mode of gratifying his sensual desires. And so matters still continued.

Beholding the Shaman.

§ 4. And so it came to pass that six days more elapsed during which the prince remained in his palace. Then again the Devaputra stirred him up to desire once more to go abroad to enjoy the pleasure of beholding the gardens beyond the city. On this occasion, as before, the prince directed the coachman what to do, who in his turn acquainted Suddhôdana Râja with the circumstances, who gave orders as before.

Then the prince, having set out on his excursion, the Devaputra by his spiritual power caused to appear, not far in front of the chariot, a man with a shaven crown and wearing a Sañghâti robe, with his right shoulder bare, in his right hand a religious staff, in his left hand holding a mendicant's alms bowl, and so going with measured pace along the road. The prince having observed this figure before him, asked the coachman—"Dear coachman! who is this man in front of me, proceeding with such slow and dignified steps, looking neither to the right or the left, with fixed attention, his head shaven, his garments of a reddish earthen colour, unlike the white-clad mendicants, his alms dish too of a purplish shining hue, like the stone 'toi'?"

Then the Devaputra T'so-Ping excited the coachman to answer thus—"Holy youth and illustrious prince! this person is called a mendicant (parivrâjika)."

Then the prince asked again, "And what is the calling and conduct of a mendicant?"

The coachman answered, "Great prince! this man constantly practises virtue, and avoids wrong; he gives himself to charity, and restrains his appetites and his bodily desires; he is in agreement with all men, and hurts nobody, neither killing nor poisoning any one; but, as far as he can, he does good to all, and is full of sympathy for all. Prince! for this reason he is called a mendicant." "If this be so," said the prince, "and he is of such a disposition, drive up to him, O coachman! and let me speak to him." This done, the prince addressed the mendicant and said, "Honoured Sir! tell me, I pray you, what man you are!" At this time the Devaputra T'so-Ping by his spiritual power caused him to answer thus—"Great prince! I am called a mendicant!" "And what is that?" inquired the prince. "It is one," the mendicant rejoined, "who has left the world and its ways, who has forsaken friends and home in order to find deliverance for himself, and desires nothing so much as by some expedient or other to give life to all creatures and to do harm to none; for this reason, O prince! I am called a mendicant (parivrâjika, homeless one)."

Then the prince, resuming the conversation said, "Venerable one! and what is the character of the preparation necessary for arriving at this condition?" (To which the mendicant replied), "Illustrious youth! if you are able to behold (or regard) all objects of sense (sansara) [*or the Samskâras, vide Introd.*, p. 505, n.] as impermanent, to think no evil and do none; but, on the contrary, to benefit all creatures (by your life and teaching), then this will lead to the condition of a mendicant; as the Gâtha says—

"'To regard all earthly things as perishable;
To desire above all things the condition of Nirvâna,
Done with hatred or love, the heart equally affected,
Freed from all earthly objects of desire;
Frequenting the solitary pits or forests or beneath a tree,
Or dwelling on the cold earth in the place of tombs,
Thoroughly emancipated from all personal consideration,
This is the way to regard the character of a mendicant.'"

Then the prince, having descended from his chariot, proceeded to the spot where the mendicant stood, and bowing his head to the ground worshipped him, and having performed three circuits round him in token of respect, he re-mounted his chariot, and being seated, ordered his coachman to drive homewards towards the palace.[1]

Then Suddhôdana Râja, being surrounded by the circle of his ministers within the palace, suddenly the prince entered the assembly and came up beside the King, his hands clasped and his body bent, and spake thus—"Would that your majesty would hear me! I wish to become a mendicant, and to seek Nirvâna! All worldly things, O King! are changeable and transitory."

"Then Suddhôdana Râja, having heard these words, trembled as a tree shivers that is struck by the whole weight of an elephant's

[1] Here follow some "verses of emancipation," which proceed from the air;—these I omit.

body, and the tears coursed down his cheeks, while he gave way to his grief in these words—"Alas! alas! my son, let not such thoughts as these prevail with you; for, my son, you are young, and the time for your becoming a recluse is not arrived. After a few years more, I shall give up my kingdom and retire to the forest, and then you, my son, will succeed me. Let not my son think of giving up the world at his tender age!"

Then the prince answered, "Your majesty cannot prevail against my resolve! for what is it? Shall a man attempt to prevent another escaping from a burning house, and he not resist? Mahârâja! all earthly things are changeable and transitory; and a man who knows this, and yet does not attempt to get free from the trammel of worldly occupations, is no wise man." Then for the sake of the King, he uttered the following Gâtha [*a mere repetition of the above sentiment*]. Still Suddhôdana Râja continued to urge his plea, and the ministers also addressed the prince and showed him how, according to the Vedas, every youthful monarch should fulfil his kingly duties, and afterwards, when old, forsake the world and become a recluse.

Then Suddhôdana, hearing the words of his great ministers, burst again into tears and looked beseechingly at his son with an earnest countenance.

On this the prince, overcome with hesitation, retired to within the palace.

And so the women, seeing the prince, were exceedingly rejoiced; they clapped their hands and sang and danced, etc. Then the prince, having sat down, they surrounded him, and began to show such blandishments as in the Palace of Ishwara the Apsarasas use. Then the prince, by displaying the beautiful signs of his person (the superior and inferior marks), so overawed the women that they could but whisper among themselves—"Surely this is Chandra Deva, the Moon God, come down to earth;" and so by his power he restrained in them all tendencies to sensual pleasures, that they were neither able to desire any indulgence or even to laugh![1]

Then Suddhôdana Râja, after his son had left his presence, called for the coachman and asked him the circumstances of the

[1] Such appears to be the character of the group in Fig. 1, Plate lxxiii, *Tree and Serpent Worship*.

last excursion. After which he resolved once more to increase the temptations to pleasure within the palace; he also surrounded it with additional enclosures, and at every gate placed guards of various descriptions to prevent all possible intercourse betwixt the prince and the outer world.

[Kiouen XV. contains 6,360 words, and cost 3.18 taels.]

CHAPTER XIV.

The Exhortation of Udâyi.

At this time the Chief Officer of State[1] had a son called Udâyi, a young man of distinguished ability and rising talent. Suddhôdana Râja, having called this youth to his presence, laid the case of the prince before him, seeking counsel and advice. "By what stratagem," said he, "can we keep Siddârtha in the palace, and prevent him becoming a Recluse?"

At the same time, the Râja summoned all the Sâkya princes and begged [laid the same case before them] them also to use such expedients as they thought necessary to effect the same purpose. Then the Sâkya princes undertook to assist in carrying out any measures necessary to prevent Siddârtha leaving his home.

And now Suddhôdana and the Sâkya princes surrounded Kapilavastu with additional guards, placing at the head of each cross-road patrols of chariots, horses, elephants—who continually circumambulated the royal palace, so as effectually to prevent any escape.

Then again Mahâprajâpati Gôtamî within the palace assembled all the women of pleasure and upbraided them with their want of influence over the mind of the prince—"Let none of you," she said, "fail to provide amusement for him night and day; let there be no interval of darkness, and never be without wine and burning perfumes; let there be guards at every door to prevent ingress or egress. For, remember, if the prince escape, there will be no other sources of pleasure within the palace."

---

[1] That is, Mahânama or Basitu.

Then Udâyi also entered into the quarters of the women, and urged them to use every desire to keep the prince engrossed in pleasure.[1] And when he saw them all sitting silent and sad he likewise reproached them and said, "Why sit ye thus silent and dejected, so incomparably fair and accomplished in every art of discourse as you are?" And then he reminded them of the Rishi's Devayana and Ekasringa[2], and others, who were all overcome by the fascinations of fair women, "and shall not you be able to enlist the affections or excite the desire of the prince with whom you live?" Then these women, having heard these words, conceived in themselves a very strong desire, and forthwith set themselves to employ every art to enamour the prince. Some postured themselves before him, others offered him flowers, others with their fingers in their mouths produced every sort of bird-like whistle, others told him different kinds of lascivious story. And yet amidst all this the prince was unmoved, absorbed in his thoughts about disease, old age, and death. "How may I hope to escape these, he thought?"—and paid but little heed to the wiles of the women. Now there was one woman amongst the rest who, with her own hand taking a Malika flower from the front of her head-dress, fastened it on to the breast of the prince. The prince, looking on with a sort of vacant stare, forthwith drew the flower out and, twirling it in his hand, scattered the leaves on the ground.[3]

Then Udâyi, seeing that all these means were useless, besought

---

[1] This appearance of Udâyi in the interior of the palace seems to be the subject of Fig. 1, Plate lxxiii, *Tree and Serpent Worship*.

[2] This story of Ekasringa (Unicorn) is one frequently alluded to in Buddhist books (*Catena*, p. 260; *Eitel's Handbook, sub. voce*). It was probably the origin of the story of Sringha found in the Râmâyana (*Talboys Wheeler, Hist. of India*, vol. ii., p. 11). The original myth was doubtless derived from the shadow of the Sun when on the meridian, added to the Horse, the emblem of the Sun, to denote strength or juvenescence. This one-horned figure became afterwards known as the *Unicorn*. The later story of his seduction by the maids of Anga probably alludes to the Sun's passage westward, enamoured by the breezes of the evening. The connection of this myth with the mediæval story of the Unicorn being capable of capture only by a chaste maiden is too evident to require proof. (*Vide Yule's Marco Polo.*)

[3] This also seems to be the case in Fig. 1, Plate lxxiii, *Tree and Serpent Worship*.

the prince to listen to his friendly advice, and repeated this Gâthâ—

"I will recount in brief the marks of a friend,
When doing wrong, to warn; when doing well to exhort to perseverance;
When in difficulty or danger, to assist, relieve, and deliver.
Such a man is indeed a true and illustrious friend."

Then Udâyi, having uttered this Gâtha, continued his conversation thus—"Great and holy Prince! as I have now undertaken to act as a friend to your Highness, it would be unfriendly if I remained silent after observing that which I consider commendable, or the contrary, in your conduct. I wish, therefore, to speak plainly on the present occasion, and I ask you to bear with me—as with a friend. I observe that your Highness is wrong in not yielding to the importunities of the ladies of your palace; but that you rather hate, avoid, and dislike their society. But why should you think it wrong to act according to our natural tendencies? The very first principle of a woman's being is to allow her the privilege of loving some one, and seeking the gratification of her desire. Respect to a husband is won only by his being capable of participation in pleasure. If your Highness persistently refuses to indulge yourself in these objects of desire, then the world, rich and poor, however well they may speak of you with flattering lips, as courteous, will find it difficult to honour you at heart." Then he added this Gâtha—

"The happiness of a woman is to respect[1] (her husband);
This respect is the highest source of her content.
Without respect, having only beauty,
Is to be like a tree without flowers."

Then the prince, having heard the discourse of Udâyi, replied in words of deepest meaning, and in tones like the thunder-roll, and said, "Udâyi! I accept your offer of friendship, and I reject none of your advice; but yet what are these pleasures of which you speak to me? I see only one thing, that worldly enjoyments are perishable, and therefore the thoughts of my heart are sad and not tending to outward exhibition of joy." Then he added a Gâtha—

[1] That is to respect in the discharge of all conjugal duties.

> "The glories of the world though they be joy-giving,
> Yet there is birth and old age, disease and death;
> These four—only extirpate them,—
> And my heart—whom will it not love?"

And then he continued—"Udâyi! only regard these women in another light! see them as they will be when they are old, their skins wrinkled, their beauty faded and gone, and on seeing one another think how sad their reflections then! how much more stupid of a man in such a place and surrounded by such companions to be merry and amorous!" Then he added this Gâtha—

> "The condition of birth, death, old age, disease,
> Fix (the mind on) these (three), birth, old age, disease—
> If thus fixed, nevertheless an amorous desire is present,
> A man is but as a brute-beast or a bird."

And so they discoursed until the sun went down; on which the prince, seeing the darkness coming on, went once more into the chamber of the women, who surrounded him on every side as they practised their arts in causing pleasure. [*On this night the Queen Yasôdharâ found herself about to be delivered.*[1]] On this night, also, the Queen Mother Gôtamî, called Prajâpatî, in her sleep had the following dream—she thought she saw a white ox-King in the midst of the city going on in a wistful way bellowing and crying, whilst no one in the place was able to get before it to stop it or hinder it. Again, Suddhôdana on that night dreamt that he saw in the midst of the city a royal standard like that of Indra fixed in the ground. It was adorned with every kind of jewel and beautifully formed. It appeared even like the Royal Mount Sumeru standing up from the midst of the watery earth, and reaching high up into space. Again, it seemed that from the midst of this royal standard a bright light shone out, which lit up the world on every side. And then from the four quarters of heaven he thought he

---

[1] This is an ambiguous sentence. According to the subsequent narrative Yasôdharâ was not delivered till six years after. Doubtless the passage in the text is an attempt to reconcile the accounts found in the different schools. We may observe, however, that the agreement of the passage cited from the Abhinishkramana by M. Foucaux (*Lalita Vistara*, p. 389, n.), with the events narrated in the subsequent pages, proves that the work we are now translating is known in Thibet.

saw some clouds rising, and these, gathering together over the standard, distilled a soft rain above it, whilst flowers fell round it and soft voices sang sweetly, and a beautiful white umbrella with a golden handle appeared over it, and at last the four Kings of heaven, with their retinues, appeared coming towards the city, and having taken the standard the gates opened and they went out.

The same night Yasôdharâ was greatly troubled in her sleep, and had twelve dreams which disturbed her exceedingly. Being unable to rest, the prince turned to her and said, "Yasôdharâ, beloved! why are you so restless and alarmed? Your breathing indicates distress, and your heart is oppressed; what is it affects you that you start so? My Yasôdharâ is not in a Sitavana (cemetery), nor in a place for burning bodies, nor amidst the mountains, or in a desert; but you are within the city surrounded by guards, in the King's palace, well protected; there are no wild beasts here, or robbers to frighten you; but in this place there is peace and safety and no cause for alarm! But yet I see my Yasôdharâ's heart is greatly affected, filled with doubt and anxiety; tell me, then, as you have just awoke, the cause of all this?" Then Yasôdharâ, with many tears and almost choked with sobbing, replied as follows—"My prince! in my sleep this night I have beheld twelve visions—oh! let me tell them! and bear with me whilst I speak. Sacred one! in my sleep I saw all the great earths around us shaking and trembling! I saw the great standard of Indra, broken in twain, fall to the earth. I saw the Sun and Moon, and all the stars falling through space. I saw a very beautiful umbrella spread over myself and affording me a grateful shade—when, suddenly, that son of the slave, whose name is Tchandaka, came and snatched it away and went off with it. I saw all the choicest jewels that adorn my head-dress, cut off and dispersed here and there. I saw the various ornaments worn on my body, necklets and bracelets (scattered) as the water is driven, I saw my body, naturally so graceful and attractive, suddenly become perfectly horrible and ugly. I saw my hands and my feet of themselves drop off from my body. I saw myself suddenly stripped to the skin and left without clothing. I saw my chair, on which I have sat for so many years, suddenly overturned. I saw the couch on which I have so often reposed with you, and enjoyed your caresses, suddenly, deprived of its four legs, fall to the earth. I saw a great mountain, composed of all the precious substances, suddenly burst into flames from its four corners and fall down in utter ruin. I saw a beautiful tree within the Mahârâja's Palace enclosure, blown down by the wind. I saw the moon and all the stars which surround it suddenly fall down and perish. I saw the Sun, with its glorious light, disappear, and the entire world left in pitchy darkness. I saw a lighted torch which was in the city depart from it. I saw the guardian spirit of this city, who protects it on every side, his person so beautiful and so magnificently attired, suddenly stand without one of the gates and raise his voice in lamentation and wailing. I saw the city of Kapilavastu suddenly converted into a waste, frightful to behold, without one spot of delight. I saw all the trees and flowers scatter their leaves and the tanks all dry up. I saw a number of fully-armed men hastening in every direction towards the four quarters of the world.

"Such were the dreams, O Prince! which cause me this distress, and indeed I cannot tell whether they be indications of good or bad fortune—or what will be the result, whether my life is coming to an end, or whether your love and society is to be taken from me; on these accounts I was troubled in my sleep, and am still distressed in mind."

Then the prince began to reflect, and thought thus with himself—"It is because I shall soon leave my home and become a Recluse, that these dreams have appeared to Yasôdharâ."

Then he addressed her and said, "Dear wife! though you had seen a thousand standards broken and fall to the earth, or a thousand suns and stars showering through space, yet let none of these things trouble or alarm you—dreams are but the empty products of a universal law; return, dear wife, to your rest! You are young in years and your body delicate and soft, let not such anxieties as these molest you or cause you distress!" Then Yasôdharâ, having heard the words of the prince, returned to her couch and slept, whilst the prince reposed by her side.[1]

Moreover, on the same night the prince himself had five dreams,[2]

---

[1] The original is more explicit. Sufficient at any rate to show that up to this time the prince was not weaned from the gratification of his senses. But the text explains this by saying that he desired to hush Yasôdharâ's suspicions.

[2] These five dreams are given with slight variation by Spence Hardy, *Manual*, p. 167.

which were these :—first, he dreamt he saw the great earth stretched out for him to use as a bed, his head reposed on Mount Sumeru as a pillow, the great sea on the East supported his left arm, his right arm rested on the great Western Sea, and both his feet stretched out to the great Southern Sea. Secondly, he dreamt that he saw a certain plant called *Kin-leh*[1], growing up out of his navel, and the top of it reaching even to the Akanishta Heaven. Thirdly, he dreamt that he saw four birds, flying from each Quarter, come towards him, they were of every colour, but as they came and fell at his feet, they all became white. Fourthly, he saw in his dreams four head of white cattle, black from their feet up to their knees, come and lick his feet. Fifthly, he saw a lofty and wide mount of impure substance, on which he reposed and went round it on foot without pollution.

The Flight from the Palace.

§ 2. At this time, whilst the Prince dwelt within the palace and slept, the chief officer of the guard, who protected the precincts, told the persons composing the guard that during the watches the pass-words should be these, "Komperah," "Mudra," "Angana." And he, moreover, warned them to be especially watchful throughout this particular night, to see that the prince did not escape, informing them of the anxiety of Suddhôdana, and the predictions of the soothsayers respecting his either being a Chakravarti or a Recluse.

Then the first watch being passed, at midnight the guard exclaimed in a loud voice, "Prosperity to his Sacred Majesty—long life and happiness!" And so the first half of the middle watch went by, and it was just beginning the second half.

At this time all the Devas of the Suddhavasa Heavens came down to Kapilavastu. The men of the city were wrapped in sleep, and all within the palace was still and quiet. One of the Devas,

---

[1] The Sinhalese account says it was an arrow that proceeded from the navel. I do not know what plant *Kin-leh* can be. Compare this with the story about Vishnu.

called Dharmâcharya Devaputra, then approached the palace, and by his spiritual power entered it, and caused all the women who were asleep in the chamber around Siddhârtha to contort their bodies into every kind of unseemly position, some half clothed, others partly in bed and partly out, lying in all directions, some with their eyes half-closed, others dribbling from their mouths, grinding with their teeth, snorting through their throats, etc.

Then the prince, suddenly waking up and seeing the braziers and lamps all untrimmed and defiled with oil, and in the lurid light observing the women lying about in the unseemly attitudes just described, and the instruments of music scattered here and there in utter disorder, seeing all this, he reflected thus—"It is only the fool who is deceived by the outward show of beauty; for where is the beauty when the decorations of the person are taken away, the jewels removed, the gaudy dress laid aside, the flowers and chaplets withered and dead? The wise man, seeing the vanity of all such fictitious charms, regards them as a dream, a mirage, a phantasy."

And then he repeated this Gâtha—

"How impure the world! how false and deceiving!
And nothing more so than woman's appearance;
Because of clothes, and the decorations of jewels,
The fool is filled with mad desire.
But if a man bring himself to consider
'All these charms are but a phantasy, unreal as a dream,'
And so put away ignorance, and do not permit himself to be deceived,
That man shall obtain deliverance and a body free from contamination."

And then the prince proceeded further to reflect in this way—"Alas! what great misery is this! What an impure place is this! like a vessel filled with filth. Oh! what madness is it to desire such pleasures as these! This place is hateful—this place is deadly as poison," etc., etc.

And again he reflected, as he still gazed on the scene in the chamber, "This sight should give me joy! as far as it steels my heart to resolve to aim at the highest religious happiness, and to vow to deliver all men who are left as it were without a Saviour, and to cause them to find a refuge and a place of safety in their present distress! I see in the spectacle before me a sign that the time of my own rescue is at hand!"

At this time, T'so-Ping Devaputra, seeing that the prince was awake, approached him and said, "Prince! the vows you have made from time to time, to be born in the Tusita Heaven, to descend to earth, to be incarnated in the world, to abide in the palace and enjoy the pleasures of life; all these vows have been accomplished. And now all the Devas and men are looking to your leaving your palace and becoming a Recluse!"

Then the prince, having heard the words of T'so-Ping Devaputra, immediately put on his richly-adorned and invaluable slippers for the purpose of rising to look round the place once more. Then beholding the precious couch on which he had been accustomed to lie, he struck it with his hand as he uttered these words, "Never again will I indulge in the pleasures of sense—never again —this is the last time; from henceforth I entertain such thoughts no more!" Then taking in his right hand the richly-adorned net-like curtain which divided the chamber from the outer hall, he raised it and proceeded slowly through the outer apartments, and then, standing at the eastern door with closed hands, he paused and invoked the Universal Spirit,[1] after which, raising his head, he looked up into heaven and beheld the countless stars of the night.

Then the four guardian Deities of the world and Divine Sâkra, perceiving that the time was come for the prince to leave his home, began to assemble from the different Quarters with their followers, designing to come to the spot where the prince was. Then Dhritarâshtra, with an innumerable retinue of Gandharvas discoursing sweet music, proceeded from the Eastern quarter, and having encircled the city of Kapilavastu three times, he descended to earth, and standing with clasped hands he bent his head towards the spot where the prince was standing. Then Virûdhaka Devarâja, with an innumerable retinue of Kumbhândas, holding in their hands vases full of perfumes, proceeding from the Southern quarter of space, came to the city and did likewise. And so also the Western

---

[1] "*All the Buddhas*"—a phrase introduced by later Buddhism —to signify "the Universal Spirit."

and Northern Kings [the first accompanied by Yakshas holding burning torches, &c.; the second accompanied by Nâgas holding every kind of gem and jewelled ornament, etc.] came and did likewise. Then also Sâkra Devânam, with innumerable Devas, holding every sort of heavenly flower, precious chaplet, costly perfume, etc., came from the Trâyastriñshas Heavens and did likewise.

Then the prince, looking up into the Heavens at the stars of night, beheld these countless beings assembling round the city, and just as the star Kwei was in conjunction with the moon, he heard the Devas chanting this song—"Holy Prince! the time has come! the star is now conjoined, the time has come to seek the Highest Law of Life; delay no longer amongst men, abandon all and become a recluse!"

Then the prince, still gazing upwards into heaven, thought thus with himself—"Now, in the silence of the night, the star Kwei in conjunction, all the Devas are come down to earth to confirm my resolution, 'I WILL GO—THE TIME HAS COME!'" Thus resolved, he called his coachman Tchandaka, born on the same day with himself, and addressed him thus—"Tchandaka! bring hither, without noise, my horse Kantaka, born on the same day as myself." Then Tchandaka, having heard these directions, and seeing the prince thus looking up into the Heavens during the depth of the night, began to doubt in his mind, his body trembled, and the hairs on his body stood erect, and he spake thus—"What fear, or what foe alarms my master that thus in the night time he orders me to bring his horse?" "Tchandaka!" the prince replied, "you shall soon know all! but now bring me my horse Kantaka!"

[Kiouen XVI contains 6,368 words and cost 3.184 taels.]

CHAPTER XVII.

On Leaving the Palace to become a Recluse.

§ 1. AT this time Tchandaka, having heard the prince speak as he did, made up his mind that he had now resolved to become an ascetic; desiring, therefore, to shake the determination of the prince, he addressed him in a loud voice with a view to attract the attention of the guards of the palace—"Holy Prince! surely there is a right time for doing every thing! Is this then a time for having your horse harnessed and equipped. If your Highness really desires to go forth to visit the gardens, this is not the right time. What foe or rebel or traitor do you fear! The world is at peace! There is no public commotion, or distress! The whole earth is under the rule (umbrella) of one Holy Prince! Why then do you require your horse Kantaka to be brought? Prince! within your palace at the present time are numberless women! They lie around you on every side, coveting nothing so much as your attention. As the Lord of Heaven, Sâkradevanam, rejoices in his garden, surrounded by his lovely Apsarasas, so are you, O Prince! in this palace, seated on your jewelled throne. Why then call for your horse? Let your heart be content in the midst of these your fair companions; listen to their charming songs, and partake of their pleasures, and rest at ease!" Then Tchandaka proceeded to pluck the head-dresses (or hair), and with his foot to move the limbs of the women, in order to rouse and wake them, but all in vain! for by the power of the Devas they were still bound by sleep, and were affected by none of the efforts made to arouse them.

Then the prince, fearing lest the people should be aroused, addressed Tchandaka in a soft voice, thus—

"Tchandaka! born on the same day with myself, be assured
That all within this palace is in my sight as a grave!
As a pit filled with noisome insects and worms!
As an abode in which Rakshas dwell together!

* * * * *

Tchandaka! I realise the misery of these delights,
And my desire to remain here is gone!
Tchandaka! bring me my horse Kantaka!
My heart is fixed, I am resolved to become a recluse."

Tchandaka, on hearing this, again replied, "But, O Prince! all the world says that hereafter you will certainly become a Chakravarti Râja, how can this be, if you now are determined to give up your—" But here the Prince, interrupting him said, "Psha! what folly, Tchandaka! for if formerly when I was a Deva in the Tusita Heavens, I vowed to give up all that glory, in order to be born in the world and become a recluse, in consequence of my sense of the evil and misery of impermanence and birth and death, shall I now prefer the short life of a man, even though a universal monarch, and give up the aim which then actuated me?"

Again Tchandaka urged the age of the prince's father, and the unutterable grief he would feel if his son carried out his purpose. To which the prince replied, "My love to my father is not less than his to me, nor do I love all my relatives less; but I feel my heart filled with awe and fear in consideration of the misery awaiting them all if they continue in this condition of birth and death, and I desire to find out the Law of Deliverance to prove my love to them to be greater even than theirs, for I aim to rescue them and all men from their misery, and every future consequence of it."

Tchandaka then said, "Are you, O Prince, thus resolved? Do you really purpose to leave the world and to become an ascetic?"

The prince answered, "Yes! Tchandaka, of propitious birth! my purpose is fixed!"

"And why are you so influenced?" urged Tchandaka, once more.

"Because," said the prince, "I see the evil of worldly things, everything is impermanent; for this reason, O Tchandaka! I am bent on seeking that higher and more excellent platform (found alone in the religious life)."

"And how do you prove the superior excellency of that life?" rejoined Tchandaka.

"Because," answered the prince, "if the world can secure freedom from birth and death; from old age, disease, the changes and alternations of love; from enmity; and attain to a royal condition, without taint or pollution, then may I well be drawn to strive after such a state. But now, worthy Tchandaka! contradict me no further; but go, as I exhort you, and harness my horse Kantaka, and bring him hither."

Tchandaka having heard the prince's entreaty, and seeing the deep purpose of his heart—notwithstanding the commands of the King that the Prince should be kept within the palace, made up his mind and said, "I shall obey your commands, oh Prince!" And so the Gâtha says:

"Tchandaka, by the power of the Heavenly Spirits,
Firmly bent on disobeying the King's command,

With a view to the accomplishment of Bôdhisatwa's ancient vow,
Resolved to harness in all his trappings the horse Kantaka."

Then Tchandaka forthwith proceeded to the stable, and from over the manger took down the beautifully adorned bit (kavika) of Kantaka, and putting it into his mouth he led him forth from the stable, and then tying him fast to a stake, he rubbed down his back before placing across him his beautifully soft and pliable saddle-cloth, adorned with gold and gems of every description; and then above this he placed a gold net-work covering. Thus having equipped the horse, he led him round forthwith to the place where the Prince was awaiting him.

Then Kantaka, king of horses, born on the same day with the Prince, seeing his master standing there in his youthful strength, filled with a transport of joy, neighed loudly as he came up. The sound of this neighing could be heard at the distance of half a yôjana, but all the Devas of the Suddha (pure) heavens, by their spiritual power, caused the sound to be deadened and destroyed, fearing lest any one should be aroused, and so put an obstacle in the way of the Prince's departure.

Then the Prince, filled with unutterable delight, with the soft silky fingers of his right hand, smooth as the leaves of the lotus flower, of a bright colour, even as that of red ore, patted the back of his Royal steed, and said in an encouraging tone, "Now then, my own Royal steed, Kantaka! your master desires to seek the ever life-giving law (law of sweet dew, *i. e.*, ambrosia). You must put forth your strength and advance bravely, nor permit any one to place an obstacle in the way. You, my brave Kantaka! in the hour of battle know how to exert yourself, even to death, to secure victory; show yourself now equal to this struggle after the joys resulting from the sacrifice of home in pursuit of a religious life. The joys of this world are brief and transitory, and when passed, then comes sorrow again. To exert oneself in religious pursuits is difficult; but now, because I am earnest in seeking how to afford universal deliverance from misery—exert yourself bravely, oh Kantaka! It is for the sake of the world, and all that lives, yea! even for you and those like you I am now struggling—then advance bravely, my horse!"

Then the Prince, standing there on the ground, vowed a mighty and earnest vow, and said, "This shall be the last time I mount a horse whilst leading a secular life—from henceforth, after this, no steed shall bear me, as I now am." Having said this, holding on to the saddle cloth, he leapt on to the back of Kantaka, and then bade him go on and bear him well for this last time.

At the time when the Prince mounted on to the saddle cloth of Kantaka, countless Asuras, Garudas, Kinnaras, Mahoragas, Rakshas, Earth-dwelling Pisachas, Heaven-dwelling Devas, belonging to the Suddha Heavens, and even up to the Akanishta regions, flocked round the royal steed Kantaka and accompanied him as he went. Then the Devas, holding in their hands umbrellas, flags with golden bells, etc., surrounded the Prince.

Thus he advanced slowly towards the outside gate of the Palace, the Suddha Devas deadening the sound of Kantaka's feet, which generally could be heard at the distance of a krôsa.

Now there was at this time a space-dwelling Yaksha, called Patrapada; this Patrapada and the older Yakshas dwelling in the air, came together at the time of the Prince's departure, and each one held the feet of Kantaka underneath, so that he might go quietly.[1]

Again, when the Prince first made up his mind to quit his home, there was a Devaputra who uttered this sentence in a loud voice, "Oh! would that good fortune may attend the Master of the ship, who now desires to deliver the countless creatures of the world from the sea of trouble." Another Devaputra spake thus, "Oh! may there be no obstacle placed in the way of the Holy and Reverend one, who now desires to leave his home and cross the sea of Life and Death."

Then the Prince addressed Tchandaka and said, "Oh! Tchandaka, of propitious birth, proceed in advance and observe the way." The inner gate of the palace, on ordinary occasions, when opened could be heard at a krôsa distance; on this occasion it opened noiselessly of itself. On this, Tchandaka exclaimed, "Wonderful portent! on ordinary occasions it requires an exertion of great strength to open this gate; but now, on the approach of the Prince it unbars itself and stands open for him to pass, even as a

---

[1] This scene is evidently the subject of Plate lix, "*Tree and Serpent Worship.*"

fierce wind divides and opens the cloud which has collected in heaven."

Then the Prince, passing through the gate to the outside, vowed a vow. "This is the very last time that I will pass through this gate." The Prince having passed this gate, rode on slowly towards the Vyâla gate, in front of which there was a Yaksha chief on guard, whose name was Shen-jih (good or propitious entrance), he had five hundred other Yakshas in attendance; these seeing the Prince coming slowly onwards, towards the gate, said one to another, "What means this, that Siddartha should be advancing towards our gate at this time of the night? Surely this is not a fitting time for such an excursion." After reflection, however, they resolved to open the gate—when lo! it silently flew open of itself!

. . . .

At this time, Mara Râja, of the Kama loka, the cruel and Malignant (Pisuna), seeing the Prince leaving his home, fearing the consequences of his so doing, caused by his spiritual power all sorts of strange shrieks and noises to be heard, like the rolling of thunder in the air, or the crashing of things together; again, he made the appearance of a great torrent rushing from a rock, right in front of the Prince; again, he caused the appearance of a great and rugged mount; also of a fiercely burning conflagration; but all these alarming appearances were overpowered and removed by the spiritual energy of the good Devas of the Suddha heavens.

Then the Prince, having got beyond the city, turned round and looked at it, and with his lion's voice, he exclaimed "Rather would I have my body crushed by a rock, rather would I drink the deadliest poison, or starve myself to death, than not fulfil my vow to seek to save all flesh from the fearful ocean of birth and death. I enter not the city again."

The Devas, hearing this resolve, were filled with joy, whilst all the spirits that kept guard at the gates and ramparts of the city exclaimed "Even so! even so! may the Prince fulfil his purpose," and then with raised hands they addressed him and said, "Oh! valiant youth! to have thus gone forth from the city, and now to look back!" The Prince hearing these words, feared not nor was alarmed, but rather was filled with joy; and his hair was moved with the earnestness of his resolve, as he said, "Never again will

I enter this city till I have attained the draught of sweet dew (the gift of Life), and entered on the road to Nirvâna—then I will return!"

Now on the spot where the Prince stopped without the city and uttered these words with his lion voice, men in after days erected a pagoda (tower) and called it "the tower of the lion voice utterance." On that spot also there was a great Nyagrôdha tree, the Deva of which tree on this occasion uttered these Gâthas:

"If a man should desire to destroy the tree,
He must first thoroughly kill its root,
As to destroy a living creature one cuts off its head!
Cross over the water and you shall reach the other shore.
But words unless they are fulfilled are vain,
They breed troubles, and in the end destroy happiness."

At this time the prince replied to that Deva in the following verses—

"You may remove from their base the Snowy Mountains,
You may exhaust the waters of the Ocean,
The Firmament may fall to earth,
But my words in the end will be accomplished."

At this time also the Devas of the Suddha Heavens added these Gâthas—

"Behold! here is the great Medicine King
Able to destroy the poison caused by Sorrow;
Is any one wounded by the arrows of Love,
Here is one able to draw them out at once;
Behold, here is the great Physician
Who can thoroughly heal the maladies of all men;
Whether it be sickness, old age, or death,
He is able to cure and completely remove the disease!
Behold! here is the great Torch of Wisdom
To illumine those who are deceived or in doubt,
Whoever dwells in the darkness and gloom of ignorance,
To him the brightness of this glorious light shall soon appear.
Behold! here is one highly gifted,
Able to instruct the entire world
By the brightness of his perfect wisdom and full knowledge,
Able to shed light throughout the universe.

Behold! here is the great Master of the ship,
Able to deliver and take across every class of living thing," etc.

Then the Suddha Devas, after these stanzas, immediately opened their mouths, and said, "All hail! (Namo) highly honourable!" and then they went before him and scattered the glorious light of their persons on every side, to show him the way, dispersing the gloom, and lighting up the path even as the Sun, bursting forth from a dark and heavy cloud, shines forth in its strength.

Then the Devas of the Kama Lokas likewise assumed bodies like young men (manavas), and went on before the Prince, leading the way. And so also Mâha Brahma, and his attendants, surrounded the prince, and all the Trâyastrinshas Devas and the four heavenly kings, besides countless Gandhervas, Pisatchas, etc. All these accompanied the prince as he went, arrayed in their several manners, and scattering flowers, incense, and sandal-wood as they advanced.

Meantime the women of the palace gradually awoke from their sleep, and suddenly began each to cry out, "I do not see the prince!—I do not see the prince!" And then Yasôdharâ, having awoke, and seeing herself alone on the couch, cried out with a lamentable voice, "Alas! alas! and have we at last been deceived by the prince!" and then she uttered a great cry and fell to the ground, beating her breast, tearing her hair, and casting away from her the jewels and ornaments that adorned her person, etc.

Then the women conveyed the news to Suddhôdana that the prince had fled, and that Tchandaka, and Kantaka, the horse, were missing.

Suddhôdana, on hearing this, uttered a great cry, and said, "Alas! alas! my son—my dear son!" and so fell fainting on the earth. Then the minister in attendance raised him with his hand, and sprinkled over him cold perfumed water, until, after a short interval, he recovered. Sending then for the captain of the guard of the city gate, he commanded him to dispatch soldiers in every direction, to find out where the prince was concealed. And so, in obedience to this command, search was made, but the prince, protected by the Devas who accompanied him in his flight, remained undiscovered.

The Onward Progress of the Prince.

§ 2. The Prince, having left the city, directed Tchandaka to proceed before him onwards in the direction of the village of Lo-má (Râma?). And so the horse Kantaka proceeded, with a light and easy pace, from the middle of the night to the time of the rising of the morning star, for a distance of two yôjanas. [*The Mahâsanghikas say twelve yôjanas. The Mahâstaviras say a hundred yôjanas.*] Then they arrived at a village called Mi-ni-ka, and as the sun rose, they came to the place where the Rishi Po-ka-pi dwelt. Then the prince asked Tchandaka, "What place is this?" to whom Tchandaka replied, "Great prince! this is a spot close to the village of Lo-ma (Rama)."[1] Then the prince, seeing the forest, and the place where the old Rishi dwelt, and also the birds and beasts and the flowing water, and pleasant fountains; and, knowing that Tchandaka and Kantaka were now weary, he addressed the former, and said: "I will alight here, and rest;" then the prince, springing from his horse on to the ground, uttered this vow: "This is the last time I will ever dismount from my steed; and this is the spot where for the last time I have alighted." And then he addressed Kantaka with affectionate words, and also assured Tchandaka of his love and kindly feeling, which was without any selfish or personal consideration, repeating this Gâtha—

"We nourish children to found a house;
We obey our fathers, to receive in return support;
We build a trade to get profit—
All men are engaged in seeking their own good."

Then Tchandaka replied, "But why, O prince, have you acted as you have, and come to this Mount?" Then the prince, having first enlisted Tchandaka's serious attention, replied, "I have given up my kingly estate from no consideration of fear or dread of its responsibilities, but with a view to seek deliverance from the bondage of the world. Tchandaka, my heart rejoices to escape from the condition of royalty, because I have now found peace; and, by becoming a mendicant, I do, in fact, escape from the endless toils

---

[1] Probably Râmagâma.

of birth and death. Now then, Tchandaka, do you take my horse Kantaka, and return to the king's palace. My mind is completely fixed. I will become a religious mendicant." And then he repeated this Gâtha:—

"No further conversation do I purpose to hold;
You know my heart and my love to you;
I am now freed from the love due only to relatives.
Take the horse Kantaka and depart."

Then Tchandaka addressed the prince as follows: "Oh, mighty prince! men generally become mendicants after four circumstances have occurred. 1. When the body begins to get old and feeble. 2. When they have become worn by disease. 3. When they are left without friends. 4. When stricken by poverty. But in your case none of these things are so. Moreover, when you were born, O prince! the soothsaying Brahmans, skilful in the art of casting horoscopes, able thoroughly to understand and explain the discourses and books which treat on the subject, all predicted that you should become a Chakravarti monarch, king of the whole world, and possessor of the seven insignia of empire. First of all the discus jewel, then the pearl jewel, the elephant, the horse, the woman, the master of the treasury, and the ruler of soldiers; moreover, that you should have a thousand valiant sons able to subdue all enemies, and establish the universal empire of their Father." [*By means of the precious discus the Chakravarti is able to travel through space, and go whithersoever he lists;—by the precious jewel he is able to light up the darkness for a distance of seven yojanas*].[1]

"Thus, O Prince, as a universal monarch, you should govern the entire earth, without an enemy, or any cause of fear, without any interruption or cause of disquiet, in perfect peace and righteousness, possessed of the greatest happiness.

The Prince replied: "And when this prediction was uttered, was there nothing else said?" Tchandaka allowed that there was, and on the prince urging him to say what it was, he added—"All the soothsayers agreed that if you gave up your kingly state, and became a recluse, that then you would arrive at perfect enlightenment, and having attained this condition that you would then estab-

1 Here follows a description of the other insignia.

lish a kingdom of righteousness, by declaring the sublime doctrines of religion."

Then the prince added: "O Tchandaka, speak idly no longer. You know perfectly that the Rishi Asita gave but one certain prediction, and that was that I should become a preacher of the sublime doctrine of religion."

Then Tchandaka, in astonishment and fear, addressed the prince thus: "Oh, mighty prince! and are you really able to recollect this prediction?—for it was agreed amongst all your kinsfolk that this prediction should never be named in your presence, lest it might awaken in you a desire to attain to the condition of supreme wisdom (Bôdhi)."

Then the prince rejoined: "Tchandaka! in former days I descended from the Tusita heavens to assume a body in the womb of my mother; and whilst in this state, everything that happened is perfectly known and remembered by me; how much more should I recollect all that occurred after my birth. Moreover, Tchandaka, all the Devas in that heaven assured me that I should arrive at perfect enlightenment, and establish the kingdom of the Highest Truth upon earth—so that I am certain that such is my destiny. And, listen, Tchandaka, to my last words—I would rather be cut in pieces, limb by limb, and piece by piece; I would rather be burnt in a fiery furnace; I would rather be ground to pieces by a falling mountain, than forego for one instant my fixed purpose to become a religious recluse, or to return again to my home. For, alas! all earthly pleasures are transitory and perishable—this alone endures."

[Kiouen XVII contains 6,559 words, and cost 3.279 taels.]

CHAPTER XVIII.

Cutting off the hair and wearing the soiled garments.

At this time the prince, with his own hand, took from his royal head-dress the priceless Mani pearl that adorned it, and, giving it to Tchandaka, spoke as follows: "Tchandaka, I now give you this precious Mani pearl, and bid you return with it to my father Suddhôdana Maharâja; and when arrived in his presence, after due salutation, bid him dismiss all grief or useless regrets on my account; assure him that I am influenced by no delusion in leaving him thus, nor by any angry or resentful feeling; tell him that I seek no personal gain or profit by what I do, that I look for no reward—not even to be born in heaven—but that I seek solely the benefit of men (all flesh), to bring back those who have wandered from the right path, to enlighten those who are living in dark and gloomy error, to save them from the constant recurrence of birth and death, to remove from the world all sources of sorrow and pain—for these purposes I have left my home; and so my loving Father, seeing me thus rejoicing in carrying out this purpose, should shake off every feeling of regret and sorrow on my account." And then he added this Gâtha:—

"Even supposing there were love and affection for a long time,
A period of change must come sooner or later,
Seeing the existence of this impermanency every moment,
I on this account am seeking for deliverance."

The prince, having repeated this Gâtha, continued in these words, "Because I am desirous to get rid of this source of sorrow, therefore I have left my home, and am about to adopt a religious life. Let not my father grieve on this account. A man bound in the fetters of lust and self-indulgence is the victim of grief and useless regrets—for such a man one may be distressed."

(The same ideas are repeated through a succession of arguments with Tchandaka. At length Tchandaka, having fallen at the feet of the prince, and embraced them, and Kantaka, the horse, having licked them with his tongue, and wept many tears, consents to go back. Then the narrative continues.)

At this time the prince greatly commended Tchandaka, and said: "You do well—you do well, illustrious Tchandaka, by consenting to return as I desire you, and it will be much for your own advantage." Then the prince, taking from off his person the jewels and precious ornaments that he wore, uttered this vow—"Never again shall my body be adorned with such things as these—never more shall my body be so adorned;" and then, handing them all to Tchandaka, he bade him take them back, and deliver them into the hands of his kinsfolk.

Then Tchandaka, having taken them, answered and said, "I

wish to know, O prince, what answer I shall give to Suddhôdana Râja and your kinsfolk when they ask me where you are living, and what further messages you sent to them." To whom the prince said, "Go back, Tchandaka, to the palace, and salute my father, and my foster-mother, Mahâprajâpatî, and all my kinsmen; and tell them that I am bent on the acquisition of supreme wisdom, and that, having attained to this, I will return again to Kapilavastu."

Then the prince, having delivered the gem from his head-dress, and the other decorations, into the hands of Tchandaka, drew forth his sword from its sheath, and, holding it in his right hand, he seized with his left hand his rosy curling locks, in colour like the Utpala flower, and severed them from his head; then, casting them into the air, Sâkra, with a joyous heart, caught them before they fell to the earth, and, ascending upwards, paid them divine honour in company with the other Devas.

At this time all the Devas of the Suddha Heavens—a great congregation—were assembled together not very far from the spot where the prince was seated. Among them was one who transformed himself into the appearance of a hairdresser, wearing on his head a wreath of Sumana flowers; and, with a sharp razor in his hand, he approached the prince, and stood still. Then the prince, having perceived him, spake thus—"My friend! is it convenient to you to attend to me or not?" to whom he replied, "It is quite convenient." "Then be good enough to do so at once," said the prince. Then the hairdresser, with his well-sharpened razor, shaved from off the prince's head his bright curling hair, whilst Sâkra Deva raja, with a joyous heart, collecting the rosy curls, and not permitting one hair to fall to the ground, gathering them all in his heavenly robe, carried them to the thirty-three heavens, and paid them religious worship; and from that time till now a festival has ever been observed by those Devas, called "The festival for honouring the hair-diadem of Bôdhisatwa."

Then the prince, having with his own hands taken off all his jewels, and having also had the hair that covered his head, like a diadem, clean shaved off, still perceived that his garments were rather those of a Deva than a recluse. Considering this, he said, "These garments are not those of a religious mendicant, such persons live in the midst of the mountains; who is there can provide me with a Kashya robe such as is worn by the hermits who frequent the mountains and forests, that I may be clad according to the rules of religion?" At this time one of the Suddha Devas, having perceived the thoughts which troubled the prince, transformed himself into the appearance of a hunter wearing a dirty and much-soiled Kashya garment. In his hand he held his bow and arrows, and thus gradually approaching the spot where the prince was, he came to within a short distance of him, and then stood still.

The prince, having perceived him thus attired, with his bow and arrows in his hand, addressed him in these words—"Oh! worthy man of the lonely mountains! will you exchange your Kashya robe with me for my Kasika garments? the price of this robe is at least one hundred thousand lakhs of gold pieces, perfumed as it is with every kind of sandal-wood scent; if you possess yourself of this, what use would that dirty Kashya robe be to you?" and he repeated this Gâtha—

"This is the robe of a holy recluse
Not becoming one to wear who carries the bow;
Bestow it, therefore, on me, and cause my heart to rejoice,
Grudge not to give it me in exchange for this heavenly garment."

The hunter replied, "I am quite agreeable, respected sir, to comply with your request." And the exchange was accordingly completed. Then the Prince, receiving the Kashya robe, was filled with joy, and forthwith he clad himself therewith, and gave his Kasika robe to the other, who, on his part, being a Deva, by the exercise of his spiritual power flew away with the precious garment, and mounting up through space proceeded at once to the Brahma Devas (or to Brahma Deva) to give them the opportunity of paying it religious worship—which when Bôdhisatwa perceived his heart was filled with joy.

Now being thus shorn and robed, Bôdhisatwa spake as follows—"From this time I swear that I will be known by no other name than 'the Recluse' (Muni)."

Then Bôdhisatwa, having dismissed the weeping Tchandaka, proceeded alone, clad in his Kashya robe, towards the place where the Rishi Bagava (Po-ka-pi) dwelt.

Meanwhile Tchandaka, having beheld Bôdhisatwa clothed as a

recluse, and with shaven crown proceeding alone, stood still and raised his voice in bitter lamentation. He embraced the head of Kantaka as he wept. And again he sighed and wailed with grief. Thus gradually advancing, overwhelmed with grief, he at last reached Kapilavastu; but the horse Kantaka, through grief and weariness, was occupied eight days in the journey, which had before only occupied half a night. As the Gâtha says:

"Bôdhisatwa on first leaving his home proceeded on for half the night,
Tchandaka exhorting Kantaka to proceed apace;
But overcome by grief, and deprived of all energy
On returning, after eight days they reached the palace."

But when Tchandaka entered Kapilavastu, it was like entering an empty and deserted abode. Within and without on every side there was naught but desolation. The fountains, trees, and flowers were robbed of their beauties; the very gardens were dried up, and, as it were, afflicted with sadness on account of the absence of the Prince.

Then when the people saw Tchandaka return with the horse, Kantaka, but without Siddartha, they came in succession and enquired "Where then is the Prince?" Tchandaka weeping and overwhelmed with grief could make no reply. Then the people, raising their voices in lamentation, followed Tchandaka and Kantaka as they went on through the city towards the palace—still exclaiming "Where! where is Siddartha?" At length Tchandaka replied to the citizens as follows: "How could I disobey the orders of the Prince; and it was he who commanded me to return with his horse to the city. Alas! the Prince himself now dwells as a hermit in the mountains." The people on hearing this were filled with astonishment and with awe; and as they looked one at another in bewilderment, the tears coursed down their cheeks, whilst they exclaimed "Alas! alas! let us go and trace the steps of the Prince (Lion) to the place whither he has gone; it would be better for us to dwell there with the Prince, than here without him! for alas! in his absence all beauty has left the place, and there is no longer inducement to remain here. It has become like a wilderness, for his presence alone it was that lent it grace." As the Gâtha says:

"The men within the city hearing the words,
With their mouths exclaimed 'Wonderful! strange!
Without Siddartha this city is a wilderness,
The place where he dwells has become the favor'd city.'"

Now it came to pass that when the horse Kantaka was re-entering the Royal precinct, that he neighed in recognition of his home—on which the people within doors, and the females within the two Palaces (of the King and Prince), attracted by the sound, crowded to the windows, and cried "the Prince has come back! the Prince has returned!" But when they saw the horse and Tchandaka, but no Prince, they left their places of observation in sorrow and retired within the precincts, weeping and with great lamentation.

Now Suddhôdana on account of his great love to the Prince, was overwhelmed with grief at his loss, and had entered into the Hall of Penitence to practise the rules of purity and self-discipline, with a view to propitiate the Devas and Divine Spirits—using every sort of religious expedient to effect his one desire to see his son again. Then it was that Tchandaka, filled with sorrow, holding Kantaka by one hand and in the other the priceless jewels belonging to the Prince, entered the precinct of the Raja's Palace, just as he would have appeared if the Prince had been slain by his enemy in combat—so it was, weeping, he passed the Palace gates, and as he observed the familiar spots where the Prince had walked, sat down, or slept, "Oh! sad," he exclaimed, and his grief was intolerable.

Meanwhile the thousand kinds of birds that were kept around and within the Palace, hearing the well-known sound of Tchandaka's voice, with one accord attuned their throats to a joyous song; for they believed in truth that the Prince had returned, and so were filled with delight. And the horses also whinnied with joy. And so also Mahâprajâpati and Yasôdharâ, with the other ladies of the Palace, who had been prostrate with grief, and had neither adorned their persons nor used any care in arranging their garments or jewels since the departure of the prince—on hearing the sound of Tchandaka's voice, all of them started up and exclaimed "Beyond doubt, the Prince has returned. The Prince has come home again!" And then filled with joy, both Mahâprajâpati and Yasôdharâ, with the other ladies of the palace, crowded on to the balconies and gazed through the open lattices, desiring to see the Prince; but when they beheld only Tchandaka and the horse Kantaka, with both arms raised in anguish they wept and lamented, whilst the frequent tears coursed down their cheeks as they spake of the absent Prince. And so the Gâtha says:

"Those ladies of the palace, their hearts overwhelmed,
Looked through the windows to see the Prince returned.
But seeing the horse and the servant only,
The tears fell in thick succession from their eyes.
Casting away their jewels and their choice garments again,
Their head dresses and other decorations scattered,
With both hands raised above them in the air,
See how they weep! hearken to their sad lamentations!"

[Kiouen XVIII contains 5964 words and cost 2.982 taels].

CHAPTER XIX.

Respecting Tchandaka's Return.

At this time Mahâprajâpati and Gotamî, having seen the bright gem belonging to the Prince's head dress, and the other personal ornaments belonging to him, with Tchandaka and the Royal horse Kantaka, were both of them filled with distress; they raised their hands and smote themselves in their anguish, as they exclaimed, "Oh! Tchandaka, where hast thou taken our beloved Prince? Where is our Siddartha?" etc., etc. To whom Tchandaka replied "Oh mighty queen! the Prince Siddartha has forsaken the world, with its pleasures, for the purpose of seeking Supreme Wisdom; and now he dwells in the mountains far away, with shorn locks and soiled garments."

Mahâprajâpati having heard these words of Tchandaka, like a cow bereaved of its calf, uttered every kind of lamentable cry, unable to control herself, she raised her hands and said, "My son! her of! alas, my child!" The tears coursed down her cheeks, and at length, overcome with grief, her limbs lost their power and she fell to the ground as one dead.

Then all the ladies of the Palace seeing Mahâprajâpati in this condition, and hearing her lamentations, themselves gave way to unrestrained grief; they wept and wailed as they cried "alas! alas! where is our Lord? Alas! alas! where is our Prince?" and in this way they gave vent to their feelings—some rolled their eyes with grief, some looked at each other and wept, some smote their bodies, some smote their breasts, some twined their arms around each other, some tore their hair, some wandered disconsolate hither and thither, weeping and wailing the while, just as the stricken deer wanders at random through the brake, the poisoned arrow in his side—so did they wander to and fro, weeping and bending their bodies in grief, as the wind bends the tender palm—others, like the fish on the ground, writhed in anguish on the earth; thus in every way they showed their grief at the loss of the Prince.

Thus it was Tchandaka and the horse Kantaka stood, whilst on every hand were heard the sounds of lamentation.[1]

Meantime, Yasôdharâ, giving way to her grief and indignation, reproached Tchandaka with having stolen away from her in the middle of the night her lord and husband (in various ways).

Then Tchandaka, unable to bear the reflections of the weeping Yasôdharâ, with his head bowed and his fingers closely intertwined, replied "Your slave, oh Yasôdharâ! deserves not to be reproached; for he has committed no fault indeed, neither has Kantaka, the noble steed, done wrong. For I opposed with all my power and with many tears, the Prince's resolution to leave his home. I vainly tried to arouse you, oh! lady, from your sleep. I fruitlessly attempted by force to awake you and the others from their torpor—calling them by their names and plucking at their hair—but in vain. And so, after the Prince had mounted his horse on the way, I raised a thousand difficulties, calling with my might to those around, and endeavouring to obstruct the horse's advance—but there was no sound heard, and all my efforts were useless! Taking it for granted, therefore, oh lady! that this was the work

---

1 The repeated details are omitted.

of the Gods, I dared no longer oppose it." And so the Gâtha says—

" Unable to bear the tears (of the Royal lady) any longer,
With clasped hands and bowed head, I replied,
Your ladyship should not thus reproach me and the horse,
For indeed we deserve not your anger."

(Tchandaka then proceeds to relate to Yasôdharâ all the circumstances of the flight of the Prince,[1] and after this he acquaints Suddhôdana Râja with the same circumstances, who in his turn gives way to excessive grief, and finally falls senseless to the earth.)

[Kiouen XIX contains 6570 words and cost 3.285 taels].

CHAPTER XX.

The same subject, continued.

§ 1. Then Suddhôdana Râja spake thus, "Oh! that the Devarâjas who rule over the earth (the four regions) and defend the inhabitants thereof, would now protect and prosper my son. Oh! that Sakra râja, the ruler of heaven, possessed of a thousand eyes, the husband of Sachi, Mahâbala Devarâja, and all the Devas who surround him on the right and left, would assist my son to accomplish his desire; oh! that all the spirits of the wind, of the water, of fire, of earth, and the spirits of the eight divisions of space would aid in this great undertaking, that my son having really left his house and become an ascetic, may soon arrive at the highest degree of sanctity, and attain to Anuttara Samyak Sambôdhi."

And then again, whilst lying on the earth, the disconsolate monarch broke out into frequent reproaches against the horse Kantaka, "Oh! ungrateful steed! who heretofore received from me every mark of affection and proof of kindness, why didst thou bear from me my much loved son, the pride of the Sâkya race? Death should be your lot,[2] or else take me to the place where my

---

[1] After this follows an account of Yasôdharâ's grief.
[2] Or it may be—"the only reparation you can make is to die."

son dwells, and I will share with him his mortifications. Oh! my son, apart from thee my life is but for a moment!" And so the Gâtha says:

"Kantaka! thou steed of mine, quickly go
And take me whence thou hast returned!
Without my son, my life is but a burthen,
As that of a man sorely afflicted without a physician."

Thus Suddhôdana afflicted himself, lying on the bare ground in recollection of his son, weeping and wailing with a lamentable voice.

At this time there was a certain wise minister, who in company with the chief Brahman, counsellor of state, seeing Suddhôdana Râja thus giving way to grief as he lay upon the earth, turning from one side to the other, his heart heavily afflicted, his body and mind both indicating his misery—these ministers aforesaid approached the king together and said "Maharâja! it is time you should overcome this grief, and again recover your self-command! It is not right that you should thus exhibit the feelings and the conduct of ordinary men. Recollect, Maharâja, that in former days other kings gave up their royal estates to become hermits, as for example, Wie-hwa-man (drooping-flower-band). And, moreover, it was Siddhartha's plain destiny thus to become a recluse. Remember, Maharâja! the words of the soothsayer Asita, that nothing could prevent him leaving his home, and finally attaining to the condition of Supreme Wisdom. If, in recollection of this, your majesty still desires your son to return, and your heart still is afflicted to this degree, then bid us go in search of him and bring him back—we dare not disobey you!"

Then Suddhôdana Râja replied, "go then, ye two, and bring back my son; for in his absence I have no pleasure in life, and my days are a burthen to me."

Then these two ministers in obedience to the King's words immediately set off in search of the Royal Prince to bring him back. As the Gâtha says,

"It was the destiny of the Royal Prince to be thus!
Recollect, oh King! the words of Asita!
That the Prince would not desire to be a Chakravarti Râja,
How much less to indulge in sensual worldly pleasures."

The ministers having thus set out, the horse Kantaka having

heard the reproachful words of the King in his affliction, unable to bear the sorrow that afflicted him, lay down and died. Afterwards he was born in the Trâyastriñshas Heavens, and when he discovered from that abode that Tathâgata had attained to Supreme Wisdom, he left the Heavenly region and descended to earth, and was born in the city of Na-po, in Central India, as the son of a celebrated Brahman of remarkable piety; and so, gradually as he grew up, he came into the company of Tathâgata, who knowing that he had formerly been the horse Kantaka, and had been born in heaven, immediately explained to him the system of cause and effect (the Nidânas), who having heard it, obtained perfect release and entered Pari-Nirvana.

The consideration of different Religious Systems by the Prince.

§ 2. Now then the prince, having with his own hand cut off his flowing locks and clothed himself in the soiled garments of a hermit, the countless Devas who surrounded him were filled with an exuberance of joy, and with their voices uttered his praises as they sounded their joyous instruments of music. And their strain was this—"Now then Siddârtha, the Royal Prince, has truly left his home! Siddârtha, the prince, has now become a recluse indeed! He will assuredly attain to Supreme Wisdom, and so bring salvation to all living creatures. He will assuredly banish the sorrow and pains of life, and bring deliverance to all!"

Now a tower of commemoration was erected on the spot where the prince cut off his hair, and its name was the "cutting-off-hair Tower;" and so also on the spot where Bôdhisatwa put on the Kashya garment there was in later time a tower erected, called "taking the Kashya garment Tower;" and so where Tchandaka and Kantaka left the prince to return home, a tower was afterwards erected called "the Return of Tchandaka and Kantaka Tower." Now as Bôdhisatwa went along the way in deep meditation, there were some men who ventured to ask him some question or other; but he remained silent, and answered them not. Then these people speaking to one another said, "This Rishi must be one of the Sâkya race;" hence he got the name of Sâkya muni.

Then Bôdhisatwa (as he went) reflected thus with himself—"I have now for ever given up my royal estate. I have left my kindred and my home; there is now no room for repentance or change—the thing is done!"

Having reflected thus, his heart was strengthened. Then Bôdhisatwa proceeded forward from that village of Ho-ni-mé-ka[1] (Anumegha?) and gradually directed his course towards Pi-ye-li (this is for Pi-che-li, *i. e.* Vâisâli). Now in the midst of his way thither there was the abode of an old Rishi whose name was Bagava (Po-ka-pi). And it came to pass when Bôdhisatwa entered within the place of this Rishi that a miraculous light spread on every side through the hills and the woods around; and as Bôdhisatwa had discarded his jewels and his Kasika garments it must have been from his body that this glory proceeded, and met the eyes of the hermits who occupied the place; as the Gâtha says—

"The Elephant-King Bôdhisatwa, with his Lion-step,
Deprived of all jewels or costly robes,
Clad in his poor hermit garments of brown colour,
His body emitted a light dazzling the eyes of the Rishis."

Then the Brahmans, who rigorously practised the Rules of a religious life within the grove of trees, looking up and perceiving the glorious person of Bôdhisatwa as he approached them, were filled with joy; and yet they were in doubt what to think. There were also other old Brahmans in the neighbourhood who were employed in gathering all sorts of roots, flowers and various kinds of wood[2]; these, without any hesitation or doubt, having heard the sound of Bôdisatwa's voice, were filled with a feeling of reverence, and leaving everything they were engaged about, they hurried straightway to the spot where Bôdhisatwa was, and stood before him. And all the birds around, when Bôdhisatwa entered the grove began to pipe their various notes, in indication of their joy; whilst the other living creatures indicated their feelings of delight. And so also the kine which the Brahmans kept for religious and sacrificial purposes, although their milk had just before been exhausted,

---

1 Bigandet, p. 62, gives Anupyia, in the country belonging to the Malla Princes, *i.e.*, Vâisali.

2 That is, for medicinal purposes; these, no doubt, would represent the Ἰατρικοὶ of Megasthenes.

yet when Bôdhisatwa appeared, their udders again filled themselves with milk, which ran of its own accord from their teats.

Then those Brahmans, seeing all these wonderful portents, said among themselves, "This surely is one of the Vasu Devas;"[1] whilst others said, "He is one of the Star Devas(?), for ever since he entered the wood, there has been a supernatural light shed around us;" and so the Gâtha says—

"This is either one of the Pasuva Devas,
Or one of the Devas dwelling in the storied-heavens,
For otherwise whence comes this light,
Bright as the sun first rising on the world."

Then all those Brahmans, practising their religious austeries within that wood, took of all that they had, and respectfully approaching Bôdhisatwa offered their gifts to him with great reverence, and as they bowed themselves before him they said, "Welcome, O Holy one. We all respectfully request your Holiness to take up his abode with us in this wood. Whatever fruits, or medicinal plants, or roots, or flowing streams are here—these all are at your service. Here it was all the old Rishis dwelt who sought after final deliverance. Here it is easy to obtain peace and rest, etc."

Then another Brahman of the company, having observed the grace and force of Bôdhisatwa's manner, addressed one standing by and said, "Venerable one! it seems to me that this is no other than a child of Heavenly birth, thoroughly acquainted with the human heart, who now by means of this expedient desires to accomplish some illustrious purpose. For why? we find that in the world men speak thus—'I must nourish and bring up my sons in order that when they grow up they may help to establish and benefit my family name, in buying and selling and getting profit for me, so that when I am old I may be able to devote myself to religious inquiries and practices.' It is thus men generally think and speak, they have a reference in all they do to their own advantage. But with this one it is not so, he seeks the good of others and not his own, he provides nothing for himself."

To him another Brahman answered—"It is even as you say, reverend Sir! in the world men do nothing but think of themselves,

---

[1] Or, perhaps, Pasuva. *Vide Colebrooke*, p. 262.

saying, 'To-day I must set about this, and to-morrow about that, and so on; and thus there is no real profit to the world, for men think of nothing but about themselves.'"

[*Now when Bôdhisatwa descended from the Tusita Heavens, and was conceived in the womb, to be born as a Sakya Prince, it came to pass that in the grove where these Rishis dwelt there sprung up of themselves two golden-coloured trees, which gradually increased in size and strength down to the night when Bôdhisatwa left his home to become a recluse. On that night they suddenly decayed and disappeared. Then one of the Rishis, observing this phenomenon, was filled with grief and began to think within himself, as he hung down his head, that this was a bad omen, and portended some calamity about to happen. At this time Bôdhisatwa, observing the Rishi's anxiety and his absent manner, approaching by degrees to his side, asked him and said, "Venerable Sir! why is your brow thus clouded, and your head hung down in grave reflection as you sit?" Then that Rishi answered Bôdhisatwa and said, "Illustrious child of Heaven! in this place where I dwell, in former days there sprung up two golden-coloured trees, which grew, and increased as they grew, in loveliness and grace; but now suddenly they have disappeared, and are no longer to be seen, therefore my heart is sad, and my head drops as I sit here lost in thought." Then Bôdhisatwa inquired further—"Venerable Sir! at what time did those trees first appear?" The Rishi answered, "It is now just twenty-nine years ago." Then Bôdhisatwa again asked, "And when did they disappear?" Last night, towards midnight, they began to decay and to die." Then Bôdhisatwa addressed him and said, "Those two trees were first produced by the power of my religious merit, and when I attain to the condition of Supreme Wisdom and begin to preach, then in this very place I will set apart a spot (garden) for my own use, where I may expound my doctrine. It was because I left my home last night bent on this object, that those trees decayed and died; let not your heart then be troubled, venerable Rishi!*]

Thus it was Bôdhisatwa dwelt among these Rishis, and beheld their religious practices day by day.

Now there was one Rishi particularly bent on his religious duties, to whose abode Bôdhisatwa proceeded, and seated himself. After observing the way in which the community was engaged, Bôdhisatwa entered into the following conversation and said, "I have but just entered on a course of religious discipline. Venerable Sirs! I desire to ask some questions, if you will permit me so to do."

"Venerable brother!" they replied, "you may ask any questions you please respecting our religious discipline, and we, as far as possible, will explain everything to you in detail. Amongst us there are some who mortify themselves by eating nothing except edible herbs (tsae), or sprouting shoots of plants (t'he), or the tender stems of the Nyagrodha tree, or of the Dukûla (?) tree, or of the Kanikala tree; whilst others eat nothing but the stems of one particular tree (ekadruma), others eat the excrements of the ox, others nothing but the roots of certain plants, or the mashed fibres of different shrubs; again there are others who take just water enough to preserve life, etc.; some clothe themselves with hempen vesture; others with the fleece of the black sheep; others with grassy robes; others with the cotton of the wild caterpillars; others with the dragon-beard plant; others with deer skins; others with the rags off corpses, or with filthy rags; some again sleep on boards, some on chips, some on tree-trunks, some on pestle-hammers; some again dwell in cemeteries; others in holes; others under the open heavens; others stand in water; others use fire to their inconvenience; others turn always to the sun; others raise both arms above their heads and keep them so; others sit in one fixed posture on the earth; others cleanse not their bodies from filth; others have their hair spirally-twisted; others pull out the hair of their heads; others pull out the hair on their faces; thus it is these different Rishis practice self-mortification, whilst in turn they give themselves to profound meditation and ardent prayers and vows to be born in Heaven, or to be born again amongst men, etc."

Then Bôdhisatwa addressed the Rishis once more and said, "I perceive that your system, although it promises the reward of Heaven to certain persons, yet provides no means of final deliverance; and so the Gâtha says—

"'You give up all, friends, relatives, and worldly delights,
And suffer pain that you may be born in Heaven,
Not considering that after being thus born on High,
In future years you may return and be born even in Hell.'"

And then he continued, "If a man, because of the sorrows of life, desiring earnestly to find some higher destiny, seek after a birth in heaven to enjoy there the happiness he covets, he forgets that in the distant future he will not escape the recurrence of evil, and that those very Rishis who now afflict their bodies will once more return to the same condition of sorrow and pain as that from which they are now striving to escape. So it is when men come to die, because, being overcome with fear, they seek some happy state of birth, because of this very desire they return again in brief space to that inconstant state of life they have left. They do not consider the ever-recurring evil of future births. Coveting the joys of Heaven, they consider nought about the very nature of the body, that its condition involves the necessity of decay and therefore of change. They strive by penance to fit themselves for joy, instead of striving to get rid altogether of the body, and be born in a condition that can never change. And so the Gâtha says—

"'Because of the ever-changing mind, the body is excited,
First bring the mind to be quiet, and so get rid of the suffering body;
The body is like a stone or tree, knowing nothing at all,
Permit the mind then to exercise its office, and let the body decay and perish.'"

Again Bodhisatwa continued—"If what you just now affirmed about abstention from sufficient food as a ground of merit, be true, then surely the wild beasts who are contented with grass and roots, ought to be most meritorious—or, again, the man who now suffers poverty and hardships ought necessarily to enjoy future happiness as a consequence of his present affliction; but these things are not so."

Then the Rishi answered Bôdhisatwa thus—"What fault then, oh, venerable and learned Sir! do you find with our system of religious discipline?"

Bôdhisatwa answered, "You afflict yourselves to-day with every kind of mortification, and hereafter again you will return into this very condition that you now hope to escape from."

They added again—"But our system involves other rules than those we have named."

"And what good will these do," argued Bôdhisatwa, "as long as you are not satisfied about final escape, what satisfaction or peace (absence of fear) can such a system afford?"

They replied, "Oh, venerable Sir! speak not thus! say not so! For this very pain we suffer gives us assurance and peace! There is great merit attaching to it, and we are confident that by this religious discipline we shall get rid of these ungainly bodies of ours, and obtain beautiful and excellent shapes elsewhere."

"And yet what assurance have you," said Bôdhisatwa, "that after obtaining the excellent and beautiful bodies of which you speak, that you have escaped the necessity of returning to the same condition you are now in? what assurance have you that you have for ever got rid of sorrow?"

They replied, "Venerable Sir! Not so! it does not follow that we shall hereafter return to sorrow! for the express purpose of our present discipline is, that we may secure happiness and joy as a certainty."

Bodhisatwa replied, "But there is no wisdom in this, for would a wise man seek for something apparently profitable if he knew that it involved as a consequence future loss, would this be the work of wisdom?"

Then one of the Brahmans of the company exclaimed, in a loud voice, "Wonderful! wonderful! This Râjaputra tells the truth! this is true wisdom! for would a man eat something sweet and agreeable if he knew there was poison concealed in it? And so with us. Although these rules of ours may secure for us some immediate reward, yet they do not destroy the necessity for birth and death, disease, and old age. How can we help, then, returning to a condition of sorrow hereafter?"

Then Brôdhisatwa resumed: "Unhappy world! hating the demon Death, and yet seeking hereafter to be born in heaven! What ignorance! what delusion is this!"

The Rishis replied: "Illustrious Râjaputra! you have but a partial knowledge of our system. In days gone by, countless holy men practised this method of self-discipline in this very place. Countless Rishis of regal birth, myriads of such persons, by undergoing these mortifications, sought to attain to future bliss!"

Bôdhisatwa said: "A thousand myriad years (perhaps you would say)! Oh, wonderful delusion! Alas! alas! what deceptive speech! for where is the promise of escape in the end? the future joy involves the necessity of birth and death, and therefore of future misery!"

The Rishis continued—"Venerable Râjaputra! the monarch of this region, who rules over the city of Mithila, desiring to make an inviolable compact, sacrificed to the gods countless victims of various kinds, hoping hereafter to attain the happiness of heaven."

Bôdhisatwa replied—"This system of religion, which consists in offering up sacrifices slain by the hand of those engaged in it—tell me, what is the character of this system?"

They replied—"It is a custom which has been handed down from very remote time, that those who worship the gods should do it in this way."

Bôdhisatwa asked—"How can the system which requires the infliction of misery on others be called a religious system? Surely, if the body were polluted and filthy, it would not be made pure or clean by returning again to the filth and rolling in it. How, then, having a body defiled with blood, will the shedding of blood restore it to purity. To seek a good by doing an evil is surely no safe plan."

The Rishis answered—"This, nevertheless, is a true system of Religion."

Bôdhisatwa said again—"But in what way, and by what reason?"

The Rishis answered—"According to the Vedas, and what we find the old Rishis said."

Bôdhisatwa said—"Pray explain what this was." They replied —"The system is simply this, that all men who worship the Gods must sacrifice."

Bôdhisatwa said—"I will ask you, then, if a man, in worshipping the gods, sacrifices a sheep, and so does well, why should he not kill his child, his relative, or dear friend, in worshipping the gods, and so do better? Surely, then, there can be no merit in killing a sheep! It is but a confused and illogical system, this."

At this time Bôdhisatwa, observing that not far from the place where they were seated there was a clump of trees, the space beneath which was used as a cemetery, he asked the Rishis, and said —"Venerable sirs! and what place is that yonder?"

They said—"In that place the corpses of men are exposed, to be devoured by the birds; and there also they collect and pile up the white bones of dead persons, as you perceive; they burn corpses there also, and preserve the bones in heaps. They hang dead bodies also from the trees; there are others buried there, such as have been slain or put to death by their relatives, dreading lest they should come to life again; whilst others are left there upon the ground, that they may return, if possible, to their former homes." And then the Rishis explained how that those who tended the dead in these cemeteries, and performed these various offices for them, did so with the hope of being hereafter born in the world as men in eminent and wealthy positions.

Then Bôdhisatwa rejoined—"That men should practice these modes of self-inflicted pain for the purpose of securing such returns! Sad! sad! What ignorance and what delusion!—what inconstancy and unrest!—to suffer, and then to be born again to suffer! These foolish men are like those who thrust themselves into a fire, or willingly enter the jaws of some devouring serpent!"

Thus it was Bôdhisatwa discoursed with wise and choice speech in the company of these Rishis, and so discoursing, the time of sunset approached. Then Bôdhisatwa, returning to the abode of the Rishi who had first addressed him, remained there that night. On the morrow, at sunrise, all those Rishis followed him as he went from place to place. Bôdhisatwa, perceiving them thus following him, immediately selected a certain tree, and sat down beneath its shade, whilst they came up, and some sat and others stood surrounding him. Amongst them there was one very ancient and venerable Rishi, who had conceived in his heart a great respect for Bôdhisatwa, and addressed him thus—"Venerable sir, of Royal birth! from the time you came amongst us the place in which we dwell seemed to be filled with a self-born pleasantness, but now you have gone it seems like a wilderness. Oh! would that your reverence might be persuaded not to forsake our company. For, indeed, all those who seek for birth in heaven come here to practice their religious duties, and in a short time attain their wish by going to heaven. Venerable sir! you should not leave the place where so many holy men in days gone by have carried out their daily duties;" and so the Gâtha says,

"Venerable sir! this wood of ours that was so pleasant,
Now you have left it becomes suddenly like a desert;
For this reason, then, turn not your back nor leave us,
As a man who loves life, desires to preserve his body."

Then all the Rishis added their requests that, if Bôdhisatwa would not remain with them, they might follow him, and accompany him whithersoever he went.

To whom he replied, as he perceived they desired to make him their chief and follow his instructions, that these things could not be so; for although his mind was somewhat divided, yet there would be no peace for him in the pursuit of their aim, and that he must go elsewhere and seek for a more complete release. "Meanwhile," said he, "follow out your system taught by the old Rishis, and by your religious practices may you obtain your desire, and be born in heaven!"

Then an old Brahmachari, who was in the habit of sleeping on ashes, and wearing the polluted garments of the dead, his eyes bleared, his nose long, his body shrivelled, and in his hand the hermit's water-pot (kwan, kundika), having heard Bôdhisatwa speak, addressed him thus—"Virtuous one! your resolve is a high one; and if you are so purposed, you had better go. Not far hence there lives a Rishi whose name is Alara, who has obtained a great renown for wisdom. Repair to him, venerable one! and receive his instructions, "and may you in the end attain your aim, and arrive at the condition of Perfect Wisdom for which you now seek."

To whom Bôdhisatwa replied "Venerable Brahmachari, may it be so—even as you say!"

So it was Bôdhisatwa left the company of the Rishis, and hastened on to the spot where dwelt Alara; and so the Gâtha says,

"The holy king-born son of the great Sâkya race,
Having conversed in lucid speech with all the Rishis,
Resolved with fixed mind to go onwards to the abode of Alara,
And to return to the Rishis when in possession of Perfection."

The King's messengers return home.

§ 3. At this time the two messengers, mentioned above, moved with pity for the king, immediately set out in a well-appointed chariot from Kapilavastu to trace the progress of Bôdhisatwa. Thus, by degrees, they came to the abode of the Rishi Bagâva, who, perceiving them, rose up and advanced towards them, offering ripe fruits and cool water as an inducement to remain there for a short time. Then these two men, having paid low reverence at the feet of the Rishi, took a seat on one side. Having rested awhile, the Rishi employed every means to alleviate their fatigue. Then the two messengers explained the object of their journey, and said, "We are the ministers of Suddhôdana Râja, of the Ikshwaku race, whose only son Siddartha, through a terror of birth and death, disease, and old age, has left his home for the purpose of searching after complete deliverance; and having heard on the way that he had tarried in this place, we have come to inquire of you about him."

Then the Rishi answered the two messengers, and said—"It is true what you have heard; that eminent person did stop here with us, and having asked various questions, and being dissatisfied with our religious system, has now gone onwards towards the abode of the Rishi Alara;" and so the Gâtha says—

"The aspirant after complete merit,
Having come here, and being dissatisfied with our doctrine,
Desiring to find complete Nirvâna,
Leaving us, has now gone on to the abode of Alara."

The two messengers having heard this, being anxious to fulfil the king's commands, without any delay, either to partake of the ripe fruit, or to drink the cool water of the place, set out after Bôdhisatwa, and gradually advancing, they saw him sitting beneath a tree in the midst of a grove, and resting. His body, bereft of all its jewels, nevertheless emitted a soft and dazzling light, like the beams of the sun piercing through a dark cloud, and spread all around the brightness of its glory. The two messengers, immediately descending from their chariot, approached towards Bôdhisatwa, and respectfully saluted him, and said, "May every prosperity attend you, sacred youth;" and then they stood before Bôdhisatwa. At this time Bôdhisatwa, having spoken to them kindly, invited them to sit down by his side. Being so seated, they addressed him and said—"Your Royal Father, overcome with grief at your departure, has sent us to beseech you not to enter on your religious life in the desert mountains without some further trial. We beseech you, therefore, return with us to our abodes, and take possession of the

Empire; and if, after some further consideration, you shall determine to give up the kingly office, then after that you shall be at liberty to undertake the life of a recluse."

[Kiouen XX contains 5,706 words, and cost 3.285 taels.]

CHAPTER XXI.

§ 1. MOREOVER, Suddhôdana Râja added this to his former arguments, "My wise son, although you entertain but little love for all your kin, yet for my sake, at least, return to your home, and do not permit me to end my days in sorrow on your account. Dear son! the practice of religion involves as a first principle a loving, compassionate heart for all creatures; and for this reason the very name of a religious life is given to it. Why, then, should you consider a religious life as a term to be applied only to those who dwell in the lonely mountains. In former days men lived at home, and yet practised religion. They did not then cast away their jewels, or shave their crowns; and yet they were able to attain to complete emancipation; for nothing is necessary for this but wisdom and perseverance. But now, contrary to my wishes, you persist in leading the life of a hermit in the solitude of the mountains. But let me recount instances of those who have attained emancipation without thus giving up their home and all their possessions. There was of old the venerable *T'sui shang*, etc. There was King Rama, and so on—all these numerous kings were able to attain a condition of salvation without leaving their home, And therefore you, my son, may do the same. Return, therefore, oh, my son! etc. I willingly resign to you the kingdom; you shall be anointed king, and thus my joy shall be complete." And so the Gâtha says—

"It is difficult to give up the pleasures and sweets of a kingdom,
Yet for your sake I renounce all claim to mine;
To see you in possession my greatest joy,
Once beholding this, I would willingly be a recluse."

The Minister of State and his companion, having delivered their instructions, such as are contained in the preceding section, to

Bôdhisatwa, moreover addressed to him arguments derived from his duty and affection to his Royal Father, as also his love to his mother[1] and to his wife, beseeching him to return and to assuage their grief, and cause them to rejoice again. To whom Bôdhisatwa, after some reflection, answered thus—"I have long known the character of a father's affection, and I am sure of Suddhôdana Raja's very great love for me, his son; but then I tremble to think of the miseries of old age, renewed birth, disease, and death, which shall soon destroy this body! and if possible I desire above all things to find a way of deliverance from these evils, and therefore I have left my friends and my home, and forsaken my kin with a view to search after the perfect possession of Supreme Wisdom.

"If you tell me that my father's grief arises from his great love to me, this consideration has no power to change my conviction; for this is just like a man seeing in a dream his friends all together, and when awaking finding them all gone again; a wise man regards his friends and relatives just as fellow travellers, each one going along the same road, soon to be separated as each goes to his own place. And if you speak to me about a fit time and an unfit time for becoming a recluse, my answer is that the Demon Death knows nothing of one time or the other, but is busy gathering his victims at all times. I wish, therefore, at once to seek escape from the power of birth and death, disease, and old age, and have no leisure to consider whether this be the right time or not." And then he continued—"As to what my father requests that I should return and be anointed King of his Empire, let my father strive earnestly to put away the thought of my ever becoming his successor; for in truth I desire to escape from, rather than to be bound by, these fetters of kingship and relationship, I seek deliverance from all such ties. For to seek such things is like the conduct of the foolish man who eats some delicious food (not thinking of the poison it contains)." And so the Gâtha says—

"Like a house of gold filled with fire,
Or sweet food concealing poison,
Or a lake covered with flowers, hiding a dragon,
Such are the miseries connected with the joys of sovereignty."

---

[1] That is, his foster-mother, Mahâprajâpati.

And then he continued—"Just as we read of kings in olden time, who, after enjoying their position for a few years, have voluntarily given it up, and sought happiness in the condition of hermits, so is it with me. I have given up all the fancied joys of my palace, and I am searching for enduring joys in the solitude of the desert; shall I then return? Will the man who having eating poison and vomited it up, return to the tempting dish again? Will he who has escaped from the burning house, voluntarily go back to the flames? Neither would any but the most foolish, having forsaken the world, return to its unsatisfying pleasures." And so the Gâtha says—

"As a man who has escaped from a house on fire
Afterwards in a moment resolves to go back again,
So is he who having left his home and become a recluse,
Goes back from the solitude of the forest to the world."

And then he proceeded to say—"As to what you tell me respecting those Kings who my Royal Father says arrived at deliverance, even whilst holding their sovereignty—this cannot be; for it is impossible to conjoin the cares of Empire and the perfect mental quietude of the man who seeks deliverance; the two are incompatible, even as fire and water cannot co-exist; they are as far apart as Heaven and earth; it is impossible to reconcile the enjoyment of sensual pleasures with the attainment of complete emancipation of soul. And it was for this cause that those old kings gave up their kingdoms to seek deliverance, because the one could not be held and the other obtained. So, then, I am resolved to persevere in my search, and never more to return to the enjoyment of merely worldly pleasures, or even to the position of the king of my Father's Empire."

Then the two messengers, having listened to the resolute replies of Bôdhisatwa, still urged their request that he would return to his home, in the following words—"Great and Holy Prince! your resolution to search after Supreme Wisdom (law) is a good and commendable one, but under the present circumstances, in consideration of your Royal father's grief, it is not a proper opportunity to continue the quest, in contradiction to his express wishes, for this is not right; and so the Gâtha says—

"'There is profit in seeking out at once the claims of religion,

But still there are opportunities when even this should be done,
When the heart of your Royal father is overpowered with grief,
Surely filial piety forbids you to persevere in your aim.' "

And then they continued—"As it seems to us, Holy Prince, there is no discordance between searching after religious truth and yet continuing in the world. For to give up a certainty for an uncertainty, to seek the fruit without being sure about the way, is the work of no wise man. For in the Siddha[1] there are various opinions as to the real existence of a future state or not—great doubts hang over the subject. If, then, there should be no future condition, what advantage will it be to give up the certain possession of the present. Again, there are others who say, it is certain that in the present condition there is both good and evil, and therefore in the future also the same confusion will exist, and therefore to endeavour by religious discipline to attain deliverance from any such necessity, is merely foolish. For surely if things shape themselves under the influences of an inevitable fate, to attempt to avoid this necessity, or to escape from the conditions of it, is futile. And so, again, whilst the embryo is in the womb, the different members—the feet, hands, bones, etc., with the hair and nails—are all successively formed of themselves under the direction of fixed laws; and so, again, a man thus perfected in his body, returns to decay and destruction, and then to restoration and perfection, under the direction of laws equally fixed; and so it is one of the old Books says—

" 'Who is it gives the sharpness to the thorn,
Or who is it paints the varied plumage of the bird?'[2]

It is necessity:[3] it is not man's doing; and so in all other things, it is not for us to desire perfection, it is all pre-arranged and fixed. And so the Gâtha says—

" 'Who is it sharpens the prickly point of the thorn?
Who is it gives variety of colour to birds and beasts?
All these things result from the working of destiny—
They are independent of man, or his efforts.'

---

[1] Siddanta, *i.e.*, established truth, *vide* J. A. S. B., 1837, p. 67; also *Jut.* ii, 72, n.

[2] *Vide* Hodgson, *Collected Essays*, p. 107, § 9.

[3] That is, *Swabhâva*.

"Again, there are people who say that things are arranged by the intervention of Isvara Deva[1]; and so follow their appointed order. But, if so, what need have we to labour and disturb ourselves, for things will certainly be as they are ruled to be of old. Again, there are others who say that things are produced by capricious selection; so we come into existence, and so we cease to exist—without any choice or effort of our own, we are created and we perish. Again, there are others who say that men are born as Devas, or as Rishis in consequence of their fathers having paid the debt due to their ancestors and begetting them into the world as men. In all these cases there is no room for individual effort, for deliverance comes not from ourselves, but from causes independent of us. Thus it is all the old Books and Shasters, speak according to their various sections (Siddha). If then, Holy Prince! you seek deliverance, seek it according to reason and precedent; listen to what the old Books say, and so be directed, for their authority is sound and indisputable. Holy Prince! your Royal Father, Suddhôdana, because of his love and affection to you, grieves to think you should thus forsake him. Holy Prince! think not on returning to your palace that there will be any cause for regret or sorrow on account of an appearance of inconstancy. For how many of the old Rishis, who had been in possession of royal dignity, after forsaking the world returned again to its enjoyment. There are many such, and these are some of them, to wit, Ambarisa Râja, who having left his kingdom and become a resident in the solitudes, was brought back in the midst of all his attendant ministers and officers of state. Again, Ramarâja, provoked by what he saw of men's wickedness, left his mountain retreat, and came back to rule his kingdom in righteousness. Again, there was that old king of the city of Vâisali, called Drûma, he also left his hermit-cell, and went back to govern his kingdom with justice. Again, there was the Brahman—Rishi Râja Sakriti, and Rigdeva Râja, and Dharmayasa Râja—all these illustrious kings, after becoming hermits, returned again to their homes. Let your Royal Highness therefore not hesitate to do likewise, and come back to your palace." As the Gâtha says—

"As the kings whom we have named,
Having left their wives, retired into solitude,

[1] That is, *a Creative God.*

Yet afterwards, forsaking their retreat, returned home,
So let the Holy Prince do likewise and return to his palace."

To whom Bôdhisatwa replied, "What you say has no reason in it; for why should I doubt about the result, when I *have* no doubt. Those questionable theories you have named are not worthy the attention of a wise man. But those who follow them are like a blind man going along the road without a guide—he can neither tell what is right or what is wrong; how, then, can he go with any certainty. So is the man who doubts in the practice of religion. But my heart is fixed, and though I may not yet attain my end till after long and wearisome discipline, yet will I never return to the pleasures of the world or immerse myself in the pollutions of sensual indulgences. For what happiness can a pure-minded man (holy man) find in these. And then, again, you refer me to the case of Ambarisa Râja, and others, who returned to their homes after once beginning a life of solitude. But in truth those kings used no true discernment in their religious life and search after deliverance. For they sought merely after spiritual qualities, such as the Rishis possess; but they knew nothing of the laws of self-discipline and mortification. And therefore they went back. But remind me, I pray you, no longer of such cases, for I swear a great oath—'Let the Sun and Moon fall down to earth, let these snowy mountains be removed from their base, if I do not attain the end of my search, viz.—the pearl of the True Law.' There is no room, therefore, for further parley about returning home, I would rather enter a burning furnace, or a fiery lake, than give up my aim and go back."

Bôdhisatwa, having sworn this oath, got up from where he was sitting, and, leaving the wood, turned his back on the messengers. Then they, perceiving his fixed purpose, raised their voices in repeated lamentations, continually exclaiming "Alas! alas!" and vainly beseeching him to alter his mind and return with them. At length seeing the uselessness of their entreaties they engaged four men to follow Bôdhisatwa wherever he went, and watch him from place to place. And then, again yielding to their grief, they wept and lamented, to think of their Royal Master's sorrow on hearing the news of the prince's resolution. And so the Gâtha says—

"Those two messengers knowing the resolution of the prince,
That he was firmly resolved not to return home,

Deputed four men to accompany him wherever he went,
Whilst they, going back to the king, considered what they should say."

The Discussion with Alâra (Arâda).

§ 2. AND now Bôdhisatwa, leaving these two deputies sent by his father in the midst of their sorrow, slowly advanced towards the city of Vâisali. Just before arriving at that city in the very highway towards it, dwelt a certain Rishi, engaged in his religious duties, called Alara, his family name being Kalada. Now this Rishi had a brother who observed Bôdhisatwa a long way off approaching the spot, who, after seeing him, was filled with awe, never before having seen such a thing as he then witnessed. Immediately repairing to the place where his Master's disciples were seated, on arriving, he exclaimed in the presence of them all, calling them severally by name—"Mitra ma(nava)! (and so on) let your heart rejoice, give up your present service and worship of the Gods; for the son of Sûddhôdana, the Lord of the Sakyas, desiring to escape from sorrow and attain Supreme Wisdom, is coming here, bright and glorious as a golden pillar, his body full of grace and beauty, his shoulders straight and upright (t'ang-t'ang), his hands reaching below his knees, underneath his feet the symbol of the thousand-spoked wheel, his gait slow and graceful as that of the Ox-king, his body encircled with glory like the shining of the sun, clad in a Kashya garment, his appearance venerable and reverend beyond measure, gradually he is coming this way, towards us. Let us then strive to pay him due homage, and show him ungrudging reverence."

Then those Manavas sounded forth this strain of praise—

"Graceful and perfectly at ease in every step,
Advancing like the King of the great Oxen,
His body perfectly adorned with every distinctive sign,
Ever single hair properly disposed,
The thousand-spoked discus beneath the soles of his feet,
The curling circle of white hair between his eyebrows,
Keeping his strength as one aiming to be self-dependent,
This can be no other than the Great Lion among men."

After they had uttered these stanzas, the first person spoken of addressed the others thus—"Ye Manavas! let us now as a body proceed together to the presence of our Master." After arriving there, and having repeated the above stanzas, suddenly Bôdhisatwa reached the spot where Alara was; seeing whom the Rishi exclaimed in a loud voice—"Welcome! holy youth!" and so they stood facing one another with some degree of uncertainty, until Alara invited Bôdhisatwa to sit down on a grass mat; as the Gâtha says—

"The two looking at one another with great joy,
Saluting each other with a sort of reserve,
Were unable to speak one to the other,
Till Alara requested him to sit down on the clean grass mat."

Then, Bôdhisatwa being seated, Alara observed his person from head to foot, and conceived great delight in his heart, and immediately addressed him in soft and courteous words—"Venerable Gôtama! long ago I heard of your intention to resign the kingdom, leave your home and become a recluse, to cast off the trammels of love and affection even as the elephant breaks away from his bonds, and asserts his freedom. Even so! illustrious youth, have you this day done. But, Gôtama! your conduct appears to me somewhat singular. Other Kings have forsaken their Empires, but only after a long course of enjoyment; but you, whilst yet of tender age, are doing so. And yet the estate of Royalty is not a thing to be despised; it was through the desire after this that in old time the Râja Teng-sing[1] (Agrajâti?), having obtained universal empire on earth, was translated to Heaven, and there shared with Sâkra the government of the Trâyastrinshas Heavens! but afterwards through coveteousness again fell down to earth; and so with Najasa Râja and others, all of whom appear to have lost their dignity through excessive coveteousness, which burns in man's heart like a fire burns in the midst of dry weeds; but with you there seems to be no such desire, for you have given up all, though possessed of Royalty itself."

To which Bôdhisatwa replied, "Great Rishi! all these earthly dignities appear to me unstable as the fruit of the plantain tree, without any real substance or solidity; destined to destruction;

[1] *Head-born, or, born from the excrescence at the top of the head.*

and, therefore, I seek other things, and look for the true road to happiness, even as a man who has lost his way in the midst of a great solitary wild, searches deligently for the road by which he may escape from it."

To which Alara replied, "I plainly perceive, Gôtama! that you have a great destiny awaiting you, and that your religious life will be no ordinary one!"

Then one of the Manava youths, a disciple of Alara, broke out into the following eulogy, his hands clasped together in token of reverence, as he addressed Bôdhisatwa, "Oh! rarely seen is such wisdom as thine; in olden times indeed many kings, satiated with worldly pleasures, have forsaken their homes, and sought for religious perfection in the solitudes; but thou! so young and in the vigor of your age, to give up the certain enjoyment of Royalty, and to prefer the harshness of a life in the desert—the companion of wild beasts, and the unfettered birds! wonderful indeed is this!" And now Alara, addressing Bôdhisatwa, said, "Venerable Sir! seeking what way and in pursuit of what object, have you bent your steps hither?"

Then Bôdhisatwa replied—"I find that all men are fettered with the chains of birth and death, old age, and disease, unable to free themselves, and therefore I am earnestly seeking a way of escape."

Then Alara, having commended the intention of Bôdhisatwa, one of the youths who surrounded the Rishi furthur inquired of Bôdhisatwa, what had induced him to give up his home and leave his relations? "Simply because all these associations of friendship and kinship are destined to be broken and destroyed; therefore, he said, I search for that which is imperishable and permanent." (Then Alara pointed out to Bôdhisatwa that the secret of all human weakness and folly resides in the presence of concupiscence, which, like a dragon, lurks in the heart, and destroys every good intention or virtuous effort of the life. To which Bôdhisatwa assented. And afterwards Alâra enters on the exposition of his own doctrine, showing that men are allured to their own destruction by some outward aim, as the mountain goat is cheated by the false cry of the hunter, the moth by the brightness of the flame, and the fish by the bait.)

[Kiouen XXI contains 6,650 words and cost 3.125 taels.]

CHAPTER XXII.

Further discussion with Alâra.

§ 1. In this chapter Alara proceeds with the explanation of his Religious system. Relying on the general testimony of the Shasters, he instructs Bôdhisatwa that the first condition of all religious discipline is, that the life be strictly that of an ascetic—without any bodily indulgence, and the mind subjected to the strictest rules of thought and contemplation—thus passing through various grades of abstraction, corresponding to the different conditions of the inhabitants of the superimposed heavens, the full joy of complete Dhyâna is at length attained, and from that the condition of Nirvâna. Thus, by the use of means, we arrive at complete deliverance.

Bôdhisatwa, having accepted the instruction of Alara so far, and himself arrived at the condition described, sought further from him something yet higher—for this deliverance seems imperfect because it is not final —there is still a possibility of returning even from this condition and receiving life again; even as the seed sown at an untimely season, may revive under certain conditions, although in the absence of those conditions it appears to have ceased to be. So it is in the case of this deliverance, there is still the idea of *I*—"I have attained Nirvâna;" and so long as this is the case, it is not final or lasting; just as in the case of burning anything, a piece of wood for instance, the two ideas cannot be separated—the wood and the fire; so when there is "deliverance from personal existence," the *I* and the *deliverance* cannot be divided, and so there is a possibility of again becoming subject to birth.

The discourse then proceeds to a consideration of the power called self-existence (Isvara), and the consequent possibility of *creation*. Bôdhisatwa objects to creation by Isvara, because then there could be no succession of events, no causes of sorrow, no variety of Gods; but all men would regard Isvara as their Father—there could be no disputes about this very subject, whether Isvara exists or not—in short, if Isvara created all things, then all things must have been Good, and there could have been no possibility of evil.

On this, Alara commends the great wisdom of Bôdhisatwa, but deprecates further discussion on the ground that unless there be a power beyond ourselves capable of creating and sustaining the world, that the great problem of the source of evil or trouble can never be solved; for he said, either Karma or the Body existed first—if Karma was not caused by the previous existence of the body, then who made it, and whence came it? But if the body existed before Karma, then it existed independently of it. In either case there must have been a Creator.

To which Bôdhisatwa replied, "I dispute not with you on this ground, but as a man who participates in the great mass of evil which exists, I seek only a physician to give me health, I throw no further difficulties in the way."

On this, one of the ascetics greatly commends Bôdhisatwa, on the ground that all religious disputes and controversies, where the object is victory only, certainly lead to hatred and greater evils than any good they can effect.

"But although," Bôdhisatwa says, "I desire not to wrangle, nevertheless, I seek a condition of escape that admits of no return to life and its troubles;" on which Alara speaks of his system as teaching this. "But how?" enquires Bôdhisatwa, "at one moment you speak of your discipline leading to a definite condition of Being (bhuva), and the next you say it admits of no return—this is strange."

"And so it is," said Alara, "for this condition of which I speak is that of the Great Brahma, whose substantial existence is one of perfect quietude, without beginning, without end; without bounds or limits, no first or last, his operations inexhaustible, his form without parts or marks—immutable, incorruptible."

"But if this be so," said Bôdhisatwa, "what becomes of him, and who is He when at the end of the Kalpa, this heaven and earth, even up to the abode of Sakṛa, is burnt up and entirely destroyed—where then is your Creator?"

Alara remained silent, with a quiet smile on his lips, whilst one of his disciples greatly commended the wisdom of Bôdhisatwa, but reminded him that in old time the great Rishis all attained perfect wisdom in the way described by Alara—for instance (here follows a list of Rishis), all of whom entered into the brightness of the sun, and attained the straight path.

"What then is this 'entering into the brightness of the sun?'" enquired Bôdhisatwa, "and if I worship these, how can I admit the idea of an Isvara or Supreme God, who alone deserves worship?" Then the conviction seized Bôdhisatwa, that this system of Alara could not be a final and complete exhibition of deliverance, and his heart became sad.

Alara perceiving this, rose from his seat and addressed Bôdhisatwa, "What then is the system of deliverance, beyond the one I have illustrated, after which you look?"

To which Bôdhisatwa replied, "I seek a system in which questions about the elements shall have no place—in which there shall be no discussion about the senses or their objects—no talk of death or birth, disease or old age—no questioning about existence (bhuva) or non-existence, about eternity or non-eternity, in which words shall be useless, and the idea of the *boundless* and *illimitable* (realized), but not talked about."

Then he added this Gâtha:

"In the beginning there was neither birth or death, or age or disease,
Neither earth or water, fire, wind, or space,
Then there was no need of a Teacher for the three worlds,
But a condition of perfect freedom, lasting, pure, and self-contained."

On this Alara invited Bôdhisatwa to divide with him the duties of Master, and instruct his followers in the doctrines he advocated. Bôdhisatwa, although rejoiced to hear such an invitation, was still dissatisfied with a system which could reach no further than this, and so arose and left the company of Alara and his followers, on which they escorted him a little distance, and wished him lasting happiness.

Discussion with Udra Râmaputra.[1]

§ 2. At this time there was a distinguished teacher living as a hermit not far from Râjagriha, whose name was Udra Rama. Bôdhisatwa, having heard of his fame, determined to seek his company, and inquire into his system of religion.

Proceeding, therefore, in a deliberate manner from the presence of Alara, he advanced towards the river Ganges, having crossed which he came to the place where Udra Rama was, and addressed him as follows—"Virtuous sir! I have sought your company, that I may receive instruction from you in the discipline of the Brahman!" To whom he replied—"Most virtuous Gôtama! as I judge, you are able to receive my instruction, and to practise this discipline of the Brahman; but if you really desire this, you must first of all lay a right foundation to secure the desired result."

To whom Bôdhisatwa answered, "Would that you would explain what I must do, and what is your system of deliverance!"

On this Udra explains that his system hinges on the absence of all questions of relationship (relative truth)—that there must be neither thought (sanjnya-skandha), or the absence of it; and in this state of absolute indifference lies the highest deliverance.

Bôdhisatwa, in a brief time, realised in himself this mode of

---

[1] In the original, Yeou-to-lo (Udra) Lo-Ma-tsen (Râmaputra).

deliverance, but was dissatisfied with it, on the ground that it was not final, and admitted the possibility of return; and, notwithstanding Udra's reference to the final deliverance of Rama, his Father, Bôdhisatwa left his company and went his way, as the Gâtha says—

"Bôdhisatwa, considering, perceived that this system
Was one which, from old time, Rama had practised,
But was no means of final and complete deliverance;
Therefore, he turned away and left him (Udra) alone."

The sojourn in Mount Pândava.

§ 2. THEN Bôdhisatwa, leaving the place where Udra Ramaputra dwelt, went forward with thoughtful mien, and came to the mountain called Pândava [*this signifies yellow-white colour*]. Having arrived there, he sought for a shady spot whereon to rest, and then sat down, with his legs crossed, beneath a tree. How beautiful his body, and his mind composed to a state of perfect rest! His condition was as that of the man above whose head there had been a burning fire, when that fire is removed! So Bôdhisatwa was at peace.

Then he began to reflect: "How long before I shall entirely rid myself of this weight of accumulated sorrow—when shall I destroy this secret power of delusion, and attain complete emancipation?—and when shall I be able to rescue the world from the bonds of perpetual birth and death?". Thinking thus, the glory of his person shone forth with double power.

At this time there were various people scattered about on the mountain side, some gathering shrubs and roots, others collecting the dry dung of the ox, others engaged in hunting, others tending their herds, and others travelling along the way. All these afar off beheld Bôdhisatwa sitting under the shade of the tree, his body glorious as a bright golden image. At the sight they were filled with a strange feeling of reverence, and one spake to another thus —"Respectable sir! believe me, this is no every-day person; whence has he come, and how did he arrive at this Mount? Surely he is the guardian spirit of this Pandava mountain." Others said, he is the Rishi of the place; others said, he is the guardian god of Mount Vibharo; others said, he is the guardian spirit of Gridhrakuta;[1] others said, this is the great earth spirit, come up from beneath; others said, he is the spirit of the upper regions of space come down to earth. So they were all in doubt who this could be that shone out so gloriously, as the brightness of the sun and moon in the midst of the mountain, and in whose presence the flowers of the Palasa trees opened and displayed their sweets. At least, said they, this is no mortal man, for never yet did man possess such beauty, and shed abroad such glory, as this man.

[Kiouen XXII contains 6420 words and cost 3.21 taels.]

CHAPTER XXIII.

Bôdhisatwa visits Râjagriha.

§ 1. Now Bôdhisatwa, having passed the night in this place, at the early dawn put on his outer robe, and proceeded from Mount Pandava towards Râjagriha to beg his food, desiring to rid himself of every remnant of earthly pollution, and to attain a condition of perfect purity and rest (Anupadhisesa Nirvâna).

Then he remembered that he had no alms-bowl (Patra) in which to receive his food; wherefore looking around him in every direction for some substitute, he suddenly saw a place where there was a pond covered with great flowers; seeing which he forthwith addressed himself to a certain man who was passing by, and said, "Respectable sir! may I ask you the favour of picking me one of those leaves[2] of the lotus flower growing in yonder pond?" Having heard the request, the man immediately entered the pond and procured the leaf, and presented it respectfully to Bôdhisatwa, having received which he went forward to the city of Râjagriha to beg his food.

Then the people within and without the city, seeing the incom-

---

[1] Ki-che-kiu, evidently an abbreviation from the *Pali*, Ghedjakato.

[2] Patra. This seems to intimate the origin of the word *pâtra*, an alms-bowl.

parable grace of Bôdhisatwa's person as he approached, and the spiritual lustre which shone from him, were filled with awe, and spake one to another thus—"Surely this is the great Isvara, possessing three eyes,[1] come down from heaven to earth." Then from every part the people came together, and whatever their engagements, they forgot all, and assembled around Bôdhisatwa to pay him honour, filled with immeasurable joy. [*Now at this time, Bôdhisatwa was in the freshness of his youth; and, moreover, since the time of his leaving his palace to become a recluse, there had formed on his forehead, between his eyes, a circle of hair, from which was constantly emitted a flood of light, whilst his hands and his feet were so admirably proportioned, and the fingers and toes so beautifully connected together, as by a network filament, that his very appearance was enough to convert and restrain all who beheld him.*] And so the Gâtha says—

"Bôdhisatwa, moving along the road,
Whatever men beheld him thus,
His body perfectly bright and glorious,
Conceived great joy in their hearts.
Between his eyes the silky hair-circle, like the new moon,
His eyes, blue and soft as those of the King of Oxen,
His body always emitting light,
His hands and feet beautifully proportioned;
Beholding such rare beauty as this,
Not thinking what their engagements were,
But lost in admiration at what they beheld,
All their hearts were filled with joy."

Thus, surrounded by a vast crowd, Bôdhisatwa advanced steadily onwards, his body perfectly erect, his eyes fixed before him, and his garments all strictly arranged. And as he passed through the streets, those who were engaged in buying or selling, or others who were drinking in the wine shops, all left their engagements, and were wrapped in awe as they beheld Bôdhisatwa, and followed him on his course.

So, also, countless women in the city gazed at Bôdhisatwa from the corners of the door-posts, from the windows, from the balconies, and tops of the houses; and as they watched him go from

---

[1] Siva Trinayana.

door to door, their hearts were filled with unutterable joy, as they spake one to another—"Who is this that has come hither—his person so beautiful and so joy-giving as he moves? What is his name? What caste or family does he belong to? Is he Brahman or Shaman?"

At this time, the King of Magadha, who reigned at Râjagriha was named Bimbasara, of the family Srenika.[1] Now this monarch, before obtaining the kingdom, had made five earnest vows, which were these:—1. May I obtain the Royal dignity early in life. 2. May there be born a Buddha during my reign. 3. May I be permitted to see him and give him charity. 4. May I hear him preach. 5. May I arrive at the knowledge of the Law.

At this time, Bimbasara Râja was on the top of the city-gate, surrounded by his ministers; as he sat there, lo! afar off he saw Bôdhisatwa, accompanied by the crowd as he went, advancing towards the city with dignified pace. Seeing him thus, his heart was filled with doubt; and so, descending from the tower, he went forth from the gate, and approached Bôdhisatwa, whose body was glorious as the stars that shine in space throughout the darkness of the night, or as the brightness of the Mani gem. The King then addressed his ministers, and said, "Never since I was born have I seen such a perfectly beautiful and dignified person as this. Go forward, my lords, and inquire who he is, and whence he comes, and what his name?"

Then some said, it is Devarâja, others it is Sâkra, others it is a Mahânâgarâja, others it is Vemachitra Asura Râja, others it is Bala Asura Râja, others it is Vaisravana Râja, the protector of the world; others it is Suryadeva, others said it is Chandradeva, others Maheshwara, others Brahmadeva, whilst one of the wise ministers declared it was no other than a Chakravarti Râja. But at length one of the councillors explained the whole circumstance of Bôdhisatwa's birth at Kapilavastu, and the horoscope that had been cast, and declared that this stranger approaching the city could be no other than he.

Then Bimbasara thought, "this is nothing more than the accomplishment of my vow;" and so forthwith he commanded two of his attendant ministers to go watch where Bôdhisatwa finally

---

[1] *Lal. Vist.* 229, n.

took his abode, that he might himself go and pay reverence to him. Accordingly they went and joined themselves to the company of Bôdhisatwa's followers, with a view to obey the king's commands.

Now, Bodhisatwa, as he passed through Râjagriha, asking alms, seeing the vast multitude of the people which thronged every part of the city, began to reflect within himself, "All these people are without any means of salvation, without any hope of deliverance, constantly tossed on the sea of life and death, old age and disease; with no fear or care about their unhappy condition, with no one to guide them or instruct them; ever wandering in the dark, and unable tò escape from the net of impermanency and change."

Thinking thus, his heart was moved with love, and he felt himself strengthened in his resolution to provide some sure ground of salvation for the world.

Thus, proceeding slowly through the city, with his eyes fixed before him, and his body erect, he begged his food from house to house, after which he returned to Mount Pandava, and sat down in the shade beside a running fountain of water, to eat his meal. After having washed his hands and feet, he ascended the mountain, and looking to the south, he sought out a shady spot, where, with his face to the east, he sat down, with his legs crossed, surrounded by the birds who flew from tree to tree, and the flowers that carpeted the earth; whilst his garments gathered over him shone forth like the sun in his glory. And so the Gâtha says—

"Surrounded by the fragrant trees of the mountain,
The birds and beasts disporting themselves in gambols;
The man, clad in his Kashya garment,
Shone as the sun in his early strength."

Seated thus beneath the tree, he reflected thus—"I must now learn even more thoroughly the vanity of such names as Pudgala, Jantu, Manushya, Manava, that the five Skandha are unreal, that all phenomena are false and illusory names.

Meantime, the two messengers of King Bimbasara, having followed Bôdhisatwa to the spot where he was seated, the chief minister approached to within a little distance of the place, and sat down. Meantime, the other returned to the king, and told him that Bôdhisatwa was seated on the southern slope of Mount Pandava.

Then the king, mounting his chariot, proceeded towards the place, and soon arriving there, he beheld Bôdhisatwa seated as we have said, his body bright as the stars that shine through the dark night, or as the fire that burns on the top of some hill, or the lightning that gleams from the cloud. Then the king's heart was filled with reverence and awe, as he saluted him with much respect. And so the Gâtha says—

"The king, seeing Bôdhisatwa glorious as Sâkrarâja,
His body bright and shining; his heart filled with joy;
He saluted him, and wished him the four compliments,
Health, happiness, freedom from pain and care."

Then Bôdhisatwa, with a voice soft and sweet as that of Mahâ Brahma, returned the salutation of the king, and wished him all happiness and prosperity, as he asked him further the purpose of his visit, and invited him to be seated. Then Bimbasara Râja proceeded to seat himself on a large stone near to Bôdhisatwa and addressed him thus—"Respectable sir! I have some doubts in my mind—would that you would solve them for me, if it be not troublesome to ask you so to do! In the first place, who or what are you?—are you a God, or a Nâga, or Brahma, or Sâkra, or a man, or a spirit?"

Then Bôdhisatwa, having entirely got rid of all crooked ways, answered plainly and truthfully, "Maharâja! I am no god, or spirit, but a plain man, seeking for rest, and so am practising the rules of an ascetic life."

Then the king rejoined—"But why are you thus living when your youth and your beauty would entitle you to the enjoyment of all the pleasures which men hold so dear.

"Your body, bright as sandal-wood,
You should not wear this Kashya robe,
Your hands fit to control the wills of men,
Should not be carrying that alms-dish."

Bimbasara then proceeds to urge Bôdhisatwa to give up his purpose, to share the kingdom of Magadha with him, and indulge in the pleasures of life.

Then Bôdhisatwa, unmoved by anything the king had said, perfectly collected, and pure in thought, word, and act, replied as follows—

"Maharâja! you should not indulge in such foolish talk? Such arguments as you have used can have no possible weight with one like myself. The pleasures of which you speak are perishing and illusory! They are as thieves and robbers; they are but fancies of an empty mind; the dreams of a madman; the follies of one who hates the truth. Even as the Gâtha says—

"'The five pleasures are inconstant, poisoners of virtue;
The six objects of sense are illusive and false—
The inheritance of fools and madmen;
But the sage! he alone has a firm standing-ground.'"

Bôdhisatwa then proceeds with various arguments, comparisons, and illustrations, to impress on Bimbasara his fixed and unchangeable purpose to pursue the life of an ascetic, and seek for final deliverance.

[Kiouen XXIII contains 6550 words and cost 3.275 taels.]

CHAPTER XXIV.

The argument with Bimbasâra (continued).

In the first part of this chapter, Bôdhisatwa proceeds with his argument with Bimbasâra Râja. He urges the folly of pursuing earthly happiness, whilst the inevitable evils of death, and old age, and disease, and renewed birth, are still undestroyed. The following are the Gâthas used at intervals to illustrate his argument:

"Wounded by the arrows of sorrow,
I desire only to find a lasting remedy;
Supposing the palace of Sâkra were mine to choose,
I would not covet it—much less worldly dignities."

Religion (Dharma), he says, is the only thing worth seeking, the only true source of profit;

> "Where there is neither birth, old age, disease, or death,
> This is the true and only sound philosophy;
> To seek wealth, or pleasures of the world,
> The thoughts of these things I dismiss—I seek religion."

Neither can final deliverance be found in the worship of gods, or in sacrifice;

> "For if a man born in the world,
> Destroy life to secure present happiness,
> The wise man considers this unbecoming,
> How much more (to destroy life in sacrifice),
> For the purpose of being born hereafter in heaven."

Bimbasâra then inquires in astonishment who and what he is—of what race and caste, etc. On which Bôdhisatwa tells him plainly his history and family. On this Bimbasara with tears beseeches him not to expose his body thus to the hardships and dangers of a hermit's life; but Bôdhisatwa declares he has no fear either of wild beast or other danger—his only fear is of the demon Death, old age, disease, and renewed birth. Bimbasara further asks what is the end for which Bôdhisatwa gives up all his possessions, and what it is he seeks? On this, Bôdhisatwa explains that his end is to attain the condition Anuttara Samyak Sambôdhi, and to establish the Kingdom of Religion (turn the wheel of the Law).

Then Bimbasara, seeing his firm resolution, doubts not of his ultimate success; but begs him to come daily to his palace to receive in charity the four necessary provisions (food, drink, medicine, clothing). Bôdhisatwa excuses himself on the ground that he must shortly remove from his present abode elsewhere. Then Bimbasara, with closed hands, entreats that when Bôdhisatwa has arrived at complete enlightenment he may become one of his disciples; moreover, he begs him to receive his confession of sins and his resolution of amendment. Bôdhisatwa, with a slight smile, listens to the Râja's words, and then gives him consolation and wishes him all success. Finally, having performed three circumambulations, and prostrated himself at the feet of Bôdhisatwa, the king, rising up, departed, and returned home. So the Gâtha says—

"Bôdhisatwa assured Bimbasara in these words,—
'When I have attained enlightenment, I will instruct and convert the king.'
Considering with great joy the conduct of the Sage,
He left the mount and returned home."

Then Bôdhisatwa, proceeding from Mount Pandava, went onwards to the city of Gâya, and having arrived there he ascended the hill Gâyasirsha, wishing to enjoy rest of mind and body. Having arranged a seat of leaves he sat down beneath a tree.

Seated thus, he began to reflect, and these three ideas presented themselves; that as it is impossible to obtain fire from boring wood that is wet, or by using dung that is sodden; so, though a Shaman or a Brahman may not practise lust, yet so long as there is the least love of it in the heart, he cannot obtain Supreme Wisdom (the dampness of the wood and the dung must be got rid of). Again, he thought, that though a Shaman or a Brahman may use every measure to overcome evil desire, and practise all the fasts and keep the rules of penance, yet so long as there is the least remnant of covetous desire in the heart, he cannot attain perfection. Again, he thought, that when a Shaman or Brahman, in addition to abstention from evil, has experienced in his heart a feeling of universal love, and desires to arrive at perfection that he may profit others, then like dry wood and dry dung, the fire may be easily kindled.

Bôdhisatwa then descended from the Mount, and passing through various villages, he came at last to one on the southern side of Gâya called Uravilva, and it being now time for seeking food, he entered that village to beg. Having obtained at a potter's house an earthern dish, holding this in his hand, he went round from house to house to beg some food.

He came at length to the house of one of the village lords, whose name was Nandika, and standing in front of it,[1] he remained silent. Now, this Nandika had an only daughter whose name was Sujatâ, a girl of great beauty and grace; it happened then that Sujatâ had seen Bôdhisatwa, holding his alms-dish in his hand, approach the house, and as he did so, take his stand before the door, and remain in silence. Having seen this, lo! the milk exuded from both her paps (from very joy and reverence), and she proceeded to address Bôdhisatwa thus—"Most excellent and illustrious Sir! what is your name, and of what family and tribe are you? who are your father and mother? and whither go you now? For in truth your Divine appearance has so affected me that the very milk from my breasts exudes of itself!"

Bôdhisatwa replied, "Illustrious sister! my name is Siddârtha, my father and mother are so-and-so, and I am now in search of the highest condition of Wisdom, known as Anuttara Samyak Sambhôdi, having obtained which I desire to turn the wheel of the Law which is above every Law. Then Sujatâ, having heard these words, took the alms-dish from the hands of Bôdhisatwa, and entering the house filled it with every kind of choice delicacy and most luscious fruit; and bringing it out she respectfully offered her gift to Bôdhisatwa, and spake thus—"Most excellent Sir! I vow to minister always to your wants; and I pray that when you have attained the end of your present search that I may become one of your followers." To whom Bôdhisatwa replied, "Illustrious sister! be it as you desire!" Having said this, he departed, and having selected a clean place, according to the religious rules he had adopted, he sat down and ate his food.

Having finished his meal, he proceeded onwards, and selected a most delightful spot, smooth and free from inconveniences, in sight of the river which ran by in peaceful flow, at a moderate distance from the village, so that he might easily resort thither for the purpose of begging, he there sat down and composed himself to severe contemplation. [*Now Gâya is so called because this was the spot where an old Rishi king called Kâya* (the Chinese interprets it by "Form," and therefore it must be Kâya) *founded a town and dwelt.*]

---

[1] Ekamantam.

Bôdhisatwa, having, therefore, prepared himself a seat of leaves. sat down and began to consider thus with himself—"What countless methods there are by which men hope to obtain final deliverance, by rules as to eating, clothing, sleeping, undergoing every kind of penance and self-mortification; alas! that such false views should be entertained." Thinking thus, Bôdhisatwa was overpowered with grief; and so the Gâtha says—

"Bôdhisatwa seated beside the Nairañjana River,
His heart composed as he remained on the shore;
When he thought over the various systems of false religions,
His heart was grieved and filled with sorrow."

Thus thinking, Bôdhisatwa composed himself to contemplation—his mouth closed, his teeth joined, and his tongue pressed upwards against the palate.

Now there was living near the place where Bôdhisatwa was a certain Brahman of a high caste, called Senayana, who had obtained from Bimbasara authority to govern a certain town close to Uravilva, and had adopted this name as his title after taking possession of his dominion; and there was another Brahman called Deva, born near to Kapilavastu, who had for a time come to lodge in the house of Senayana, to transact some business. Whilst there he had occasion to go to the wood where Bôdhisatwa was practising austerities. Whereupon, this Deva, seeing Bôdhisatwa, immediately recognised him and said, "This is Siddârtha, our Prince Royal, who is now living the life of a hermit;" and his heart was filled with joy at seeing him. Then Bôdhisatwa, having seen the joy of Deva, addressed him and said, "Great Brahman, will you undertake to provide me with millet, sufficient for me to take a daily meal and so to support me in life." On which that Brahman, with a narrow and illiberal disposition, hoping to obtain merit by this act of charity, promised to do so; and thus, day by day for six years, Bôdhisatwa received this modicum of millet sufficient to keep him alive. Thus it was his skin became wrinkled, and his body attenuated and his eyes hollow as an old man's; whilst his limbs were unable to support him as he moved, and all who beheld him were filled with a strange feeling of awe and reverence at the sight of the penance he was thus enduring.

[Kiouen XXIV contains 6786 words and cost 3.393 taels.]

CHAPTER XXV.

The Exhortation to Return.

§ 1. Now at this time, when the spring was just in its prime, it came to pass that Suddhôdana Râja went forth from his palace to enjoy the beauties of the gardens that were near his Royal city—the opening flowers, the budding trees and the chattering birds. Whilst thus enjoying the delights of the gardens, a melancholy recollection of his son overwhelmed him, and he exclaimed, "Alas! my son, it is now six years since you left your home; where art thou now? Alone, in the wild mountains, surrounded by the roving beasts, and the tenants of the forest!"

Meanwhile, the Devas, observing that Bodhisatwa was practising such severe penance, so that he could not long survive, deputed one of their number to go quickly to Suddhôdana; who, coming to Kapilavastu, declared to the king that the prince was dead. But another Devaputra immediately came and contradicted this, but told the Râja that his son could not endure such affliction beyond seven days more. Whereupon the king was overpowered with grief, and gave way to his sorrow with lamentable cries.

On this, Suddhôdana, assembling the Sâkya princes, who had heard the expression of his grief, related the news to them, and besought them to seek some mode of finding out if the prince were still alive, and if so to induce him to return to his home. [*The number of the Sâkya princes was ninety-nine thousand.*]

At last, when all of them had failed to suggest any method for effecting this, Udâyi undertook to search after the prince and bring him back.

Then Udâyi, leaving Kapilavastu, proceeded to Uravilva, to the banks of the Nairañjana River, and there first of all encountering Kaundinya[1] and the other hermits, he asked of them saying, "Illustrious Kaundinya! can you tell me where Siddârtha abides?" To whom Kaundinya replied, "Siddârtha is practising austerities in yonder grove." Then again Udâyi inquired and said, "And what

---

[1] Kaundinya and four other Rishis had associated themselves with Bôdhisatwa during his penance.

is the name of that attendant of yours?" to whom Kaundinya replied, "His name is Asvajit." Then Udâyi requested Asvajit to enter the wood and tell Siddârtha that a messenger from his Royal Father had come to inquire for him. But Asvajit declined to accede to such a request, and desired Udâyi himself to go into the wood. At length Udâyi complied, and found Bôdhisatwa asleep on the ground; but how altered his appearance! Then, raising a great cry, Udâyi exclaimed, "Alas! alas! that one so beautiful and full of grace should ever come to this!" etc. Then Bôdhisatwa, hearing these cries, demanded, "Who are you?" On which Udâyi explained why he had come; but Bôdhisatwa replied, "I seek Nirvâna, and will have nothing more to do with the troublesome world;" and, he added, "may my body be ground to powder small as the mustard-seed if I ever desire to return to my home! If indeed I die before the completion of my vow, then, Udâyi, take back my bones to Kapilavastu, and say, 'These are the relics of a man who died in the fixed prosecution of his resolve;' but, as it is, go tell my Royal Father that I am resolved to persevere. For, in truth, in my dreams the Devas come to me, and they tell me that within seven days I shall indeed attain to the perfection I seek. Go, then, Udâyi! return home, for there can be no further communication between us." Then Udâyi, having heard these words, arose and left the wood and returned to Kapilavastu, and told Suddhôdana Râja that his son was still persevering in his aim, and was alive; on this the king said, "My son is yet alive, and my heart is filled with joy."

The Conclusion of his Severe Fast.

§ 2. Now during the six years' penance which Bôdhisatwa endured, Marârâja Pisuna[1] had come once and again to try and tempt him to the commission of some small sin, but with no success. And so the Gâtha says[2]—

---

[1] That is, "the Wicked Mâra." Mâra is the same as the Lord of the World of Pleasure (Kama loka). He is sometimes identified with "Death."

[2] These Gâthas are almost identical with the Thibetan. *Lal. Vist.*, p. 251.

"To the east of the village of Uravilva,
Beside the banks of the Nairañjana river,
Firm in his resolve to obtain deliverance
He sat with his legs crossed as a hermit.
Then Marârâja Pisuna, coming to him
With blandishing words, addressed him and said,
'Oh! that you would lengthen your days!
And by so doing be able to practise religion.
It would indeed be for your profit so to do,
And afterwards you would repent not of it;
Your body, oh, virtuous one! is weak and worn,
You cannot indeed live as you are for long,
It were better far to live than die;
To become a Recluse is no easy task
To subdue one's heart is difficult,
Listen then to me, and give up the quest!'
To whom Bôdhisatwa replied in excellent words,
The sounds of which were scarcely heard—(*owing to his weakness*),
'Pisuna! your attempts are vain!
You seek only your own, as you wander to and fro!
You speak of death! but what is that?
I fear not death, nor the end of the world,' " etc., etc.

Then Bôdhisatwa reflected thus—"It is because men seek continually their own things and their own profit that sorrows come; and what am I doing but this?" And then he thought of the incident of the ploughing-match, and how as he sat beneath the Djambu tree he enjoyed the bliss of Dhyâna; and he thought with himself—"Why do I not now experience these joys?" Then he resolved to strengthen his body by partaking of sufficient food, wheat and oil and milk, and also by bathing and caring for his health.

Then Bôdhisatwa addressed the Brahman, whose name was Deva,[1] and said—"Great Brahman! I have resolved to break this long and trying penance, and partake of other food—wheat and honey, and oil and milk! prepare these things for me, I pray."

---

[1] Deva was the niggard Brahman who had supplied Bôdhisatwa with the few grains of millet he ate daily. *Vid. ante.*

To whom Deva replied—"Virtuous sir, indeed I have no such things at hand to offer; but if Bôdhisatwa will follow my advice, it will be easy to procure them."

"And what is your advice?" he said. "To come to the house of the Brahman Senayana, and receive them there?" On this Bôdhisatwa consented.

Accordingly Deva, returning to Senayana, said—"Oh! great sir, not far from this place is an illustrious Shaman, who is about to break through his long and rigorous fast, and to come to your house to beg for some wheat, oil, and honey, and water, wherewithal to refresh his body. Can you, oh, virtuous sir! provide these things?"

Now Senayana had two daughters, one called Nanda, the other Bala, both of them very beautiful, and in the prime of their youthful days. These girls had long ago heard about the Sâkyas who lived at Kapilavastu, beneath the northern mountains, and of Suddhôdana, and Mâya, and their graceful son; and having heard all this, they had besought their father to try to get for them the graceful youth, the child of Suddhôdana, as a husband.

Then Senayana, having heard from the Brahman Deva that Bôdhisatwa was coming to his house to beg for food, ordered his two daughters to prepare at once provision of wheat and oil, and milk and honey, and take it, said he, "to the place where the great Shaman is, and carry him warm water for his body, for thus perhaps you may obtain the desire of your hearts, and become the wives of that beautiful Sâkya Prince." The girls having received this intimation, forthwith proceeded to prepare the necessary food, and afterwards they carried it to the place where Bôdhisatwa was undergoing his penance. Arrived there, they bowed down their heads at his feet, and offering their food to him, spake thus—"Illustrious and honourable sir! deign to receive this offering of food at our hands." Then Bôdhisatwa, having received the gift at the hands of the two maidens, ate according to his desire. Then, taking the butter and the oil, he rubbed it into his body, and afterwards using the tepid water, he washed himself as he purposed. Then his body, absorbing the oil, like the thirsty ground drinks up the rain, from that moment he began to revive, and his frame resumed its youthful appearance.

And now Bôdhisatwa, having eaten and drunk, addressed the

two maidens thus—"My sisters! you have wrought a meritorious deed by thus ministering to my wants; tell me, then, have you any wish you would have fulfilled?" On which they replied—"Of old time we have heard of a certain beautiful Sâkya Prince, whose equal it would be hard to find; we would wish to become the wives of that prince." Then Bôdhisatwa answered—"My sisters, I am that Sâkya Prince! but I have vowed never again to participate in the five pleasures of sense—for my object is to obtain supreme enlightenment, and to preach the insurpassable Law." To which the maidens replied—"If this be indeed the case, beyond all doubt you will obtain your end; when this is so, come, we pray you, to our house, that we may become followers of yours." On which Bôdhisatwa said, "My sisters, it is well—it is well; your wish shall be accomplished."

From that day forth these two maidens continued to bring food and water to Bôdhisatwa, until his body had once more resumed its wonted beauty.

After this Bôdhisatwa desired them no longer to bring him food.

Now at this time a certain shepherd boy, having observed the invincible purpose of Bôdhisatwa in practising his penance, approached him, being filled with reverence and joy, and bowed before him and said, "Oh! virtuous and honourable sir! may I be permitted to make you some offerings of food." On obtaining the desired permission, he took of his goat's milk and offered it to Bôdhisatwa, and anointed his body therewith; whilst, cutting down some branches of the Nyagrodha tree, he wove a covering over the head of Bôdhisatwa, as a shelter from the wind and the rain. Meantime, in virtue of the spiritual power of Bôdhisatwa, these branches took root, and bore flowers and leaves as they sheltered him.

Now it came to pass that the five men, seeing Bôdhisatwa's altered mode of life, and his appearance of revived grace and health, thought with themselves that he had lost his power of Dhyâna, and also his purpose of attaining supreme wisdom; they were therefore incensed against him, and left him with many reproaches. After a time they came to Benares, and entering the deer-garden, they gave themselves up to severe contemplation. And so the Gâtha says—

"Those five Rishis practising severe penance,
Seeing Bôdhisatwa partake of various kinds of food,

Spake thus among themselves, 'This is no contemplative discipline—
He has given up the quest, and now nourishes his earthly body (5-element-body)'."

Now from the day when the daughter of the village lord had first given Bôdhisatwa the food in charity, which we have described, through the whole of the six years that he had practised his severe penance, she had ever ministered her substance in bestowing charity on all the Brahman and Shaman mendicants who came to her door; and in each case she uttered this vow—"May the merit of this charitable act accrue to the benefit of that Sâkya mendicant who is now undergoing such severe penance, and may he in the end attain his earnest desire."

Now the six years being over, on the 16th day of the second month of spring-time, Bôdhisatwa began to reflect thus, "It is not right that I should continue thus eating, and not aiming to attain the end of all, the perfection of complete wisdom; where, then, shall I obtain fitting food for the purpose, which may nourish me, and at the same time not unfit me for that great end of all?"

Thus reflecting, a certain Devaputra, knowing the thoughts of Bôdhisatwa, went straight to the house of the village Lord, Sujata,[1] and his two daughters, and spake thus—"Sujata, now is your opportunity! Bôdhisatwa desires some choice food, after partaking of which he desires to devote himself to the attainment of supreme wisdom. [2] Ye, then, should now prepare some exquisite cream for the purpose of ministering to his wants."

Then the two daughters of Sujata, the village lord, having heard the Devaputra's words, quickly assembled a thousand milch kine, and with their milk fed five hundred others, and with their milk fed two hundred and fifty others, and so on down to fifteen cows; taking the milk of these cows and mixing it in a dish with some of the purest rice, these two maidens proceeded to prepare a lordly dish for Bôdhisatwa. Then appeared all kinds of wonderful portents; every kind of appearance presented itself on the surface

---

1 But Sujata was given before as the name of one daughter, and the village lord was called Nandika.

2 Here again the expression denotes *two*, "ni-tang."

of the mixture, whilst Brahma, Sâkra, and the other Devas appeared in attendance.[1]

At length, on the 23rd day of the second month, Bôdhisatwa, having arranged his garments very early in the morning, proceeded towards the village of Uravilva, to beg his food. Arrived there, he at last came to the house of Nandika, the village lord, and there stood silently before the principal door of the dwelling, awaiting charity.

Then Sujata, the daughter of the village lord, seeing Bôdhisatwa standing thus silently before the gate, immediately sent for a golden dish, and filling it up to the brim with the delicious food, with her own hands came and presented it to Bôdhisatwa. Having taken her place before him, she spake thus, "Would that my lord would accept from me this dish full of deliciously prepared rice milk." Then Bôdhisatwa, seeing the character of the food, thought thus with himself, "This is a token that I should henceforth strive after the true nectar (sweet dew) of the right law. I vow from this moment to deliver the world from the thraldom of death, and of the Wicked one. I will procure salvation for all men, and conduct them to the other shore." Then, having accepted the gift of Sujata, she likewise urged him to keep the golden dish. Thus Bôdhisatwa departed from Uravilva, having received the charity of Sujata, and step by step advanced towards the Nairañjana river, where he partook of the food, after which he entered the river and bathed, whilst all the Devas showered down upon him every kind of flower and perfume. Afterwards, Bôdhisatwa, taking his Kashya garment, washed it in the stream, and attempted then to proceed to the other shore of the river; but his strength had been so reduced by the penance which for six years he had endured, that he was unable to reach the opposite bank. Then the Deva of a certain great tree which was called Pinjuna,[2] the Deva's name being Akuba, stretched forth his jewelled arm to assist Bôdhisatwa.[3] Then Bôdhisatwa, having taken the outstretched hand, reached

---

[1] These portents I omit, *vide* M. B., 167-8.

[2] Observe that Foucaux gives the name of the tree *Kakoubha* (*Lal. Vist.*, 257). Compare also Pancu(kulasiva)na with Pinjuna (in the Text).

[3] It seems plain that this incident is the subject of the sculpture on the right hand pillar of Plate lviii, *Tree and Serpent Worship*.

the shore in safety. Meanwhile, all the Devas, taking portions of the water of the river in which Bôdhisatwa had bathed, returned therewith to their several palaces.

Now the lord of that Nairañjana river had a certain Nâga daughter of the same name as the river, who, with her hand advanced from a spring that bubbled up from the earth, presented to Bôdhisatwa a seat,[1] on which, taking his place, he finished the delicate food of Sujata, the village lord's daughter. Having concluded his meal, he forthwith cast the golden dish on the river stream, which the Nâga, who was lord of the river, at once seized and conveyed to his palace; but King Sâkra, observing this, assumed the form of a Garuda, and forthwith snatched it from the hands of the Nâga, and transported it to the Trâyastriñshas heaven, where it is still an object of worship.

Then Bôdhisatwa arose, and, step by step, advanced towards the Bôdhi tree; whilst the Nâga Râja's daughter, taking the seat she had provided for Bôdhisatwa, carried it to her own palace, as an object for future worship. And so the Gâtha says—

"Bôdhisatwa, having partaken of the choice food, as the laws of religion direct,
The food which Sujata had piously prepared,
Filled with joy, proceeded onward to the Bôdhi tree,
Determined to attain to Supreme Wisdom."

[Kiouen XXV has 6,480 words, and cost 3.24 taels.]

CHAPTER XXVI.

The advance to the Bôdhi Tree.

§ 1. Thus refreshed with the food he had taken, and the water of Nairañjana river, Bôdhisatwa set his face toward the Bôdhi tree, and proceeded onward—slowly and with dignity, like all the former Bôdhisatwas had done. (Here follows a long description of the method of walking adopted by the Bôdhisatwas.) And as he

---

1 A sort of basket-seat, confer, *Tree and Serpent Worship*, Pl. xxiv, Fig. 2.

advanced in this way, he began to reflect with himself thus—"I am now proceeding to that sacred arena of the Bôdhi tree; what, then, is the method of sitting adopted by other Bôdhisatwas when engaged in the attainment of the highest wisdom?" Immediately he recognised the truth that he ought to make a cushion of grass for a seat.

At this time certain Devas of the Suddhavasa Heavens addressed Bôdhisatwa, and said—"Even so! even so! Holy and reverend one, the former Bôdhisatwas have all made their seat of grass arranged for the purpose, and thus have attained complete enlightenment." Then Bôdhisatwa thought, "And who is there to give me this grass?" Thinking thus, he looked on every side of him to see if any one were near him who could supply the want. At this time Sâkra Râja, of the Trâyastriñshas Heavens, by his divine wisdom knowing the thoughts of Bôdhisatwa, immediately transformed himself into the shape of a grass-cutter, and taking his stand not far from Bôdhisatwa, he remained there on the right hand side of him, cutting some beautiful grass, shining as the peacock's feathers, of a beautiful blue-like colour, its points all turning to the right.[1] When Bôdhisatwa perceived him thus engaged, he approached to his side and said, "Excellent sir, and what is your name;" to which the grass-cutter replied, "My name is Kih-li[2] (Santi?)" On hearing this, Bôdhisatwa thought thus with himself, "This name is an assurance to me that I shall attain my aim;" and then, in a soft and melodious voice (here follows a long description of the different qualities of his voice) he addressed the grass-cutter and said, "Can you give me some of this grass?" The supposed grass-cutter immediately answered, "I can." Then Sâkra, under the form of Santi, came forward and respectfully offered some of his grass to Bôdhisatwa. Having taken one handful of it, he proceeded onwards. Then the earth quaked six times. And now, just as Bôdhisatwa took the grass, suddenly five hundred blue birds, coming from the ten quarters of

---

[1] This, amongst numerous other notices of a similar character, will explain many Buddhist symbols and emblems; the lines, which turn to the right in the composition of various figures, constitute the emblem a fortunate one, *e.g.*, the *conch*, the volute of which twists to the right, the *swastika*, etc.

[2] That is, "good luck," or "fortunate."

space, flew up, and turning to the right, circumvented Bôdhisatwa three times, and then followed him as he advanced. Again, five hundred Garuda birds, coming from the four quarters, did the same. Again, five hundred peacocks (and, in short, every kind of bird and beast) coming up, did the same. Thus, surrounded by Devas, Nagas, Asuras, and creatures of every grade and kind, Bôdhisatwa marched onwards.[1]

Now at this time there was a Nâga Râja belonging to that region whose name was Ka-cha (Kâlika).[2] This Nâga Râja was very old, and in ages and kalpas gone by had seen many Buddhas. He had now been asleep for some time, when he was suddenly roused by the shaking of the earth, and by hearing the noise of the earthquake. Proceeding outside his palace, with some anxiety, he looked round on every hand to see the cause of the commotion, and there, not far from his dwelling, he saw Bôdhisatwa proceeding onward with dignified gait towards the Bôdhimandala.[3] Observing this, the Nâga Râja feeling sure that Bôdhisatwa, like the former ones, would reach Supreme Wisdom, with great joy began to utter the following stanzas:

"How full of grace and dignity this great and virtuous person!
Just as I have heretofore seen
All the Bôdhisatwas coming towards this central point,
So this one is now advancing in the same way.
I clearly see that this illustrious youth as he proceeds
Will certainly attain to supreme enlightenment.
His walk and bearing indicate him as the Lord of the World;
First raising his right foot, and so moving onwards.
See him now looking round with an inquiring gaze;
He surely must attain the perfection of Buddha.
And now see him by the side of the grass-cutter, Santi,
Begging a handful of grass—holding which
He now with straight course advances to the Bôdhi Tree!
He certainly will now attain the state of Sambôdhi!
And now from all the quarters of heaven blows a cool air,

---

1 The description here is very florid and exaggerated. I have not thought it worth my while to translate the whole. *Vide Lal. Vist.*, p. 263.

2 The interpretation is "the black one."

3 That is the arena round the Bôdhi tree.

Sounding like the distant voice of the King of the Oxen;
And now behold the birds come flying towards him,
On every hand they surround and circumvent him.
From out the darkness and the gloomy night of the world,
The gross darkness and the ignorance that envelope mankind,
This holy one, having attained the perfection of wisdom,
Shall cause to appear the brightness and the glory of his own light.
And now again see all the beasts of every sort approach,
And in their infinite varieties surround him as he goes;
Surely as they turn thus before him in the direction of the right hand,
This virtuous one will accomplish his aim and become the Lord of the World.
And now again the elephants and horses and such domestic creatures,
And all the turbanned[1] crowd approach his side.
See them thus together advance and greet the Bôdhisatwa,
Ah! surely he must soon become a perfect Buddha, Lord of the World!
And now the Devas of the Suddhavasa Heavens,
Of pure and lovely form and person,
Bending before the virtuous one as he advances!
Pay him reverence! soon will he become a perfect Buddha," etc.

Having uttered these stanzas, the Nâga Râja, filled with the greatest joy, proceeded with hands clasped together to meet Bôdhisatwa, and humbly pay him reverence. On which Bôdhisatwa addressed him thus: "Be it so! be it so! great Nâga Râja as you say! I am now bent upon the acquisition of the highest wisdom." And then he repeated the following Gâthas:

"Great Nâga Râja! these words of thine
Cause my resolution to increase still more,
I now am fixed, and soon shall reach perfection!
The state of which the world has no equivalent.
These various signs and portents you have named
Are all of lucky omen, to assist me.
I now must soon cross over this sea of sorrow
To the other shore; of this there can be little doubt."

[1] Devas.

Then this Nâga Râja's wife called Kin-Kwong (Suvarna Prabhâsa ?), taking with her countless dragon girls, surrounded Bôdhisatwa, each holding in her hand some choice flower, or unguent, or coloured garment, or flag, and every kind of tinkling jewelled ornament, with which they kept up a perpetual chant of praise; from the midst of which some such words as these were heard:

"Go forward! Lord of the World! firmly fixed in thy resolve,
Without anxiety or fear, perfectly established;
Rejoice and be very glad—thou who hast banished desire!
Free from all doubt or anger (raga and moha) or covetousness (tanha).
Thou art the Lord able to heal the world,
And therefore we adore thee and we worship thee."[1]

The dreams of Mâra.

§ 2. THEN Bôdhisatwa having heard these stanzas, proceeded onwards towards the Bôdhi Tree, and then he began to think that Mâra Râja, the wicked one, Lord of the Kama Lokas, ought also to be a witness of his victory over the world and attainment of Supreme Wisdom. On this, emitting a bright ray of glory from between his eyebrows, which penetrated to the abode of Mâra, this voice was heard where the ray penetrated throughout the vast chiliocosm:

"There is one born now amongst men
Who has practised the rules of piety for ages,
The Prince Royal, son of Suddhôdana Râja,
Who has resigned the royal dignity and become a recluse;
He, desiring to open the gates of everlasting life,
Is now proceeding towards the Bôdhi Tree.
If you are able to do so, and equal to the task,
Repair straightway and see him there beneath the tree,
For now he is about to cross over to the other side
And desires above all things to save others with himself;
Bôdhisatwa, himself enlightened,
Desires also to enlighten others," etc., etc.

---

[1] The whole of this description agrees with plate lviii (*right-hand pillar, upper group*)—*Tree and Serpent Worship.*

At this time Mâra Râja, the Wicked,[1] Lord of the Kama lokas, hearing these stanzas sounding out of the middle of the supernatural light, in the midst of his sleep, was greatly moved, and in his night dreams beheld thirty-two kinds of portents, which were of an unlucky character. And now, what were these portents? 1. He saw all the heavens darkened with a deep gloom. 2. He saw his own palace greatly polluted with stones and filth. 3. He saw his own body trembling with fear, and his heart devoid of strength. 4. He saw himself galloping fast away on horseback towards the four quarters of heaven. 5. He saw his crown fall from his head, and tumble to the ground. 6. He saw himself with fevered breath and burning throat, but his body icy cold and numbed. 7. He saw all the trees and flowers in his palace garden withered and dead. 8. He saw all the lakes which were covered with lovely flowers, dried up and gone. 9. He saw all the favourite birds in his gardens fall to the ground, their feathers scattered here and there. 10. He saw all the musical instruments within his palace mutilated and broken to pieces. 11. He saw all his attendants, who had hitherto surrounded him to do him service, flee hither and thither, and leave him alone, lying on the earth. 12. He saw his lovely concubines tearing their hair and rolling on the ground. 13. He saw all his children prostrate at the feet of Bôdhisatwa, beneath the Bôdhi Tree. 14. He saw four of his favourite women, with both arms raised, weeping and lamenting, and saying, "Alas! alas! woe is me! woe is me!" 15. He saw his royal garments covered with dirt and filth. 16. He saw his own body begrimed with dust and dirt. 17. He saw the glory of his body fade, and all its beauty disappear. 18. He saw the walls, windows, and towers of his palace all destroyed and falling down. 19. He saw all the Yakshas, Kumbhandas, Nâgas, and so on, drop on their hands and raise their heads and weep through grief. 20. He saw all the Devas of the Kama Loka proceed weeping towards the place where Bôdhisatwa was, and when arrived there stand in front of him. 21. He saw these Devas within the sacred enclosure driving away, with clubs and swords, Mâra Râja, who was fleeing with his followers in every direction.[2] 22. He saw the

---

[1] That is, *Pisuna*.

[2] This seems to be the subject of Pl. lviii, *Tree and Serpent Worship; left hand pillar.*

various vessels of good augury broken and destroyed. 23. He saw the Rishi Narada uttering unpropitious words. 24. He saw a certain Divine Spirit, whose name was "fun-hi" (joyous), standing in front of the door and crying out "call me not joyous." 25. He saw the expanse of space filled with clouds of dust and smoke. 26. He saw the guardian spirit of Mâra's palace, whose name was Kung-tih (merit), raise a doleful cry, and weep. 27. He saw that which before had been self-sufficient, no longer so. 28. He saw those who had been (his) friends now quarrelling and fighting. 29. He saw the palaces of Mâra burning with fire, and finally wrapt in darkness. 30. He saw all the rooms in the palace moving and rocking to and fro. 31. He saw the trees and forests uprooted, and the earth covered with their branches. 32. He saw the world come to an end.

Now it came to pass that when Mâra Râja, the Wicked, had seen these thirty-two unlucky dreams that he awoke out of his sleep, and as he awoke his whole body trembled with fear, and his thoughts were exceedingly troubled. Forthwith, he called to his side the entire assembly of his household, and all his ministers and guards, that he might tell them the visions he had seen. And thus he addressed them—"Be it known to you all who are here assembled, that yesternight, in my dreams, I beheld these visions, and am thereat greatly troubled and distressed, for they are not propitious, but, on the contrary, of evil omen, for it seems to me they indicate that soon I shall lose my dominion through the power of some great man, who is to be born within my domain." And so the Gâthas say—

"Last night there shone around a self-caused light,
From which a voice spake out these words—
'The child of the Sâkyas has become a recluse,
His body adorned with 32 marks of pre-eminence;
And now he has fulfilled six years of penance,
And is gradually advancing to the tree of knowledge,
Self-enlightened, to enlighten others with the light of wisdom.
Now, then, if you have strength, go! strive with him!
His virtue the growth of infinite ages,
He now is about to attain the true and only lasting wisdom.
He it is who will destroy thy kingdom for ever!
If you cannot meet and overpower him;

When once he has attained the eternal and everlasting body,
Then he will overturn your dominion and authority.'
Now, then, ye children and associates of Mâra! I say,
If ye have any power or strength, go straight to him,
The Shaman who aims to gain Divine Power at the foot of yonder tree;
Go quickly there, and overwhelm him, that he succeed not.
If ye will attend to my words of loving counsel,
Take now your host of every kind.
The world has many holy men (Pratyeka Buddhas),
But this man aims at Nirvâna itself (Divinity),
Despite of me he presumes by himself to be Dharmarâja,
And defies me to cut off the seed of the Tathâgatas."

At this time the chief son of Mâra Râja Pisuna, whose name was Shreshti, rose up and addressed his father in the following words:—

"Why, my father, are your cheeks so pale?
Your heart in trepidation, and your body without glory!
I see these proofs of some great cause of anxiety,
But as yet we have not heard any reason thereof.
Would that you would tell your children the reason
Why thus you look, in very truth."

Then Mâra Râja answered his son Shreshti, and said—

"Listen, then, my son, and understand:
Last night I had such ever varying dreams,
That if I should narrate them in your midst,
Ye all would fall upon the ground through fear."

To whom Shreshti replied—

"Say not that we should fall upon the ground,
For then 'twere useless to engage ourselves to fight;
If your dreams were of this unlucky sort,
It were better not to seek to overcome that man."

To whom Mâra Râja replied—

"Let him who fights resolve to conquer,
For if he doubts, 'twere better not to fight.
What can that solitary hermit do?
I myself will go and meet him underneath the tree."

To whom Shreshti rejoined—

"There may be strength and much brute force,
But Wisdom is the only assurance of victory.
The universe may be full of fire-flies,
But one sun eclipses all their brilliancy.
If a man puffed up with idle thoughts,
Make no inquiry as to what his adversary is,
Then all wise men, presaging what will happen,
Regard such person as one difficult to deal with."

And now Bôdhisatwa, advancing toward the Bodhi tree, on his way observed a certain Amra tree, seeing which and thinking it was the Tree of Knowledge, he approached to it, intending to sit down. At this time the earth shook as though it would dissolve, in consequence of the glory of the person of Bôdhisatwa. Then he reflected thus with himself—there are but two occasions in the world on which the earth shakes in this way, viz., when a man gives up every remnant of virtuous principle; and, secondly, when a man's virtuous principle is fully grown and his merit as great as it can be. Neither of these cases applies to me, and, therefore, this cannot be the Bôdhi tree.

Then the Devas of the Rupa loka worlds, dwelling in the Suddhavasa Heavens, in order to denote the true Bôdhi tree, began to hang upon it flags and banners, and also on the branches of the trees that led towards it. Then Bôdhisatwa, recognising from these signs the true Bôdhi tree, proceeded slowly forward from the Amra in the direction indicated. Now when Bôdhisatwa had just arrived there, a certain Yaksha called Hiang-shan, who was guarding the precinct not far from the tree, seeing Bôdhisatwa approaching, called hastily to another Yaksha, whose name was "red-eye" (chih ngan), and said to him, "My dear friend, go as quickly as you can to Mâra, the Lord of the Kama lokas, and tell him that just as in days of yore Krakusanda, and Konagamana, and Kâsyapa approached this tree, and afterwards attained Supreme Wisdom, so now there is advancing towards it a man of invincible determination, whose appearance indicates the greatest religious merit, and whose person is marked by the thirty-two significant signs, encroaching on the dominion of Mâra; and in truth this is none other than Siddârtha, the son of Suddhôdana Râja, who has undergone a long course of self-discipline, and now is coming here to this most distinguished place with a view to take up his abode here. Let your Majesty, therefore, beware of what is taking place." Red-eye, having heard this from Hiang-shan, went straight to Pisuna, and on coming into his presence delivered the message just as it was given to him.

Then Mâra Râja, the Wicked, Lord of the Kama-lokas, having heard from the Yaksha, Red-eye, the news of this event, immediately proclaimed to all the Devas of the different heavens belonging to the Kama loka the tidings of Siddârtha's attempt to attain Supreme Knowledge, and of his own intention to go forthwith to the spot, and prevent the prosecution of his purpose.

Then Shreshti, son of Mâra, addressed his father in these words—"My Father! this project of thine gives me no satisfaction, for I fear that after a while you will repent of your undertaking when you find that naught can be accomplished." To whom Mâra Râja replied, "Tush! you are but a child, and you know nothing of my spiritual power and facilities in transforming myself as I please; you are completely in the dark and without any knowledge." Then Shreshti rejoined, "Not so! my father! I am not ignorant of your powers; but I fear you are ignorant of the spiritual resources of Siddârtha, for you have not seen the religious power Bôdhisatwa possesses; you had better repair to the spot, and see and examine for yourself."

Then Mâra Râja Pisuna, disregarding the words of his son Shreshti. forthwith gave orders to assemble his host, armed for the strife. Then indeed might mortal man be terrified to see the vast assembly of warriors all caparisoned and belted for the struggle. How fearful the sight! there were some who, with but one body, had a hundred thousand faces (mouths) through each of which came forth every kind of snake-like body, which twined around the arms and legs of the monster-fiend; oh! dreadful sight! And then they were all armed with bows and swords, falchions and axes, spears and lances, morions, and every kind of club! Then there were some whose bodies, heads, eyes, hands, and feet, were all of hideous and misshapen form. Some had above their heads a flaming fire; others emitted forked flames from their paps and breasts! others uttered ribald curses and taunts, as they grasped the plough-like club or shook the pestle-shaped mace. And then how dreadful were their eyes!—their eyeballs bursting forth or bent askew, looking upwards and downwards! their mouths again distorted, and filled with monstrous teeth! their tongues lolling out and of every shape! their eyes gleaming with a lurid light as those of the black snake; their heads wreathed with living serpents, whilst in their hands they held the writhing forms of other snakes on which they fed, even as the Garuda bird devours the Nâgas of the sea. Others held in their hands the flesh of men recently dead, and their various limbs, with cups full of blood. Others were holding the entrails and garbage on which they fed. Some of them had green eyes, like that of the lion, fearful to see; some had sunken eyes; others goggle eyes, their ears like those of sheep, or the elephant, or the fox, &c., pot-bellied, bandy-legged, flat-nosed, crinkle-skinned, slobbering, and blood-stained;—such were the forms of the warriors who followed Mâra, an army dreadful to behold, fearful to meet as they marched onward to the scene of the coming strife!

[Kiouen XXVI has 6,604 words and cost 3.32 taels.]

CHAPTER XXVII.

The attack of Mâra.

§ 1. Then Mâra Râja addressed the Yaksha, Red-eye, in these words and said, "You see before you this army of mine, who is he then that would wish or dare to usurp the authority I possess over this world?" Then the Yaksha, Red-eye, answered Mâra Râja and said, "He is one named Siddârtha, son of Suddhôdana, who, from the time that he received the food of Sujata, the village maiden, has not ceased to advance onwards in the presence of many omens, towards the tree of knowledge.

Then Mâra entertained the thought that he would tempt Bôdhisatwa to rest, and spread his grass mat beneath some other tree, and not proceed onward to the Bôdhi tree. Having thought of this, he called all the host of the Yakshas and said, "Go! all ye Yakshas, assemble at once beneath the Bôdhi tree; nor suffer this child of the Sâkyas to approach near it." They replied, "We go, O mighty King! to execute your commands;" and so they proceeded to take their stand around the Bôdhi tree. Then it was these Yakshas beheld Bôdhisatwa gradually approaching the sacred precinct, his body shining like a mountain of pure gold, incomparable for beauty. Then the Yakshas, seeing him thus advancing, uttered the following verses—

"Surely this is the glory of the newly-risen sun,
Shining as a golden mountain shines!
In deep commiseration both for Devas and for men.
See! like a Lion, how he slowly nears the tree!"

Then the Guardian Spirit of the Wood replied as follows (verses to the same effect) to the Yakshas.

Then as Bôdhisatwa approached the sacred spot, holding the grass in his left hand, he arranged it with his right hand on the eastern side of the tree, and so sat down, and as he took his seat he vowed that he would never rise again till he had attained enlightenment.

Then the earth quaked six times. Upon this Mâra Pisuna, Lord of the Kama-lokas, repaired to the place where Bôdhisatwa was seated and said, "Thou son of a Kshattriya! it is not agreeble to me that you should make your seat here, under this tree, nor is it safe for you; for in the middle of the night there are countless Pisatcha fiends and Putanas and Yakshas and Rakshas who come here to devour the flesh of men and quaff their blood; but to the north of this tree there is a grove where all the great Rishis dwell, it is close to the village of Uravilva, a very delightful spot indeed; go, therefore, thou son of the Sâkya race, and take up your abode there."

To which Bôdhisatwa replied, "And dost thou not know, Mâra Pisuna! that I have for years dwelt as a hermit in the midst of the solitary mountains and woods, and in the hollows and dells of the lonely wastes, and yet have never feared such midnight visitors; and now I have come here not without purpose and design, for I know full well that beneath this tree all the Buddhas have attained to the condition of Supreme Wisdom, and for this reason and with this end in view, I have come here and taken up my abode." Then a certain Yaksha, who stood on Mâra's right hand said, "And why, oh, child of the Sâkyas! should you select this tree for your further sufferings, there are others on every side better than this one. Get thee hence! to some other place." To whom Bôdhisatwa replied, "I am persuaded that beneath no other tree but this can I fulfil my vow, but only beneath this one—I am resolved therefore to remain here!" And so the Gâtha says—

"Bôdhisatwa, seated with his legs crossed beneath the tree,
Even as the mighty snake coils himself up and rests,
Strong in his resolve, made this vow—
'Until my aim be accomplished I will rise no more.'"

Then Mâra Râja, having disappeared for a moment, transformed himself into the figure of a messenger, with disordered garments and dishevelled hair, panting as if with haste and anxiety, and holding in his hands a bundle of official notices as if from all the Sâkya princes. With these he approached to where Bôdhisatwa was, and opening his mouth he said, "These notices, oh! Manava! are from Sâkya princes to you; this one is from Nandika, this from Aniruddha, this from Devaka, this from Nandi, this from Ananda." Now, on all these letters was written the false report that Devadatta had usurped the government of Kapilavastu, and entered the palace of Bôdhisatwa, taken his goods, ravished his wives, and placed Suddhôdana fast bound in prison. They urged Bôdhisatwa, therefore, to return, to restore peace and order to the government.

Then Bôdhisatwa reflected, that lust had caused Devadatta to act thus to the women, and natural malice had made him imprison Suddhôdana, whilst the Sâkyas in not defending their king had shown a cowardly and hateful disposition. Thinking thus on the follies and weakness of the natural heart, his own resolution to attain something higher and better was confirmed and strengthened within him.

Then, as Bôdhisatwa sat thus beneath the tree, the Deva who resided there to protect the precinct, filled with unutterable joy, cast all her ornaments before Bôdhisatwa, and with encouraging voice entreated him to persevere in his purpose. Then all the Devas of the surrounding trees coming to that Tree-Deva inquired who the glorious being was that sat there beneath the shade of the branches, and on hearing the circumstances they scattered all sorts of flowers and perfumes above Bôdhisatwa, and with their hands clasped above their heads, they encouraged him by their words and laudatory verses to persevere, and soon to accomplish his aim. Then Mâra Râja, filled with rage, thought thus with himself, "This child of the Sâkyas, of the Kshattriya race, desires now to overthrow my power and the dominion I hold over the world, he aims to drive me back and trample me underfoot; if he prevail he will teach all men the way to Nirvâna, he will show them by various methods how to attain it, and my kingdom will be at an end, but he has not yet accomplished his aim. I will, therefore, by every possible expedient and stratagem prevent him from doing so, and drive him away from this spot." And so the Gâtha says [as before].

Then Mâra assembled around him his thousand sons; on his right were five hundred, of whom Shreshti was chief, and on his left five hundred, of whom "Wicked-mouth" was chief.

Then Mâra addressed them all in these words—"My sons! I have summoned you to this spot that I may know your opinion respecting the best method of overthrowing and destroying this Bôdhisatwa who sits there beneath the tree!" At this time Shresti began, and addressed his father in the following Gâthas—

"Would you dare to touch the great dozing snake?
Would your strength be enough to meet the mad elephant?
Would you fight with the king of the beasts?
Then you may also destroy this Shaman."

To whom "Wicked-mouth" replied—

"If a man but see me his heart sinks within him!
All the trees at my touch fall to the earth!
How much more, then, shall this Shaman, seeing me,
Flee away at the sight and hide himself."

(And so the discussion continues from right to left, the former deprecating any attempt to conquer Bôdhisatwa, the latter encouraging it.)

Mâra Râja then addresses his great minister Bhadrapati, who also dissuades him from attempting to prevent Bôdhisatwa attaining his object, on the ground that he is protected and worshipped by the occupants of all the Heavens, and that every good omen is in his favour. He also reminds Mâra Râja of the misfortunes that have ever attended those who molest or attempt to injure the great Rishis and Saints; as, for example, the fire that burnt up the lovely garden of Brahmadatta, on account of his opposition to Vyasa Rishi, so that nothing would grow on the spot. Finally, he pointed out that, according to the Veda, whosoever possessed the thirty-two characteristic signs which appeared on the person of Bôdhisatwa, would, if he became an Ascetic, certainly attain to Supreme Wisdom.

At this time, Mâra Râja Pisuna, having heard these words of Bhadrapati, his great minister, was filled with sorrow and regret; whilst those around him were equally afraid. At length, his eldest son, Shreshti, addressed his father, and besought him to give up his object; for though it were possible for a man to paint the empty void of space with richest colours, or to move Mount Sumeru with a finger, or to pass over the vast ocean without sinking, or to chain the wind—or, though the sun and moon and stars might fall to earth, or the whole family of created beings possess one heart and mind—yet it would not be possible to overcome the fixed resolve of Bôdhisatwa. Then Mâra Râja addressed Shreshti as follows—

"Begone! thou child of contradiction!
Look no more upon my face,
Thine heart is altogether with this Shaman;
Go, then, and join thyself with the son of Sâkya."

Then, turning to his female attendants, he bade them use all their wiles to induce Bôdhisatwa to relent, and give way to his passions. On this, in obedience to their Lord's command, they went with mincing gait towards the spot where Bôdhisatwa sat beneath the tree, and standing at a short distance from him, they proceeded to put into practice every ogling way and lascivious art they could.

Some of them with their heads covered, others with their heads bare; some showing half their faces, others their entire face; some with dainty smiles to display their white teeth; some with eyes askance looking at Bôdhisatwa; others kneeling down before him and looking upwards into his face, others drooping their heads so as to conceal their faces, and looking at one another; some raising their eyebrows, others opening and shutting their eyes; others combing out their dishevelled hair; others spreading out their arms, others raising their arms so as to show their person; others with their hands toying with their breasts; others half uncovered, with their breasts and hips bare; others with their hands clapping their stomachs; others again entirely nude; others again just dressing, others with their garments so arranged as to show their buttocks; others again toying with their jewels and earrings; some again playing with their suckling children; others amusing themselves with various kinds of birds; others walking to and fro, with their heads turning this way and that, and their eyes darting side glances; others sighing, and pining for love; others with their knees bent, drawing figures on the ground; some again singing, some dancing, some moving their bodies amorously, other indulging lascivious thoughts; others lying down, and thinking over their past experiences in love; again there were some who disported themselves as virgins, others as newly-married women (the rest is of the same tenor). But, notwithstanding all these temptations, Bôdhisatwa remained unchanged in face and appearance—tranquil and at perfect rest he sat; even as the full-moon when it emerges from the hands of Rahu, the Asura Râja, pure and spotless; or the sun when first he scatters his dazzling rays to the morning; or as the lily that reposes on the placid waters; or as the brightness of the flame; firm as Mount Sumeru, so Bôdhisatwa was unmoved, even as the iron walls that surround the Universe; without the least agitation, his heart and his mind at perfect rest—without fear or anxiety, and entirely self-possessed.

[Kiouen XXVII contains 6,126 words, and cost 6.063 taels.]

CHAPTER XXVIII.

At this time those attendants of Mâra, having practised all these beguiling arts, began to address Bôdhisatwa in the following words—

"This early spring-tide, how fair the season!
All the trees beginning to bud, and flowers to bloom!
Surely this is the time for pleasure and love,
Whilst you are in the prime of your beauty and youth—
Your appearance so graceful, your years so few,
This is the time for you to indulge your desires.
Your present search after supreme wisdom is hard to accomplish;
Turn, then, your thoughts from it, and take your pleasure—
Look at us, and behold our beauties and charms—
See our bodies, so perfect in shape, and so fit for love,
Our locks so brightly shining, of a rich auburn tint,
Our foreheads broad, and our rounded heads,
Our eyes so beautifully even and full,
Like the blue lotus flower for depth of colour.
Our noses curved like the beak of the parrot,
Our lips red and shining as the ruby for colour,
Like the choicest coral in tint; and see our graceful necks,
Our teeth so white, and free from all disfigurement,
Our tongues so fresh, like the leaf of the lotus flower;
Listen to the soft and charming voices we possess,
Even like the sound of the Gandharvas for melody;
See our bosoms, so enticing, white, and lovely!
Round as the fruit of the pomegranate tree!
See our waists, so lithe and slender, like the handle of the bow,
Our buttocks, broad and glossy (fat), placed evenly,
Just as the rounded forehead of the elephant king;
Our flanks, so soft and white, of graceful shape,
Smooth as the trunk of the elephant;
Behold our legs, so round and straight and tapering,
Beautiful as those of the King of the Deer!
And see how full and plump our feet beneath,

A reddish white in colour, like the shining petal of the lily.
How beautiful and joy-affording, then, our forms!
Adorned with all these marks of excellence!
Our fingers deft in every kind of music,
Our voices able to produce the softest sounds,
Our feet to dance and give delight to every heart—
What joy the Devas feel to see us thus!
How ravished with the thoughts of love they are!
Why feel you not, O youth, the same delight!
Why covet not the same enjoyment!
But like a man who finds a treasury of gold and gems,
Leaves all, and goes away far off,
Not knowing the happiness which such wealth can give;
So, Youth, your heart seems utterly estranged!
You know not what the joys of love and pleasure are,
But sit, self-wrapped, unmoved—and heed us not!
How can such folly and such ignorance be thine!
Why not partake of the world's joys and bliss!
And let Nirvâna and the path of wisdom be delayed."

At this time, Bôdhisatwa, unmoved from his fixed purpose, and without any appearance of disturbance, but firm as Mount Sumeru, replied thus to the women, his voice soft as that of the Kalabiñka Bird, or, as the voice of Brahma—

"All those pleasures in which the world indulges
Are sources of sorrow, sin, and distress!
By reason of this, the worldling loses all spiritual discernment;
Clouded with ignorance, he lives in darkness and gloom.
Men are never satisfied with the enjoyment of these things,
But I long ago have utterly discarded them, and escaped from their slavery,
As a man flees from a burning furnace, or a poisonous drug;
I have long since given up these sources of sorrow.
I have tasted of the water of eternal wisdom;
My heart enlightened, I desire to enlighten others,
And to declare the doctrine of the most excellent law.
But if I were to partake of these polluting pleasures,
Then I should in the end fail to attain wisdom,
For it is by continuing in these deceitful pleasures,

That a man acquires the infection of folly and sin,
Neither profitable to himself or able to profit others;
I, therefore, desire not these things—I cast them away.
It is these pleasures that burn up all living things,
Even as the fire at the end of time burns the world.
They are perishable as the bubble that rises on the water,
Light as a dream, unreal as a phantom,
Hollow and false, deceiving the worldly-wise;
But the man of true wisdom finds no delight therein.
Just as you see the child with his fellows
Playing and polluting himself with filth,
So is the ignorant and besotted man polluted by these;
He sees the dazzling sheen of the jewelled trinket,
And forthwith there arises in him a covetous desire.
That hair of yours which grows from the brain,
What pollution, sores, and ulcers it generates;
Your teeth, that are secretly shed one by one;
Your lips and nose and mouth and eyes,
They are but as the bubble for permanence.
Your waist and loins, your buttocks and hams,
What pollution is here, proceeding from the blood;
And what impurities, the effect of indulgence.
The man who delights in these is foolish
As one who makes a millstone to grind his own body.
And therefore every one who is wise,
Distinguishing these matters, as I have shown,
Will reject and forsake all such false delights.
He will behold his body, day and night circulating its blood,
As the receptacle of that which is unclean, and find no joy in beholding it.
So it is I see you, standing before my eyes
As a phantom, a dream, an unreal appearance—
For all things spring from connection of cause and effect.
These pleasures are in themselves false and delusive;
By these, men are drawn away from the path of happiness,
And led captive along the ways of misery—
They are as a fiery furnace,
As vessels full of poison—
As the head of an angry snake not to be touched,

The causes of ignorance and delusion and death;
Whoever tampers, then, with these,
Deserting the path of purity and wisdom,
Shall in the end, without doubt, perish in Hell.
So, then, having let go these things, and forsaken them,
I am now free as the air or as space, which cannot be bound with
a chain, etc."

The three daughters of Mâra then suddenly appear and enter into a similar controversy with him, of which the following is a summary:

"Illustrious son of Sâkya, the kingly office is yours,
Why, then, sit you thus beneath this spreading tree—
For like the spring-tide buds and flowers appear,
So now should man and woman join in love;
See how the birds delight in mutual fellowship:
It cannot be that Love's true course should cease.
The time is fit; you also may indulge in love;
Why, then, with guarded heart, do you behold us not!
We three have come, that now and henceforth,
There should be one accordant purpose between us and you."

Then, like the sun first rising, the illustrious saint,
By the accumulated merit of ages past,
Unmoved in heart, sat firm as Sumeru,
His words reverberating like the thunder-roll,
His mien like the lion for quiet dignity,
His speech so full of profit, thought (or spake) thus—

'Because the world is full of covetous desire,
This causes endless quarrellings and disputations,
And this again leads on to litigation;
And thus the ignorant and the besotted
Are immersed in countless troubles and vexations;
The wise man follows none of these things,
But rejecting all, forsakes his home and lives apart,
And finds his pleasure 'mid the lonely hills and glens;

So I continue to restrain myself,
Desiring to abide for ever in the True Eternal Law.'

Then spake again those daughters three of Mâra—

'O youth! your face and eyes, bright as the opening flower,
Listen, we entreat you, to the words we speak.
Go! take the office of a king of men,
Without a peer, the most exalted monarch.
And whether sleeping, sitting, or arising,
Surrounded ever by the sounds of melody!
To attain the wisdom you desire is difficult,
How much more so that of all the Buddhas.
To find deliverance, and walk along the path of rectitude is difficult.
If, fair youth! you see all this, then give it up!'

At this time Bôdhisatwa once again replied—

'I am resolved to gain my end, and become a king of religion,
First among men and gods,
To turn the most excellent wheel of the Law,
To gain the ten superior qualities (dasa balas),
To dwell the only truly great one in the three worlds,
To be surrounded ever by innumerable disciples,
Whose mouth shall ever praise me thus—
"The great and holy one has come into the world, to deliver men from doubt and fear;"
Then I will on their account declare the Law—
Going from place to place as my heart prompts;
For this reason, then, whilst in the world,
I never will partake of its indulgences.'

Then spake the daughters three of Mara once again—

'We promise you shall reign, as Sâkra does in heaven,
On every hand surrounded by lovely damsels;
Yea! like the gods in all the heavens,
Unequalled, with no competitor or any rival,
If only you will not refuse our love.'"

Then Bôdhisatwa replied in these Găthas—

"Pleasure is brief as the lightning flash,
Or like the autumn shower, but for a moment;
I fear you women as I fear an angry snake;
And as for all the gods ye name, through all the heavens
They all are prone to change—no constancy;
Why should I covet, then, the pleasures you describe."

To whom they rejoined—

"Youth! see you not these trees and flowers,
These butterflies, these birds with mellow notes!
The earth is carpeted with glossy green,
The trees and all the woods produce their varied tints;
Hark to the pleasing sounds, like angel-trills,
Oh, what a pleasant time is this for joy and love!"

To whom Bôdhisatwa replied—

"The trees in season bear their fruits and flowers,
The butterflies and birds sip nectar and enjoy the sweets;
The sun progresses to its height, the earth is parched,
The joys of heavenly wisdom still abide the same."

Again the women spake:

"Oh youth, our face is shining as the silvery moon!
Look then on us, bright as the lotus flower!
Behold our teeth so white, without a fault,
Few in the heavens to be compared with us;
Much less on earth—come then, possess the prize,
And shun us not, oh youth! let us be one."

To whom Bôdhisatwa replied:

"I see your bodies full of all impurity,
Disgusting worms in every pore I see.
Your bodies destined to unnumbered ills,
Birth, death, disease, old age, are yours.
I seek the highest prize, hard to attain with men,
The true and constant wisdom of the wise."

And so unmoved as Sumeru, the women finally left him and wished him success in these words:

"That which your heart desires, may you attain!
And finding for yourself deliverance, deliver all."

Then, despite the counsel of his son Shreshti and his daughters, Mâra forthwith himself repaired to the Tree beneath which Bôdhisatwa was seated, and when he had arrived there, he immediately addressed him and said: "Thou son of the Sâkyas! solitary Shaman! what seekest thou here? This place abounds with noxious insects, evil dragons, beasts of terrible appearance; when the dark night comes on, oh Bhikshu! there are fearful robbers here, who will murder and plunder you!"

To whom Bôdhisatwa replied: "Oh Mâra Pisuna! I am now seeking to attain the repose of Nirvâna, in the way and place in which all former Buddhas have done so! I have no fear whatever! all places are alike to me in my search, and I therefore sit here in solitude beneath this tree."

Then Mâra spake thus:

"Oh! Shaman dwelling here alone as an Aranyaka hermit,
It is a work of extreme difficulty to endure long penance.
The ancient Rishis, thoroughly versed in all manner of expedients,
Frequently lost their power of abstraction and failed of their end.
How much more you, a mere stripling, and in the freshness of life,
How can you expect to find this most excellent gift?"

To whom Bôdhisatwa replied:

"From old times the Rishis practising penance,
Because of their want of resolute perseverance,
Their spiritual power was not great or lasting;
But I, from the first have resolutely carried out the precepts,
And now if I do not attain my end, O Pisuna,
Never more will I rise from underneath this tree."

To which Mâra rejoined:

"I am the Supreme Ruler of this world of desire.
Sakra, who protects the world, derives his power from me.

Asuras, Kinnaras, the Nâga Râjas,
From the time of their origin have been my people.
And so thou (art mine) dwelling in the midst of my dominion;
Begone then, this moment begone, and depart from this tree."

Then Bôdhisatwa replied again to Mâra:

"Thou, although supreme in the world of Desire,
Hast no authority or power in the Spiritual world.
Thou art acquainted only with the wretched beings in Hell;
But I belong not to either of the three material worlds.
It is I who hereafter will destroy thine abode, O Mâra!
And wrest from you your power and your dominion."

Then Mâra Pisuna continued his address to Bôdhisatwa thus: "Oh thou son of Sâkya, rise up and begone quickly from this place. Of a very truth you shall become a supreme Chakravarti monarch, governing the four quarters of the world, lord of the great earth, possessed of the seven imperial insignia, ruling over all hills and vales. Is it possible, oh Sâkyaputra, that you do not recollect the true and notable predictions of all the Rishis respecting you! how they declared that you must become a King. Rise then quickly; take the power given you over the world; receive the homage and reverence of those over whom you shall reign with righteousness. Oh! Sâkyaputra, thou art yet young and of vigorous body—go, enjoy the sweets of your palace. There are but few people in this wild desert; the beasts prowl about for their prey. I fear much for your safety; arise then, Oh son of Sakya! return to thy palace, leave this place—search no longer after that wisdom which is so hard to find; but indulge in the pleasures of life, and forget thy present quest."

Having so spoken, Mâra stood silently before Bôdhisatwa awaiting his reply. Then Bôdhisatwa rejoined, "Waste no further words, Mâra! for well do I know the miseries attending the indulgence of pleasure and the gratifications of sense. How inconstant and perishable are such things, empty and unreal as the dew on the leaf—to be avoided as the touch of an angry snake—filthy as the secretions of the body, leading to strifes, murders, and bloodshed. Yea, just as the ripe fruit ready to fall to the earth (and there to rot), or as a dream, a phantom, a bubble, a lightning flash—they are without any true being or endurance, and so, like the fire placed around the dung-fuel, these shall speedily burn up the men who partake of them. Pisuna! I have done with such things; I search after a higher state than this. Thou knowest, O Pisuna, how, long ago, I gave up all the pleasures of life, and shall I return to these? Would a man surfeited with unwholesome food, even to sickness, return again to that which caused him such distress of body? Shall I go back then to the pleasures of which I have seen the evil and felt the burden? Mâra! not long hence I shall attain the Highest Wisdom. I shall soon become Buddha. I shall have done for ever with birth, old age, disease, and death. Return then, oh Pisuna! from whence you came—it is useless to remain here; your words are without profit, they are fit only for the foolish and the besotted—not for me!"

Then Mâra thought, it is useless to tempt this man by offering him pleasures or sensual delights. I must try other expedients, and by gentle and persuasive words move him to depart. Having thought thus, he addressed Bôdhisatwa again: "Oh youth! descendant of the Ikswaku family, thou son of Sâkya! rise quickly and leave this spot; in a little while such sights will meet your eyes, as should not be seen. Armies fighting one with the other —terrible to behold; return then, O son of Sâkya to your palace, and prevent these things by your righteous government!" And so the Gâtha says [to the same effect].

Then Bôdhisatwa thought thus with himself, "Ah! thou Pisuna! this advice is for thine own profit, and not for mine;" having thought thus, he added, "Mâra râja Pisuna! having taken my seat here, seated as I am, my legs crossed, immovable and firm, it would be difficult, by any prospect of pleasure, to move me! for my aim is to obtain the Nectar of true Religion (immortality). Mâra râja Pisuna! do what you list; pursue your own design (but it will be in vain)."

Then Mâra, enraged, rejoined, "Thou mendicant son of Sâkya! why sittest thou here as a solitary recluse beneath this tree?" Having uttered this angry question, and receiving no reply, he continued, "See you not, oh Shaman! my army of warriors approaching—see yonder Yakshas that feed on the reeking flesh of men! each holding his terrible bow and his arrows—see those clubs and knives and swords! see yonder host of elephants, horses and chariots. Listen to the sound of their approach—see those Nâgas, each riding on a pitch-black cloud, and launching forth the fiery lightnings! see how the world shakes at their approach." Then Mâra snatching a sword from his side, clutched it in his hand, and rushing onward toward Bôdhisatwa, he exclaimed, "Thou Sâkya mendicant! I will smite thee in twain with my sword, as the warrior youth divides the plantain tree at a stroke!"

And so the Gâtha says:

"I, with my precious diamond sword,
Grasped in my hand before your very eyes,
Will smite thee in twain as a plantain branch,
Oh! Shaman, if thou dost not quickly depart!"

And to this Bôdhisatwa replied in the following Gâthas:

"Though all this world were filled with Devils,
Each grasping his sword, heavy and large as Sumeru,
Not one hair of my head should they injure,
Much less be able to divide my body in twain.
Your sword, oh Mâra, may be great and strong,
But I am bent on the acquisition of Supreme Wisdom.
If you can prevent it, oh Mâra! do so;
Hesitate not—but follow out your plan, and do your worst."

Then follows a further altercation, summed up in the following Gâthas:

"Though all the void of space rained swords upon my head,
Though limb by limb and joint by joint my body were divided,
If I attain not to the other shore of life and death,
Never will I leave this Bôdhi Tree."

To whom, with the roar of a lion, Mâra rejoined:

"My soldiers, horses, elephants, chariots,
All equipped with spiritual arms,
Accoutred, cap-à-pied, grasping their clubs,
Are coming on to take thy life.
It will be hard for me henceforth to rescue thee,
However much I would; to help thee now is far too late."

To which Bôdhisatwa rejoined:

"My helpers are the Devas of the pure abodes,

My sword is wisdom; strategy, my bow and arrow;
With these to conquer thee is easy, Mâra!
Easy as for the drunken elephant to trample down the plantain bough."

Then Mâra summoned all his host, enraged with greatest fury, Yakshas and Rakshas! and addressed them thus, "Now then ye braves! go quickly, bring hither mountains, rocks, and trees—bring bows and arrows, swords and clubs; clutch your diamond maces, spears, and halberds—every kind of implement, and hurl them down on yonder Sâkya youth of the Kshatriya caste. Crush him to powder—rain your arrows down as hail from heaven!" Then these Yakshas, having heard Mâra's commands, forthwith hastened to obey. They hurried to the front 10,000 myriad Yakshas and Rakshas, Pisatchas, Kumbhandas, of every shape and form, of every colour and appearance, of changing hue terrible to see! What cries and shrieks were heard! some headed like the elephant, others of horse-shaped front, others like camels, some like the ass, others with horns and head of ox, some like rams and lions, some like wolves and foxes, monkeys, and desert stags; some like birds, others like the vast Maka turtle, some with snake's head, others of reptile shape, others half horse, half elephant! [and endless other monstrous combinations.] Some with three heads on one body, some with many heads, some with heads but no face. Others all face[1] and no head, some with half a head and no face, others with half a face and no head! Some with two heads, but neither with face, etc. Some with a face without eyes, others with one eye, others with two and three eyes. Some without ears, others with one, two, three, and many ears. Some without hands, others without arms; some with one, two, three, and many hands and arms. Some with no feet, etc. Some with their heads below and their feet upwards. Some with their hands and legs dangling by the skin; others with eyes protruding from their heads; others with ears as large as the mountain sheep or ass; others with monkey-ears, etc.; others with teeth like swords and tongues like spears; others with bellies vast, others with none, etc. Thus this vile army gathered around Bôdhisatwa.

[Kiouen XXVIII contains 6365 words and cost 3.181 taels].

[1] This is the scene represented on the North Gate at Sanchi.

CHAPTER XXIX.

ADVANCING thus, mounted on horses, camels, buffaloes, or in chariots, they came from the four quarters. Of every shape, kind and colour, uttering every kind of unearthly sound, armed with every sort of weapon, they came. Then darkness filled the air, and the earth quaked, whilst the seas on every side bubbled up with affright. And so the Gâtha says:

"The four great seas swelled their waves, the earth shook,
On all sides the lightnings gleamed, and strange sounds were heard.
The moon and stars in the void of space withdrew their light,
And dark as midnight nature hid her face."

Then a certain Nâga Râja, named Chi-ti (holding-earth) secretly wishing that Bôdhisatwa might overcome Mâra, vomited forth a pestilential vapour, and afflicted his body so that he could not rest. The Devas of the pure abodes also exercised their influence of love and beneficence in favour of Bôdhisatwa, while all the Devas of space, in strong faith and reverence for Bôdhisatwa, shouted in derision at Mâra and his army. And so the Gâtha says:

"All the Devas assembling beneath the Bôdhi tree,
Seeing Mâra and his army desiring to destroy Bôdhisatwa,
Exercising faith in the power of the law to save men,
Uttered derisive shouts and jeers, hoo! hoo! ha! ha!"

Then Bôdhisatwa, unmoved, and with perfect composure, addressed Mâra thus, "Oh, Mâra Pisuna! I am born a Kshatriya, and therefore I scorn to lie.[1] I tell you then my determination is fixed. Do thy worst without delay!" Then Mâra said, "Even so! now then I will grind thy body into fragments, prepare thyself for the fight!" Bôdhisatwa replied, "I have neither bow nor sword wherewith to smite thee; nevertheless, oh Mâra! I will conquer thee, ere I attain the aim of my life, supreme enlightenment!" Then Mâra hurried on his followers and said, "Haste ye! use your utmost strength—show no pity for this child of the Sâkya race—

---

[1] That is, on account of the oath taken by the Kshatriya. It has been well observed that this is the origin of the "word of honour" in chivalry.

use every means in your power to fill him with affright." Then they advanced belching forth fire and flame—with barbed and fiery tongues and sharpened teeth, wishing to grind Bôdhisatwa to bits, even as a lion tears his prey. Such fearful sights they exhibited, fit to alarm the soul; but Bodhisatwa still remained unmoved. And so the Gâtha says:

"The armies of Mâra came in terrible array,
But the Holy One remained unmoved and calm,
Even as a wise and prudent elder when a child
Disports before him; so Bodhisatwa looked on Mâra."

Then an angry demon advanced towards Bôdhisatwa with a long sword (spear?) to cleave him down, when lo! the sword stuck to the demon's hand and would not move; and so, with rocks and mountains, which they tried to hurl upon him, these also would not leave their hands, whilst others broke in fragments and dispersed themselves through space; meantime, the weapons, which they hurled thick as the rays of the sun when it shines forth from a dark cloud, these changed themselves to flowers, and fell at the feet of Bodhisatwa. Moreover, some were rendered blind so that they could not see, and others were unable to move, so that they could not approach to Bodhisatwa. And so the Gâtha says—

"The army of Mâra, confused and dazed,
Used every stratagem to slay the saint;
But they could not shake the seat he occupied,
By reason of his vow, in virtue of his firm resolve."

Then such awful sounds and screams and yells were heard—like beasts and birds and demons all combined—but yet 'twas vain. At length the son of Mâra, Shreshti by name, embraced his father's knees, and begged him to desist in the attempt to injure Bodhisatwa, but uselessly! for Mâra now advanced toward the seat beneath the Bodhi tree. Then an angel of the Pure Abodes, invisible to the eye, seeing Mâra advancing, uttered the following words with pleasant voice—"Attempt not, O Mâra! to disturb this holy one! Give up your phantom show! return to your own abode! for never can you move this holy saint; as well might the wind lash against the sides of Sumeru, and hope to overturn it. And so the Gâtha says—

"The fire will as soon lose its power to burn,
And the flowings of the water cease and stand still;
As soon will the earth lose its power to hold and sustain,
Or the wind forget its power to blow and rest,
As the power of this one's virtuous life and conduct
Fail in the end to lead him to attain his vow.
* * * * * *
Desist, then, from your efforts, for this holy one
Shall certainly accomplish all he seeks to do."

But still Mâra, maddened with rage, advanced. Then the eight guardian angels of the place, whose names were these [eight names given] encouraged and comforted Bodhisatwa in various ways.

And so numerous other Devas came to strengthen him.

(The rest of this book is occupied in detailing the temptations of Mâra, and the supporting influences of the Devas.)

[Kiouen XXIX contains 61,57 words, and cost 3.078 taels.]

CHAPTER XXX.

At this time, Bodhisatwa, having defeated and overpowered all the evil influences and devices of Mâra and his companions, proceeded to pass through the various grades of perfect self-abstraction (dhyâna), and so having put away for ever all remnants of selfishness and evil desire, the first three watches of the night being passed, on the dawn of the fourth watch he attained to the perfect state of Enlightenment known as Anuttara Samyak Sambhôdi. And so the Gâtha says—

"Three parts of that eventful night were gone,
The stars that indicated the fourth part just appeared,
All source of sorrow now destroyed, Bodhi attained;
This is what men call "perfect Enlightenment."

At this time the heavens, the earth, and all the spaces between the encircling zones of rock, were lit up with a supernatural splendour; whilst flowers and every kind of precious perfume fell down in thick profusion around Bhagavata, who had now attained perfect enlightenment; and whilst the earth shook six times, the Devas sang together in the midst of space, a joyous song, and rained down upon earth every kind of sweet flower—the Mandara, the Mahamandara, and so on; all kinds of garments, gold, silver, precious stones, and so on, also fell at the feet of Buddha. There was no ill-feeling or hatred in the hearts of men; but whatever want there was, whether of food, or drink, or raiment, was at once supplied; the blind received their sight, the deaf heard, and the dumb spake. Those who were bound in hell were released; and every kind of being,—beasts, demons, and all created things,—found peace and rest. And so the Gâtha says—

"At this time there was no angry thought on earth;
All sorrows disappeared, and there was great joy;
The mad and drunken came to their right mind,
And all who were in fear, were comforted."

Then the world-honoured one, having arrived at perfect enlightenment, uttered the following Gâthas—

"Through ages past have I acquired continual merit,
That which my heart desired have I now attained.
How quickly have I arrived at the ever-constant condition,
And landed on the very shore of Nirvâna.
The sorrows and opposition of the world,
The Lord of the Kama lokas, Mâra Pisuna,
These are unable now to affect me, they are wholly destroyed;
By the power of religious merit and of wisdom are they cast away.
Let a man but persevere with unflinching resolution,
And seek Supreme Wisdom, it will not be hard to acquire it;
When once obtained, then farewell to all sorrows,
All sin and guilt are for ever done away."

This was the very first utterance of Tathâgata after attaining Supreme Wisdom.

[Kiouen XXX contains 6,540 words and cost 3.27 taels.]

CHAPTER XXXI.

§ 1. At this time, when Bôdhisatwa, pointing to the earth at early dawn, overcame and destroyed the devil and his followers, the earth shook six times, and up to the very highest point of space was the reverberation heard.

Then all the people of the world, observing these strange phenomena, inquired anxiously one of another as to their meaning, and further, they consulted the Rishis and soothsayers as to the meaning of these strange portents. At length these various Rishis and soothsayers replied, "In the country of Magadha, near the village of Gaya, there has been a deadly contest betwixt one who has left his home to become a king of the highest law, and one who seeks to be king of the world of sin; and the former has just prevailed, and beaten down the latter; and soon he will begin to preach and establish his kingdom amongst men, by declaring the tidings of his most excellent doctrine. And so the Gâtha says [to the same effect].

At this time also, Suddhôdana Râja, unable to sleep through restlessness and fear, was informed by his Brahman soothsayers that if he would wait awhile with patience, they would explain the cause. Meanwhile, Mâya, the mother of Buddha, who had acquired a heavenly body, taking the form of a hand-maiden, descended from heaven to the spot where Suddhôdana, and Yasôdharâ, the mother of Rahula, were, and spake thus, "Mahârâja, be it known to you that on this night, your son, Siddârtha, has attained supreme wisdom, and on this account the earth shook."

Again the Devas of the Rupa worlds, perceiving all the phenomena we have before named, were also filled with doubt as to their meaning, on which the world-honoured one uttered the following words with his own lion voice—"Now have I entirely cut myself away from the bondage of all impure desires. The lustful heart is entirely destroyed, and all sources of sorrow; the waters shall no longer flow, no further form of life shall I receive, no more to be tossed upon the waves of misery, I have crossed over and for ever escaped."

Then all those Devas, having heard these words, reflected that Tathâgata had obtained complete deliverance, and then their hearts rejoiced, they exulted and were unable to repress their feelings of triumph, they scattered flowers and poured down the choicest unguents and perfumes. Meanwhile, Mâra Pisuna, witnessing all this, sat down at some distance from Tathâgata, his heart filled with grief, and whilst he pretended to draw something on the ground, he thought with himself thus—"How is it that I, who am able to hold in my power both Sâkra and all the other Devas, have been defeated, with all my host of followers, by this Shaman of the Sâkya race?"

The Story of the Resolute Merchant.

§ 2. In explanation of this we must have recourse to some subsequent teaching of Buddha, when all the Bhikshus were gathered round him and inquired thus—"Oh! seldom-seen Tathâgata! we fain would know by what power of resolution and fixed determination the world-honoured one has attained to this glorious condition of perfection." On which Tathâgata rejoined, "Know ye, O Bhikshus! it was not on this occasion only that I have exercised this resolution and power of fixed determination (virya), so as to arrive at the condition of Sambôdhi and the seven[1] Bôdhyangas; but I remember, in years gone by, how by the same power of perseverance I recovered a very precious Mani gem." Then all the Bhikshus requested Buddha on their account to explain the particulars of this event. At this time Buddha addressed them as follows—"Attend, then, O ye Bhikshus, and consider well what I say. I remember in years gone by that I was a merchant prince who entered the sea in order to gather precious gems, and whilst so engaged I obtained one Mani gem of inestimable value; but suddenly, after getting possession of it, I let it fall into the sea, and so lost it. Then, having taken a ladle, I began with fixed determination to empty out the water of the great sea, wishing to dry it up with a view to recover the gem. Then the Sea-spirit, observing what was done, forthwith reflected thus with himself—'This man is foolish and ignorant; he has no wisdom or judgment; for how can he hope with a ladle to empty out the water of the

---

[1] *Vide* Eitel, *sub-voce.*

wide and boundless ocean, and then the Sea-spirit began to recite the following Gâthas—

"'There are many sorts of men and other creatures in the world,
Who will do all sorts of things to get wealth thereby;
But now I see you are a man wholly bereft of sense,
Beyond all I have ever seen amongst mortals!
This great ocean is eighty-four thousand yojanas in width,
And do you hope to dry it up and empty it with a ladle?
If you were to work from the day of your birth
Till death in emptying out your ladlefuls,
The water you emptied away would be but a drop
Compared with this wide and profound ocean,
You are ignorant, therefore, and void of reflection,
Like one who would take Mount Sumeru for an earring.'

"At this time I (the merchant prince) answered the Sea-Spirit thus—

"'Divine Being! this is not well said on your part,
Desiring as you do to prevent me from emptying the sea,
You may now watch me with fixed mind, and see
How soon I will empty the ocean and make it dry;
But you, because the long delay you expect in waiting
Would weary you, therefore you grieve and fret.
But I swear that my resolution shall never flag,
I will empty this ocean, I will render it dry,
The precious gem which I have lost in its depths,
On its account I desire to dry up these waters,
Then shall I recover my priceless gem,
And, having obtained it, I will return home again.'

"At this time, the Sea-spirit, having heard these words, was filled with anxiety, and reflected thus—'This man, so firm in his resolution, will really empty out the sea and make it dry;'—and so, having reflected thus, forthwith he gave back to me (the merchant prince) my priceless jewel; and, in so doing, repeated the following Gâthas—

"'All men should encourage a resolute and firm determination,
And vow that what they undertake they will never give up,
I see now the power of this principle—
Having recovered your lost gem, go to your home.'"

At this time the world-honoured one also uttered this Gâtha—

"In every way and on every occasion encourage a resolute heart.
Irresolution and vacillation bring with them sorrow;
But when once the mind has been made up for good,
The wise man hereby soon acquires perfect knowledge."

Then Buddha said, "That merchant prince was myself in a former birth, and by the same resolution which I then displayed, have I now acquired the Highest Intelligence and the seven species of Supreme Wisdom" (Bôdyangas).

The Story of the Two Parrots.

§ 3. THEN the Bhikshus again addressed Buddha and said, "It is wonderful indeed and incomprehensible, O Tathâgata, that one man should be able by himself to overcome the combined temptations of Mâra and all his associates (as you have done);" and, having thus spoken, they remained silent. Then the world-honoured replied—"It was not on this occasion only, but in days gone by on many occasions, did I overcome by myself the efforts of Mâra to destroy me. I remember in years gone by, ages ago, there were two macaws,—brothers one to the other, the name of one was Malligiri (hair-wreath-mountain), the other called Sutagiri (or Sudagiri). Suddenly, whilst these two parrots were seated together on the top of a tree, there swooped down a great falcon, and caught up the little one and flew away with it into the air. Then the one brother said to the other—

"'One man alone may cause much grief;
One man alone may cause great joy;
Then bite and tear as best you can the falcon's flesh,
As soon as he perceives the pain he will release his hold.
Your body indeed is little, and my strength is light,
But only persevere, nor give up what you undertake.'
The little parrot, having heard these words of his brother,
Put forth his utmost strength and force,
Wishing to make his efforts felt as much as possible,
He bit the falcon's body in the most tender part.
No sooner did the falcon feel the pain and anguish,

Than he quickly let the parrot slip from him,
And on account of what his body felt,
He flew around and round, seeking to escape,
From the cunning parrot,
Who fled away thro' space;
Then the falcon, seeing the parrot thus fly off,
Departed, seeking some other means of getting nourishment.
Now, as to this parrot that attacked the falcon,
It was myself who by myself alone
Thus conquered and escaped that enemy.
How much more now by my accumulated merit
Should I not conquer and defeat the power of Mâra?
So learn this lesson well! ye Bhikshus here assembled!"

The Story of the Cunning Tortoise.

§ 4. AGAIN the world-honoured one proceeded to narrate the following Jâtaka: "I remember in years and ages past there was a certain river called Paryata; on the banks of this river there lived a man who gained his livelihood by making flower-wreaths; moreover, he had a garden bordering along the side of the river. Now, at this time there was a certain tortoise which was in the habit of coming up out of the water, and, going to the middle of this man's flower garden, he used to eat what he could find here and there, and by so doing he trampled down and destroyed the flowers; and then he departed. The gardener seeing this, and observing the tracks of the tortoise in every direction, perceiving how his flowers were destroyed, immediately formed a device to catch the tortoise. Accordingly, he made a wicker cage, and soon entrapped him. Then when he was about to kill and eat him, the tortoise thought thus with himself—'What can I do to escape from this danger? What device or cunning plan can I adopt? How can I take this gardener in?' Having thought thus, he immediately addressed his captor in these verses—

"'I have but just come from the river, and am covered with mud,
You should put aside your flowers and proceed to wash me,
Lest my body, covered with impure mire,
Should perhaps pollute your basket and its flowers.'

"Then the gardener thought thus—'This is good advice. I never thought of that. I will go and wash his body in the stream, and get rid of the dirt.' Immediately then he went and dipped the body of the tortoise in the river, thinking to wash him, and putting him on the top of a stone for this purpose, he flung water over him, when suddenly the tortoise, exerting his whole strength, jumped off the stone, and escaped into the river. Then the gardener, seeing the tortoise paddling away into deep water, thought thus with himself—'Wonderful indeed! that this tortoise should have been able thus to impose upon me! but now I will repay him in his own coin, and deceive him also, with a view to get him on land again;' on this the flower-seller spake this Gâtha to the tortoise—

"'My dear tortoise! listen whilst I tell you my idea.
You no doubt have plenty of relations and dear friends,
I will make you a beautiful wreath and hang it round your neck,
That when you return home there may be much joy at the sight of you.'

"Then the tortoise thought thus—'This flower-seller is telling me a great falsehood—he wants to delude me. His mother is ill abed, and his sister, so-and-so, is busy making garlands to get money enough to support them all; and yet he tells me that he will make a garland and give it me for nothing. It is all false; he only wants to catch me and eat me.' So the tortoise replied to the flower-seller in these words—

"'Your family are busy in brewing wine to have a feast,
They are getting all sorts of tasty food to eat, no doubt;
Go home, then, and give your orders, my friend;
Let the tortoise be boiled, with forced-meat balls in plenty.'"

Then Buddha added, "I was the tortoise at that time, the flower-seller was Mâra Pisuna, he wished to entrap me with delusive speech, but was not able."

The Story of the Foolish Dragon.

§ 5. Again Buddha related this Jâtaka—"I remember in years gone by, ages ago, there was a certain dragon (kau—a dragon with horns), living in the great sea, whose wife being pregnant, suddenly took an extraordinary desire to have a monkey's heart to eat, and because of this longing her body became sorely afflicted so that she had no rest or ease for a moment. Then the male fish, seeing his wife thus afflicted and her natural beautiful colour fading away, and all her appearance changed, asked her and said, 'My dear! what is it troubling you so, what food is it you desire, seeing that you eat nothing that I provide; why is this?' Then the female dragon was silent, and answered not a word. Again her husband asked the same question, and pressed her for a reply; on which she said, 'If you could give me what I want, then I would tell you at once, but if you are unable to do so, why should I trouble you about it?' To this he replied, 'Only tell me what you want, and if it is possible by the use of any device or craft to get it, trust me, you shall have your desire.' To this she answered, 'I am longing for a monkey's heart to eat; can you get me this, do you think, or not?' Then the husband answered, 'What you want is a thing very difficult to get; for, in fact, I live here in the great sea and monkeys live in the mountain forests, on the tops of the trees; how, then, can I get at them?' To which the wife replied, 'This only I know, that if I cannot procure what I long for, my time will come prematurely, and I fear I shall die.' Then the husband said, 'My dear! be patient. I will go and try to accomplish it, and I cannot tell you how delighted I shall be if I succeed!'

"Forthwith the dragon went to the shore, and going up on the bank he saw, not very far off, a large tree called the Udambara. Now, it so happened that at that time there was a great monkey living on the tree top and partaking of the fruit and eating it. Then the dragon, having espied the monkey thus feasting on the top of the tree, gradually approached till he came under it, and then, looking up, he spoke in gentle words and said, as he saluted the monkey, 'All hail! all hail, thou shining one (básad?), what art thou doing up there? art thou not afraid to move, lest in seeking thy food thou shouldst tumble down and come to an untimely end?' To whom the monkey replied, 'No, dear sir! I have no such fear as that.' Then the dragon went on to say, 'What, then, do you find to eat up there?'—to which the monkey answered, 'I am living here in this Udambara tree, and feeding on its fruit (seeds).' Then the Dragon said, 'I am filled with inexpressible joy in seeing you thus, and I beg your leave to form a close friendship with you; let us from this time be allies; but, why, let me ask, do you live in this place, feeding on the scanty fruit of this solitary tree. What pleasure can you find here? Come down, I pray you, and let me conduct you. I will carry you over the great sea to yonder shore, where there are vast forests of every kind of tree with flowers and fruit. There is the Amra tree, and the Djambu tree, and the Lakaja (*likusa*, or, *lakasa*, a bread-fruit tree), and the Banava (*phanava ?*), and the Tinduka tree, and many others besides.' Then the monkey said, 'But tell me, pray, how am I to reach that place, the water is deep and wide, and very dangerous, how can I possibly float myself across it?' Then the dragon said to the monkey, 'I will take you on my back and carry you over. You have only to come down from the tree, and get on the top of my back and all is done!'

"Then the monkey, because he had no fixed mind, and had little knowledge or experience of the world, came down from the top of the tree, and got on the back of the dragon. Then the dragon thought thus with himself—'Well done! I have managed this business exceedingly well!' and immediately he proceeded to make his journey homewards. Then he plunged into the water, and began to dive downwards towards his dwelling-place; on which the monkey cried out, 'My dear friend, where are you going, diving down in this way all of a sudden?' On which the dragon replied, 'Never you mind!' On which the monkey said again, 'Oh, pray tell me what you are going to do?' Then the dragon said, 'I have a wife very sad and ill, and she has taken a strong fancy to have your heart to eat, and that's the reason I am taking you to her in such a hurry.' Then the monkey thought thus with himself —'Alas! alas! this is a very unlucky job for me! I have brought this ruin on myself; alas! I must think of some crafty expedient to get myself out of this difficulty, if I can.'

"Thinking thus with himself, he addressed the dragon and said, 'Illustrious and dear friend! I am extremely sorry, but as a matter of fact my heart at this moment is on the top of the Udambara tree, where you first saw me, and I didn't think of bringing it with me when I left. Why did you not tell me the truth at the time that I might have brought it with me? But now, my dear friend, if you will just return for a moment, I will go and fetch my heart, and then go back with you to your wife.' The dragon, having heard the monkey's speech, immediately complied with his request, and the two went back together. No sooner had they got within a short distance of the shore than the monkey with all his strength gave a leap off the dragon's back, and scampered with all his might up to the top of the Udambara tree, whilst the dragon took up his position below. After a while, perceiving the monkey made no move as if to come down, the dragon addressed him and said, 'Come, my dear friend! be quick and come down, that I may carry you to my house as we agreed.' But the monkey remained quite silent, and gave no sign of an intention to come down; and so the dragon, after a long time, seeing no prospect of his coming down, began this Gâtha and said—

"'My excellent monkey-friend, having taken your heart,
Come down quickly from the top of the tree,
I want to take you over to yonder forest,
To the place where there are trees and fruit of every kind.'

"Then the monkey thought with himself, 'what a fool this dragon is!' and immediately answered in a Gâtha:

"'Your plan, old fellow! is a very excellent one;
But your wisdom is very little indeed.
Just think now for a moment and reflect:
Did you ever know a single creature without a heart?
As for those forests—no doubt the fruits are beautiful,
The Amra fruit, and all the rest you talked about,
But do you know I prefer just now not to visit them,
I would rather stop here and eat the Udambara fruit.'"

Then Buddha said to his followers, "You should know that at this time I was the monkey, and that the dragon was Mâra Pisuna, and as he could not catch me then by his stratagem, so neither has he now been able to entice me by his promise of bodily pleasures."

The Story of the Prudent Quail.

§ 6. Then the Bhikshus said again (as before). On which Buddha replied, "it was not on this occasion only that I was enabled to defeat Mâra; but I remember in years gone by, ages ago, there was a certain hunter, who having found out a secluded spot where the birds were in the habit of alighting to feed, he himself proceeded to the place, and having arrived there, he made a certain covering of twigs and branches, and put it over himself as he lay in wait, seated on the ground. Then the birds seeing this green looking fabric when they came, alighted on the top of it, whilst the hunter seeing them on the top, slily put his hand through, and dragging them in killed them at his leisure. Then one bird having observed what happened, thought thus with himself: 'This hut-like covering seems to be able to move about from place to place, whereas all the trees are fixed and immovable; it is certain that there must be somebody beneath the covering.' And so this bird kept at a distance from it, and the hunter was not able to catch him. And so the Gâtha says:

"'I observe that all the trees of the forest,
Whether it be that which is called the Vîra,
Or the Aralu, or the Djambu tree,
Or the Motchara, or the Tchanda tree,
Are ever fixed and remain in one place,
Even from the time they first began to grow.
But this tree-like structure ever moves from place to place;
There must be some one alive beneath it,
And if that some one have an evil intention,
It is better that I should keep as far away as possible.
My heart is full of doubt and fear;
This wicked plan augurs no good to any of us;
For if he catches me he will certainly kill me,
Even as I remember in days gone by,
How I escaped from the net of the fowler.
Having gained wisdom by this experience, I will be off.'"

Then Buddha added, "at that time I was the wise bird, and Mâra Pisuna was the hunter; and as I then discerned the stratagem of the fowler, so also was I able to perceive all the varied and hideous forms of the army of Mâra." And so he ended with this Gâtha:

"If there be no deep reflection with men,
How is it possible to obtain superior wisdom?
Now, because of deep and long consideration
Have I escaped the toils (of Mâra) and obtained a condition of rest (wou-wei)."

The Offering of Food by the Two Merchants.

§ 7. Now at this time, after Buddha had arrived at Perfect Enlightenment beneath the Bôdhi tree, he remained seated there during seven complete days and nights, ravished with the happiness of his condition, and he ate nothing.

After this interval, having aroused himself from his rapture, seated on his lion throne, on the first night he considered (or realised) in their right order the twelve Nidânas, and then in a reverse order, he identified these as one and the same; he traced them from the first cause and followed them through every concurrent circumstance. From ignorance he ascertained came merit and demerit (sanscara); from these came consciousness (vijnyâna); from this came names and things (nama, rupa); from this the six ayatanas; from these touch (sparsa); from this sensation (vedana); from this came love (trishna); from this cleaving to existence (upadana); from this reproduction; from this old age, and disease, and death; and from these the whole category of sorrows. Then the world-honoured one having recognised these laws of connection, uttered the following Gâthas:

"Whoever, practising the rules of a Brahmana, observes the world around him (tchu-fă, *ye damma*),
Sees at once that these things are produced by mutual relationship;
Perceiving that the world around him is produced by this mutual dependence,
He recognises then that all phenomena are but the result of cause and effect."[1]

Then the world-honoured one, in the middle of the night, having fully gone through these successive links of the chain, began to return in a reverse order, and he concluded thus: destroy ignorance, and you destroy the cause of merit and demerit; destroy this, and you destroy consciousness, and so on. Then the world-honoured one again uttered these Gâthas:

"Whoever practises the rules of a Brahmana, and observes the world around him,

---

[1] This seems to be the well-known stanza, "Ye damma hetu prabhasa," etc.

Immediately perceiving that things are produced by the laws of mutual relationship;
Seeing that things are thus the result of dependence on one or the other,
He concludes also that by destroying this relationship things will come to an end."

Then the world-honoured one, after the night had passed, having thoroughly investigated these laws, and perceived clearly that by destroying ignorance all is destroyed, and by the power of ignorance all is produced, repeated the following Gâthas:

"If there be a man practising the rules of a Brahmaṅa, and observing the way of the world,
Who forthwith perceives the rules of production and the consequent method of destruction,
This man firmly fixed, having overcome the fascinations of Mâra,
Stands like yonder Sun Deva, illustrious in the midst of the vault of space."

Then the world-honoured one, having arisen from his lion throne, and going a short distance from the Bôdhi Tree, sitting down with his legs crossed, remained immovable during other seven days, beholding the Bôdhi Tree without removing his eyes; and as he sat he thought thus, "Here have I loosed myself from all the concourse of sorrows, and have cast away the burden of them." [*In after time a tower was erected on this spot, and called "not lifting the eyes."*] Then after seven days, the world-honoured one, arising from his ecstasy, uttered the following Gâthas:

"In this sacred arena I have got rid of every source of sorrow,
And seated here beholding that sacred throne on which I sat,
I remember it was there I fulfilled my vows, I arrived at the other shore,
In that place it was I reached the full enjoyment of Bôdhi."

Then the world-honoured one, proceeding from the tower called "the eye unmoved," proceeded slowly and with dignity to the place called Marîchi (ray of light), where he walked up and down, and then sat down and again for seven days sat still with his legs crossed, enjoying the delights of emancipation. After seven days, having come from his condition of ecstasy, then Kâla Nâga Râja (*black color*), having come to the place where he was, paid homage to the world-honoured one, and took his place on one side and addressed him thus: "World-honoured! from remote ages, I have ever presented a place of abode (hall or palace) to the Buddhas on this very spot, and they have all deigned to accept the offering at my hands; deign then, oh Lord! to receive from me on this occasion also, this glorious palace in which you may abide."

Buddha accepts the gift, and after seven days he delivers for the benefit of Kâla, the triple refuge, and the five laws, on which Kâla becomes a disciple. After this a Nâga Râja, called Muchalinda, comes to the spot, and presents him with a similar abode; and when a storm occurred, wound round the hall with seven folds, and spread his seven-fold hood over Buddha to shelter him; and when Buddha arose from his ecstasy, he appeared before him as a Brahman youth, and told him what he had done. He also received the three refuges, and the five commandments, and became a disciple. After this the shepherd boy, who had protected Bôdhisatwa, during his six years' penance, by planting some boughs of the Nyagrodha tree over him, and had in consequence been born in the Trâyastriñshas heaven as a Deva, now came and worshipped the world-honoured one, and besought him to sit beneath that tree in contemplation. This the world-honoured one consented to do, and remained in rapt contemplation beneath that Nyagrodha tree for seven days. After this he delivered to the Deva the triple form of refuge and the five commandments, and he also became a disciple, the first of all the Devas.

[Kiouen XXXI contains 6,360 words, and cost 3.18 taels].

CHAPTER XXXII.

At this time time the world-honoured one, having sat for seven days beneath the Nyagrodha tree, arose and proceeded slowly towards a grove called Ktchirnika,[1] where he remained for another seven days enjoying the fruition of deliverance.

It was now forty-nine days since Sujata, the village girl, had given him the milk and rice, and since then he had eaten nothing. Now, it so happened that at this time there were two merchant princes of North India, whose names were Tripusha and the other Bhallika. These men were very prudent, and had taken five hundred wagon loads of valuable goods to Middle India, and were now removing to North India with a corresponding amount of valuable property. Now, when they were not far from this Ktchirnika grove, each of these merchants had an ox that went before the caravan, and whenever there was a place of danger they showed symptoms of fear, and so warned the merchants beforehand. Now it came to pass that the Guardian Spirit of that Tchirnika grove just at this time assuming a bodily form and standing in front of the oxen, they were afraid to go on. Then the two merchants, gently striking the oxen with a twig of the Utpala flower, would have them advance, but they still refused, and so all the other oxen were brought to a standstill; moreover the wheels of the various wagons remained fixed, and the whole caravan was obliged to halt. Then the two merchantmen were filled with fear, and the very hairs of their bodies stood erect as they spake thus one to the other—"What unlucky circumstance is this which has befallen us!" Then each of them going two or three paces from where they stood, with clasped hands and prostrate forms paid reverence to all the Gods[2] and all the spirits with their utmost strength, and as they adored they said, "Oh! that we who are involved in this calamity and in fear of death, might find a swift deliverance!" Then the Guardian Deva of the grove, assuming a body and appearing to the merchants, addressed them thus—"Be not afraid, oh merchantmen! there is no cause for apprehension in this place; but the world-

---

[1] Fouceaux gives it Tchîrikas, p. 356.

[2] Tien.

honoured Tathâgata, having arrived at Supreme Wisdom, is now dwelling in this wood; and it is now forty-nine days since he has eaten anything. This, then, is your opportunity for making some offering of food to him that you may obtain an enduring recompense of peace and rest." Then those merchants, obedient to the words of the Deva, prepared an offering of honey and wheat, and brought it to the place where Buddha was. Then the merchants, beholding the glory and grace of the body of Tathâgata, were filled with faith, and adored at his feet. They then addressed him thus—"Would that the world-honoured one, on our account, would accept this pure offering of honey and wheat." Then the world-honoured one, reflecting that all former Buddhas had first received the offering of an alms-dish, considered thus with himself—"But in what vessel am I to receive this offering?" Then the four Heavenly Kings, each bringing a golden alms-dish, came to the place to present them to Buddha, and besought him to accept them. But he refused, as such costly dishes were unbecoming a recluse. Then they brought silver dishes, and emerald and ruby dishes; but yet he would not accept them. At length they brought four earthen dishes and offered them, on which Buddha, causing them to unite in one (lest there should be jealousy), accepted the one from them all. At this time, the world-honoured one repeated the following Gâthas:—[a Gâtha to each of the four kings].

Then Buddha, having accepted the offering of the two merchants, delivered to them the triple Refuge, and they became his disciples. Finally, he delivered their caravan from its difficulties and presented them (in consequence of their request for some memorial of him) with a hair and fragments of his nails, telling them that hereafter a stone should fall from heaven near the place where they lived, and that there they should erect a pagoda and worship the relics as though they were Buddha himself. On their feeling some doubts, he related to them what had happened when Dipankara was the Supreme Buddha (the story of the five-stalked flower), and how the Devas had taken his hair after he had become a recluse, and erected a pagoda over it in the Heavens: after this they took the relics with joyful heart and departed. After this, having partaken of the food of the two merchants, Buddha was visited with a sickness and colic, on which a medicine-Deva brought him an Amra fruit, which healed him; and in consequence of this good act, Buddha delivered to him and his wife, the Devî, the triple formula of Refuge, which led her to become a female disciple—the first who became so among women. Then Buddha, having buried the Amra stone, immediately there sprung up a tree covered with fruit and flowers. Then the world-honoured one felt his disease perfectly removed.]

[Kiouen XXII contains 6,568 words, and cost 3.284 taels.]

CHAPTER XXXIII.

The Exhortation of Brahma Deva.

§ 1. At this time, the world-honoured one reflected thus with himself—"The condition (Law) to which I have arrived is certainly a deep and mysterious one, difficult to perceive, even as the finest dust is hard to see, and its mode and place of existence hard to determine. No teacher or cunning man of wisdom has brought me to this condition. But this system of the twelve Nidânas[1] is not for man to comprehend, but for Buddha alone; although I could desire to proclaim this Law to men, yet how can they receive it? it would be useless for me to make the attempt."

Thinking thus, that he had acquired this knowledge from no human source at any time, the world-honoured one remained in that place lost in thought; as the Gâthas say—

"Through much sorrow and suffering have I attained to this condition.
How then can I make it known to others in a moment or without preparation.
How difficult for men to receive such a Law, bound as they are by the chain of evil desire, doubt, anger, and hate, etc."

So Tathâgata, perceiving the gravity of the circumstances in which he was placed, desired to remain where he was in the place

---

[1] The twelve Nidânas are the well-known links in the chain of existence, taught by Buddha.

of solitude (aranya[1]), and not declare his Law to others; as the Gâtha says—

"Seeing all flesh weighed down by sorrow,
Oppressed by the weight of false teaching and heretical beliefs;
He thought,—how difficult to release them by declaring this inscrutable Law of mine,—
Thinking thus, he desired to remain as a solitary hermit (aranya)."

At this time, the Lord of the Sahalôkadhatu, Mahâ Brahma, the King of Heaven (Devarâja), whilst dwelling in his palace, perceived this condition of things, and having perfect cognizance of the intention of Buddha not to declare the Law, he assumed the appearance of a martial youth, with outstretched arms, and appeared thus before Tathâgata. Having saluted him by kneeling at his feet, he stood on one side and addressed him thus—"All hail (Sadhu)! honoured by the world! See now the world without a refuge—the seeds of virtue utterly gone: whilst the world-honoured one has arrived at perfect wisdom, he has acquired that unequalled Law, he has become perfectly enlightened, and yet he has suddenly resolved to enter an Aranya[2] place of abode, and not declare his Law for the good of men! Oh, let me exhort the excellent Tathâgata not to act thus; be not thus silent, oh world-honoured! but, for the sake of men sunk in sin, declare Thy Law! Let the love of Tathâgata constrain him so to do; let the compassionate heart of Sugata move him to declare his Law! for though the world be naughty, yet there are many prepared to receive this message of love, and to be converted, many who otherwise will perish; let the world-honoured one, therefore, resolve to preach his Law for the good of these!" And to the same tenor are the Gâthas.

[*These are omitted, being only another form of the same exhortation.*]

At this time, the world-honoured one, having heard the exhortation of Brahma Devarâja, was moved by love for all flesh to exercise

---

1 O'-lan-jo (*Méthode*, p. 477); does this explain the Tarâyana of Foucaux, p. 364?
2 That is, a hermit's cell—apart from men.

his Divine power of sight,[1] and so to ascertain the condition of the world around him. Thus by the power of his Divine Wisdom, he beheld men in the various conditions of ignorance, prepared for instruction, or advanced in knowledge, just as in a tank of different Lotus flowers, some are just emerging from the mud, but not yet above the water; others above the water, but not yet opened; others just opening, waiting for the power of external influences (the four elements) to complete their development; thus beholding by his wisdom the various conditions of men, and their several capabilities for further instruction and enlightenment, having thus acquainted himself with these circumstances, he addressed Brahma Devarâja thus—

"Oh! Brahma Devarâja, attend carefully!
I am willing now to open the gate of immortality[2]
If any will listen, let them come gladly;
Let them hearken to me as I declare the tidings of this Law (Religious System)."

Then Mahâ Brahma, having heard these words and understanding their purport, was filled with joy beyond expression, he rejoiced exceedingly and exulted at the news; and then, having respectfully walked round Tathâgata three times, suddenly he disappeared!

Then the world-honoured one began to consider with himself who was worthy first of all to hear the words of his teaching, and in a fit state to accept them. Considering thus, he remembered Udraka Râmaputra and his companions, and wished to preach to them first, but then a voice of an invisible Deva proclaimed to him from space that Râmaputra had already been dead six days; then, considering in what place he was now born, Buddha perceived that he was now an inhabitant of one of the Arupa worlds, the life of the inhabitants of which extends over eighty-four thousand great Kalpas. Then, by the exercise of his wisdom, Buddha saw that at the expiration of this period of time Udraka Râmaputra would return to this world and be born as a flying fox, and after that he would be born

[1] This exercise of the Divine power of sight is alluded to by the Priest Migettuwatte, in his "Controversy" with the Christian advocates held at Pantura, in Ceylon, Aug. 1873, *vide* p. 70 (*op. cit.*).

[2] Amrita.

in hell; on which Buddha exclaimed, "Alas! alas! for Udraka Râmaputra! Oh, that he had survived to hear the saving words of my Law! alas! alas!"

Then Buddha considered also what the condition of Alâra was; and a Deva, invisible in the air, exclaimed that Alâra Kalâma had died but yesterday, on which Buddha, by his eyes of Wisdom, found that he also had been born in one of the Arupa Heavens, where he would live for sixty-three thousand great Kalpas, after which he would be born on earth as a Râja, and after that in hell; on which again Buddha exclaimed, "Alas! alas! would that Alâra had survived that he might have heard the saving words of my Law! alas! alas!"

On Turning the Wheel of the Excellent Law.[1]

§ 2. Buddha, having thus considered who of all living creatures was in a condition first to hear his Law, remembered the five Rishis who had dwelt with him during the time of his severe penance, and perceiving their fitness for it, he resolved to turn the wheel of the Law first for their benefit. He then considered where they dwelt, and using the power of his Divine sight he perceived that they were living in the Deer park near Benares, occupying one part of it and another according to circumstances. Then the world-honoured one, having stood for a little time near the Bôdhi tree, turned away, and then gradually advanced towards the country of Benares; as the Gâtha says—

"The world-honoured one, wishing to preach to Râmaputra,
Bending his mind to discover where he was living,
Found that his present life ended, he was now in Heaven,
Then his mind turned to the five Rishis, and he desired to go to them."

---

[1] This expression "turn the wheel of the Law" (dhammacakkam pavatteti) is better rendered "establish the dominion of the Law," in other words "the dominion of Religion." The evident contrast between Buddha, as a Chakravarti Râja, and a Spiritual Teacher or Ruler, observed throughout this work, will help to show that "dhammacakkam" is only an expression used for religious dominion, instead of Regal or Secular authority. *Vide* Childer's *Pali Dict., sub voce Dhamma.*

Then Mâra Râja, the Wicked one, seeing Buddha's intention to leave the neighbourhood of the Bôdhi tree, was filled with sorrow and consternation, and forthwith hastened to the spot to meet him; having arrived, he addressed him thus—"Hail! world-honoured! I pray thee leave not this spot! but let the world-honoured remain here in rest as he desires." To whom the world-honoured one replied, "Mâra Râja Pisuna! trouble not yourself further about me! In days gone by, you desired to perplex and baffle me in vain; at the present time, possessed as I am of Supreme Wisdom, your efforts will be worse than useless."

Then the world-honoured, having advanced from the Tree of Knowledge, proceeding by easy stages, came first of all to the village called Chandra [*beautiful and bright* (*Ch. ed.*)]. From this he advanced to the village of Tchundajira [*without-horn-strike* (*Ch. ed.*)]. In the middle of the road, leading to this place, he met a mendicant Brahman called Upakama[1] [*come* (*or, future*) *business* (*Ch. ed.*)]. This Brahman, having looked at Buddha, addressed him thus, "Venerable one! offspring of Gôtama! whence comes it that thy form is so perfect, thy countenance so lovely, thy appearance so peaceful? What system of religion is it that imparts to thee such joy and such peace?" To whom the world-honoured replied, as he proceeded on his way, in these Gâthas—

"I have conquered and overcome all worldly influences,
I have perfected in myself every kind of wisdom,
I live now in the world, spotless and without taint,
For ever have I cast off the trammels of desire," etc.

Then Upakama, the Brahman, further inquired of Buddha whither he was going, and on hearing he was going to Benares, he inquired for what purpose he was going there, to whom the world-honoured replied in the following Gâthas:

"I now desire to turn the wheel of the excellent law;
For this purpose am I going to that city of Benares,
To give light to those enshrouded in darkness,
And to open the gate of Immortality to men."

---

[1] Named "Upagana" by Burnouf (*Introduction*, p. 389) and "Upaka" by Spence Hardy (*Manual of Buddhism*, p. 184), *vide Etudes Bouddhiques*, by M. Leon Feer, p. 15.

On this, Upakama again inquired as to the meaning of what Buddha had said, that he had become a Rahat, and had overcome sorrow; to which the world-honoured one replied in these Gâthas:

"Know then that I have completely conquered all evil passion,
I have for ever got rid of the remnants of all personal being;
Every evil law throughout the world destroyed,
I am, therefore, called the True and Perfect Teacher (Lord)."

[There are other Gâthas also which speak of the folly of one, who, though himself enlightened, seeks not to enlighten others—even as a lamp enlightens all in the house—so Buddha, by the light of his religious system desires, to dispense light to all.]

Then Upakama cried out, "Venerable Gôtama, yonder is your way," and himself turned to the eastward.

Then a certain Deva, who in days of yore had been a relative of Upakama's, on this account wishing to do him some benefit, and to point him to the way of deliverance and of rest and peace (without fear) came near and uttered the following Gâthas:

"You have now met with the Supreme Teacher of gods and men,
You know not that this world-honoured one has attained the true condition of Bôdhi;
Whither goest thou then—immersed in heresy;
Wheresoever thou goest, sorrow and disappointment will be thine.
Rejecting thus the advances of the one true teacher,
Deserting him and offering no religious alms,
What service can thine hand or foot render thee,
In him alone can be found the source of the true faith."

Then the world-honoured one gradually advancing from Tchirnasatra [*the same as Tchundajira (Ch. ed.)*] came to the village of Karnapura [*the city of the ear (Ch. ed.)*]; from thence he advanced to Sarathi [*harmonious-royal-city (Ch. ed..)*], thence he proceeded to Rohita vastu [*obstruction-city*[1] *(Ch. ed.)*]. From this city he advanced straight to the banks of the Ganges, and there encountering the owner of a ferry boat, he addressed him thus, "Hail! respectable sir! I pray you take me across the river in your boat!" To whom the boatman replied, "If you can pay me the fare, I will willingly take your honour across the river."

---

[1] Compare Attak, "Archæolog. Survey," ii, 7.

To whom Buddha said, "Whence shall I procure money to pay you your fare, I, who have given up all worldly wealth and riches, and who am now of no more worth than a broken pot or a cracked earthen jar; my heart now is beyond the influence of favour or dislike; the man who would kill me, or would bestow upon me all honour, both are alike to me—where then shall I get the money you ask of me as a fare?" To whom the boatman answered, "If you can give me the money I will ferry you across; for this indeed is my only means of livelihood, for the support of my wife and children." Then the world-honoured one, perceiving a flock of geese flying from the south to the north bank of the Ganges, immediately addressed the boatman in the following Gâthas:

"See yonder geese in fellowship pass o'er the Ganges,
They ask not as to fare of any boatman,
But each by his inherent strength of body,
Flies through the air as pleases him.
So, by my power of spiritual energy,
Will I transport myself across the river,
Even though the waters on this southern bank
Stood up as high and firm as Sumeru." (*And so he flies across.*)

Then the boatman, having witnessed this miracle, began to upbraid himself, saying, "alas! alas! that I should have seen the great religious merit of this holy one, and not have given him a free passage across the river. Alas! alas! what an opportunity have I lost!" and reproaching himself thus he fell to the ground in a swoon. At length coming to himself, he arose from the earth and went straight to Bimbâsara, King of Magadha, and told him all that had happened, hearing which the king made the following decree: "It is impossible to know in every case whether this spiritual ability of locomotion exists or not. Wherefore, I command that in every case when a religious mendicant desires to cross the river, that he be ferried over free of charge."

Then the world-honoured one, having transported himself thus over the river, kept up his flight towards the city of Benares. Now in that neighbourhood there was a certain dragon-tank, the dragon's name being "Sankha" [*this means "serpent"* (*Ch. ed.*)]. The world-honoured one having come to this spot and there alighted, the Nâga Râja raised on the site a tower which was called Medika [*this means earth-tower* (*Ch. ed.*)]. And as Tathâgata remained there, awaiting the time for asking alms, another tower was erected, called "awaiting-time-tower," even as the Gâtha says:

"All the Buddhas at night time go not among men,
They await awhile till the time of fasting be over.
Those who beg at improper times have great sorrow;
Therefore it is an ordinance for ever, to abide the time."

Then Buddha entering in at the western gate of the city, proceeded in order through the streets asking alms — afterwards leaving the city and taking his place beside some water (the river), he sat down and ate; and then washing his (hands and feet) he proceeded northward by easy steps to the grove of Deer. As the Gâtha says:

"In the Deer park, the carols of the various birds resounding,
The place where the holy ones of old have ever dwelt,
The shining body of the world-honoured one also
Slowly advanced towards that sacred spot, as the sun for glory."

Now when the five Rishis saw him approaching, they said one to another, "This is none other than that Shaman of the Gautama clan; he has lost all his spiritual power, and is now approaching with his body full of strength and grace; let us disregard him—let us offer him no reverence, let us not offer him an abode in our company." [Now Adjñata alone did not feel these sentiments in his heart, nevertheless he said nothing]. And so the Gâtha says:

"See this Gôtama now approaching,
Let us Rishis not disagree,
We will pay him no reverence or worship,
For he is a man who has broken his vow."

So it happened that in this mood the five Rishis awaited the approach of the world-honoured one as he slowly advanced; but, at the same time, as they sat one beside the other, they were distressed beyond measure in their hearts, and desired above all things to rise to salute him. Even as the Sakuna bird (the eagle), caught in an iron net surrounded by fire, frets and tears his prison chains to get away, so did those five men vex their hearts to rise and pay the world-honoured one due reverence. At length, unable longer to restrain themselves, they rose and offered him water for his feet and all other necessary provision after his journey, and then they exclaimed—"Welcome! welcome! our old friend Gôtama! sit down and rest, and halt awhile in our company!" And so the Gâtha says—

"They presented to him an alms-dish and the three garments,
And they bowed themselves down at Buddha's feet;
Moreover, they arranged a place for him to sit,
And offered him a water vessel and a pitcher."

Then Buddha, slowly approaching the place appointed for him, took his seat; and being seated he reflected thus—"What sad weakness is this of these five Rishis unable to keep the vow they had just made together!"

Then they addressed Buddha as follows—"Venerable Gôtama! your body is of a beautiful appearance, your face and your eyes round and fresh, and all your senses in perfect accord; you must indeed have found the elixir of immortality, and the way of life."

Then the world-honoured one replied, "Ye Rishis! mock not Tathâgata by calling him 'the venerable Gôtama.' Ye are indeed in the way of death, and shall reap sorrow and disappointment by continuing therein; but I have found the way of Immortality, and am now abiding in it. I am able also to instruct you therein, if you will but attend and consider my words, if you will but walk according to my directions; if a man or woman will leave the world, and follow me, desiring to find that highest condition of a true Brahmana, to reach the fountain head of such a condition, then such an one shall surely find it, and arrive at the desired goal; his faculties perfected, he shall cut himself off from further birth and death; and well-founded in his religious life he shall hereafter receive no other form of temporary existence (bhava). This is what ye should meditate on." And so the Gâtha says—

"Those five Rishis mockingly spoke of Buddha as Gôtama,
The world-honoured one in pity taught them, saying,
'Let not your thoughts be so proud and high;
Let go that pride of self, and obey and reverence me,
There is no pride of self in me, but perfect self-composure;
I desire to change in you the ground of your destiny,

I, who have become Buddha, honoured by the world,
For the sake of all living things, I would bring this good.'"

Then those five Rishis answered thus—"Venerable Gôtama! In days gone by you vainly sought (by austerities) this condition of Supreme Wisdom, you obtained it not then, how much less now, weary as you are of the practice of abstract meditation, your body in the full possession of its faculties and enjoying the complete tide of its life!"

Then the world-honoured one, chiding these Rishis, said, "Speak not thus! Tathâgata wearies not in the practice of religion, nor loses his power of meditation nor relaxes his bodily discipline! but ye Rishis! I have now attained the end of all, the condition of 'Araha-Samma-sambudda.' And because I have thus attained the way of life, ye Rishis should attend to my instruction, and not oppose your minds to my instruction, for I am able to teach you the one way by which alone ye may hereafter escape all (personal) existence."

Then the five Rishis rejoined, "Venerable Gôtama! surely in old days you sought this Law and this condition of Supreme Wisdom, till your body relaxed from very weakness its efforts." To whom the world-honoured one replied, "Did ye, then, oh Rishis! know me ever lie or speak falsely in my instructions?" To which they answered, "No!" At this time, the world-honoured one, projecting his tongue from his mouth caused it to reach to both his ears, and to the nostrils, and then to cover his whole face, after which he withdrew it again,[1] and said, "Can a man, oh Rishis! guilty of lying, perform such an act as this?" To which they replied, "No!" "Mock not, therefore, Tathâgata, by saying that he became weary of his bodily discipline, or that he has lost his power of meditation; whereas, in fact, he has attained a condition of Supreme Enlightenment, and is ready to instruct you in the way of life." [*In the end the Rishis submit to be taught, and assume the robes and the personal preparation fit for a follower of Buddha.*]

[Kiouen XXXIII contains 6148 words and cost 3.074 taels.]

---

[1] This extraordinary power of lengthening the tongue is constantly attributed to Buddha, as one of the peculiar marks of his person. Sometimes (as in the *Lotus* and elsewhere) it is exaggerated grotesquely into a power to cover the worlds of the universe with the same member.

CHAPTER XXXIV.

§ 1. THEN the world-honoured one began to reflect as to where the previous Buddhas had first turned the Wheel of the most excellent Law, and in what manner, and what the truths first declared were. Then the spot where he was seated began to heave and quake, and at the same time five hundred lion-thrones appeared in the garden. The world-honoured one, having respectfully circumambulated three of these, took his seat on the fourth, with his legs crossed, without fear, in perfect composure. And then considering what truths the former Buddhas had first taught, he found they were the four truths triply explained.[1]

At this time, being the fifteenth day of the month Vaishya, at mid-afternoon, the world-honoured one began to preach the most excellent Law of the four truths, which neither Brahman or Shaman had been able to preach before.

On which occasion he addressed the five Rishis as follows [*here follows a description of the peculiar characteristics of Buddha's voice*]: "Ye Bhikshus! who have left your homes, there are two things ye should finally and for ever renounce—all worldly sources of pleasure and bodily gratification, and also excessive mortification of body, which neither tend to self-profit nor the profit of others!" And so the Gâtha says—

"Reject and forsake places and modes of excessive penance;
Check and entirely control sensuous gratifications;
If a man is able to follow these two lines of conduct
Immediately he will attain the true way of eternal life."

Then the Buddha continued his address—"Bhikshus! be assured that I have given up each of these erroneous methods, and this is the middle path to which I have attained; thus am I enlightened, thus my eyes are able to see and my mind to know, and therefore I have gained a condition of rest (santi), and am in possession of complete spiritual life, and have accomplished the acquirement of perfect intelligence, and am now a true Shaman, and have reached Nirvâna and am perfected. If then, Bhikshus, ye wish to reach

[1] This is the *Evolution duodécimale des vérités* referred to by M. Leon Feer, *Etudes Bouddhiques*, p. 213.

this condition, ye must also use this middle path which I have used, and your eyes shall be opened, and wisdom shall spring up within, and you shall enjoy rest and reach Nirvâna, and the eight paths of holiness (As'htanga Marga), viz.—Samyak-drishti, Samyak-samkalpa, Samyagvâk, Samyagadjîva, Samyak-karmanta, Samyagvyâyâma, Samyak-smriti, Samyak-samâdhi. This, Bhikshus! is the middle path, which having attained to, my eyes are opened, and I have found rest, etc. To this, therefore, ye ought to tend; as the Gâtha says—

'Because of these eight paths leading aright,
A man casts off the trammels of life, death, and fear,
Having entirely got rid of all the effects of Karma,
Through eternity he shall no more receive migratory existence.'

And now, Bhikshus! listen and consider well what I have to say respecting the four great truths. And what are these four? 1. The Sacred Truth that sorrow exists. 2. The Sacred Truth of the accumulation of sorrow. 3. The sacred truth of the destruction (of sorrow). 4. The sacred truth of obtaining or finding the path (of complete deliverance). These are called the four Holy truths. What, then, oh Bhikshus! are the reasons they are so called? The sacred truth that sorrow exists is this, that there is in the world the sorrow of birth, the sorrow of death, of disease and of old age; the sorrow of loving that which cannot be had or of hating that which cannot be avoided, this is the sacred truth of sorrow. And what is the meaning of the accumulation of sorrow? This is the second sacred truth, Bhikshus! and it is this, that the force of desire (trishna) compelling the mind to seek fresh sources of enjoyment in every place and on every occasion, that this leads to every sort of anxious reflection and constant thought, and so results the accumulation spoken of. And what is the destruction of sorrow mentioned before? This is the third sacred truth, and it is this; the removal of and utter rejection of desire, so that it is destroyed and put away for ever, the heart then has no anxious thoughts or reflections, and in consequence attains the fixity of rest. This is the third sacred truth. And what is it to attain the path (of deliverance)? This is the fourth sacred truth, and it is this; to be able to acquire and walk in the practice of the eight rules aforesaid, viz., Samyak-drishti, etc. This is called the sacred truth of the "way." These truths, oh Bhikshus! have been on no occasion taught to me from without, they are self-revealed, known by intuition, not acquired from any human source, but of my own inborn power. [*These assertions are again and again repeated in the Sanscrit original; here only a digest is given* (*Ch. ed.*)]. Neither the first nor the second or either of the others have I learned from other sources, I have heard them from no one, they are all self-revealed, they spring only from within myself. So it is I have attained the condition of enlightenment I now enjoy; so it is my eyes behold the truth, so it is I have acquired complete wisdom; it is alone by my own power, by myself, by intuition from within, and from no human source of instruction. [*These assertions are repeated in many ways, in the original Sanscrit* (*Ch. ed.*)] It was thus, oh Bhikshus! by thrice turning these four sacred truths and arriving at the very bottom of the matter (which I had not done when ye first sought my company), by simply perceiving the sacred truths aforesaid, I arrived at the condition of Samyak-sambôdhi and at perfect enlightenment. Bhikshus! by thus comprehending the twelve relationships (*i.e.*, the twelve Nidânas) resulting from the complete consideration of these four sacred truths I arrived at Anuttara Samyak Sambôdhi, and so I have accomplished my aim and become Buddha.

"Then it was, oh Bhikshus! wisdom was born in me, I was able to see, my mind no longer confused or fickle, I obtained deliverance. Bhikshus! I have now reached my last birth; hereafter there is no more individual existence for me (bhava)."

When Buddha was thus declaring the marks (or, relationships) of the Law, the aged Kaundinya, as he sat attentively listening, arrived at a condition of supreme knowledge; he was able to cast away and reject the influences of sense (dust) and defilement, to free himself from all trammels and bonds and obtain pure sight, just as a garment freed from defilement is easily dyed and retains its colour, so with him he cast away the defilements of sense, and let go the hold of sorrow, and having done so, he stepped forth a free man, his eye purified, he beheld the Truth.

At the same time, sixty thousand Devaputras also attained the same condition of purified sight and perfect knowledge.

Then the world-honoured one, with his lion voice, spake thus—

"No words can reach the depth of the law which I preach;
The absolute,[1] the ever-peaceful Nirvâna, hath no name or title,
The most excellent Kaundinya hath first attained to it,
The way I have sought and found is not an empty[2] one."

And so the Gâtha says—

"Thus, at the time of the preaching of the profound law,
As the first and most excellent result of the love of the world-honoured,
Kaundinya arrived at the possession of the pure eyes of the law;
And afterwards innumerable Devas were equally blessed."

At this time all the Devas sang together and said, "Brother Devas! be it known that to-day, Bhagavata Tathâgata Arahato Samma Sambuddha, dwelling in the park of Deer, where, from remote time, the Rishis have resided, has began to preach the most excellent and sublime law, which neither Shaman or Brahman has hitherto been able to declare." And so the Gâtha says—

"Verily! the world-honoured, gifted with Divine sight,
Turns the wheel of the Law of Immortality, for men!
* * * * * *
He declares the one true and most profound system,
He establishes this wheel, honour'd by the three worlds.
He dwells near the city of Benares,
In the midst of the Garden of Deer he preaches thus."

Then all the Devas dwelling in that neighbourhood, having chanted this song, the sounds thereof ascended to the abode of the four great Kings, who took up the strain, and from them they ascended to the thirty-three Heavens, the Devas of which on their part took up the words, the sound ascending upwards to the Yama Heavens [and so throughout the successive Heavens, to the highest point of space].

[*Here follows an account of prodigies which ensued, the falling of delicious flowers, the sighing of gentle breezes, and the quaking of the earth.*]

---

[1] In the original the phrase is "chin ju," which is an expression denoting the nature of Tathâgata, *i.e.*, the Universal and the Absolute.

[2] That is, "fruitless," or, "insufficient to convert others."

At this time, Kaundinya, rising from his seat and falling prostrate at the feet of Buddha, addressed him thus—"World-honoured one! I accept thy Law! World-honoured, take me as a disciple, I vow to obey and follow thee perfectly."

Then Buddha answered and said, "Welcome! oh Bhikshu! enter into my Law, act the part of a true Brahmana, and extinguish all the causes of sorrow."

Kaundinya, having assumed the character of a disciple, began to address the other Bhikshus, according to their several capacities, and exhibit the nature of the Law to them; in this way, three of them having gone a-begging, when they returned, and the six (including Buddha) were together, then in regular order Bhadraka, Basava, Mahanâma, Asvajit, became disciples and assumed the robes of ascetics; and so the Gâtha says—

"Bhadraka, Basava, Kaundinya,
Mahanâma, and Asvajita:
These five first arrived at enlightenment,
And tasted the sweet-dew of Tathâgata."

Then the world-honoured one addressed these five Bhikshus and said, "Ye Bhikshus! it is because I have through every successive birth, constantly practised the rules of right-recollection (Samyak smriti), and because of this have been able to walk in the right way (samyak karmanta), and by this means have attained complete deliverance and perfect inspiration. So do ye also! walk in the same way, and ye also shall attain the perfect condition of supreme intelligence!"

[*Then Mâra Pisuna again appears, and addresses Buddha in taunting language*[1]; *to which Buddha replies*, *in terms of quiet defiance; on which Mâra, disconcerted, vanishes out of sight.*]

[*Buddha then proceeds to address the Bhikshus, and shows them the non-reality (individuality) of all the constituents of finite existence (the five Skandha): "It is impossible to say that either of these is 'I,'*[2]

---

[1] The verses used by Mâra are precisely those found in *Bigandet* (*Burmese Buddha*), p. 124.

[2] That is "attá" or "atma." Thus, in the *Brahmajâla Sutta*, Buddha says, "Priests! some Samanas and Brahmins hold the eternity of existences, and in four forms maintain that the soul and the world are of eternal duration." Where Gogerley observes

or that 'I' am either of these; rejecting this thought, therefore, the causes of sorrow and impermanency are perceived, and destroyed, and hence comes complete deliverance." Having uttered this discourse, the five Bhikshus obtained salvation and became Rahats; so that now, including Buddha himself, there were six persons in the world enjoying this condition.]

The previous History of Kaundinya.

§ 2. At this time, the world-honoured one addressed the Bhikshus and said, "Listen, oh Bhikshus, and weigh my words well. I remember, in days gone by, that there was dwelling in this place, where the city of Benares now stands, a certain potter who offered to receive into his house, during the interval of the summer rest, a Pratyeka Buddha, who was suffering from some grievous bodily ailment, and supply him with the four necessary articles required by the religious (food, clothing, bedding, medicine). The potter, therefore, constructed, not far from his own abode, a convenient pansal[1] for the Pratyeka Buddha, and there lodged him and supplied all his wants. Now, it came to pass that the Pratyeka Buddha on that very night entered into the ecstasy known as the 'ecstasy of fire;'[2] and the potter, seeing the brilliancy of the flame as it shone forth from the Pansal, thought thus with himself—'What can be the meaning of this fire burning in the Pansal so brightly, and yet not disappearing, is it possible that the Pansal itself is on fire?' So then the potter, hastening to the place, looked inside through a crevice in the walls, and there he saw the Pratyeka Buddha sitting cross-legged on the seat, and his body shining like the brilliancy of fire, and yet not consumed.

---

that "Attá" properly signifies the "self," and is either the soul, being a material form, or the soul, being sensation, perception, reason and consciousness, (*i.e.*, being the aggregate of the Skandhas). If this Buddhist definition of the "soul" [the self (attá) which is named the eye, the ear, &c.] were kept in sight much vain controversy would be avoided.

[1] That is, a "leafy hut," or a "sheltered abode."

[2] Agnidhâtu Samâdhi."

Seeing this, he returned to his house, and on the following day, thinking over the wonderful sight he had seen, he arrived at a firm condition of faith. Thus, during the whole season, the potter attended to the wants of the Pratyeka Buddha; he procured the advice and medicines of a learned physician, and provided all things necessary for the restoration of his guest, but all in vain! and so at last the Pratyeka Buddha died. The potter, having seen him thus enter Parinirvâna, was filled with sorrow, and exclaimed, 'Alas! alas!' as the tears coursed down his cheeks. Then, the people around hearing the potter's lamentations, began to assemble together, and inquire the reason of his sad grief; on which he told them all about it. Now at this time there were other Pratyeka Buddhas, five hundred in number, less one, who came flying through the air with sandal-wood offerings to attend the funeral obsequies of the one who had died. Coming thus, they addressed the potter and said, 'You should rather rejoice, and be filled with joy; for, because of your pious attention to this Rishi, you shall in ages to come enjoy a complete reward. Perceive you our spiritual capabilities or not?' The potter replied, 'I see them.' Then they said, 'As we are, so was he! he was one of us.' The potter then said, 'But whence come ye, and where is your abode?' To which they replied, 'Not far from a city called Rajagriha there is a Mountain called "the mountain where Rishis dwell" (Rishigiri), it is there we dwell and have our abode.' Then the potter said, 'Welcome then, oh Rishis! receive the best my house can afford, and when you list, take your departure!'

"After having thus been entertained, they spake to the potter as follows—'In future times long hence there shall be born a Buddha in the world, and you shall be privileged to enjoy his company and receive his instruction.' To whom the potter said, 'Venerable sirs; as the Pratyeka Buddha who came to my door was old, and worn out with age; oh! that I may when old at least obtain the blessedness of receiving the instruction and profiting by the teaching of that Buddha, Sâkya Buddha, whom ye name! oh! that I may become one of his followers, and the first to receive the deliverance he will confer on his disciples!' Then the Rishis, having given the potter a distinct assurance that all this would be the case, forthwith departed, flying through space as they came at first.

The potter, beholding this miracle, with his hands clasped together, bowed down on his knees and worshipped. Then taking the relics which remained after the cremation of the Pratyeka Buddha, he raised over them a stupa of magnificent proportions, surrounded by successive wheels of railings, and capped with banners, flags, and streamers of every kind; and he offered sandalwood offerings and scented unguents of the orthodox description as he worshipped before it. Thus, owing to this root of merit, this potter was afterwards born as Kaundinya and became the first of my disciples, and received the deliverance he now enjoys as the first of the Rahats."

The History of Yasada[1] (Ye-shu-to).

§ 3. At this time, not far from the city of Benares, amongst other trees, there was a certain Nyagrodha tree, remarkable for its luxuriant growth. This tree was an object of veneration to all the people, rich and poor, who dwelt in the neighbourhood, all of whom, at certain seasons of the year, came to offer gifts and religious worship to it. And it came to pass that whatever prayer or vow a man made whilst in the act of worship, the same was certain to be granted. But the fact was, that the previous Karma of the worshipper was the sole cause of the fulfilment of his vow or prayer; yet men, not regarding or considering this, attributed it entirely to the tree, and so continued to frequent the spot to offer up their prayers, and to present their offerings.[2] From this circumstance, the tree was commonly known as the "Divine tree that granted all that was asked of it." Now at this time there was dwelling in the city a certain wealthy nobleman whose name was Supra Buddha (shen-hioh); this man was possessed of every kind of wealth; cattle, elephants, horses, sheep; every kind of

---

[1] The same as the Burmese Ratha (*Bigandet's Legend*, p. 112) and the Singhalese Yasa, M. B. 187.

[2] Here we have an instance of the old faith (tree worship) of India, brought into contact with Buddhist principles, which are entirely opposed to the worship (properly so called) of any material object.

grain and other produce; besides gold, silver, and jewels. His palace was of exquisite beauty, even like that of Vaisravana, king of the northern region. But he had no child. His friends, therefore, who visited him, besought him to pay religious worship to the aforesaid tree, and to offer up his prayer in its presence, that he might have a child born to his house. But he replied, "how can that senseless tree, which is nothing more than a piece of wood, hear my prayer or answer it; but we know that the accomplishment of every prayer depends only on the character of the previous karma of the person offering it up, and if one desires to have offspring, this also depends on the karma of both father and mother. I decline therefore to betake myself to any such refuge as this."

But the nobleman's relations urged their request, and cited instances to prove the truth of their allegations, and said, "You cannot doubt the truth of what we say—it is impossible not to believe these things—we know many undoubted instances in which the prayer for offspring made to that tree has been granted; do you therefore go, make your request known with strong vows, and you may be sure that a child will be born."

[Kiouen XXXIV contains 6320 words, and cost 3.16 taels].

CHAPTER XXXV.

§ 1. Then Supra Buddha, the nobleman, overpowered by the entreaties of his kinsfolk, having collected certain of his household together, he put into their hands hatchets and other instruments for cutting and digging, and proceeded with them to the spot where the Nyagrôdha tree was standing. Arrived there, he spake thus: "You tree! I have heard from certain persons that you have the power of granting the request of those who pay you religious worship! I would have you know, therefore, that if you will procure for me the birth of a well-favoured man-child, I will offer you every kind of offering, and pay you becoming veneration; but if you cannot procure this boon for me, then I will cut you down, and root you up, and utterly destroy you, branch by branch, and bit by bit, till there is nothing left of you, and the very ashes remaining after you are burnt I will scatter to the winds and on the waters, till you are utterly annihilated, and put clean out of remembrance."

Now, when the Deva of the tree heard these words, he was greatly distressed, and in much perplexity; and thought thus with himself: "What power have I to give this man a child? all that depends on his previous conduct and the destiny attaching to him from his former works. And yet men persist in saying that this tree, in which from old times I have taken my residence, has the power to do this or do that, and if I do not give him a child he threatens to cut down my abode. Alas! alas!" The tree Deva, thus weeping and lamenting, resolved to go straightway to Sâkra, King of the Gods, and lay his case before him. Then forthwith he ascended up to the Trâyastriñshas Heaven, and falling down at Sâkra's feet in humble adoration, he spake thus: "All hail! illustrious King of Heaven! Oh! that you would help me! A certain nobleman threatens to cut down the tree in which I dwell, and root it up, destroy and burn it, unless I grant him his request that he may have a son! Pity me, illustrious king! Give me some mode of escape; nor permit that tree to be thus destroyed and burnt for want of some expedient by which the desire of this nobleman may be gratified!" Then the Lord of Heaven (Tien Chu),[1] Sâkra Mahâ Râja, spake thus to the tree Deva: "Utter no such words as these, oh Deva! as though I had power to procure such a boon for this nobleman; for all this depends entirely on his own individual merit. But fear not, nor tremble thus, oh Deva! for I will forthwith examine into this matter, and see what the character of his destiny is."

Now, at this time there was a certain Deva Putra dwelling in the Trâyastriñshas Heaven, whose sojourn there was just about to expire, as was known by the five signs of decadence, which are these: the flowers in the head-chaplet begin to fade; there exudes a perspiration from beneath the arms; the garments begin to grow old and soiled; the brightness of the body pales; and the Palace couch of that Deva no longer has charms for him, but he wanders restlessly this way and that.

---

[1] *Tien-chu*, as is well known, is the expression used by the R. C. Missionaries in China for "God".

Then Sâkra, seeing this was the case with the Deva Putra in question, addressed him thus: "My son! your destiny here is fulfilled, and, according to your Karma, derived from former births, you are now about to descend to earth and to be born amongst men! but you shall be born in a distinguished family!" Then the Deva Putra replied: "Would that I knew in what place and position I am about to be born." Then Sâkra Râja answered: "In Jambudwîpa there is a certain city called Benares, in which dwells a nobleman very rich and prosperous; his name is Supra Buddha; but though so rich, he despises all because he has no child! Pray, then, make up your mind to be born in that city and in his house!" Then that Deva Putra, who had long set his mind on the acquisition of final deliverance, answered Sâkra Râja thus: "Great and illustrious King of Heaven, I desire to be born in a house not far from where Prabhâpâla Deva, who lately inhabited this Heaven, now abides; for he has arrived at perfect enlightenment, and is now able to deliver all who come to him from the misery incident on continual transmigrations. I prefer, therefore, not to be born in the house of that rich man of Benares." To him Sâkra Râja replied: "But it so happens that in the neighbourhood of that very place, the enlightened-one is about to preach the excellent Law, so that here is your opportunity at once to become his disciple and arrive at the Deliverance you seek." Then the Deva Putra consented to be born there. On this, the mighty Sâkra addressed the tree Deva, and said: "Go and tell that nobleman that his prayer is answered! he shall have a son, who shall in his turn leave his home and become a Shaman."

And so the Deva Putra descended from Heaven and was incarnated in the womb of the nobleman's wife, on which she acquainted her Lord with the fact, and invited him to rejoice in prospect of the birth of a child. Then the Lord nourished and cherished his wife, giving her every sort of food and nutritious support, in order to procure a propitious birth; he also distributed alms at the four gates of the city to all the poor, with every other necessary. So, at the end of the ninth month, the child was born—his skin bright as gold, his head round, his nose like that of the parrot, etc.—of perfect beauty. He had four nurses appointed to take special charge of him. And then, when the time came to fix his name, they called him "Yasada", because of the glory that appeared above his head when he was born. And so he remained the only child of his parents. And thus he gradually increased in stature and also in all useful knowledge.

Meantime, his father built for him three magnificent palaces, one for the winter, one for the summer, and one for the spring and autumn. He was supplied with every sort of pleasurable indulgence, and surrounded by an ever watchful retinue.

Now it so happened that the world-honoured one had just begun to preach the law at Benares, when Sakra Râja, descending from heaven, came to the palace of Yasada, and entering into the inner apartments stood there, and addressed the youth as follows: "Dear Yasada! it is full time for you now to leave your house and become a religious mendicant!" Yasada having heard the summons in silence, immediately at dawn ordered his chariot to be prepared for him to go forth in it to view the beauties of the adjoining gardens!

Now it so happened that on this very morning, the world-honoured one, having robed himself in the orthodox way, carrying his alms-dish in his hands, proceeded to the city of Benares in company with Asvajit, to beg his meal for the day. Walking along with a dignified gait he entered the city, and as it so happened, he encountered Yasada as he was proceeding towards the gardens. The latter, beholding the beautiful appearance of Buddha's person, was filled with inexpressible joy; he descended from his chariot and bowed down in reverence at his feet, and having three times circumambulated him in token of respect, he again mounted his chariot and proceeded on his way.

Then Buddha, with a gentle smile on his face, addressed Asvajit, and said: "Did you see this youth, Yasada, and the way in which he behaved?" Asvajit replied in the affirmative; on which the world-honoured one continued: "On this very evening this youth, Yasada, will become a recluse, and soon will become a Rahat."

Now, Yasada having gone round the gardens, it happened that Sâkra transformed himself into an old and decrepit woman, just dead, and ready to be buried, from whose body the worms came out, and entered in everywhere, feeding on the carcass. Yasada, beholding this disgusting sight, his heart was filled with sorrow, and he thought thus: "What pleasure can there be in any such condition as this." He returned to his palace full of these thoughts.

and lay down to sleep. Then Sâkra, by his Divine power, caused all the women to be overpowered with sleep, and the lamps of the palace to burn with a sort of supernatural light. Meantime, Buddha, perceiving by his innate power that Yasada on this night would become a recluse, proceeded towards a certain river called Varnâ (or Varanâ). [*This signifies "to separate and exclude".*] Crossing over this river, he made for himself a small Pansal (leaf-hut), and there sat down cross-legged. Yasada having awoke, and seeing all the women lying about in disorder, arising from his couch, passed out. Meantime, Sâkra caused a bright light to go before him as he pursued his way to his Father's palace, and there seeing the women lying about in disorder, as in his own, he proceeded on and came to the gates of the palace, which opened of themselves without noise; then, proceeding to the gate of the city, which was called Bhadra-pati, this too opened of itself, without any noise; on which Yasada advanced slowly to the bank of the river Varanâ. Now, at this time the river had suddenly become very shallow, and all along the banks the birds were feeding in great numbers; when lo! the light which had gone before him suddenly disappeared, and Yasada was left alone in the gloom. He then began to bewail his unhappy condition, on which Buddha, from the other bank of the river, caused his body to emit a dazzling brightness, and with his arms stretched out towards Yasada, he exclaimed "Welcome! welcome! oh! Yasada. There is nothing to fear here! there is no danger here! nought but rest and peace! and perfect independence!" and so the Gâtha says:—

"Tathâgata, having perceived his state of mind,
And having heard his lamentation, accosted him thus—
'Come, then! come, then; oh, my Yasada!
Take this way towards the fearless Nirvâna!
The world-honour'd one perceives all things,
The world-honour'd one knows all things,
He can, therefore, read the thoughts of every heart;
And so his words are full of hidden meaning.'"

Then Yasada, hearing these words, lost all fear, and experienced a feeling of perfect rest, just as the thirsty and way-worn traveller, who lights upon a lake of pure water, cool and refreshing, bathing in which and drinking thereof, forgets all his former griefs, so Yasada, hearing the words of Buddha, lost every remnant of fear and anxiety, and experienced a sense of complete repose. Then Yasada, filled with joy, took off his jewelled slippers, laid them on the bank, and entered the river Varanâ to cross over it; he left them there just as a man who rejects some spittle from his mouth leaves it, nor thinks of it again! Then, on account of the shallowness of the water, Yasada soon passed over, and having approached towards the spot where Buddha was, and beholding all the excellencies of his person, he fell down before him in humble adoration and worshipped him. Then, arising, he stood on one side. Hereupon Buddha, having preached to Yasada, and declared to him the character of the four sacred truths, behold! he received enlightenment, and, like pure water, his heart was cleansed from every remnant of care.

Meantime, his wives, having woke up and perceiving that their Lord was absent, began to raise a great outcry with much lamentation, and hastened to his mother and said, "Dear Mother! your son is gone! he was here yesternight, but now we cannot find him in the palace!" His mother, filled with fear, then aroused her husband and said, "My Lord! your son Yasada is nowhere to be found in the palace!" On this, he sent for the wise men and soothsayers, and told them the circumstances, on which proclamation was made from the four gates of the city, saying—"Whoever will bring me news of my son, Yasada, where he is, or in what direction he has gone, that man shall receive one hundred thousand lakhs of money as a reward." On that very night the nobleman, Yasada's father, distressed with fear and grief, was wandering forth in his perplexity towards the Varanâ River, having passed through the Bhadrapati gate, when he came to the very spot where the priceless jewelled slippers which Yasada had left there, were lying; on seeing these, he said, "Then, my dear son is not dead; for if he were dead these slippers would not be here!" Leaving them where they lay, the father forthwith crossed the river in search of his son. Buddha, perceiving the approach of the nobleman, determined to exercise his miraculous spiritual power, and so he caused Yasada to become invisible. On this the father, approaching, addressed Buddha with great respect and said, "Have you, venerable sir! seen my son Yasada pass by this way, or not?"

To which the world-honoured one replied, "If you have leisure, respected sir! sit you down here awhile and rest! and soon you shall see your son!" Then the nobleman reflected thus—"It is impossible for this Shaman to speak falsely—what he says must be true!" and so he was filled with joy, he bowed his head at Buddha's feet and sat down. Then Buddha began to preach to him, and to explain in order the various truths of his system; on which, like a clean garment that easily receives the dye, he attained joy and release, and accepted the three refuges and the five commandments of the lay disciple. Then Buddha, by his miraculous power, caused Yasada to appear; on seeing him, his father exclaimed, "Dear son! your mother is weeping, and filled with grief on your account. Dear son! pity her condition and return to her lest she die of a broken heart!" Then Buddha addressed the nobleman and said, "Illustrious sir! how think you? can a man who has accepted the three modes of refuge, and taken on him the vows of a religious mendicant, can such an one return to his house and family again, or not?" To which he replied, "He cannot." Then Buddha said, "Even so this Yasada, having obtained emancipation from the world, can no more return to its pleasures; he is free from all family ties, and can no longer be subject to them."

Then the nobleman, having entreated Buddha to partake of his alms, arose and proceeded a little way homewards; on which Yasada also arose from his seat and, bowing down at Buddha's feet, besought him to receive him fully as a disciple. On which Buddha said, "Welcome! oh Bhikshu! walk perfectly in the Law which I declare, and thus become a perfect Brahmana." Buddha, having said this, Yasada received perfect deliverance, and arrived at the condition of a Rahat. There were now seven Rahats in the world.

Then, early in the morning, the world-honoured one, having put on his robe, and holding his alms-bowl in his hand, having desired Yasada to wait upon him, proceeded to the city and to the house of the nobleman, Yasada's father. Arrived there, he entered into the house and sat down. Then the mother of Yasada and his wife, having come into his presence, bowed down and saluted Buddha's feet. On this the world-honoured one proceeded to explain in detail the rules of the system, and preached to them as well on charity as on purity and rest. After this he expounded the four great truths. And so it came to pass that they were able to cast off the defilement of sense, and to realise the inward cleansing power of these truths; and as a pure garment which is dyed easily, so they also attained enlightenment.

These two, viz., Yasada's mother and his wife, were the first female disciples of Buddha who took refuge in the threefold gem, and took upon them the five commandments of the lay-disciple (Upasika).

Then the nobleman and his wife, with their household, presented with their own hands to Buddha the choicest food and drink, wheat and honey and rice, of which he freely partook. Then Subrabuddha and his wife, having taken the alms-bowl of Buddha, carefully washed it, whilst Buddha himself remained resting. After which, carrying with them smaller cushions, they arranged them in front of Buddha, and themselves sat down to listen to his further exhortations. Then Buddha, seeing their conduct in exact conformity with his Law, freely preached to them, and caused them to understand his doctrine fully. They on their part were filled with joy, and accepted all they heard with sincere hearts. Then the world-honoured one, rising from his seat, prepared to depart from the city, and, followed by Yasada, he left the abode of his entertainer.

[Kiouen XXXV contains 6,310 words, and cost 3.155 taels.]

CHAPTER XXXVI.

The subsequent conversion of Yasada's friends.

§ 1. Now at this time there were in the city of Benares four exceedingly rich and prosperous householders—the name of the first Vimala [*no pollution* (*Ch. ed.*)]; of the second Subhada [*illustrious, or, good, shoulder* (*Ch. ed.*)]; of the third Purnaka [*full and enough* (*Ch. ed.*)]; of the fourth Gavpati [*Lord of Oxen* (*Ch. ed.*)]. These four, having heard of Yasada's conversion, and that he had become a Shaman devoted to the practice of a Brahmana,[1] having heard this, began to reflect with themselves thus—"This is very singular, there must be something very superior in the system of that great Shaman to induce Yasada to behave in this way; we will go for ourselves and see what it is that great Shaman teaches."

[1] That is, devoted to a pure life.

Having thought thus, they set out together and proceeded to the place where Yasada was dwelling.

Arrived there, they respectfully saluted him and spake thus—"Noble Yasada! there must be something very superior in the system of this great Shaman, to induce you to join yourself to his company, and enter on the life of a Brahmana; tell us, we pray you, what his system is." Then Yasada brought these four, the householders of Benares aforesaid, to the place where Buddha himself was. Arrived there they respectfully bowed down at his feet, and then took a place on one side. Then Yasada addressed his master as follows—"Mahâ Buddha! honoured by the world! these four eminent persons—Vimala, Subhada, Purnaka, and Gavpati—are very old friends of mine, and they have come here desiring to learn what your system of doctrine is, in order to attach themselves to your person as lay disciples; would that my Lord would teach them and expound the truth in their hearing!" Then the world-honoured one, of his great love and compassion, began to explain in consecutive order the great principles of his system, to wit, the character of true charity (Dana), morality (sila), patience (kshanti), and so on; he went through the whole, step by step, and explained his entire Law. So it came to pass, that these four also received enlightenment, they cast off the defilement of sense, and, as a pure garment is readily dyed, they also were changed in heart. Then they arose and prostrated themselves at the feet of Buddha, and respectfully addressed him thus—"Oh! Mahâ Buddha, world-honoured one, permit us, we pray you, to become your disciples also, to leave our homes and take upon us the rules of a Shaman."

Then Buddha replied, "Welcome, oh Bhikshus! enter on the course of true Brahmanas! and follow me."

Then they received the accustomed tonsure, and after seven days put on the three garments, and accepted the alms-bowl of mendicants. Then, having passed some time in the woods as hermits (arañyaka), they also arrived at the condition of Rahats. There were now eleven Rahats in the world.

In the same way fifty other persons, all friends of Yasada, who were in the habit of coming to him from different countries, to converse and discuss questions of importance, were all converted and became Rahats; so that the number of Rahats altogether amounted to sixty-one.

§ 2. AND now the world-honoured one, having converted these sixty persons in the Deer park near to Benares, desired to visit other countries also, whereupon he spake to Yasada as follows—"Dear Yasada! I wish you now to remain here and not to follow me, for you are but young and ill-prepared to bear the toil and privations which the life of a travelling mendicant will require of you; remain, then, I pray you, in this place, and receive the nourishment and other necessaries you require at the hands of your father and mother, who will care for you that you want nothing." On this, Yasada, with reverence, replied, "I dare not disobey your wishes, honoured by the world!" And so he remained there at Benares. Now at this time there happened to be five hundred merchant men at Benares who were formerly well acquainted with Yasada's family; these, having returned home from a distant expedition, heard the news about Yasada's conversion, and began to reflect thus—"There must be something very superior in the teaching of this great Shaman, to induce Yasada to leave his home and become a disciple; we will go and inquire at his hands, and learn what this doctrine is." So, having repaired to Yasada's abode, they addressed him thus—"Dear Yasada! we were formerly well acquainted one with the other, but we have not met for a long time, for in truth we merchants have only just returned from a long voyage. But now, having come home, the first thing we hear is, that you have become a recluse; we have come to inquire, therefore, from you what it is that induced you to take this step, and what the doctrines of your master are." Having said this, they stood on one side. Then Yasada entered on an explanation of Buddha's teaching, and in consequence these five hundred merchants also became his followers, they left their homes, received the five precepts of the lay disciple; but, nevertheless, for many years they tried in vain to obtain perfect enlightenment (*i.e.*, acquire Bôdhi, or become Rahats).

Buddha visits Sravâsti.

§ 3. Now it came to pass that Bhagavat, having gone through various countries, at last came to Sravastî (Savatti), and had taken up his abode in the garden of Jeta[1] (Jetavana), within the Vihara erected there for his accommodation. Then Yasada, having passed many seasons at Benares, hearing that Buddha was located at the Jetavana, set out, accompanied by the 500 merchant men, to join him there. And so these wandering Bhikshus at length arrived there. Then they were received according to custom, and were entertained in the Vihara (or monastery) attached to the garden. Whilst thus entertained, however, it so happened that they made much noise with their chattering and shouting, and caused considerable confusion in the establishment by their disorderly conduct. At this time Bhagavat, although perfectly acquainted with the reason of it, yet asked Ananda whence proceeded these shouts and disorderly noises. On this Ananda related how that these 500 merchants had arrived at the monastery in company with Yasada, and had claimed hospitality and shelter. On this Bhagavat commanded Ananda to go to them and reprove them for their conduct. After this they all came into the presence of Bhagavat, and bending at his feet, they worshipped him; and then, rising up, stood on one side, in silence. Then Bhagavat addressed them—"Ye Bhikshus, the noise and disorderly shouting I heard just now reminded me of the clamorous disputatious ways of men, some saying 'Hoo! hoo!' others 'ha! ha!' just like the shouting of fishermen one against the other, when they are hauling in their nets! Such conduct does not become this place. I desire you therefore to depart hence at once!—it is impossible for you to dwell with me!"

Then these Bhikshus, with submission, bowed down again at Buddha's feet, and having circumambulated him three times, departed from the Vihara. And so it was that they came to the banks of the river Paragomati, and there sitting down, they re-

---

[1] The gift of this garden by Anathapindana is a well-known event in Buddhist history. It is curiously illustrated in a sculpture at Bharahut, lately brought to light by the Archæological Surveyor of India.

mained together, practising themselves in the pure rules of the life of a Brahmana, and giving themselves up to constant reflection and self-examination, until at length they all were able to shake off mundane influences, and became Rahats.

Then Bhagavat, having remained for some time longer in the Jetavana of Savatti, resolved at length to go through the country and visit other towns and villages; and so, travelling on, he came at length to the town of Vâisali; and there, taking up his abode in a leafy hut by the side of the Monkey Tank, he dwelt. Then, as the sun was going down, Bhagavat, arousing himself from the religious reverie in which he had been lost, went forth from his pansal into the open ground, and making a grass seat for himself, he sat down, the priests, his followers, being arranged in order around him. Then Buddha declared how he had seen in his reverie those five hundred Bhikshus by the side of the Paragomati River, and a great light shining round them; and he bade Ananda to signify to them that they should come into the presence of Buddha. Then Ananda dispatched a young Bhikshu with this message. He, having heard the commands of Ananda, immediately prepared himself to obey, even as the warrior braces on his armour and clasps his helmet, in readiness for the expected strife. And so, in like manner, those five hundred Bhikshus, when they had heard the message, prepared to obey; and thus they all came to the place where Bhagavat dwelt in the pansal beside the Monkey Tank at Vâisali.

The previous History of Yasada.

§ 4. Then the world-honoured began to relate the previous history of Yasada and these five hundred merchants in the following words—"I remember, in days gone by, there was a certain man living in Benares who thought thus with himself—'If this business in which I am engaged succeeds, and that other matter turn out well, then I vow to give away in charity to Shaman or Brahman every variety of choice food, as a token of my gratitude, as much as ever he wants.'

"And so it came to pass that, his efforts having been crowned with success, one morning, very early, he took every variety of choice food with him, and went forth to the city gate, and there sat down with this intention—'Whoever shall come first to this spot, whether Shaman or Brahman, to him will I offer this food in charity.' Now it so happened that outside the city gate there was a Pratyaka (Pasé) Buddha dwelling, whose name was Nagarasikhi [*perfect hair, or chaplet* (*Ch. ed.*)], who, on this very morning, had arisen early, and arranged his dress, etc. in order, with a view to go a-begging within the city of Benares. Then, as he approached the gate, the citizen beheld him coming on with dignified mien and measured pace, looking neither to the right nor left; and as he beheld him thus, his heart was filled with joy and satisfaction, and taking his food, he offered it forthwith to this Pratyaka Buddha. Then the venerable personage, having received the food, thought thus with himself—'It is still early, and I have met with this supply unexpectedly. I will, therefore, give myself up to thought and self-examination for a time before eating.' And for this purpose he went down to the river's bank, and selecting there a shady spot beneath a spreading tree, he sat down with his legs crossed, and gave himself up to inward contemplation. Now it so happened that the King of Benares at this time was called Brahmadatta [*Virtue of Brahma* (*Ch. ed.*)], a very celebrated monarch; and on this very day he was proceeding in his chariot, surrounded by the four kinds of military cortege, beyond the precincts of the city on a certain business. Just then a villager, travelling towards Benares with an umbrella in his hand to shelter himself withal, was advancing along the same road, when lo! he saw the King Brahmadatta coming onwards towards the very spot where he was. Seeing this, he thought with himself, 'I will get out of the way of the King'; and so, stepping down into a byepath, he went onwards through the wood till he came to the riverside; and then, following the river's course, he went on towards the city. As he was thus going, suddenly he came to the very spot where the Pratyeka Buddha was sitting, lost in reverie, under the tree, and his food by his side. And now it so happened that the sun had risen so high that the spot where he was sitting, motionless and lost in contemplation, was no longer in the shade, but exposed to the full glare and heat of the day. And so the perspiration was bursting from every pore, and trickling down his face.

Seeing which the villager thought thus—'This Rishi is evidently lost in abstraction, fulfilling some religious purpose; and the sun's rays, as they light on his body, must be a source of inconvenience. I will stop here, and shelter him with my umbrella.' At length the Pratyeka Buddha, perceiving that the time for taking food had fully come, thought thus with himself—'It is now time to take food (12 o'clock)! I will shake off this ecstasy and arise.' Having done so, lo! he beheld the man by his side holding an umbrella over his head to shade him from the sun. In return for this act of consideration, the Pratyeka Buddha immediately ascended into the air, and exhibited before the eyes of the villager some wonderful transformations; he caused fire and water to proceed from his mouth, and many other astonishing changes; so that the villager, overcome by what he saw, was filled with faith, and bowed down at the feet of the saint, uttering these words—'Oh! that I, in future states of existence, may fall into no evil kind of birth![1] but may be able to offer food, and provide other necessaries for this Pratyeka Buddha.'

"Then he asked the saint where he lived, on which he replied, 'I live in such and such a place.'

"Then the villager at once proceeded to the place where his pansal was; he swept it and watered it with great care, and having cleansed it from all pollutions, he requested permission to offer to the Pratyeka Buddha the four necessary articles, viz., food, drink, clothing, and medicine. After this he returned to his home, and told his father, mother, and wife what he had witnessed; and taking them to the pansal of the Pratyeka Buddha, they also beheld, and finally requested permission to leave their homes and become disciples, whereupon Nagarasikhi instructed the villager to go and join himself to the company of some Parivrajakas (wandering hermits) who were located near that spot, and 'after learning from them,' he said, 'how to subdue your appetites and to practise complete self-control, then you may be in a condition, when a future Buddha called Sâkya comes into the world, to join yourself to his company and become a Rahat.'

"After this, the Pratyeka Buddha died, and entered Nirvâna, on which they burnt his body, gathered together his relics, and

[1] That is, be born either as a beast, or an Asura, or in Hell.

erected a tower over them, and having decorated the tower with flags and surmounting canopies they worshipped before it, offering flowers and burning incense. So it came to pass that this villager, having for a long time practised the discipline of these Paribrajakas, became a recluse, and on one occasion, as he went to the city of Benares to beg, he accidentally saw the corpse of a woman covered with a loathsome disease, and awaiting to be burned; worms and disgusting insects covered it—it was altogether a loathsome sight. This spectacle so affected him, and impressed his mind with the vanity and misery of life, that he uttered this vow: 'Oh! would that when Sâkya Buddha appears in the world, I may become his disciple and undertake all the rules of a religious life, and so obtain deliverance.' And so, after his death, he was born in the heaven of Brahma; after that he was again born in the world, and so successively through many births, till at last he was born a great minister, rich and prosperous in this very city of Benares; but still his vow was not perfectly accomplished. Afterwards, however, having been born as the king of the country of Kasi, known by the name of Narakhi, he was devoted to Kâsyapa Buddha, and erected over his ashes a Stupa, adorned with the seven precious substances. This Stupa was called Dasavrika (*ten marks, Ch. ed.*), and was surmounted by seven encircling discs placed there by the king and his different relatives. On this account that king is now born as Yasada; and because formerly he held that umbrella over the head of the Pratyeka Buddha, there is now over his head 'a precious chatta ever appearing of itself,'[1] and his father and mother and wife have become my first lay disciples." At this time the world-honoured one pronounced these Gâthas:

"Thus by nourishing and tending holy men,
Great merit and corresponding recompense is acquired.
At present this reward may be as a man or Deva,
But hereafter it shall secure complete Nirvâna."

[Kiouen XXXVI contains 6270 words and cost 3.135 taels.]

---

[1] This seems to relate to the origin of Yasada's name.

CHAPTER XXXVII.

The History of Pûrna.

Now there was in a certain village between Kosala and Kapilavastu a great Brahman, whom Suddhôdana had made first minister of the country. He was exceedingly rich and prosperous, and his palace was beautiful as that of Vaisravana,[1] the king of the Northern Region. He had one only son whose name was Purnamaitrayani putra, of great personal beauty, unequalled for grace, and perfectly acquainted with the Vedas and Shasters. He was born on the same day as Siddârtha, and was of a most gentle disposition. Now it came to pass when he grew up that Pûrna, becoming dissatisfied with worldly occupation and pleasure, resolved to become an ascetic. Accordingly, on a favourable occasion, without naming his intention either to father or mother, he left his home with thirty companions, and having reached the slopes of the Snowy Mountains, they practised the life of the Paribrajakas (*i. e.*, hermits).

After a time, having acquired spiritual faculties, he was able to enter dhyâna and perceive hidden truths. Being so gifted, he said that he would use his spiritual power to find out what had become of Prince Siddârtha, and whether, as yet, he had gained the dominion of a sacred Chakravarti monarch. On this, exercising his faculty of divine sight, he perceived that the prince had now become completely enlightened, and was preaching the law for the good of Devas and men in the Deer park near Benares. On this he was filled with joy, and communicated the intelligence to his thirty companions.

Afterwards, setting out from the Snowy Mountains, they all flew through the air, even as the Royal Hansa king pursues his flight, and thus arrived together at the Deer Park. Then Pûrna going to the side of Bhagavat, bowed down before him, and placed his foot upon his head; and then raising his face, he kissed the foot of Tathâgata, as he prostrated himself before him, and afterwards uttered these laudatory stanzas :

"Oh thou! who in former days dwelt in the Tusita Heavens,
And thence came down in the shape of a white elephant,

[1] The same as Kuvera, the God of wealth.

To be incarnated in the womb of the Divine Mâya,
To be born in the royal house of the Sâkyas;
As the lotus springs uncontaminated from the water,
So was thy body pure and spotless in the womb.
What joy and delight was it to thy mother,
Desiring no carnal joys, but rejoicing only in the Law,
Walking in perfect purity, with no stain of wickedness,
Beholding her son dwelling in her womb, as in a golden casket," etc., etc.

Then after some time, Pûrna and his thirty friends all became Rahats. It was this Pûrna of whom the world-honoured spake as follows: "Bhikshus! know ye that of all my disciples, this Pûrna will be the first for preaching the law amongst men;" and so the Gâtha says:

"The world-honoured dwelling at Benares,
Spake in gentlest words to the great congregation,
This Bhikshu Pûrna, a true disciple,
Shall be the most distinguished of those who preach my law."

Story of Narada.

§ 2. Now there was in South India, in this continent of Jambudivipa, a country called Avanti; and in the middle of that country there was a village called "Monkey-food"; and in this village a rich and prosperous Brahman of the family of Katyayana; his palace like that of Vaisravana, and himself perfectly versed in all the literature of the Vedas and Shasters, so that the King made him chief minister of the realm. Now, the eldest son of this nobleman, having gone forth on his travels to complete his education, returned, after a time, perfectly versed in all the polite learning of the day; able to repeat the Vedas and Shasters, and acquainted with all the learned works of the time. Then the father said to his second son, who was called Narada, "You too, my son, may now proceed on your travels and, like your brother, perfect yourself in the literature of the day." Then Narada, having heard these words, replied, "Noble father! I am already perfectly acquainted with all these works; so that if my honourable father will now assemble together the people, I will repeat the Vedas from beginning to end." On hearing this, his father was greatly rejoiced, and having convoked a large assembly, his son Narada repeated before them all the Vedas and the various Shasters, as he had promised to do.

Then all the assembly exclaimed, "Well done! well done! clever youth!" and his father, filled with joy, bestowed on him great stores of wealth and jewels. But his elder brother, being vexed at the celebrity which Narada thus acquired, began to plot against his life; on which his father made the following plan for his younger son to escape the malice of his brother. There was a certain city in that southern region called "Oudyani," and not far from the city was a mount called Pandu (or, Pandagiri), in a cave of which an old Rishi called Asita was living. This Rishi had so thoroughly mastered the Vedas and the Shasters that he was able to exercise every supernatural power, and to practise the four sorts of ecstatic reverie. Then the rich Brahman and his wife brought Narada to this old man and entreated him to take him as a disciple, and perfect him in all the knowledge necessary for the acquirement of supernatural power.

Then the Rishi, accompanied by Narada, went to the neighbourhood of Benares, and having made a leafy Pansal outside the city, he dwelt there, and during six hours of every day continually repeated this exhortation, "Narada! Narada! a Buddha has now been born; go, then, shave your head, leave your home, practise the conduct of a Brahmana, and become a follower of the sage, for your own and others good." Shortly after this the Rishi died, nevertheless, Narada, blinded by the adulations of men, was unable to seek the refuge afforded by Buddha, the Law and the Church.

At this time, Elapatra, a Nagarâja, conceived a strong desire to forsake sin and become a religious person. This desire had haunted him ever since the time of Kâsyapa Buddha Tathâgata, who had told him that after a certain number of years Sâkya Muni Tathâgata would be born; but as yet he knew not whether this had come to pass or not. Now there was also another Nâga Râja, called Sâgara, at whose palace were frequent assemblies of the Nâgas, and to these assemblies Elapatra repaired. On one occasion, meeting a certain Yaksha Râja at the palace of Sâgara, he asked him if Sâkya Buddha was already born in the world; to whom the Yaksha replied, "I know not indeed; all I know is this, that in a certain desolate region there is a Yaksha city called Arkabandu, and in this city there is a couplet of verses inscribed, which are to this effect—" If no Buddha is born in the world, then no man can read these verses;" and, "if they can be read, still no one can explain them except Buddha alone." Then Elapatra addressed that Yaksha Râja and said, " Dear Yaksha! go, I pray you, and see if you can read these verses, and, if so, bring me an account of them." Then the Yaksha Râja, having gone to this city of Arkabandu, soon returned to the palace of Sâgara Râja and said, " Rejoice, oh Elapatra! for I can read the verses, and therefore be sure that Sâkya Tathâgata has been born! And if any one can be found able to explain their meaning, be sure that he is Buddha himself."

Then Elapatra, with great joy, received these Gâthas from the Yaksha.

Meanwhile, the two dragon Râjas, taking with them a Nâga maiden of exceeding beauty, and vessels full of the choicest food and other rare offerings, went to the banks of the Ganges and standing in the open space adjoining the river, repeated these Gâthas in the hearing of all passers by—

> " In what does true independence consist?
> What is it that causes pollution?
> How can one attain perfect purity?
> What is it that deludes men most?
> Why is the deluded man so utterly deceived?
> And who is the really wise?
> From what associations must one be freed,
> Before he can be said to be free indeed?"

Then these Dragon Râjas offered the gifts of rice and money, and the Nâga girl as a wife, to any one who could answer these questions. At length Narada, who was now dwelling in Magadha, knowing that the people would despise him if he did not undertake to answer these Gâthas, went boldly to the Nâga Râjas and asked them to repeat the verses in his hearing; then, having heard them, he promised after seven days to return with the true interpretation of them.

And so it came to pass that the six heretical teachers who resided at Benares endeavoured to find out the hidden meaning of these lines, in vain; till at last Narada, hearing that Buddha was residing in the Deer park near the city, went to him, and respectfully requested him to explain the Gâthas as he recited them.

Then Buddha said—

"Because of the 'six' (Abhidjñas) a man becomes independent,
The pollution of Kingship is the great pollution;
To be thus polluted and yet to know it not,
Is the great delusion of the world;
To empty the great River (of transmigration),
This is the end of all expedients;
And he who is able to do this
Is the only Wise man."

Then Narada, having brought this explanation, Elapatra, the Nâga Râja, besought him to say where and from whom he had received it; for, said he, "Whoever communicated it to you, he is the true Buddha come into the world." Then Narada answered,

"As you say, oh Nâga Râja, the explanation is not mine,
It is the great Sage, the Holy Buddha, who has revealed it,
Whose body is marked by all the distinguishing signs;
He alone was able to unravel its meaning."

Then Elapatra, having inquired where Buddha was dwelling, Narada again replied in verse—

"The great independent one (Isvara)[1] among gods and men
Is now dwelling within the Deer garden of Benares;
There he is declaring the doctrines of his system
With a voice like that of the lion in the forest."

Then Narada, having further bared his right shoulder and bent his right knee in adoration towards the spot where Buddha was residing, Elapatra also in the orthodox manner made obeisance towards the same quarter, and repeated the formula, "Namo Bhagavata Tathâgataya Arya Sambuddha" (three times).

Then Elapatra resolved not to use any spiritual transformation but in his own natural body to behold Buddha; on which, extending his body from Taxasila to Benares, a distance of three hundred

[1] The word "independent" means here "self-dependent," or "self-sufficient" (*swayambhu*).

and sixty yojanas, his head reached to the spot where Buddha was, while his tail was still in his palace. Then his head, like the prow of a ship, or the trunk of an elephant, emitting all sort of flame and lightning flash, and uttering every sort of terrible sound, bent before the world-honoured one, who, on his part, only said, "Welcome, Elapatra! It is long since I have seen you. Welcome, oh! Nâga Râja!"

[Kiouen XXXVII contains 6,167 words, and cost 3.083 taels.]

CHAPTER XXXVIII.

§ 1. THEN Elapatra, perceiving that he was known, transformed himself into the shape of a Manava youth, and approaching Buddha, bowed down before him, and then, standing apart, repeated these verses—

"In what does true independence consist?
What is it that really pollutes and deceives a man?
And who is the pure and unspotted man?
And what is it that brings delusion?" etc. etc.

(Then Buddha replies as before.)

Then Elapatra added, by way of inquiry, the Gâtha following—

"By doing what, and observing what rules,
And acquiring what ground of merit,
May one attain an excellent condition as Deva or man,
And so lay up in store future blessedness?"

To which Bhagavat immediately said, in reply—

"Ministering to the worthy! doing harm to none!
Always ready to render reverence to whom it is due,
Loving righteousness and righteous conversation,
Ever willing to listen to that which may profit another,
Rejoicing to meditate on the true Law,
And to reflect on the words of Divine Wisdom,
Practising every kind of self-discipline and pure life,
Always doing good to those around you.
* * * * * *
This is indeed the wisdom of a true disciple."

Then Elapatra, regarding Buddha with attention, began to weep; on which Buddha inquired why he did so. On this Elapatra rejoined, "I remember in days gone by, that I was a follower of Kâsyapa Buddha, and because I destroyed a tree called 'Ila' I was born in my present shape, and was called 'Elapatra.' Then this same Kâsyapa told me that after an indefinite period, when Sâkya Buddha came into the world, that I should again receive a human shape, and so by becoming a disciple attain final deliverance, and it is for this reason I weep!" Then Elapatra, having taken refuge in Buddha, the Law and the Church, departed, having first offered to Narada the money, and the Nâga girl, both of which he refused.[1]

After this, Narada and his companions became disciples, and because he was of the family of Katyayana, he was called "the great Katyayana;" and of him it was Buddha said—"He of all my disciples shall be most distinguished in the definition of words, and fixing their true meaning." And then Buddha narrated the following history respecting Katyayana in his former births—"I remember in years gone by, in the middle of this Bhadra Kalpa, when men's lives were twenty thousand years in duration, that there was a certain Buddha born, whose name was Kasyapa. This Buddha also preached the Law in this Deer park, near Benares. A certain religious person, having come near to hear this Buddha preach, made the following vow—'May I also in future years become like one of these disciples, and be privileged to attend on the person of a true Buddha.' This disciple, oh Bhikshus! was the present Narada, who is none other than the great Katyayana."

Story of Sobhiya.[2]

§ 2. At this time, in North India, there was a city called Taxasila

---

[1] This story seems to be the subject of one of the groups at Bharahut, lately discovered by the Archæological Surveyor of India, and thus described by him—"A bas-relief representing a Nâga chief kneeling before the Bôdhi tree, attended by a number of Nâga followers, with this inscription, 'Erapâto Nâgarâja Bhagavata vandate,' *i. e.*, 'Erapatra, the Nâga Râja, worships Buddha.'" *V. Report of Archæol. Surveyor of India*, 1874. *V.* also *Jul.* ii, p. 152.

[2] *Vide* "Manual of Buddhism," p. 254.

[*severed rock* (*Ch. ed.*)]. There was a certain family living in that city, in which were born unexpectedly two children—twins—the one a boy, the other a girl. Then the parents, having sent for a renowned soothsayer, had the horoscope of these children cast at once. The wise man pronounced the tokens of the female child unlucky. The mother, having heard this, began to think with herself—"This child will be the cause of much anxiety to us, she will never find an honourable condition of married life." Having thought thus, she inquired after a woman belonging to the Paribrajakas,[1] and begged her to take care of the child, and that she would pay all expenses.

So, then, it happened that this child grew up under the care of the Paribrajaka woman, and was duly instructed in all the wisdom of the day, and grew more and more comely as she increased in years. At this time a certain Paribrajaka from North India, having met this woman, and being much struck with her beauty, fell in love with her; but, to avoid a public scandal, they agreed that there should be a disputation between them, and whoever prevailed that the other should be slave and servant. Accordingly, having met, the disputation began, and the female being defeated, she joined herself to the company of the other; and taking his slippers and water-vessel, in token of her servitude, she went her way. After having come together, a change took place in the woman's appearance, which caused the man to forsake her; but before doing so she said, "It is because I have lost my beauty that you are about to leave me, and I shall die alone and neglected." On this the Paribrajaka said to the woman, "Take this golden ring, and if you give birth to a girl, use it for your mutual support; but if you give birth to a boy, then commit the ring to his care, and bid him set out and search till he find me, his father, and by this ring I shall know him." And so, taking his leave of the woman, he turned, and went on his way. Then the woman, travelling about, came at length to the village of Ma-tou (Mathura?); and there, in a secluded spot, called the White Cloud Valley, she brought forth a son, in the district-hall, and so she called the child Sobhiya [*district court* (*Ch. ed.*)]. Then

[1] *Vide* M. B. 254. The Chinese *tika* defines the word as a "wanderer" (*hing-hing*).

all the people round about, seeing her destitute condition, moved with pity and commiseration, brought every necessary article of food and clothing for her use and the use of the child. And so the boy grew up, instructed by his mother in the three Vedas, and all the liberal arts.[1]

At length Sobhiya one day asked his mother who his father was, and where he was to be found; on which his mother said, "Your sire, dear child, lives somewhere in South India; go, then, and seek for him"; at the same time she gave him the ring as a means of recognition, and forthwith the young man set out. So, travelling from town to town, and village to village, he arrived at length in South India; and there, hearing of a celebrated champion of logic, who challenged all comers to dispute with him, Sobhiya, not knowing it was his father, forthwith sounded the drum of the law, and said—"I am ready to meet in disputation any Paribrajaka, man, or woman, who dares to encounter me in discussion." Forthwith the Paribrajaka came forward, and being immediately moved with feelings of love at the sight of the youth, asked him—"Who are you, and whence come you?" On this an explanation took place, and, by means of the ring, the father was convinced that the youth was no other than his son. So, taking him, he instructed him in every religious practice, including the power of dhyâna (ecstasy), and other acquirements connected with the profession of a hermit—and after that he died.

Then Sobhiya, his father being dead, gradually journeyed on, till at last, coming to the sea-coast, he there made him a Pansal to dwell in, and took up his abode there. And so he remained for a time practising the power of abstract meditation (dhyâna) and the five spiritual faculties; and so he boasted that he had acquired the dignity and privileges of a Rahat.

Now, Sobhiya's mother, dying, was born in the Trâyastrinshas heavens; at which time the world-honoured one, having obtained supreme wisdom, was preaching in the Deer park near Benares. The news of this having reached the thirty-three heavens, it came also to the ears of the Devî, the mother of the young man Sobhiya. On this she exercised her spiritual power of sight, to find out where her son was; and seeing that he was occupying a Pan-

[1] *Tayo vede Sabbasippáni ca.* Fausböll, 5 Jatakas, p. 32 n.

sal by the sea-shore, she appeared to him in a vision by night, and discouraged him from thinking he was a Rahat, and bade him go seek the instruction of Bhagavat in the Deer park. Then Sobhiya, not being disobedient to the heavenly visitor, set out on his journey; and wherever he came he challenged all disputants to meet him in discussion. So he drew near to Benares, and there, hearing of the celebrated six teachers, Purna, Kâsyapa, and so on, he immediately sought their company, and having saluted them, he arose and stood on one side.

[Kiouen XXXVIII contains 6,234 words, and cost 3.117 taels.]

CHAPTER XXXIX.

§ 1. Then Sobhiya inquired of Purna, Kâsyapa, and the others, what their system of religion was, and proposed various questions to them respecting subjects which caused him doubt; but their answers were only confusing and unsatisfactory. He turned away, therefore, and sought the company of Masakali Gosala, and the other Nirgranthas, with the same success. At length he determined to seek the company of the Great Shaman (Gôtama), and lay bare his doubts before him, and request a right solution of them. So he came, and found the world-honoured one bright (as the moon) in the midst of the stars of heaven, glorious among the assembly of Bhikshus who surrounded him. Then, prostrating himself at his feet, he rose up, and took his place on one side; after which he addressed the world-honoured thus—

"I am Sobhiya, a man of religion (Bôdhi),
And on this account I have travelled far and come here,
Because I have doubts, and I desire to ask a learned man
On my account to explain them, and satisfy me;
Oh, would that you would solve my doubts,
And answer me, one by one, the questions I put,
And so, explaining these things as I name them,
Gradually open out to me the clear light of truth."

To whom the world-honoured one replied—

"Sobhiya! thou hast come from afar,
Desiring to ask me respecting your doubts;
Ask, then, now! and I will explain,
According as your queries are put, in order."

Then Sobhiya, struck with the calm and self-possessed appearance of Gôtama, addressed him thus with all reverence—

"Holy one! tell me what means the word Bhikshu?
What means the expression, to 'overcome and subdue'?
Seeing and knowing what things is it, that a man is called 'Buddha'.
Oh! that the world-honoured one would explain these things to me!"

At this time, the world-honoured answered Sobhiya in the following stanzas—

"A man who endures constant penance in search of wisdom,
Overcoming all doubts, and crossing over to the shore of Nirvana—
Letting go all thoughts of what exists, and what does not exist,
Thoroughly practising the rules of a Brahmana! he is a Bhikshu.
Whoever is able to forsake all systems, and practise right-recollection,
Living in the world, and doing no harm to aught that lives,
Able to acquire a body spotless and pure,
And escape all the toils of sorrow; he is called *calm*.
Able to control all the senses and objects of sense,
And to subdue all obstacles in the way; he is called *True*.
Living above this world, and all other worlds,
Awaiting the time of Nirvâna; he is called *Virtuous*.
Toiling through ages of suffering,
Receiving births and deaths in succession,
Yet not soiled by the pollution of the world;
This man is rightly called 'Buddha'".

[And much more to the same effect; after which Sobhiya becomes a disciple.]

The Story of the Chief Soldier (Senapati).

§ 2. Now at this time people from all quarters were flocking to Buddha, to hear him preach, and join his community; on which Buddha, after due consideration, resolved to send his followers through the different districts, towns and villages, to teach and explain his system of doctrine, and so prepare the way for their becoming disciples. So, early in the morning, on a certain day, he assembled the Bhikshus together, and addressed them thus—"Bhikshus! I desire to go into retirement for a time; go ye and visit the different cities and towns of the land, and prepare the way for my coming." Moreover, he gave them directions as to the mode of receiving all who sought to become disciples—that they should receive the tonsure, and wear the robes of a mendicant, and be instructed in the other rules of right behaviour, such as bending the knee and clasping the hands; and, finally, how they ought to take refuge in the threefold formula (Buddha, the Law, the Church). Then Buddha, having sent them forth, retired to the Deer park, and there rested for a time, having already signified his intention to proceed gradually towards Uravilva, and the village of the soldier-lord (Senapati), to preach the law for his sake and others.

And so the Gâtha says—

"Bhikshus! having myself escaped from all sorrows,
I desire my own profit to redound to the good of others;
There are yet a vast number of men enthralled by grief—
For these we ought to have some care and compassion.
Do you, therefore, oh Bhikshus!
Each one go forth by himself, to teach the world;
Whilst I, by myself, go from this place
Towards the village of Uravilva, to preach there."

Then again Mâra came to the spot where Buddha dwelt, and addressed him thus—

"You, oh Shaman! are bound by the same cords
As those which bind both gods and men;
You are entwined in the same meshes as they,
And from these thou canst never escape!"

Then the world honoured one recognising at once, from the words, that they came from Mâra the wicked one, replied to him in a Gâtha as follows—

"Long ago have I escaped from all the meshes of the net;
No more am I bound with the cords which bind gods and men;
My body has been released from all these trammels,
And I have conquered thee, oh wicked one! What more, then, dost thou seek?"

Moreover, he added the following Gâtha—

"The five pollutions that affect the human race—
The power of beauty, sound, odour, taste, and touch—
These I have long since cast away and rejected,
And in so doing I have conquered all thy power, oh Mâra!"

Then the devil took to flight, and left the enlightened one.

Then the Bhikshus addressed Buddha, and said—"Suppose, on our entering a town or village, we are asked what is the meaning of the word Shaman or Brahman, what answer shall we give?" To whom Buddha replied in a verse—

"A man who has for ever destroyed the source of evil desire,
And left no longer in himself a seed of covetousness,
Who is calm and at rest, both in body and soul—
This man is rightly called a Shaman and a Bhikshu, etc., etc.
Cleansed thus from all personal defilement, and coming out of the world,
He is truly a homeless one—a disciple indeed."

The Bhikshus then inquired what words they were to use when begging their food from door to door; to whom Buddha replied—

"The wise man, in begging, uses no words,
Nor does he point to this or that in accepting food;
But silently he stands, lost in thought and self-recollection.
He who thus begs is indeed a true Shaman.
Whoever sees a religious person thus begging his food,
May be sure that he is worthy of his charity, and a real disciple."

[After some further conversation, the Bhikshus respectfully salute their master and depart.]

Now the guardian spirit, who kept watch in the grove where the Bhikshus had been, perceiving that the place was now empty and without occupants, came to Buddha, and inquired of him the reason why the disciples had gone, and whither they were going; on which Buddha replied—

"These disciples of mine, perfect in self-restraint,
Have gone forth to convert the world
They have gone to Kosala,
And to Vaisali,
And to the land of Ayûdhyâ,
And to the region of the diamond-fields,[1]
To subdue and remove the doubts of men,
Respecting the truths of the law which I declare."

So it came to pass, when the time of the Summer's Rest[2] at Benares was past—the world-honoured one having sent his disciples forth to preach and teach—himself set out for Uravilva, where he had practised the austerities he endured for six years. Now, in that village of Uravilva there was a great Brahman called Senapati, who had resided there from very remote time, for the purpose of instructing and benefiting the people. So it came to pass that, as Buddha was journeying along the usual road near to this village, that he saw a copse of beautiful trees by the wayside, and, feeling fatigued, he retired to this shady retreat for a time, and sat down beneath a tree of remarkable beauty.

Just at this time there was a party of thirty young men enjoying themselves in this same wood, all of whom, save one, had a pleasant female companion as an associate. Then the others, seeing that one of their number was not accompanied by a companion, began to contrive how to find one for him, but without any success, till at last they got a common dancing girl to join herself to their company, and associate with the young man who was alone without a female friend. So they passed their time in singing and

---

[1] Literally, the region of the district of the Great Diamond country (Vajra).

[2] The Summer Rest, as is well-known, is the season of the rains, during which Buddhists met together under the cover of some friendly roof or monastery. This season is sometimes called their "Lent."

dancing, till, night coming on, they gradually sank to rest, and were soon asleep. Then the dancing woman, seeing they were all asleep, arose, and having taken such jewels and property belonging to the men as struck her fancy, she departed out of the wood. Then the young man whose companion she was, waking out of his sleep in the morning, and finding his fair companion gone, aroused his fellows, and they all set off in pursuit of her. Suddenly, under a tree, they lighted on Buddha, sitting in a perfectly composed manner, and conspicuous for his superhuman beauty and dignified mien. Addressing him respectfully, they asked him if he had seen the woman of pleasure, their former companion, go by that way? To whom Buddha replied: "Tell me, I pray, all about this woman of whom you speak; why did she come to you, and from whence?" Then they related to him the story of their adventure. On this Buddha replied to the young men thus: "Listen to me, oh youths! and I will ask you a question—whether it is better, think you, to find yourselves, or to find this woman whom ye seek?" They replied —"It would certainly be better to find ourselves." Then Buddha invited them to sit down whilst he recited to them his law [*and in the end they were all converted, and became Rahats*].

Then Buddha, passing on through the wood, came to another beautiful tree, and there sat down. Whilst seated thus, it so happened that sixty travellers drew nigh; and seeing Buddha, so beautiful in form and figure, thus resting, they drew nigh to him, and having heard his exposition of the law, they also were converted and became Rahats.

[Kiouen XXXIX contains 5,834 words, and cost 2.917 taels.]

CHAPTER XL.

§ 1. So Buddha, by easy stages, at length arrived at the bank of the river Ganges; then a certain ferryman, whose boat was on the margin of the river, seeing the venerable one approaching, hurried him and exclaimed: "Welcome! world-honoured, whence come you thus unexpectedly? Deign to enter my boat, that I may transport you to the other side!" Then Buddha, having gone on board, began to instruct the ferryman according to the purport of the following Gâthas—

"If you should allow your boat to lie useless in the sun (on the shore),
Little the profit that your calling would bring you;
So if you can let go your hold on the shore of desire and appetite,
Soon shall you attain the reward of your enterprise, and arrive at Nirvâna," etc., etc.[1]

Having thus preached to the ferryman, suddenly there appeared in his hands an alms-bowl, and his hair seemed as though it had only just been shaved, and his appearance altogether was like that of an old Bhikshu; and thus, having preached further to him, this man, too, became a Rahat.

So, by degrees approaching nearer to Uravilva, Buddha saw before him a Brahman youth, very beautiful to behold, in his left hand a golden ewer, in his right a precious staff. This was Sâkra, who had assumed this shape. And so going on his way thus prepared before him, he arrived at length at the village of the soldier-chief, and, approaching his house, he entered it and sat down. Now this illustrious Brahman had two daughters, one called Nandi, the other Bala, who went forth on beholding the venerable one, and escorted him with much reverence within the house. On their account Buddha began to explain the four sacred truths, and so they also became disciples. And forthwith they took from his hand the alms-dish which he carried, and filling it with every sort of tasty food, they brought it again to him, and desired him to eat.

Then the world-honoured one, having received the food, at once left the village, and proceeded onwards.

At this time, the great Brahman called Deva, having heard from some other quarter that Buddha, the great Shaman, had returned to the neighbourhood of Uravilva, forthwith began to reflect thus

---

[1] These Gâthas are obscure.

with himself—"I remember, in former days, having asked this great Shaman to accept at my hands an offering of food; and now I am so poor that I can present him with nothing worth his acceptance. What expedient shall I adopt?" Reflecting thus, he returned to his house, and laid the case before his wife, asking her advice. Then the woman advised him to do as follows: "I remember," she said, "not long ago that the rich Brahman, Senayana, came to my house, and used blandishments, and made promises, to tempt me to permit him soft dalliance with me; but I would not allow it, or permit him so much as to touch me; but now, my master, seeing that things are as they are, and that you have made a vow to provide entertainment for this great Shaman, you had better let me go to the house of Senayana, and, by my art and persuasiveness, I will get from him what money I please, yielding to his dalliance as I think fit." On this, the Brahman Deva replied—"Far be such a thing from me; it would be entirely contrary to the purity of my caste to permit you so to behave yourself. Such a thing can never be!"

Then Deva proceeded to the house of Senayana, and entering within, he addressed the latter as follows—"My dear friend Senayana! I beseech you lend me for a short time five hunded pieces of money. I will do my best to return it to you very soon; and if not, my two wives will undertake to repay you by working for you as slaves in your house!" On this, Senayana having lent him the money, Deva returned to his house, and bade his wife prepare a sumptuous repast for the morrow, whilst he himself went out into the neighbouring wood, to invite the great Shaman to partake of his hospitality. This having been done and his invitation accepted, Deva returned to his house and made all ready. On the morrow, going forth, he acquainted Buddha that the offering was prepared, and besought him at once to come to his house to partake of it. Escorting him thus, Deva and his guest returned home, and there his wife, having dressed the food made of the most delicious ingredients, herself waited on Buddha and placed the offering before him. After accepting it the world-honoured one arranged his seat, and proceeded to expound the system of his teaching for the sake of the Brahman and his wife. Deva, meanwhile, placed his seat close to the feet of Buddha and attentively listened. After this, the world-honoured one arose and left the house, escorted as before by the Brahman Deva.

Now it came to pass that, after they had gone, the Brahman's wife took off a robe she had worn during the feast, and which she had borrowed from a neighbour, and putting it on one side by itself, she began to sweep and clean the house and attend to other domestic duties.

Just then a thief spying about saw the robe which the woman had borrowed lying by itself, and, seeing it was a costly one, he slyly entered the room and went off with it. Then the wife of Deva, discovering her loss, was greatly distressed, and in sad perplexity. Meantime, the Brahman returned home, and seeing his wife looking so disconsolate, he inquired the reason; on which she told him all about her loss, and how she had borrowed the robe that had been stolen. On this, Deva was greatly cast down, and addressed the woman thus—"You know that I had to borrow that money to buy the food necessary for the offering that the great Shaman has accepted, and now you have borrowed a robe, and it is lost! how shall I ever be able to repay all this, seeing we are so poor?"

On this, Deva went out, and going into the wood, where dead bodies are placed, he got up into a high tree, determined to kill himself by throwing himself down.

Just then, he saw a man approaching the spot, and he detected at once that he was the very thief who had stolen the borrowed robe, which in fact he was carrying in his hand. Stopping underneath the tree where Deva was, the thief dug a hole and put the garment there, and then, having covered it, he departed. On this Deva came down, and removing the earth, he took the garment up and returned with it to his house. Meantime, his wife, searching and sweeping through every corner of the abode, found unexpectedly the mouth of a sort of hole in the ground, of which she knew nothing before; and clearing away the opening and looking down into it she saw a red copper vessel full of gold pieces, and to her great surprise, on examining further, she saw one and two and three more, all full of gold, and underneath these, others. Seeing this, she set up a great shout, and beckoning to her husband, she cried out, "My lord! my lord! come quickly! hasten with all your speed!" Deva, hearing his wife's shouts, began to think—"What is the matter with the woman now? why is she bellowing out like a madwoman, 'I've found it! I've found it?' Found what? for it is I who have found the garment and not she!" So, entering into his house, he asked his wife what she meant by saying, 'she had found it'; "why here, you see, it is I who have found it, and not you." On this, the woman continued to exclaim, "Oh! I have found it! I have found it;" and at last she led her husband to the place, and pointed to the crocks full of gold. On this, he bade his wife take back the robe to the person from whom she had borrowed it, whilst he, taking some of the money out of one of the pots, went straight to Senayana to repay him the five hundred pieces he had borrowed, On arriving at Senayana's house and offering him the money, the latter addressed Deva thus—"I agreed with you that you should not borrow this money of any one for the purpose of repaying me; but that you should wait till you could by your own effort save it from your labour, and then give it back." On this, Deva assured him that he had borrowed it of no one; and, being further questioned, he said the earth had given it to him, and at last he told Senayana all about it, and took him back to his house, and showed him all the crocks full of gold. At first, Senayana said he was mad, for the stuff was not gold, but only charred wood! But Deva, at last, taking up some of the pieces, showed them to Senayana and said, "See what good fortune is mine, and it is all in consequence of my offering made to that great Shaman!"

[*On this, Deva invites Buddha a second time to his house; and, finally, both he and his wives become faithful disciples.*] [*This story is intended to show the folly of covetousness, and the reward of liberality in religious matters.*]

The History of the Three Kâsyapas.

§ 2. At this time, the world-honoured one thought thus with himself—"What man of distinguished character is there whom I may convert to my doctrine, so that by his conversion he may bring over with him a body of disciples?" Now it so happened that there dwelt near the village of Uravilva, three celebrated Rishis of the Brahman caste (Brahmacharis), who wore their hair as a spiral head-dress;[1] their names were these—the first, Uravilva Kâsyapa, the chief of the three, who had five hundred spiral-haired followers. The second, Nâdi Kâsyapa, who had three hundred followers. The third, Gâya Kâsyapa, who had two hundred followers. Altogether there were one thousand of these disciples, all of whom were learners at the feet of these three Rishis.

Then the world-honoured thus reflected: "the fame of this Uravilva Kâsyapa is spread throughout all Magadha, and all the people hold him to be a great Rahat. I must convert this man first, so that all his followers and those who believe in his sanctity may come over to me, and so there may be much happiness conferred on the world." Then reflecting that these Rishis made much ado about self-mortification and penance, the world-honoured one transformed himself into a spiral-haired Yogi, and with 500 followers he came flying through the air to the place where Uravilva Kâsyapa and his followers were located. Alighting thus in their midst, there was no small stir amongst the followers of the Rishi, as they hurried here and there to bring water and mats and other necessaries for the new arrivals, and meantime they addressed them in hurried language saying, "Whence come ye, so suddenly, oh sirs? Why did ye not tell us beforehand of your coming?" [and so on]. Then all at once, Buddha assumed his own appearance, and stood there alone in their midst, his head shaven, with his Kashâya-coloured robe over his shoulders.

Then Uravilva Kâsyapa began to think thus—"Doubtless this great Shaman is possessed of considerable spiritual power and is of great personal dignity; but he is not a Rahat like myself."

Then he addressed Buddha as follows:—"Your excellency has doubtless come from far; if it seem good to you to stay here awhile, we will welcome you with our best; dwell in whatever place you wish, there is a pansal for you to sleep in, and a hall for worship." To whom Buddha replied, "Thanks, oh Kâsyapa! if it be not disagreeable to you, I will enter the place where you worship the Fire Spirit, whose votaries you are!" Now it had so happened that one of Kâsyapa's disciples, in years gone by, had

1 This style of head dress is observable throughout the Sanchi and Amravati sculptures.

been afflicted with a disease that rendered it impolitic for him to live in company with the others; he had been obliged therefore to leave his Pansal and dwell apart, where he died; but before he died he prayed that he might, in his next birth, come back to the place and have his revenge for the slight done to him. Accordingly he was born as a great poisonous snake, and he took up his abode in that very pansal from which he had been driven, and it came to pass, that whatever man or other creature entered that abode he slew them at once, so that no one dare go near it or rest in it. Then Kâsyapa reflected that nought but the Fire Spirit could subdue the malice of this poisonous dragon, and therefore he consecrated the place to his worship, and reverenced him with fire according to right religious usage. So Kâsyapa replied to Buddha that he could not consent to his entering there, because of the evil and poisonous snake that occupied the place, who would certainly destroy him.

Whereupon, Buddha urged his request, and Kâsyapa again objected, and detailed all the history of his disciple who had died, and had come back in the form of this fiery dragon; but Buddha replied, "Oh, Kâsyapa! if the place were full of fiery serpents, they could not hurt one hair of my body, how much less this one evil creature! permit me then to make my abode there!"

Then Kâsyapa, seeing that he had thrice urged him to comply, consented.

Then, having obtained permission, Buddha, holding in his hand some twigs from the leafy roof of the hut, entered forthwith into the Dragon's abode, and having entered, he sat down on the mat (prepared from the twigs he had taken in), spreading out his Sanghati garment on the ground above it. And thus he lost himself in meditation.

Now it so happened that the fiery dragon at this time was out seeking for food; after a while returning to his abode, he there beheld the form of Buddha seated on the ground in meditation. At this sight he reflected thus. "What man is there whilst I live here shall dare to intrude or enter within this Pansal?" On this he emitted from his mouth a fiery blast to destroy the intruder; but Buddha, still lost in ecstatic meditation, caused a counter blast to proceed from his mouth, which quite overpowered that of the Nâga. Whereupon, in his rage, the monster emitted a more terrible and destructive vapour from his mouth; but this, too, was overpowered as before. And so it came to pass that the brightness of the flames which each breathed out filled the hut, till it seemed to be wrapped in fire. And so the contest proceeded, whilst Buddha, by his spiritual power, caused flames of every colour to proceed from his body and envelope the dragon.

Then Uravilva Kâsyapa, seeing the flames darting forth from the hut,[1] thought thus with himself—"alas! alas! this Shaman is being destroyed by the monster within the hut! alas! would that he had obeyed me, and not entered there!"

Then there was one of the disciples, called Ardhagiraka, who, seeing the flames, shouted out to others and cried, "Here! Gatimuni! Yamâgni! Arnivachyana! Parivarsha! Chamrayana! Pariyana! Gatiyana! ye sons of Gôtama! Muchilinda! Basita! all of you there! come quickly and rescue this Great Shaman from the flames of the fiery dragon!" Then all these young men hurried to the spot with their water vessels, and dipping up the water from the river,[2] they hastened to pour it over the fiery pansal to extinguish, as they supposed, the flames that were destroying the world-honoured one. So, as they flung vessel after vessel-ful of water over the flames, instead of decreasing its strength, the fire increased in power, and the brightness waxed greater and greater. Then these young men standing on one side in astonishment, the first took up the conversation and said, weeping with emotion!

"Alas! for the superlatively beautiful body,
The curling locks of his shaven head,[3] the delicate fingers,
The beautifully rounded eyes, so clear and bright!
Destroyed by the Dragon, as Rahu destroys the Sun!"

Then another repeated, as he wept, the following:—

"Alas! that he, born of the most exalted race,

---

[1] This adventure is the subject of Pl. xxxii. *Tree and Serpent Worship.*

[2] It would seem as if the figures in the Plate, referred to above, were so occupied.

[3] This apparent contradiction seems to illustrate the conventional figures of Buddha with what is called the "shell-ornament" on his head: this being, in fact, the young hair curling as it grew, until shorn again.

Even of the Ikshwaku family of Kings,
That he, unequalled amongst those born of women,
Should thus be destroyed by this Fiery Serpent."

And yet another said, with tears,

"His body adorned with thirty-two excellent marks
Himself arrived at emancipation, able to emancipate others,
Destroyed by the hate of this poisonous monster,
The flames are even now consuming his body," etc., etc.

[Kiouen XL contains 6,117 words and cost 3.059 taels.]

CHAPTER XLI.

At this time, the fiery dragon seeing the four sides of the hall in flames, but the centre part alone, where Buddha was seated in contemplation, without even the appearance of fire; seeing this, he stealthily approached the spot, and then with a leap sprang into his alms-bowl and then repeated this Gatha,

"If a man, for hundreds of thousands of myriads of years,
Were with undivided heart to worship the Fire Spirit,
It would not avail to remove his wrath,
So much as the patience of this Honor'd one of the world;
Of all Devas and men who inhabit the world,
He alone is rightly called the Master;
For all their diseases and infirmities,
He alone by his patience is able to provide a cure."

At this time, the world-honoured one, after the night had passed, came forth in the morning holding his alms-dish in his hand; and with the Nâga in it[1] he approached to the place where Uravilva was, and having come nigh, he addressed him thus, "Excellent Kâsyapa, this is the fiery dragon you so much dreaded, and for fear of which you dared not enter the Hall of the Fire Spirit. I

---

[1] It seems very probable that this adventure of Buddha with the Dragon is also the subject of Plate lxx., *Tree and Serpent Worship*, and that the alms-dish, before which the Kâsyapas are there worshipping, represents the Patra of Buddha with the Dragon in it.

have overcome his poisonous blast by my more powerful breath, and now I pray take him and show him to your followers," and so the Gâtha says,

"Now after the night watch had passed,
The world-honoured, approaching the place where Kâsyapa stood,
Shewed him the poisonous Nâga in his alms-dish,
His hand holding him there in perfect security."

Then Kâsyapa began to reflect thus—"This great poisonous Dragon entered of his own will into the alms-dish of the Great Shaman, induced so to do by the spiritual power of his vanquisher and desirous to hear his instruction." At this, Buddha removed his hand from the Patra, on which the fiery snake, emerging with his nine heads, stretched out his neck in the direction of Kâsyapa, who on his part was filled with fear at the sight, and covered his face with his hands. On this Buddha chided him and said,

"Yesternight I went to teach and convert this creature,
You need not fear him therefore or tremble at his presence,
If he now were to desire to hurt you or bite,
The world might come to an end without Salvation;
No! the heavens may fall to earth,
The earth itself be triturated into fine dust,
Sumeru may be moved from its place of rest,
But my words cannot be false, or deceitful."

Still, Uravilva Kâsyapa, though he allowed the mighty spiritual power of the honoured one, denied that he was so great a Rahat as himself.

Then Buddha, taking the poisonous Dragon, bade him go and dwell in the ocean between the iron mountains that encircle the Sakwala; on which, Uravilva asked him and said, "My Lord, whither have you sent the fiery Dragon?" to whom Buddha replied, "I have dismissed him to dwell in the ocean between the great iron mountains that encircle the earth;" on hearing which, Kâsyapa, overcome with awe and astonishment, besought the world-honoured one to remain with him as his guest and receive his offerings of food and drink.

At this time, the Devas of the Suddhavasa heavens sang this song,

"Such is the might of this great and loving Lord,
That his virtue can bind the malice of the fiery Dragon;
All the labour of the three Kâsyapas in propitiating the Fire Spirit
Is rendered vain by the strength of this Great one's patience."

Now after this, the world-honoured one, having received food from Uravilva Kâsyapa, proceeded onwards a little way towards a wood called Tcharnaka (*sirrup from the bark*), and arrived there, he rested awhile. At this time the four guardian kings of the world came down from their abodes, and, resplendent with their glory, they advanced and bowed at the feet of Buddha in worship. The glory of these kings made the wood so luminous that it seemed as if on fire.

The next morning, Uravilva Kâsyapa, bringing some food to the world-honoured one, inquired who those glorious beings were who had come to the wood? to whom Buddha answered, these were the four Kings of Heaven who came to me to inquire some particulars about the Law.

Then Kâsyapa thought, "The religious merit and spiritual energy of this Shaman are very great indeed; but yet he is not a Rahat, as I am."

[After this, Sâkra, the King of the Gods, visits Buddha for the same purpose, and with the same result; and after him, the Devas of the Yama, Tusita, and other heavens.][1]

Now, whilst Buddha was dwelling in the wood before-named, all the people of Magadha, as they were accustomed to do once a year, brought their several offerings of food, etc., intending on the morrow to present them to the three Kâsyapas.

Then, that very night, Uravilva Kâsyapa bethought himself thus, to-morrow all the people of Magadha are going to present me with their offerings. I must contrive by some expedient or other to prevent this Shaman Gôtama from coming near us, lest by some superiority of spiritual power he convince the people that he is better than I.

Now the world-honoured, knowing the thoughts of Kâsyapa, on

---

[1] These visits may possibly be the subject of plate xxv, fig. 1, *Tree and Serpent Worship*, or, the incident alluded to above, *vide* p. 74.

the morrow departed to the northern country of Uttara to beg his food, and having received it, he sat down on the margin of the Anavatapta Lake and consumed it, after which he returned to the wood where he abode.

Then Uravilva Kâsyapa, having taken his meal, at the conclusion of the day, came to Buddha and excused himself on the plea of forgetfulness, for having neglected to come to call him to his meal; but, said he, "I have not forgotten now to bring you a store of our best food." On this, the world-honoured exposed the folly of Kâsyapa's conduct, telling him exactly what his thoughts had been, and how in consequence he had gone to Uttara and eaten his meal by the side of the Anavatapta Lake.

On this, Uravilva Kâsyapa thought thus with himself, "this great Shaman possesses much spiritual power and is of great personal dignity; but he has not yet attained to the condition of a Rahat as I have." [This account is according to that held by the Nijasas;[1] according to the Mahâsañghika school, the account is as follows:—At this time, there was held in the place where Uravilva Kâsyapa lived an annual assembly called *yih-suh-yih* (fair-day),[2] on which occasion, the people were accustomed to give liberally to the Kâsyapas, food and other commodities. Thousands and tens of thousands of men and women came there from all Magadha. They brought with them all sorts of merchandise for sale, so that whatever one needed might be purchased. So Kâsyapa began to think thus, "if this Shaman comes here to-morrow, then all the people will be looking at him and will think nothing about me, and, therefore, they will supply me with no food or other necessary." So he went to the place where Buddha dwelt and said,—Excellent Sir! to-morrow there will be a great concourse of people at Uravilva, and much noise and confusion. Now you, I know, prefer peace and quiet, and you would rather dwell in this your peaceable retreat than in the middle of such a crowd as will be there. Remain therefore in this place, and do not disturb yourself to come to me.]

---

[1] This is undoubtedly the school of the Mahisasakas, *vide* Wassilief, p. 232, n. 3.

[2] The preparation for this "Fair" is evidently the subject of fig. 2, Plate xxxv, *Tree and Serpent Worship.*

[Here follows an account of the visit of all the Garuda Râjas, the Nâga Râjas, etc., to Buddha, also of Buddha's miraculous appearance to Kâsyapa in a remote corner of the forest.]

And so it came to pass that the world-honoured one, having received his food from the hands of Kâsyapa, again returned to the Tcharnaka wood and took his usual seat there. At this time the Kashâya-coloured robe, which the world-honoured wore over his other robes, was completely tattered and in rags; and just then a man who had died in the house of the rich Brahman Senayana was laid in the wood where corpses are deposited. The world-honoured one perceiving this, went and took the soiled robe that enveloped the corpse, thinking within himself where he could find a tank of water in which to wash it, and so make a clean garment for himself. Whilst thinking thus, Sâkra, the God of the Trayastriñshas Heavens, knowing what occupied the mind of Buddha, caused a lake of water to appear suddenly, just fit for the purpose, filled with pure water, and then coming forward he addressed Buddha and said, "Let the world-honoured one use this tank of pure water for the purpose of washing the soiled robe of the corpse!" Accordingly, Buddha complied, and washed the robe [in the same way, a great stone is brought from beyond the iron circle of mountains, on which he might lay out the cloth to rub it, and another stone on which to dry it in the sun, whilst a tree-Deva bent down a branch of a tree for him to hang up the robe, before drying it in the sun]. Then Uravilva Kâsyapa coming to him as before, was surprised to see the lake of water, and the stones, and inquired whence they came; nevertheless, on hearing the account he was not converted, and still thought that Buddha was not such a Rahat as himself.

On another occasion, Kâsyapa having come to invite Buddha as usual to return with him to take his food, Buddha besought Kâsyapa to go on a little way in front, on which, by his spiritual power, he transported himself to Sumeru, and plucking some fruit from the Djambu tree that grows there, he returned in a moment and took his seat in the Hall of the Fire Spirit. When Kâsyapa arrived there, astonished to find his guest already seated, he asked in some surprise whence he had come, and by what way. On hearing the history of Buddha's visit to Mount Sumeru, he was lost in wonder; but yet would not acknowledge him to be a Rahat like himself. [In the same way, he went again to Sumeru and brought an Amra fruit, and other fruit and flowers, with the same effect.]

[Kiouen XLI contains 6144 words and cost 3.072 taels.]

CHAPTER XLII.

AGAIN, as in the last chapter, Buddha goes in a moment to the Trayastriñshas Heavens, and there plucks a flower called Parijataka. On another occasion, the spiral-haired disciples found themselves unable to chop the wood, or, if they were stooping down, to lift themselves up again, or, if they were standing upright, to stoop down, or, if the hatchet were in the wood, to get it out. Then they were convinced that it was all the result of the great spiritual power of that Shaman.[1] Accordingly, when Uravilva Kâsyapa went to the wood again, Buddha asked him about these misadventures, and told him that now they would be able to chop their wood as they wished; and so it came to pass. Yet Kâsyapa was not able to accept him as a Rahat. And so on another occasion the spiral-haired disciples were unable to light their fires till Buddha permitted them. And on another occasion they could not put their fires out. At another time, when the disciples of Kâsyapa had entered the Nairañjana river, and were nearly

---

[1] This is evidently the scene by the lower tablet, Plate xxxii, *Tree and Serpent Worship*.

frozen to death with the cold, Buddha caused five hundred bright charcoal fires to appear on the shore, by which they might warm themselves; and then again the fires were extinguished without any apparent cause. At another time, the disciples wished to dip up some water in their pitchers (Kundikâs), but were unable to do so. At another time, Kâsyapa found himself unable to ascend into the air as usual—or having ascended, to come down to earth. At another time, the fire pots would not stand still, but moved about in every direction. At another time, when a fierce storm came on, and all the surrounding country was flooded, the place where Buddha sat was perfectly dry, whereupon Kâsyapa, seeing the suddenness of this storm and the vast downpour of rain, began to think, "surely this Shaman must be drowned"; whereupon he took a boat to search for his body, and after a time found him peacefully seated on a dry spot of ground, surrounded on every side by water. Whereupon, Kâsyapa having addressed Buddha, he, in a moment passed through the air and alighted in the middle of the boat.[1] [The Mahâsãnghikas affirm that after each miracle, Kâsyapa still asserted that Buddha was no Rahat as *he* was (Ch. ed.)]

[1] I think it very likely that this is the scene depicted, fig. 2, Plate xxxi, *Tree and Serpent Worship*. The left hand pillar of the Eastern gateway at Sanchi seemsd evoted to this Kâsyapa history; moreover, the grouping itself is highly suggestive; the great stone in front, the *four* disciples on shore and the one in the boat (the other figure is undoubtedly Kâsyapa), and Buddha himself in the middle. Moreover, the half immersed trees show that the district was visited with a flood.

At last, Buddha plainly said that Kâsyapa was no Rahat, that he had not entered on the path, and therefore could enjoy none of the fruits of such a condition. On this, Kâsyapa professed willingness to become a disciple of Buddha, and finally opened his mind to his five hundred followers, who all confessed that they had long wished for this step, only they had been afraid to propose it. Then Kâsyapa and all his disciples went to the place where Buddha was, and respectfully stood on one side. On this, Buddha addressed Kâsyapa and said, "You must take off your deer skin doublets, and take your pitchers (kundikâs) and your staves, and your fire vessels, and all the vessels in which you held the blood of your victims, and your fanciful head dresses, and fling them all into the Nairañjana river. And so they did, whilst from the river every sort of strange noise proceeded; after this they all came and worshipped at Buddha's feet and became disciples.

At this time, Nadi Kâsyapa, with his spiral head-dress, dwelt some way down on the shore of the Nairañjana River. And it so happened that, when he observed these various implements and the leathern doublets floating down the stream, he was filled with fear and anxiety, and exclaimed, "alas! alas! surely my brother has been slain by robbers, and these are the things which they have flung in the river. I will go and see whether it is so or not." Thinking thus, he first of all sent some of his disciples before him to spy out what the calamity was. These soon returned and reported all things perfectly safe, and then Nadi Kâsyapa himself, with 300 followers, went to the spot [and were soon converted, as his brother had been]. That Gâya Kâsyapa, seeing the various utensils of the fire worshippers floating down the stream past the place where he dwelt, also thought with himself, "Surely my brothers have been slain, and these are the proofs of it, alas! alas! [Then Gâya Kâsyapa, with 200 followers, proceeds to the place where Buddha was, and they also are converted]. [In each case when the Kundikâs and other utensils were cast into the river, strange noises proceeded from them as they floated down the stream and sank].

Thus Buddha and these 1,000 disciples dwelt for some short time longer in the village of Uravilva, and then gradually going onwards to the city of Gaya, they took up their abode at the top of the Elephant-head Mount, where he taught them the mysteries of spiritual manifestations (miraculous powers) exercised by the body, the mouth, and the mind (word, thought, deed). [Here follows a list of the magical exhibitions: 1st. Of the body, making it ascend and descend at pleasure, making fire and water proceed from it, etc. 2nd. Of the mouth, showing them how to discriminate, argue, and determine. 3rd. Of the mind, showing them how they ought to regard and conclude respecting all mundane existence, with a view to reject all these things as unreal, and so to rise to that which alone is real]. And thus those thousand men became perfect Rahats.

The Story of Upâsana.

§ 2. At this time, these three Kâsyapas had a sister whose son was called Upâsana, a Brahmachari adorned with a spiral head-dress. This youth was dwelling in a mountain called Asuraganga, in company with 250 other disciples, all of them preparing themselves to become Rishis. These, having heard what had happened to the three brothers, were filled with astonishment and alarm, and then Upâsana addressing them said, "Most wonderful! to think, my friends, that those who have for so many thousand years been worshippers of the Fire Spirit, should at this time suddenly become Shamans! It is my duty on their account to go direct to the spot where they dwell and remonstrate with them on this indecorous proceeding of theirs."

Then going to the spot, behold! he saw the three brothers with shaven heads, and wearing the kashâya garments of a Shaman. On seeing which, he addressed them in the following Gâthas:

"Oh Reverend Sirs! who have worshipped for a hundred years the fire, in its pure essence!

"And have practised austerities and self-mortification in dependence on that alone.

"How is it that to-day ye have deserted this ancient religion of yours,

"And cast it off, even as a serpent wriggles out of its old skin?"

To this, the three brothers answered simply, "We have, as you say, cast away our old habiliments, even as a snake shifts its skin!" Then Upâsana, having heard this, inquired further, "Wherein resides the superior excellency of the system you have adopted?"

[Then the three brothers explained the system of Buddha, on which Upâsana and his followers resolve to become his disciples, and are received, on condition of laying aside their deer-skin doublets and their fire vessels, and vessels for holding blood. Afterwards, on hearing a discourse on the three miraculous powers of body, word, and thought, these also became Rahats.]

And now it came to pass that, in the presence of these 1,250 disciples, the world-honoured one related their previous history as follows:

"I remember in years gone by in this continent of Jambudwipa, there were a thousand merchants, amongst whom were three brothers, one of whom in his turn took upon him the office of chief merchant. The names of these three were as follows, Uravilva, Nadi, and Gaya. The first had 500 merchants in his charge, the second 300, and the third 200. Now, on one occasion, these merchants undertook a voyage of great importance, and embarked with a very rich cargo, proposing to return with one of still greater worth. Having sacrificed to the sea-spirit, they set sail, and were soon borne by a storm into mid-ocean, where they were becalmed."

[Kiouen XLII contains 6,232 words, and cost 3.116 taels.]

CHAPTER XLIII.

At length, having completed their voyage, and possessed themselves of a very valuable freight, they set out on their return homewards. And it so happened on their mid-passage that they saw a Stûpa, erected to the memory of Kâsyapa, in ruins and falling to pieces. Then the senior of the three merchant princes addressed the others as follows:

"You know, my comrades, that I am always ready to risk my life in these ventures of ours, and now we seem to have had a very successful voyage and are returning home in safety, let us not forget then that it is our duty to do something, not only for our own benefit, but for the good of those who shall come after us; let us not forget the burthen of the old saying which wise men have handed down to us,

"A man by good fortune obtains much profit,
Obtaining this he becomes idle and listless,
From this he is careless about his religious duties,
And from this he gradually sinks lower, till he goes to hell."

And so the senior merchant proposed that out of the abundance of their wealth they should devote some portion to the restoration of the sacred Stûpa, containing the relics of Kâsyapa. So they severally contributed according to their means, and restored the building to its original beauty and perfection, and then they put up the following prayer: "Oh! would that we in ages to come may have the privilege of hearing the words of Buddha, the successor of this Kâsyapa, and so may receive the benefit of his preaching!"

Know ye then that at the present time these three Kâsyapas and their followers are the thousand merchants and their chiefs. And according to the proportion of money contributed by each of those chiefs towards the restoration of that Stûpa, so is the excellency of these three brothers in point of disciples and priority of conversion.

§ 3. Again, in relation to this subject, the world-honoured related the following story. I remember in years gone by there was a country called Videha [*this means "not graceful body," Ch. Ed.*] in which was a Kshatriya monarch, called Anghada [*this means "to give parts of his body"*]. He was a regularly anointed (baptised) king, and possessed of wealth and means in abundance, but he was a heretic. Now it came to pass on a certain night, being the 15th of the month, when the moon was full and bright, that this king summoned all his great ministers to his presence. The first was called Vijaya (pi-che ye) [*Various Excellences, Ch. Ed.*] The second Sumana [*Excellent thought, Ch. ed.*] The third Arvata [*before-spoken, Ch. Ed.*] These three chief ministers having come into the king's presence he said to them, "Tell me, my ministers, what is your opinion; what other plan except the enjoyment of the society of my courtesans is there, by which I may be kept awake during this night?"

Then one answered and said, "My Lord King! engage your attention about the subjugation of your enemies, plan some method of attack by your army by which the countries yet unsubdued may be brought under the yoke." The second answered and said, "My Lord King! it seems to me that all your enemies being subdued, you may now amuse yourself with music, dancing, and the other pleasures of sense which are usual under such circumstances, and so keep yourself awake." The third said, "I advise my Lord King to send for some Shaman or Brahman, and let him discourse before you on the merits of religion." The king, adopting this last suggestion, further inquired, and "where shall I meet with such a man?"

The king is then informed of an ascetic, living in the Deer Park, called Kâsyapa and surnamed the naked,[1] who convinces the king of the unreality and folly of all positive assertions respecting the relation of things one with another—such as "father and son," "king and subject," "present and past." This sceptical view is supported by the ministers, who refer to their former births, and declare that there has been no influence exerted by these on their present condition. The king hereupon returns home, gives up the anxieties of government to his three ministers, and retires himself to a house of pleasure (*beautiful—colour*) in the neighbour-

[1] This is evidently the same as Purana Kâsyapa, vid. *M. B.* 291, and *Fa koue ki*, p. 149.

hood, and there abandons himself to a life of ease and unchecked indulgence. At length there comes to this palace, a certain damsel called "thought—joy"[1] (manah-priti ?); her body adorned with the most beautiful clothing, and her neck with the costliest jewels. Coming into the presence of the king, he asks whether the beauties of the garden had attracted her hither? She begs permission to speak to the king without restraint; and on permission being given, she utters the following words:

> "My reverend king (father-king) I ask your charity:
> I would bestow on all the Shamans and Brahmans,
> On the 15th day of the coming moon,
> A gift—I ask you then to give me 1000 golden pieces!"

To whom the king replied:

> "Illustrious maiden! listen now and understand!
> I have just learned this fact from an ancient sage,
> That, notwithstanding all the wealth we give, or wish to give,
> All things are vain—and bear no fruit of good or ill.
> Why then has such a thought possessed your heart,
> 'Tis but the foolish talk of a mad world, this 'giving alms;'
> For all things present, past, and future, are but nought.
> Listen, oh foolish girl! to what I say,
> The words of Kâsyapa are true and cannot change,
> There is no bond that joins the works of man to any consequence.
> What people say about good, bad, and so on,
> Men and angels, spirits, demons, ghosts, all this is nought,
> And so the words 'sire,' 'mother,' 'friends,' 'relatives," all are nought!"
>
> etc., etc., etc.

[1] Called "Rucha" in the Southern ac. M.B. 192.

On this, the maiden expostulates, and after a long exposition of the truth, as she entertained it (relating her own experience), she sees a divine messenger flying down from heaven. This messenger, called Narada, she invites to sit down on the seat she herself had occupied; and after bowing down at his feet, she appeals to him for a refutation of Kâsyapa's sceptical views. The Rishi at once enters on the subject, and declares that such scepticism is absurd and contradicted by facts. On this, the king in a bantering way says, "if, indeed, the present be but a part in the chain of the past and future, then I pray you lend me five hundred pieces of money, and I will repay it in some future birth a thousand-fold." On which the Rishi reproves the king, and tells him that if he thus trifles with religion and harbours sceptical thoughts, that he never will have the chance of returning any such gift or loan; for his body will be born in hell, and there cut by swords, impaled, burnt, ground to dust, revivified, passed out to other wretched births, again consigned to hell, and so through endless ages. "How then," the Rishi asks, "can you presume to say that you will pay my loan a thousand-fold?"

On this, the king terrified, and in abject fear, recants his wicked creed, and becomes a true and faithful disciple.

Buddha then explains that the Rishi Narada was himself the Buddha now existing; and that the Râja Angada was Uravilva Kâsyapa. "And as the Rishi was the means of turning the king back to the truth, so have I also converted this Uravilva Kâsyapa, and led him back to the right way."

[Kiouen XLIII contains 5510 words, and cost 3.757 taels.]

CHAPTER XLIV.

The gift of the Bamboo Garden [Karandavenuvana].

§ 1. Now, the world-honoured one, having dwelt for some short time on the summit of that elephant-head mount (*Pilusara ? for Pilusila ?*) began gradually to advance towards the city of Rajâgriha. Now it so happened that on the road from the village of Uravilva to Rajagriha, not very far from the latter, there was a celebrated garden, in which dwelt an old Rishi. The garden was called Dharmavarsha.[1] The Rishi, dwelling in his leafy Pansal, and surrounded by 500 disciples, who practised self-mortification, was now very old, his head white and hoar, his teeth gone, and his body bent nearly double, scarcely able to move a step through decrepitude, his breath feeble, and his whole appearance lamentable. He had thus completed a hundred years of life; and now, owing to his former good works, on the very borders of the grave, it was his fortune to meet with Buddha, and be converted.

The world-honoured one, approaching the place where this Rishi and his followers were dwelling, was moved with compassion for them, and standing outside the entrance door of the grot where they were sitting lost in meditation, he began to recite the following Gâthas.

The purport of the Gâthas is, that it were better to repeat one line which has the power of bringing light and release to the soul, than a hundred Gâthas which have no such power. That the conquest of self is the greatest victory a man can achieve. That the confes-

---

[1] Called "*Yashti*," M.B., 191.

sion of sin, and consequent triumph over it, is the one object of all religion. That the invocation of the precious objects of worship—Buddha, the law, the priesthood—and the refuge provided by these for the faithful, is the sum of all duty. And that a man, who for one day realizes the virtue and power of this religious condition, is far better than he who lives a hundred years in ignorance of it.

On hearing these verses, the five hundred ascetics coming forth from the grotto, prostrated themselves at the feet of Buddha, and immediately flying away through the air they exhibited themselves for a moment, exercising their miraculous power, and then, self-consumed, they entered Nirvâna.

Then Buddha, gathering the relics of their bodies which had fallen to the earth, with his own hand erected over them a Stûpa and proceeded onwards to Râjagriha.

At this time, the king of Magadha was called Bimbasâra, who hearing that Buddha, with his followers, was approaching the royal city, and had arrived as far as the bamboo grove (*cheung-lin*) and was resting for a time near a tower erected therein — and hearing, moreover, of his great fame as a teacher—he resolved to go forth to meet him. Sitting, therefore, in his beautifully adorned chariot,[1] and surrounded by his ministers of state and the Brahmans, with countless other persons, he proceeded from Râjagriha towards the place where Tathâgata was dwelling.

Now there was at this time a certain courtesan dwelling in Râjagriha, whose name was Sâlapati; she was of incomparable beauty, and accomplished in every female art and blandishment. This woman, having heard of the approach of the world-honoured one,

---

[1] This excursion of Bimbasâra seems to be the subject of one of the processional scenes on the pillars of the northern gateway of the Sanchi Tope. (*Tree and Serpent Worship*, Plates xxxiv and xxxv). Compare also the scene at Bharahut, described by General Cunningham, as "Prasenajita Râja, drawn by four horses in his chariot, going to pay respects to the wheel symbol, 'Bhagavato damma chakam.'"

and reflecting that he was a Prince of the Sâkya race, she resolved to go forth herself and salute his feet, if possible, before the king arrived. Then reflecting that she would be unable to push her way through the crowd that accompanied the king, she caused a breach to be made through the city wall, and so proceeded onward. Then the world-honoured one, perfectly knowing the purpose of the woman, caused the wheels of Bimbasara's chariot to fix themselves in the soil, so that he could not move onwards. Astonished at this accident, the king was filled with fear and anxiety, and exclaimed, "What demon or power of evil has brought this calamity on me, that my chariot will not move?" Then a spirit, residing in the air, without making himself visible, spake thus to the king: "Oh râja! be not dismayed or anxious, but send quickly into the city for such and such a man, and he shall deliver you." Having done this, the chariot was now able to proceed.

Arriving at length where the world-honoured one was seated, they each, in turn, saluted him, and stood on one side.[1]

Then, after some preliminary conversation between Buddha and Uravilva Kâsyapa, the latter having displayed his miraculous powers, and rendered homage to his master, Buddha began to preach for the good of Bimbasâra, who finally took upon him the vows of a disciple (Upasakawa), and declared his purpose to shed no more blood, but to be compassionate to all that lives. Then finally he invited Buddha and his followers to an entertainment on the morrow; and, offering his chariot, he desired Buddha at once to take his seat in it, and he himself would help draw him into the city. This Buddha declined. Then the king and his followers, having saluted Tathâgata, and circumambulated him three times, departed.

---

[1] This account is almost identical with that found in Spence Hardy, M. B. 191.

Buddha then relates that this was not the first time that the gift of a royal chariot had been offered him; but that formerly, when he reigned as king of Kasi, under the name Sumana (*illustrious or virtuous—thought*) he had been taken up to heaven (the Trâyastrinshas heaven) in a splendid chariot, under the guidance of an angel called Matali, and arriving there had been visited by Sâkra, and tempted by all kinds of offerings to remain there and indulge in pleasures—which he declined, and also the gift of the chariot which Matali drove.

Now it came to pass that Bimbasara, having prepared a sumptuous repast, and swept and garnished the apartments of the palace, sent forth to the world-honoured to invite him to come and partake of the feast. Then Buddha, with his robes properly arranged, his alms-bowl in his hand, and surrounded by all his followers, approached the city. At this time Sâkra, assuming the form of a young Brahman (Manava), went before the body of the disciples and recited the following verses:

"Tathâgata, the conqueror of himself, can succour others,
See all these one thousand spiral-haired converts,
Converted by him whose body is bright as pure gold,
Now enter the city, with the Supreme Lord of the world.
Himself delivered and at peace, he can deliver others!
So has he delivered these thousand spiral-haired converts.
And now," etc. etc.

Then all those within the city began to exclaim, "Wonderful! wonderful! Who is this handsome youth? Whence does he come, and what words are these he utters?" Then Sâkra continued his song, and said:

"The Buddhas alone by their virtue can subdue all!
Their condition is the highest and the most exalted!
Able to advantage Gods and men by their Teaching!
And therefore I join myself to this cortége to honour the world-honour'd."

Thus slowly and with dignified gait approaching the Royal Palace, the Lord of the World and his disciples entered into the apartments prepared for them, and, taking their seats, partook of the hospitality of the king, who himself attended to all their wants and waited on them in person. Then, after the meal, having provided water for washing, the several attendants and the royal household took smaller cushions, and placing them in front of Buddha, they also sat down and awaited his instruction.

Then the king began to reflect how he might retain the society of the world-honoured, and keep him in the vicinity of the royal city. Reflecting thus, he remembered the suitableness of the Bamboo-garden for the purpose—so quiet and shady! free from all noxious insects and pollution. He resolved, therefore, to offer this garden as a free gift to Buddha and the congregation. Having done so, the Lord accepted it at once, and the Râja, having arisen and taken a pitcher,[1] poured water on the hands of Buddha, and said, "Illustrious Lord of the World! I give in free charity to you and your followers the Bamboo garden, situated not far from my capital. Oh! would that of your condescension you would receive the same at my hands!"

Then Buddha, having recited some verses in token of his intention to preach in this grove for the salvation of men, arose and departed, exhorting his followers henceforth to resort to the Garden of Bamboos as their place of rendezvous for religious teaching.

[The above account is according to the school of the Mahîsâsakas.]

[Kiouen XLIV contains 6,068 words, and cost 3.034 taels.]

CHAPTER XLV.

§1. Now at this time there resided in Râjagriha a very wealthy nobleman, called Kalanda, possessed of untold riches, and living in a palace like that of Vaisravana, the Northern King. Now, this Kalanda had a bamboo garden not far from the city, which he had purchased and arranged for the purpose of entertaining religious persons

---

[1] This pitcher is evidently the teapot-shaped utensil seen in plates xxxiv and xxxv, *Tree and Serpent Worship.*

who passed to and fro. These religious persons (tao-sse) were called Ajîvakas.[1] [This is what the Kâsyapîyas say.]

Now at this time, the four Kings who preside over the world sent certain blue-clad Yakshas to the garden of Kalanda to sweep and adorn it, for the purpose of receiving in a proper manner the Lord of the World, who was coming there to rest. Then the Ajivakas who dwelt there, rising early in the morning, saw these blue-clad messengers performing their mission and sweeping the garden. Seeing this, they came near and said, "Sirs! who are you, and whence do you come?" Then they answered and said, "Good sirs! we are Yakshas, sent by the Kings of the four quarters for the purpose of preparing this garden for the arrival of the Lord of the World, who is coming hither to abide for a time."

Then the Ajivakas, having understood this, went at sunrise to the house of Kalanda, and said, "Honorable sir! this morn, ere the stars had yet disappeared, we saw in your garden certain heaven-sent messengers sweeping and watering it, and otherwise engaged in preparing it, as they said, for the arrival of the Lord of the World, who is coming there to dwell for a time [during the season of the rains]."

Then Kalanda, having heard this news, went forth to receive the Lord of the World, and, meeting him about half a yojana from the garden, he bowed down before him, and then rising up, he took in his right hand his water pitcher, and pouring some pure water on the Lord's hand, he begged him to receive the garden as a free gift. To whom the Lord replied, "Such gifts of land or houses, or clothes or riches, are needless for me. I have already received all things; but for my disciples in perpetuity I will accept your offering of the garden." And so it was bestowed by Kalanda, for the perpetual use of the priests [congregation]. And so, when Buddha dwelt in Râjagriha, the thousand disciples who accompanied him abode in this Kalanda-venu-vana.

The History of Mâha Kâsyapa.

§2. The Mahasañghikas say as follows:

---

[1] The Chinese *Tika* explains "Ajivaka" as equivalent to "here-

Not far from Râjagriha there is a district called Mahasudra and a hamlet belonging to this called by the same name. In this dwelt a certain rich Brahman, whose name was Nyagrodha Kava; his wealth was so great that while Bimbasara râja had one thousand yoke of oxen for ploughing, this Brahman kept only one less, for fear the king should be envious if he possessed a greater number than himself. As for other cattle, they were simply innumerable, like the sparks of the fire for number. Now, his wife having brought forth a son under a Pipal tree, the child was called Pippalayana. He was very lovely, and of a beautiful golden complexion, and it came to pass that at his birth a garment of rare workmanship was brought by the Deva for the use of the child, and hung upon the tree; hence his name of Pippalayana [*the robe being so called*]. His parents procured for him the best nurses for the various purposes required—viz., to fondle, to feed, to accompany in out-of-door walks, to play and laugh. So dearly did his parents love this their only child that they could not bear him to be out of their sight. And so he grew apace, and at eight years of age was initiated into the religious customs of the Brahman caste, and instructed in the various books belonging to his religion—to wit, the four Vedas and the various treatises on writing and calculation, the Mantras, the Chhandas, the different sections relating to the five elements, the heavenly constellations, the seasons, the casting of events (lucky and unlucky days). Moreover, he learnt all the polite arts, and acquainted himself generally with the literature of the time, so that there was no subject on which he was not fully informed. Yet, notwithstanding all this, his mind was ill at ease and dissatisfied, desiring to find rest and freedom from sorrow.

Now, it came to pass that as Pippalayana grew up, his parents wished him to marry and fulfil the duty he owed to his ancestors by continuing the race. But Pippalayana spake thus: "Papa! mama![1] I desire no such event. I wish to avoid marriage and live

---

tic." It is evident from Burnouf (*Introd. p.* 389, *n.* 2) and the Lalita Vistara (*p.* 378, *n.* 4) that the Upakama spoken of (*supra*, p. 245) was one of these heretics. From this and many other passages it would seem that the Chinese expression "tao-jin" does not always mean a "Buddhist," but a religious person of any denomination.

[1] This is the phonetic rendering of the Chinese.

the life of a Brahmana!" Then his parents began to remonstrate with him: "Let not our son say so; but first fulfil your duty to your ancestors, that you may find a place in Heaven, and then when old you may retire from the world and live as a recluse!" But their appeal was in vain! The youth replied that he desired to be free from such attachments. In vain they urged the desolation of their house and family from lack of descendants. Pippalayana still pleaded for freedom. At length, after his parents had three times repeated their entreaties, the youth took some very fine Jambunada gold,[1] and desired a celebrated artist to make from it the figure of a female, and then, taking this to his parents, he said, "Papa! mama! I desire not to marry; but if it be your wish that I should, then find me a wife as beautiful and as resplendent as this figure, and I will comply with your request!"[2] On hearing this his parents were much afflicted, and his father Nyagrôdha, going up on the roof of his house, sat down in great sorrow, and remained there in silence. At this time, a certain Brahman friend coming to the house of Nyagrodha, saluted it thus: "May continued prosperity and increased happiness attend this house!" Then, seeing the master was not there, he inquired, "Where is the lord of the house?"

On this, they told him how the matter stood; whereupon he goes at once to his benefactor, and salutes him with much respect. The Brahman householder remains silent, until his friend having urged him to open his heart and relate his grief, Nyâgrodha tells him all, and appeals to him for help and sympathy; and finally, through his friend's kind offices, a wife is found for his son.[3]

[Kiouen XLV contains 6,176 words, and cost 3.088 taels].

---

1 Heavenly gold. Vish. Pur. 168.

2 The resemblance of this narrative with the Kusa-jâtaka is singular.

3 Her name was Bhadrakâ. Both she and Kâsyapa, even after

CHAPTER XLVI.

Now it so happened that as Pippala and Bhadrakâ were sleeping in the same apartment, but separately, that the latter unconsciously in her sleep threw her arm from off the couch and let her hand touch the ground. At this time, Pippala, being awake, observed a small black snake creeping on the floor and approaching the spot where the hand of Bhadraka was exposed. Softly rising up and going to the spot, he took her hand, and, raising her arm, he placed it gently upon the couch and covered it from sight. But Bhadraka, roused by the touch of her husband's hand, awoke and began to reproach him with having had some other intention than that which caused him thus to act.

On this, he explained the circumstance and she was satisfied.

Thus they passed twelve years and lived in perfect purity. At length Bhadrakâ, in the preparation of some oil-cake for the cattle, was grieved to find the number of insects, and so on, which were destroyed with the seeds when being ground. And from this her attention was turned to the universal prevalence of suffering and sorrow in the world. Having become very sad in consequence of this discovery, she communicated her thoughts to Pippala, who, in his turn, was so impressed with the conviction that the world is full of sorrow, that he left his home and became a recluse.

Accidentally meeting with Tathâgata, he became attached to him. After a time having given his Sanghati robe to Buddha, and received the soiled and unsightly one of Buddha's in return, he became a Rahat, and because he belonged to the family of the Kâsyapas he was called the venerable Maha Kâsyapa. [*He founded a school who adhered to the Telesdhutanga*[1] *rules.*]

---

marriage, lived perfectly pure lives. Kâsyapa was the founder of the ascetic school in Buddhism; his followers were called Kâsyapiyas.

[1] E. M. 9, Catena 256.

At this time all the Bhikshus asked Buddha, saying, "Lord of the world! what previous circumstances in the history of Mâha Kâsyapa led to this happy termination of his life?" Then Buddha answered, "I remember in ages gone by that there was, a certain Pratyeka Buddha, whose name was Tagara Sikhi, who lived in the city of Benares. At that time, owing to a famine, there was scarce any grain to be had, and in consequence many men died from want, and the mendicants of the various religious orders could scarce obtain any food in alms. At this time the Pratyeka Buddha, having got up early one morning and put on his robe, took his alms-dish in his hand, and entering the city went begging from door to door. Having obtained nothing, he returned to his place of residence, washed his bowl, and sat down. Now there was a certain poor man in Benares at that time who, on this very morning, had watched the Pratyeka Buddha as he went from house to house, and seeing that he got nothing he had followed him to his place of residence, and there watching his peaceful and contented behaviour, he addressed him as follows:—"Venerable Rishi! have you obtained aught in alms during your visit to the city, or not?" To whom the Pratyeka Buddha replied that he had received nothing. On this the poor man asked him to his house, to share with him all he had, which was just one measure of coarse cockle seed. Having cooked this he gave it to the Rishi, on which the latter rose up and passed away through the air; on seeing this, the poor man fell down on his face in adoration, and with his hands clasped over his head he prayed that, if ever that Rishi came into the world as a Buddha to teach men, he might be one of his disciples. [And so it came to pass that this poor man was afterwards born as Mahâ Kâsyapa, who was converted by the preaching of that Rishi, born in the present age as Sakya Muni,] etc.

[Kiouen XLVI contains 6121 words, and cost 3.06 taels.]

CHAPTER XLVII.

THE beginning of this section is occupied by an account of Maha Kâsyapa's condition at present; being enclosed within a mountain cavern, awaiting the arrival of Maitreya Buddha.[1]

The History of Bhadrakâ.

§ 1. Now after the Lord of the world had admitted Mahâprajâpati among the number of his disciples, Kâsyapa, exercising his divine power of sight, looked abroad to see what had become of Bhadraka priya.[2] Having done so, he perceived that she had joined herself to an heretical sect, and was now leading the life of a Paribrajika, near the river Ganges.

Having therefore called a Bikshumi, gifted with spiritual power, to his side, he prayed her to go to the spot where Bhadraka was and endeavour to bring her into the number of the disciples. This Bikshuni, after receiving the commission, by the exercise of her spiritual power, in a moment alighted on the spot where Bhadrakâ was, and after describing the character of Buddha as a teacher, conducted her, by virtue of the power she possessed, in a moment to Srâvasti, where the Lord of the world was residing in the Jetavana. Then overpowered by the excellency of his presence, the newly arrived Bhadrakâ besought the Lord to admit her among the number of his female disciples. Whereupon Buddha bade Ananda to conduct her to Mahâprajâpati for instruction and initiation.

Then Mahâ Prajâpati Gotamî, having received Bhadraka at the hands of Ananda, admitted her into the number of the female disciples, and committed to her the rules of the community, and so she became a true Bikshuni, and in the joy of her heart she sang this song,

"Now am I freed from the power of birth and death,
Now all my discipline as a Brahmani is ended,
I have experienced a true and living conversion,
And shall no more be hampered by personal existence."

Then she became a Rahat and obtained final deliverance.

---

[1] *Vide Fah-hian.* Cap. xxxiii.

[2] That is, his former wife.

The Story of the Religious Servant Girl.

§ 2. THEN Buddha related further the history of Bhadrakâ in her former birth and said, "I remember in ages gone by, there was dwelling at Benares a certain rich householder, whose wife had a slave girl to wait on her in the house. One day, a Pratyeka Buddha, having come to the neighbourhood of the city, took up his abode there for a time. Early in the morning, he put on his robe, took his alms-bowl in his hand, and went forth to beg his food. Coming to the door of the householder, above named, he stood there awaiting the time when some food should be given him. Now it so happened that the slave girl had watched the movements of the mendicant, and being impressed by his dignity and self-possession, she had found her mind much comforted and pacified. On this, she came indoors to her mistress and addressed her thus—'Reverend mistress! [Holy woman or lady] There is a Bhikshu standing before the door begging food!' Now it so happened that just then her mistress was engaged dressing (combing) her hair, and as she was sitting down, her left hand holding up her tresses, she saw the Pratyeka Buddha at some little distance off. She saw that he was old and ugly, and without any graceful way with him; so having seen this, she said at once to the slave girl, 'I have taken a dislike to that ugly old man, so dirty and graceless—I have nothing to give him!' On this, the girl replied, 'Reverend and virtuous lady! pray give him a little! pray give him something! in the case of such holy persons, one does not look for comeliness of person, but purity of heart!' But her mistress said, 'I hate such ugly people, and I have nothing to give him.' On this the girl rejoined, 'Reverend mistress! if you cannot find it in your heart to bestow some charity on this mendicant, pray you! give me my daily portion of meal, and I will bestow some portion of it on him.' To this, the mistress said, 'Well, girl! you may have your food to do what you like with it.' Whereupon, having received it, the slave girl at once gave it in charity to the Pratyeka Buddha, as he stood before the gate.

[*The Pratyeka Buddhas can convert people only by displaying their spiritual powers, not by any preaching of the Law. Ch. Ed.*]

"So it came to pass that this mendicant, directly he had taken the food of the girl, was moved with compassion for her, and so mounting into the air, he flew away through space, till she lost sight of him.

"Seeing this wonderful event, the girl fell down in adoration, and clasping her hands over her head she prayed thus—'Oh, would that I, at some future time, may meet with this divine personage as a teacher who may instruct me how to avoid the evil ways of life, and be born with a graceful and attractive body, so that I may not create feelings of dislike in the breasts of those who see me, as this Pratyeka Buddha did in the mind of my mistress!' Now the lady who was dressing her hair, having watched the whole proceeding, was filled with astonishment at the sight of the spiritual power of the Bhikshu, and so coming out to the girl she said, 'My good little girl! if you will give me the merit of the charitable action you have just performed, I will give you as much food again as I bestowed just now!' But the servant refused; 'indeed, she said, dear lady! I cannot!' Whereupon the mistress offered her twice as much, up to twenty times as much food. But she still declined to part with the merit she had acquired. Then the mistress getting angry cried, 'how dare you disobey me! how dare you refuse me! I will beat you well, and make you feel for it.' Whereupon, she chastised the girl, who on her part began to weep and to scream with as loud a voice as she could.

"Now it so happened that the master of the house, hearing the hubbub, came indoors, and seeing the servant girl weeping and sobbing, he inquired what was the matter with her, in this way, 'My good girl (bhadrâ), why are you crying so?' on which, the slave girl, turning to her master, told him all about it. Then the lord being angry, called out at once for the mistress to come, and ordered her to take off her fine clothes and her jewels, and said to her, 'You know that I warned you that I would lock you up (*kim kau*, put in the stocks) if you ever refused to give charity to any Brahman or Shaman who might come to the door to beg.' Thereupon he drove her out of doors, and shut her up in the small house at the back, and then he ordered the servant girl to go wash herself and put on her mistress's clothes and jewels, and then he opened his treasures, and told her to give away just as she liked, either to Shaman or Brahman, whatsoever she pleased of all he possessed.

"Bhikshus! this slave girl was Bhadrakâ in a former birth, and in reward for her charity she was born in heaven as a most beautiful girl, for whom the very gods were jealous, and finally she was born in the house of that rich Brahman, and is now the Bhikshuni Bhadrakapriya."

The Story of the Peasant's Wife.

§ 3. AGAIN Buddha related this story—"I remember in years gone by, there was a certain poor man at work in the fields, whose wife at the proper time set forth to take him his dinner. Now, as she came down to the river bank, she saw there a Pratyeka Buddha sitting and lost in reverie: at the sight of this reverend person, the woman put down her basket, and falling prostrate, she remained adoring him with hands clasped above her head. Meantime the peasant, who had seen his wife set out from the house, and watched her a long way off as she went down to the river side, was astonished that she did not appear, after having crossed over, on his side of the stream. Whereupon, after waiting some time, he exclaimed, 'Where in the world is the woman gone! leaving me here toiling and sweating without my dinner or my drink!'

"On this he went down to the river bank, and there saw the Pratyeka Buddha and his wife. 'Oh!' thought he, 'I see the reason of the delay! this fellow has been amusing himself with my wife, whilst I have been left dinnerless!' so he took up a big stick that was lying near and began to belabor the Pratyeka Buddha with it till he was tired.

"Then the mendicant, having said nothing, rose into the air, and by his spiritual power flew through space to another spot!

"Seeing this miracle the woman turned to her lord and said, 'Alas! master, what have you done? see what a crime you have committed, and all through your own perverse thoughts, for in truth this was a good man, and incapable of anything like you wickedly imagined.'

"Then the peasant who had beaten the Pratyeka Buddha was filled with remorse, and said to his wife, 'Dear woman! I see nothing for it, but that you and I should immediately give up the world and enter on a religious life; let us give up all worldly pleasures and lead a life of purity, if haply I may thus atone for my wickedness.' His wife having consented, they both became religious ascetics, and after death were born in heaven.

"Now Bhikshus! that peasant was Mahâkâsyapa in a former birth, and his wife was the Bhikshuni Bhadrakapriya."

The History of Sari(putra) and Mulin (Mudgalaputra).

§ 4. AT this time, not very far from Rajagriha, there was a village called Narada[1] (Nalanda?), where lived a certain rich Brahman, called Danayana (or, Danyayana) [*other accounts say that his name was Danadatta. Ch. Ed.*] Now this wealthy Brahman had eight sons, the first was called Upatissa (and so on). Moreover, he had one daughter called "Susimika," who had become a recluse belonging to the heretical order of Pariprajikas. [*But the Mahâsanghikas say that he had only seven sons, the first called Damma, the second Sudamma, the third Upadamma, the fourth Tissa, the fifth Upatissa, etc. Of all these Upatissa was the most promising and talented. He was thoroughly acquainted with the literature usually acquired by the Brahmans, and his disposition was most gentle and loving. Ch. Ed.*]

Not far from the spot where Upatissa lived there was a village Kolita,[2] and in that village a Brahman, exceedingly rich, who was called by the same name, and he had an only son, who was also very accomplished and of great natural genius. Between this young Kolita and Upatissa there sprung up a close friendship, so that they were always together, and never so much grieved as when necessity kept them apart, and so the Gâtha says—

"Closely as cause and effect are bound together,
So do two loving hearts entwine and live,
Such is the power of love to join in one.
Even as the lily lives upon and loves the water,
Upatissa and Kolita likewise,

---

[1] *Vide* Fah-Hian, p. 111 n.
[2] Called Koulika by Jul. iii, 51.

These two joined by closest bond of love,
If by necessity compelled to live apart,
Were overcome by grief and aching heart."

[Kiouen XLVII, contains 6,054 words, and cost 3.027 taels.]

CHAPTER XLVIII.

Now, at a short distance from Râjagriha there is a mountain called Giriguha, on which mountain at stated periods there used to be an assembly convened for the purpose of distributing charity among the priests. There was also another mountain called Rishigiri, on which similar assemblies were held; also on a mountain called Vaibhara, and another called Panda, and another called Vaihâra. Now, on all these mountains assemblies were held in certain rotation. At this time it happened that the convocation took place on the mountain called Grihakuha (or guha) and countless people, afoot and in carriages and vehicles of all descriptions, were assembled together to witness the spectacle. Now the distance of the villages Narada (or Nalanda) and Kolika (for *Kolita ?*) from Rajagriha was not more than half a yojana. At this time the youth Tissa thought thus with himself, "I ought certainly to go to this assembly on Mount Giriguha, to see if the people assembled there can do me any good or benefit my mind in any way." So Upatissa having ordered his chariot, drawn by four elephants, to be harnessed at once, set out from Narada towards Giriguha, to see what the people there assembled were doing. At this time also the youth Kolita began to think thus, "Certainly I ought to go to that great assembly on Mount Grihaguha," and so, mounting on his elephant, caparisoned for the occasion, he set out and gradually drew near to the spot; before him were all sorts of dancing men and women, whilst the music sounded on every side as he proceeded.

Thus it was these two accomplished youths set out to visit the same spot, and moved by the same considerations.

Having arrived at the place, they were both accommodated with high chairs in the midst of the assembly. Then Upatissa observing the vast crowd, all engaged in listening to music and watching the performances of dancers and acrobats, began to reflect thus, "How strange that so vast a multitude should be amused by such trifles as these! and then to reflect that after a hundred years not one of all this multitude will be alive!" Thinking thus, he began to regret that he had come to such a place, and so rising from his seat, he left the assembly and sought the retirement of a neighbouring wood, where, sitting down beneath a tree, he gave himself to severe reflection.

Now in the middle of that assembly there was one celebrated performer, who by his amusing tricks caused great merriment among the people; then the youth Kolita, seeing that vast assembly convulsed with laughter and hearing nothing but "Ha! ha," "Ho! ho!" on every side, began to think thus—"All these people in a hundred years will be nothing but bleached bones, scattered here and there." Thinking thus, he was much depressed, and felt very sad; rising from his seat, therefore, he went his way in search of Upatissa, whom he found after a while seated beneath the tree as before described; having approached to the spot, the youth Kolita addressed his friend and said, "Why are you so sad, dear Upatissa, and why are you sitting here alone, lost in reflection, this is a time for mirth and joy, and not for grief, surely no calamity or misfortune has befallen you, dear friend, to cause you such affliction?"

And so the Gâtha says—

"Hark to the sound of drum and lute,
The voice of singing men and women!
Listen to the merry ringing laugh,
Why then do you rejoice not, too?
This is a time for happiness and glee,
And not for sorrow and despondency,
This is a time to laugh and sing
And not to weep and sigh;
Hark then! listen to the pleasant sound,
The sound of voices like the choir of Heaven!
This meeting, like the assembly of the Gods!
Surely this is not a place or time for tears!"

Then Upatissa replied, "Dear Kolita! look at that vast assembly! listen to the merry sound of music and of singing! hark to the ringing laugh, and then remember in a hundred years not one of all that multitude will be alive!" And so the Gâtha says—

"This people, under the dominion of desire and love,
Can find no safety whilst in such a state,
For all such things are weak and perishing.
What joy can people such as these possess?
These multitudes, and all things living,
Defiled by lust and fleshly appetites,
Ere long will be consigned to lowest hell.
I, therefore, in my heart can find no place for joy
But rather filled with dread, my sorrow swells and grows,
For all these pleasures, tho' repeated, cannot avert
The coming end—I, therefore, will have none of them!"

To this Kolita replied—

"In grief as well as joy we are united,
In sorrow and in happiness alike!
That which the wise man says in verse,
Is now the case with me and you,
'What your heart rejoices in as good,
That I rejoice in, and pursue:
It were better I should die with you,
Than vainly try to live where you are not!'"

Thus, these two inseparable friends agreed to become religious mendicants together, and seek the waters of immortality. Returning to their homes, therefore, after much solicitation and repeated prayers, they obtained their parents' permission, and so finally left their friends and retired apart to lead a religious life. Now, at this time there was in Rajagriha a certain heretical teacher called Parijava Sanjaya,[1] followed by 500 disciples. Upatissa, then, and Kolita, having as yet no master, at length found their way to this Sanjaya, and after inquiring into his system, gave themselves up to practise it. [This system appears to have required the use of medicinal herbs for the purpose of producing ecstasy.] Having tried this method for seven days and nights, and

[1] Jul. iii, 52. Parijava in the text is evidently a mistake for Paribajaka. With respect to Sanjaya compare *Introd. to Ind. B.*, p. 532.

thoroughly investigated it, they found no rest to their souls, and were still dissatisfied.

At this time it was that the Lord of the world was dwelling near Râjagriha, in the Kalandavenuvana, attended by the thousand Rahats, and waited on by Bimbasâra and countless thousands of people. It so happened that an old Bhikshu, called Upasana, the most reverend of all the disciples of Buddha, went very early in the morning, with his robes properly adjusted, and his alms-bowl in his hand to beg from house to house in Râjagriha. [*So the Mahasanghikas say, but the other schools say that the Bhikshu's name was Asvayujatta.*[1]] Whilst so begging, robed in his Sanghâtî and his Nirvâsana, with his alms-dish carried evenly in his hands, he was watched by the people, who all agreed that he must be one of the Sâkyas, so graceful and dignified his appearance. The two youths, Upatissa and Kolita, likewise, having beheld him were convinced that if there was a Rahat in the world that he was one, and forthwith they resolved to follow him to his place of residence, and enquire respecting the religious system he had adopted.

Accordingly, having found him, they saluted him and stood on one side. Upatissa then addressed him as follows: "Most reverend Sir, do you receive disciples to instruct them in your doctrine?"

To whom Asvayujatta replied, "I myself am only a learner (sravaka) and not a teacher." Upatissa rejoined, "Who then, reverend sir! is your master, and where does he dwell? and what is his doctrine? and what is his name?" [*Now at this time, just after the Lord of the world had arrived at supreme wisdom, he was universally known as "the Great Shaman" (Ch. ed.)*] Then Asvayujatta replied to Upatissa as follows: "My master is the Great Shaman of the race of the Sâkyas, and his religious system of complete retirement from the world is that which I have adopted, to my heart's joy."

Then Upatissa asked, "and is that great Shaman of whom you speak, as full of dignity and grace as you are?" To whom Asvayujatta answered as follows:—

---

[1] Called elsewhere Asvajita. [I derive Asvayujatta from *Jul. Méthode*, 2292.]

"As a mustard seed compared with Mount Meru,
As the pool, caused by the cow's footstep, compared with the great ocean,
As the gnat compared with the Garuda,
So am I compared with my master!"
[And much more to the same effect].

At length, Upatissa having inquired what was the doctrine taught by the great Shaman, Asvayujatta replied, "I am but the disciple of a day, and know but little of the profound doctrine of my master; but yet I will tell you in brief what I have understood." To which Upatissa replied, "Pray tell me in few words, venerable one, for I love not long discourses," and so the Gâtha says:—.

"I desire only true Reason,
I love not words and sentences;
The wise man loves sound Reason,
Relying on this, he frames his Life."

Then Asvayujatta consented to explain what he knew of his master's teaching; "My master, he said, discourses on the connection of causes and their consequences, he also touches on the path of deliverance, and so a Gâtha which he often repeats will explain, [*The above is what the Mahasanghikas say; the account of the Kâsyapiyas is a little different, and as follows*]:—"What then is this system of doctrine, venerable sir?" "My master repeats the following aphorism of the Law:

"All things are produced by cause,
All things are destroyed by cause;
Thus Destruction and Production,
Our Shaman says, result from cause."

Then Upatissa (the Paribrajika) at once comprehended the character of the doctrine involved in these lines, whilst the venerable Asvayujatta went on to explain them, thus—

"The phenomena which result from cause,
By cause also are destroyed;
Destroy this cause, and you arrive at supreme wisdom,
So teaches my master, the great Shaman."

Then Upatissa, the Paribrajika, having clearly perceived the truth of this doctrine, obtained perfect peace and was freed from all doubt; so opening his mouth, he said,

"This Dharmachariya (mode of teaching),
Which I have heard,
Thro' Niyutas of Kalpas
Has not thus been exhibited."

Then Upatissa, the Paribrajika, having uttered this stanza, bowed down at the feet of Asvayujatta, and having circumambulated him three times, departed to the place where Kolita, the Paribrajika, was dwelling.

Then Kolita, seeing the sparkling eyes and joyful countenance of his friend, asked him if he had found the deliverance he sought, and the way of immortality. [On this, Upatissa repeats the stanza above given, and Kolita also arrives at a condition of rest.] They then went to the abode of Sanjaya, and entreated his permission to join themselves to the company of the Lord of the world, and on his refusing to let them go or to come himself with them, they turned away from him and left his society.

Meantime, the disciples of the Paribrajika Sanjaya, reflecting on what had happened, resolved to follow after Upatissa and Kolita, and accompany them to the great Shaman. In vain Sanjaya cried, "Oh! leave me not! do not go!" for they heeded not his entreaties, and departed. Then Sanjaya, overcome with grief, began to vomit up blood and died.

Then the two young men, Upatissa and Kolita, accompanied by the 500 Paribrajikas, went on to the Kalandavenuvana, to join themselves to the company of the Lord of the world.

Then Buddha, seeing them afar off approaching to the place, addressed Kaundinya thus—"See you those two young men! they are coming hither, not for the purpose of disputation, but because they seek to learn a more excellent way than that in which they have been instructed;" and then, turning to all the Bhikshus, he said, "These two shall be the most distinguished of my disciples—the one for wisdom, the other for spiritual power (irddhi)." And so the Gâtha says [to the same effect].

Then approaching the presence of the Lord of the world, they besought him to admit them into the company of his disciples, to whom the world-honoured spake thus, "Welcome Bhikshus! enter into my fraternity; ye have practised the Rules of a Brahmana, and therefore have cast off the trammels of worldly sorrow;

welcome, then, to my company!" On this, the new Bhikshus were provided miraculously (of itself) with the proper garments with which to invest themselves, and having put on these, their hair fell off, so that their heads were as smooth as a child's head when first shaved.[1] They then took their places in the assembly, the venerable Kolita on the left and the venerable Upatissa on the right of the Lord of the world. [And in the course of a half month Upatissa became a Rahat, and six days afterwards Kolita likewise obtained that condition.]

Now the mother of the venerable Upatissa was called Sari, and so Upatissa was generally called Sari putra (putta). And so Kolita is called Mugalana (because this was his family name).

Then the world-honoured related the following stories in connection with the previous history of these two distinguished disciples. "I remember in years gone by there were two children living in Benares, a brother and sister, both called Supriya. The boy became a recluse and afterwards a Pratyeka Buddha, the girl became a Paribrajika heretic.

"On a certain occasion, the Pratyeka Buddha went to visit his sister, at which time she provided every kind of delicate food and drink for him, after partaking of which she then presented him with a knife and (a case of) needles. On this, the Pratyeka Buddha, by his spiritual power, rose up into the air and flew away. Whereupon the Paribâjika, falling down on the earth with her hands clasped over her head, adored him, and prayed thus—'Oh! that I may in some future birth meet with a divine teacher like this man, and so avoid falling into the evil paths of transmigration. And as the needle is able to penetrate everything by its sharpness, so may I be able to pierce through the most difficult subjects of enquiry and cut away every doubt by the acuteness of my intellect.' This Supriya, Bhikshus! is now born as Sariputta.

"Again, I remember in days gone by there was a certain shell merchant residing at Benares, who likewise fed a Pratyeka Buddha, and on seeing him fly away through the air, he offered up a similar prayer, desiring that he might possess the same spiritual power as that Pratyeka Buddha had. This shell-merchant, Bhikshus, is the present Mugalyana."

[Kiouen XLVIII contains 6,374 words, and cost 3.187 taels.]

---

[1] *Vide* Jul. iii, 52.

CHAPTER XLIX.

The Story of the Five Hundred Merchants.

§ 1. At this time, all the Bhikshus inquired of Buddha how it was that these 500 Paribâjikas, followers of Sanjaya, the heretic, were able to accept the guidance of Sariputra, and escape from the pitfalls and wastes of heretical teaching, and find deliverance in the hearty belief of the doctrines taught by the Lord of the world.

On this Buddha answered and said, "Listen well, oh Bhikshus! and weigh my words. This is not the first time that by the guidance of Sariputra these 500 heretics have been able to find escape and deliverance; but I remember in ages gone by there was a certain royal horse born called Kesi,[1] his bodily appearance most beautiful, his coat as white as the driven snow or as the brightest silver, pure as the moon when full, or as the flower of the kuta (grass). His head of a bright fiery colour,[2] his feet swift as the wind, his voice mellow as that of the softest drum. At this time, there were in Jambudwipa five hundred merchant men who wished to undertake a voyage by sea for the purpose of exchanging their goods for others and so increasing their wealth. Accordingly, having selected a wise man as their chief and leader, they came down the sea shore for the purpose of embarking their merchandise and setting out on the voyage. First of all, having paid their devotions to the Sea-God, they appointed five men to superintend the various departments. One to manage the sails[3] (sailing master?), a second to hold the oar (helmsman?), a third to pump out the water, a fourth to manage the stowing (floating and sinking, *i. e.*, the draught or stowage), and a fifth to be captain. Having then confessed to one another whatever crimes they had committed and duly repented of them, and having moreover instructed one another in all the preliminary duties before embarking in such an undertaking as theirs, they set sail for the purpose of seeking jewels and precious stones.

---

[1] For allusions to this horse Kesi refer to the *Vish. Pur.*, p. 540, also to the *Prem Sagar*, p. 73 (Eastwick's translation.)

[2] That is, the colour of the sandal wood, known as *Gosirsha*. Compare *Bucephalos*.

[3] *Vide* below, chap. 50, where the expression is "shap mi." I suppose "mi" is equal to the "main-sheet."

"Suddenly, whilst on the voyage, there arose a fierce storm, which blew their vessel toward the country of the Rakshasîs,[1] and ere they could reach the shore the tempest beat so against them, that their ship was entirely broken up and destroyed. At this time the merchants bound themselves to pieces of the wreck, and struggling with the waves endeavoured to reach the shore.

"Now the Rakshasîs having perceived the disaster and the fate of the 500 merchants, hastened with all speed to the place, intending to rescue the men and enjoy their company for a time, and then according to their custom to enclose them in an iron city belonging to them, and there devour them at their leisure. Having transformed themselves, therefore, from their real shape as hideous ogres into the most lovely women, adorned with jewels, flowers, and every kind of charming ornament, they hurried down to the spot, and when arrived there, they cried out, 'Be not afraid, illustrious strangers! be not alarmed, dear youths! stretch out your hand, lift your arm, rest yourselves here! thus! thus!' and so the merchants, half drowned in the ocean, hearing these welcome words, and seeing the pleasing forms of the women, did as they were told, and so by their help reached the shore in safety.

"Then the Rakshasîs in great joy cried out, 'Welcome! welcome! dear youths! Whence have ye come so far? But now ye are here, let us be happy. Be ye our husbands, and we will be your wives! We have no one here to love or cherish us; be ye our lords, to drive away sorrow, to dispel our grief! Come, lovely youths! come to our houses, well adorned and fully supplied with every necessary; hasten with us to share in the joys of mutual love.'

"Then those merchants addressed the Rakshasîs thus: 'Illustrious maidens! (sisters) let your hearts rest awhile! Give us a short space to expend our grief and dispel the sorrowful thoughts that afflict us!' Then those men, going apart by themselves, gave vent to their sorrow! They raised their voices and cried, 'Alas! alas!' One lamented for his father and his mother; another cried, 'Alas! my sister!' or, 'Alas! my brother!' Another exclaimed, 'Alas! my loved ones!' 'My dear kinsfolk!' 'My house!' 'My fellow-clansmen!' 'Alas! we shall see you no more!' 'Alas! for Jambudwîpa, our own dear country, unequalled for beauty and delight. Alas! alas!'

[1] That is, Ceylon.

"Uttering such lamentable cries, they relieved their burthened hearts.

"Then going on gradually with the Rakshasîs, they advanced towards their city, and as they went they observed that the ground was beautifully soft and level. There were no wild shrubs or thorns, no broken pots or stones, no dust flying about, no unsightly flowers, but all they saw was charming to the eye and grateful to the senses. The flowers, the trees, the fruits, the grass, all were beautiful!—soft to the touch, sweetly scented, and brightly painted. [Here follows a list of the trees, flowers, and birds.]

"At last they approach the city, surrounded by a four square wall of the whitest marble, bright as the Snowy Mountains or like the fleecy white clouds. Inside rose tower upon tower, as the cliffs rise one above the other on the beetling shore; from the numerous turrets, that surrounded the central towers, floated every sort of garland and flag, whilst lovely canopies (umbrellas) crowned the highest. In every direction throughout the city were placed metal censers, in which the choicest aromatic woods were kept constantly burning.

"Then the Rakshasîs, taking their guests through the city, bid them cast off their dripping clothes, and having washed their bodies in warm and scented water, they bring for them luxurious seats on which to recline.

"And now they give way to unhindered pleasure. The music ravishes their ears, and they are lulled to forgetfulness by every device that art can provide or love suggest.

"So time passed. At length, the Rakshasîs having warned the merchants against approaching a certain part towards the southern side of the city, the curiosity of the merchant chief was excited, and, being a man of very superior parts and of penetrating mind, he began to have some doubts about the matter. 'Why,' thought he, 'should these women exhort us never to go towards a certain part at the south of the city? I ought to look into the matter, and when the women are asleep endeavour to see what danger there is, so that we may avoid it, if there be any, before it is too late.'

"Having thought thus, the chief merchant waited that night till the women were all asleep, and then arising softly from his bed, without any sound, he got away, and, seizing his sword, left the house. Going onwards in the forbidden direction, he came at length to a narrow path, which had neither tree or plant growing beside it, and was altogether of a dreary and fear-inspiring character. Then, listening, he heard the sounds of groans and lamentations, like those proceeding from the wretched beings confined in hell. Hearing these sounds, the merchant chief was seized with wonderful fear; the hairs of his body stood upright, and he remained silently transfixed as it were to the ground. Thus he continued for some time, till at length recovering his self-possession, he entered on the desolate path he had seen, and cautiously advanced along it. After proceeding a short distance, he saw before him the dim outline of an iron city, and he soon perceived that the cries and groans he heard proceeded from within the walls of that place. Going round the city, he could see no gate, only on the north side of it he observed a tree, whose name was *hoh-hwen*, (united joy), which grew beside the wall and seemed to overtop it. Having observed this tree, the merchant forthwith resolved to mount it and look within the city. Having climbed to the top, he gazed over the wall, and lo! he beheld before him a piteous sight. He saw many dead men lying about—more than a hundred—and of these some were half-eaten, and others, scarcely dead, were dismembered and mutilated. Others, again, were sitting about, famished to death; others, again, sightless, their eye sockets like deep well-pits; others with their flesh half torn from their limbs, as if gnawed off by some wild beast; others with their hair matted and torn, covered with filth and dirt; and in the midst or all there arose a constant wail, as from the culprits who suffer torments in the place where Yama rules. Seeing this doleful spectacle, the merchant chief was once more overpowered by fear; his hair stood erect through terror. At length, regaining his courage, he seized a branch of the tree on which he was seated, and, waving it violently about, he raised a great shout, so as to attract attention. The sound of his voice having reached the prisoners inside the city, looking up they saw the merchant chief seated on a branch of the *hoh-hwen* tree outside the wall. Beholding him thus, they raised a piteous cry, and spake to him these words: "Who, then, are you? Are you Deva, Nâga, Yaksha, Gandharva, Asura, Kinnara, Garuda, Mahoraga, or what? or are you Maha Sâkra Kausika, or the adorable Brahma Râja, come to visit us in our misery, and bring us deliverance?" Then those miserable ones, falling down to earth, and placing their hands above their heads, worshipped the merchant chief, and said, 'Pity us! oh, pity us! and help us to escape! We are ruthlessly torn from those we love! Oh, help us, then! help us to escape from this wretched city, and once more see the faces of our dear ones!' Then the merchant chief, having heard these sad words proceeding from the miserable men within the city, his heart filled with unutterable sorrow, he addressed them thus: 'Be it known to you all, I am no god or other unearthly creature, but a man of Jambudwipa, who set out on a voyage seeking precious stones. Whilst crossing the sea, a storm came on and destroyed our ship, whereupon I and my comrades were near perishing, but were rescued by some women who suddenly appeared, and now we are living with these women hard by this, and enjoying their society to the full! But tell me, what can I do to assuage your sufferings?' Then they answered, 'Ah! dear sir! we likewise were once like you, merchants of Jambudwipa. Seeking precious pearls, we entered on a voyage, and were lost as you were. Then those Rakshasîs, having come to our rescue, conveyed us to the shore, and afforded us every pleasure for a time; but as soon as they heard of your shipwreck they carried us forthwith to this place, and here within this iron city we are doomed to lie till those Rakshasîs have devoured us alive! We were the other day five hundred men, and now we are but half that number; all the rest devoured by those infuriate demons. For a time they seem to love their companions, but all the while they live on human flesh. Their hearts are quite incapable of love. Beware, then, of their wiles; your time will soon come on!'

"Then the merchant chief replied, 'Oh! most unhappy men, know you of any stratagem by which we may escape from those Rakshasîs?'

"They answered, 'There is but one method of escaping from them.' On which the chief inquired respecting it.

"They then explained, 'Upon the fifteenth day of the fourth moon, when the Moon, Sun, and Pleiades (*Man*) are in conjunction,[1] a certain Horse King, called Kesi (the hairy one), of most beautiful form, white as the driven snow, his head a rosy tint, his feet swift as the wind, his voice mellow as the softest drum;—this

[1] Probably the conjunction of the Sun (?) with Ashâdha (June, July). *J. R. A. S.* Vol. V, pl. ii, p. 263.

horse, having partaken of some dainty food (corn or grain without husk and of aromatic flavour), comes to this shore once every year and half his body seen. He cries three times, "Whoever wishes to cross over the great salt sea, I will convey him over." Now, then if you would escape from your present danger, this is the only way —await the arrival of Kesi, the Horse Râja.'[1]

"Then again the merchant chief inquired, 'And have you yourselves seen this horse? If so, how is it ye did not escape? From whom, again, did you hear this strange story?—it may be it is false.'

"Then those captives answered, 'We heard from heaven a voice like this: "The merchants of Jambudwîpa are foolish and ignorant men, and why? How can they expect ere the Pleiades and Moon be in conjunction in the middle of the fourth Moon—how can they dare to try a northern course?[2] But then, if they would try, let them wait until they see the half-revealed form of the White Horse King Kesi, seeking food upon the sea-shore. He shall carry them across the briny sea to the other coast." But we, alas! were so besotted with the love of women that we heeded not the voice, and let the time slip, and are now here the certain victims of the Rakshasîs, for there is no escape from this city—the walls so high! If we dig to escape under the walls, the holes fill up again as soon as they are made. There can be no escape for us—we shall most surely all be eaten by the Rakshasîs. But, ah, dear friend! if you escape, and if you reach Jambudwîpa again in peace, go, we pray you, to such a town (or, village), and tell our loving friends that

---

1 The whole of this description seems to refer to the change of monsoon. The setting in of the south-west monsoon would be a signal for the land-bound vessels of Ceylon to start for the north again. The White Horse Kesi denotes the white crested waves that roll in with a remarkable sound punctually as the monsoon changes. Hence, because of his attributes, Avalokiteshwara was pictured under the figure of a white horse. We have remnants of the same idea in the expression common amongst sailors, "the white mane of the horse," when the waves break. The white horse of the Saxon sea kings may have a similar origin.

2 Vid. Jul. II, 62, "Quand le soleil se meut en dedans (de l'équateur) c'est la marche au Nord (Oudagayana)." It is still the custom at Madras, and elsewhere on that coast, to fling fruit, etc., into the sea on the full moon of August, after which the native craft set sail.

so-and-so is now condemned to die within the iron city of the Rakshasîs, and warn them all, and all you see, against the love of money and the desire for precious stones, and let them not risk their lives upon the treacherous ocean. Meanwhile, you and all your friends use every diligence to make good your escape, and when you join your loving relatives, parents and wives, be sure to pay your vows to Heaven, and lead a holy and religious life.'

"Having heard so much, the merchant chief descended from the tree, and as he went his way he listened to the piteous lamentations of the captives, who cried, 'Alack! Oh! for one more look at our dear country, Jambudwîpa! Far better, if safe there, to feed upon the very offal of the streets than risk one's life upon the sea in search of wealth.'

"Then the merchant chief returned to his abode and found the Rakshasîs asleep as he left them.

"Finally, after much thought, he determined to keep the knowledge of his night's adventure perfectly secret from his brother merchants, lest by any chance they should let it be known to the Rakshasîs, and so their condition be rendered desperate, following, in fact, the words of the Gâtha—

"'Every one who has learned a secret,
And with thoughtless heart and head
Lets out some portion of what he knows,
Forgets that those who hear will tell the same,
And so bring trouble and disgrace,
And stir up strife and enmity.
The wise man and the man of prudence
Let nothing out, but conceal the matter.'

And so the merchant chief, thinking of this, held his peace, and awaited the arrival of the joyous day of the fourth month, and then he began to reveal his plan to his comrades. Exhorting them all to constancy and determination, he begged them to cast off the unconcern resulting from a life of ease and shake off the power of love. So saying, he appointed a certain place of rendezvous on the night before the fifteenth day, and 'when the women are asleep,' he added, 'rise up and hasten to the spot, and I will tell you more.' Accordingly, they acted as their chief advised, and met at the appointed spot. [The chief then narrates his adventure before the iron city.]

"After a while the Horse King Kesi, having partaken of the pure food, came to the shore, and, raising his body half out of the waves, exclaimed in a loud voice three times, 'If there be anyone here desirous to pass over to the other side across the briny ocean, I will convey him.' Then those merchants, seeing the Horse King and hearing his words, were filled with joy and exultation. Their very hair stood erect with delight, and, bowing down to the earth, with their hands above their heads, they exclaimed, 'Oh illustrious Horse King! we wish to be conveyed across to that shore. Would that you would transport us hence to that side where we would be.' Then the horse replied to the merchants, 'Be it known that the Rakshasîs will certainly pursue you. They will bring their children in their arms and entreat you to return. If either of you relent or be moved by feelings of regret—if you say, "Ah! there is my wife," or, "Ah! there is my child," then do not suppose for a moment that I will convey you away. You will certainly fall off my back and become the prey of those Rakshasîs; but if you steel your hearts against their wiles, and cling closely to my hair, then I will convey you safely across the salt sea to the other shore.' Having said this, the Horse King invited them all to mount his back, and cling to him with their legs and feet. Then, mounting into the air, he flew away like the wind. Meantime the Rakshasîs, hearing the thunder-voice of the Horse King, suddenly awaking from their sleep and missing their companions, after looking on every side, at length perceived afar off the merchants mounted on the Horse King's back, clinging to his hair, and holding fast in every way, as they journey on through the air. Seeing this, they each seized her child, and, hurrying down to the shore, they uttered piteous cries, and said, 'Alas! alas! dear masters! why are you about to leave us desolate?—whither are ye going? Beware, dear ones, of the dangers of the sea. Remember your former mishap. Why do you leave us thus? What pain have we caused you? Have you not had your fill of pleasure? Have we not been loving wives? Then why so basely desert us? Return, dear youths! return to your children and your wives!' But all their entreaties were in vain, and the Horse King soon carried those five hundred merchants back to the welcome shore they had left, across the waves of the briny sea.

"Now at this time, Bhikshus; the five hundred merchant men

were these five hundred heretics, the followers of Sañdjaya; Sariputra was the wise chief, and I was the horse Kesi."

[*The Mahasanghikas say that after this Buddha travelled onwards through the neighbouring villages and so came again to Râjagriha. The Kasyâpiyas say he went to the Southern Mountains (Lanka?), and there exhibited many marvellous changes of person, and that in the meantime the people of Magadha thought he was dead, and began to break through the rules when he suddenly returned.*]

[Kiouen XLIX contains 5,587 words, and cost 2.794 taels.]

CHAPTER L.

§ 1. Now it so happened that Bimbasara Râja, observing the advantage got by the heretics in consequence of their convocations held for five days, during which they explained to the people their system of Doctrine and preached to them out of their law. Seeing this, the king exhorted Buddha to hold similar assemblies,[1] and so keep pace with the Paribâjakas, who were opposed to him. To this the Lord of the World consented, and Bimbasâra on his part undertook to be present at these convocations, and so draw the people together, in imitation of his royal example.

Then Buddha having ordered the leaders of his community (Sthavîras) to assemble, in the manner aforesaid, to repeat the law, they requested to be instructed what law they should repeat. On this he told them to preach upon the excellency of Buddha, the Law, and the Church; to exhort the people to charity, to the cultivation of wisdom, temperance, and complete personal discipline (Dhûtâ Rules, vid. E. M., p. 9); to avoid entering crowded towns and villages; to live in quietness and retirement [and so on].

Now it came to pass that as soon as the Bhikshus had begun to recite the law, as their master directed, during the five successive days of assembly, that the people also began to find fault with them, and say, "How is it that these teachers of ours continue to repeat the same thing over and over again, in a monotonous voice,

---

[1] There seems to be a reference here to the assemblies known as *pan-che-yu-sse*. Vid. Fah Hian, cap. v, p. 15.

just like children who have learned their lesson repeat it to their masters"? Then Buddha gave the priests permission to vary their mode of repeating the law, according to their individual character of voice and ability.

The people then complained of the want of agreement in the mode of recitation, and also of omissions and alterations made by some of the priests, and argued that they could not be true teachers if they varied so. On this Buddha ordered them to confine themselves to explanations of the Agama, and the Sûtras generally; and each priest (if there were more than one in an assembly) to take up the recitation in turn, explaining each word and sentence according to individual ability.

Buddha then permitted the priests to enclose a space within four walls, to smooth the enclosed ground and plant it.[1] Buddha then gave them permission to wash their feet [after a journey along a muddy road, undertaken for the purpose of reciting the law]. He then permitted them to use incense [perfumed cow dung] and scented water, for the purpose of purifying the place of recitation. The people then complained that the priests were transgressing the order that they should not use or possess any unguents or perfumes. On this, Buddha permitted them to receive gifts of flowers and incense from lay persons, for the purpose of assisting in the religious function; but when this permission was abused, and money and other things offered, Buddha restricted the permission to gifts of the necessary things [viz., meat, drink, clothes, medicine].

Buddha afterwards permitted *selections* of the sacred books to be read; also an elevated place to be erected, on which the priest or priests should sit, for the purpose of being heard; he forbad two preaching halls to be near one another, lest there should be confusion of sound; he also permitted those assembled to join in the recitation of certain portions of the law, such as the Gâthas, etc., but he forbad anything like irreverent or indecent singing; he also ordained that, if any Bhikshu wanted to go to any place for the purpose of reciting the law, he should first ask permission of the Achârya, and on a certain occasion, when some Bhikshus had disobeyed this order, and gone to a certain town contrary to the

---

1 Doubtless the origin of the Sañghârâmas or "priests' garden."

wishes of the Achârya (senior priest), it happened that they were robbed and beaten, and scarcely got back alive to the Sanghârâma, on which occasion, to show the fatal consequences of disobedience to parents and religious superiors, the world-honoured one related this story.

Story of the Merchant who Struck His Mother.

§ 2. "I REMEMBER in years gone by, there were 500 merchants in Jambudwipa, of whom a certain one was chief, his name was Mâitri (sse-chè). On one occasion, these merchants all assembled together, and begun to consult how they might best embark on some expedition for the purpose of getting gain. Having agreed upon a voyage in a certain direction, and settled all preliminaries as to freight and provisioning the ship, they separated for a time, returning to their homes, to take leave of their wives and families.

"Now at this time Mâitri went to see his mother, to get her permission and blessing ere he set out on the expedition contemplated. At this time his mother was living in retirement in the upper portion of the house, exercising herself in religious discipline [laws of purity and self-restraint].

"Mâitri approaching her, addressed his mother thus: 'Honoured mother! [or, honoured "parent"] I am about to undertake a voyage by sea, for the purpose of getting much profit. I hope to return home with gold, silver, jewels of every kind, and so be able to minister in every way to your comfort, and also to that of the members of my family [give me then your permission and blessing].'

"Then his mother began to expostulate with him, and to say, 'Dear son! why venture your life at sea? Surely you have wealth enough at home, and every comfort and necessary without stint. You can easily afford to give what is necessary in religious charity; there is no impediment in the way of your happiness (merit). Darling Son! dear Son! the sea is full of perils, boisterous winds, hungry and cruel monsters (fishes), evil spirits, Rakshasis, and ghouls; dear Son! darling Mâitri! all these dangers infest the ocean; and now I am getting old, and if you leave me now, although as you say you want to return a rich man to minister to my necessities, still the day of my death is so near, that all your pious intentions may be of little use to me; stay, then, dear Son! stay to be the comfort of my old age'! [And so she entreated him three times.]

"Then Mâitri answered, 'Yes! dear mother, but still I must go! think of the wealth I shall bring back, the gold and silver and jewels! think how I shall be able to nourish and cherish you in your old age, and what gifts I can bestow in religious charity.'

"Then his mother arose from her seat, and threw her arms round his neck, and embraced him, as she cried, 'Darling Son! dear Mâitri! I cannot let you go; I cannot give you leave to risk your life on the ocean just to seek for gain! we have money enough, we have all we need at home! I cannot let you go!'

"Then Mâitri thought thus—'My mother is cross with me, and does not want me to prosper, and so she forbids me go this voyage,' and then he got angry, and pulling his mother to the ground, he slapped (kicked) her head, and rushed out of the house!

"Then the merchants having assembled on the coast, and offered their worship to the Sea-God, selected five men to superintend the various departments [as before], and then set sail. But, sad to say! their ship was soon overtaken by a storm and broken to pieces, and all the merchants except Mâitri were lost. But he, having clung to a plank, after tossing about on the waves for a long time, was at length thrown on the shore of an islet called Vaisvadipa [North island or islet]. So Mâitri, having refreshed himself with some of the wild seeds and medicinal herbs growing on the shore, at length recovered his strength, and began to explore the neighbourhood of the spot where he had been cast ashore. At length, as he went on, he came to a southern division (fork) of the island, and there he saw a path leading right before him. Following the track, after a short distance he saw, from a slight eminence, a city immediately in front of him, shining like silver, extremely beautiful and glorious! it was full of towers and palaces, surrounded by a lofty wall, and in every respect perfectly adorned [with lakes, woods, censers, flags, etc., etc.], and calculated for the unbridled indulgence of love and pleasure. In the centre of the city was a charming palace (called "Merry-joy"), built of the seven precious substances, and most exquisite to behold!

"And now from within the city there came forth four beautiful women, adorned with jewels and every ornament calculated to please. Approaching the spot where Mâitri stood, they addressed him as follows: 'Welcome, oh Mâitri! let us conduct you within yonder city, there is no one there to interfere with us, and there is an abundance of every necessary for food and enjoyment. See yonder beautiful palace, called 'joy and pleasure', constructed of the seven precious substances. It is there we four live, we rise up and lie down as we like, with no one to molest us! come, then, oh Mâitri! enter there with us and enjoy our company without interference, we will nourish you and cherish you with the fondest care.' So entering into that pleasant hall, Mâitri enjoyed the society of those women, with no one (man) to dispute possession with him. Thus passed many, many years; nothing to interrupt the current of his happiness. At length, after a long lapse of time, these four women addressed Mâitri, and said, 'Dear Mâitri; remain here with us, and go not to any other city.' Then Mâitri began to doubt about the matter, and he thought 'What do those women mean when they talk about other cities, I will wait till they are asleep and then go and explore in every direction, and see whether there is good or bad luck in store for me.' So when they had dropped off to slumber, Mâitri arose, and leaving the precious tower, he went out, and passing through the Eastern gate, he entered the garden which surrounded the city, and then leaving this by the Southern gate, he struck into a road, along which he pursued his way. At length he saw before him at some distance a city of gold, most beautiful to look at, and in the middle of it a lovely palace called 'ever-drunk', made of the seven precious substances and beautifully adorned. Now whilst he gazed, lo! eight beautiful women came forth from the city to the place where he stood, and addressed Mâitri as follows: 'Dear Mâitri! come near and enter this city in our company, there is a beautiful palace which we occupy, with no one to molest us, there is no lack of any comfort or necessary within its walls; come, then, and enjoy our society, whilst we nourish and cherish you without intermission.' So he went with them, and enjoyed their company for many years, till at last, when they began to talk to him about going to some other city, his suspicions were aroused as before, and he resolved when they were asleep to explore further and find out what other cities there were. [And so he discovered two other cities, one built of crystal, the other of lapis lazuli, the first with sixteen, the other with thirty-two maidens, who invited him to enjoy their company as before.] On receiving similar hints from these, in succession, he went on further discoveries, till at length he saw an iron city, that appeared to him quite desolate, only he heard a voice constantly crying out, 'Who is hungry? who is thirsty? who is naked? who is weary? who is a stranger? who wishes to be carried?' On hearing this voice, Mâitri began to consider with himself; at the other cities I found agreeable companions, but here I see no one, but only hear this doleful voice. I must search into this. Accordingly he entered the city to see whence the voice proceeded. No sooner had he passed through the gate, than it shut behind him, and he felt that he was alone within the walls and all escape cut off. On this he was filled with fear, his limbs trembled, and the hairs of his body stood upright. He began to run to and fro in every direction, exclaiming, 'Woe is me! I am undone! I am ruined!' At length, as he ran here and there, lo! he saw confronting him a man, on whose head there was placed an iron wheel, this wheel was red with heat, and glowing as from a furnace, terrible to behold. Seeing this terrible sight, Mâitri exclaimed, 'Who are you? why do you carry that terrible wheel on your head?' On this that wretched man replied, "Dear Sir! is it possible you know me not? I am a merchant chief called Govinda.' Then Mâitri asked him and said, 'Pray then tell me, what dreadful crime have you committed in former days that you are constrained to wear that fiery wheel on your head?' Then Govinda answered, 'In former days I was angry with and struck my mother on the head as she lay upon the ground, and for this reason I am condemned to wear this fiery iron wheel around my head.' At this time Mâitri, self-accused, began to cry out and lament; he was filled with remorse in recollection of his own conduct, and exclaimed in his agony, 'Now am I caught like a deer in the snare.'

"Then a certain Yaksha, who kept guard over that city, whose name was Viruka, suddenly came to the spot, and removing the fiery wheel from off the head of Govinda, he placed it on the head of Mâitri. Then the wretched man cried out in his agony and said, 'Oh, what have I done to merit this torment?' [the Gâthas are to this effect] to which the Yaksha replied, 'You! wretched man, dared to strike (kick) your mother on the head as she lay on the ground; now, therefore, on your head you shall wear this fiery wheel, through 60,000 years your punishment shall last; be assured of this, through all these years you shall wear this wheel.'

"Now, Bhikshus! I was that wicked Mâitri, and for 60,000 years I wore that wheel for disobedience to my mother; so be ye assured that disobedience to your religious superiors will be punished in the same way!"

[Kiouen L contains 6,053 words, and cost 3.027 taels.]

CHAPTER LI.

The History of Sikhi Buddha.[1]

Now it came to pass, whilst Bôdhisatwa was dwelling on the banks of the Uravilva river, and in the exercise of self mortification had reduced himself to the one grain of millet and rice in the day, at this time his father, Suddhôdana, began to think about the welfare of his son, and spoke to one of his attendants, saying, "I wonder what my son is doing, and where he is living? see if you can find out." In obedience to this inquiry, messengers were sent to the banks of the Uravilva river, and a correct report brought back to Suddhôdana Râja as to the condition of his son.

Then the Râja's heart was oppressed, and he uttered his lamentations and said "Alas! alas! for my poor child! how can he survive this penance of six years' duration."

Then Yasôdharâ, the Sâkya princess, having heard of the privations and sufferings endured by her Lord, immediately laid aside her jewels and fine clothing, and used none but the commonest food, for she said, "How shall I enjoy the luxuries of a royal residence, and partake of delicate food, whilst my lord is thus enduring affliction and want. I will even share his self-privation and suffer the same pain."

Then, in answer to Udayi, the Lord of the world related the following story about Yasodharâ:—

"I remember in years gone by, there was a certain remote forest

---

[1] Sikhi "who wears a crown."

enclosure (district; arânya), in which a deer-king with his herd had found a place of pasture, and lived in contentment. At this time a hunter, having discovered the spot where these deer congregated, set a snare to entrap one or more of them, and as it happened he caught the king of the herd himself. At this time a certain hind, the wife of the deer-king, big with young, seeing the deer king thus in the snare of the huntsman, stopped in the neighbourhood and would not leave the spot where he was. Meantime, all the other deer having fled from the spot, the deer-mother spake as follows, in Gâthas which she addressed to the king :—

"'Deer-King! exert your strength,
Push with your head and your heel,
Break to pieces the trap which man
Has set to catch you, and escape.'

"Then the Deer-king answered in the following Gâthas and said :—

"'Although I used all my strength,
Yet I could not escape from this trap,
Made as it is with thongs of skin, sewn with silk,
In vain should I struggle to get away from such a snare.
Oh! ye mountain dells and sweetest fountains!
May none of your occupants henceforth
Meet with such a misfortune as this!'

"And the Gâtha continues as follows :—

"'At this time those two Deer,
Filled with alarm, and shedding bitter tears!
Beheld the wicked hunter approaching the spot
With his knife and club in his hand (ready to slay.)'

"Then the Deer-king, seeing the hunter thus armed approaching the place, said to the Mother-deer—

"'This is the Hunter, coming here,
His face dark and forbidding, his doublet of skin,
He will come and strip off my hide,
Cut up my flesh in joints, and depart.'

"Then the female deer gradually approaching the hunter, addressed him and said—

"'Most illustrious Hunter! listen!
You may arrange your seat of grass, and prepare

First of all to kill me, and skin my hide from my body,
Then go and kill your prisoner—the Deer-king.'

"At this time the hunter addressed the hind as follows: 'Is this Deer-king related to you?' Then the hind answered and said, 'He is my husband. I love and revere him with all my heart, and therefore I am determined to share his fate; kill me first then, hunter! and afterwards do as you list to him!'

"Then the huntsman reflected and said, 'What a faithful and exemplary wife is this! seldom indeed is such a one to be found!' Then he addressed the hind and said, 'Most respectable one! your conduct is very commendable; I will let your lord go!'

"Then there was great joy, and the huntsman said—

"'Seldom have I seen such faithfulness,
Go, then! oh, Deer-king!
And as you owe your life to your mate,
Cherish and nourish her as you ought.'

"Then the huntsman loosed the snare and let the Deer-king go, on which the hind overjoyed, addressed the huntsman and said—

"'Most virtuous and illustrious huntsman!
May all your friends and relations,
As you have caused me to rejoice
Seeing my husband escape, likewise so rejoice.'"

Then Buddha said, "This Deer-king was myself, and the hind was Yasodharâ, who, on my account, experienced much sorrow, so much indead, that for six years she carried Rahûla in her womb, till at last hearing that I was about to return and assume the dignity of a universal monarch (whereas my kingdom is of a spiritual character), overcome with joy she brought forth her son, Rahûla, and clothed and adorned him as became the child of a queen."

Then Suddhôdana, hearing of the birth of the child, was much incensed against Yasodharâ, and thought she had done his son dishonour, on which he assembled the various Sâkya princes and laid the case before them.

After consultation, they severally proposed the following punishments: That she should be whipped, burned, mutilated, blinded, impaled, buried alive, etc., etc. [But at length the Lord of the world, knowing the trouble and danger of Yasodharâ, sent to Suddhôdana and said, 'The child is my child;' and then all honour was done both to the mother and babe.]

[The rest of this chapter is occupied by an account of the conversion of Udâyi and the charioteer Tchandaka, who had been sent to the place where Tathâgata was, for the purpose of asking him to return to Kapilavastu.

These two, having taken on them the usual vows, and shaved their heads, and assumed the robes, were sent by Buddha to Kapilavastu to announce his intention of visiting the place of his birth. They gradually returned till they arrived at the Garden of the Nyagrodha-trees, where Suddhôdana, having gone for some other purpose, beheld them. Astonished when he heard that these two strange figures were Shamans like his own son, filled with grief, without further inquiries, he returned within the city walls.

Buddha then relates to Saripûtra the miracles that attended the progress of a former Buddha, called Sikhin, as he returned to his own country. The trees, flowers, fountains, rivers, and all created things combined to do him honour].[1]

CHAPTER LII.

The History of Udâyi.

§ 1. Now Buddha, at the end of the 14th day of the month, began to move towards his native country of Kapilavastu. On this occasion the earth quaked and countless Devas accompanied the cortège, showering down flowers, and producing many spiritual manifestations.

At length, having arrived in the neighbourhood, the world-honoured one took up his residence in the Nyagrodha wood.[2]

Then Udâyi and Tchandaka, having saluted the feet of the Lord of the world, related how Suddhôdana had not a believing heart, or a pure mind, and how he had no desire to have anything to do with the Bhikshus.

---

1 Compare M. B. 201, 202, etc.

2 Here follows a poetical description of his progress, similar to that of Sikhin in the previous chapter.

The Lord of the world, understanding the case, addressed all the Bhikshus and said, "Which of all your company, oh! Bhikshus! is able to go to the place where Suddhôdana resides, and convert him to the faith!"

Then some said, Sariputra can; others, Mugalan is able; others Mahâ Kâsyapa; others, Katyâyana; others, Uravilva Kâsyapa; others, Nadi Kâsyapa; others, Upâsana.

Then the lord addressing Udâyi said, "You, Udâyi! are fit to discharge this mission; go then to the presence of Suddhôdana, and use your ability to convert him to the faith."

[Udâyi then proceeds to Kapilavastu, and explained to Suddhôdana that he had come from the royal prince who is now residing in the Nyagrodha garden. The king then begins to form an affection for the Shaman, and orders food to be prepared for him; but Udâyi prefers taking the food to the Lord of the world. Suddhôdana offers to give other and better food for his son; but Udâyi instructs the king that his master will eat nought except rice and vegetables, with sugar and honey. Hereupon the king orders a special dish to be prepared for his son, and Udâyi consents to take it to him. [*There is some slight divergence here betwixt the Kàsyapiyas and the Mahâsanghîkas, but not of any importance.*] Then Buddha, having received the food of Udâyi, and heard that his royal father was about to visit him, related the following story]:—

The Story of the Two Parrots.

§ 2. "I REMEMBER in years gone by, in the country about Benares, there was a certain King of the Birds, named Suputra, who dwelt in the midst of all the birds (80,000 birds) that frequented the city of Benares. This Suputra had a wife called Suputrî. The latter, on a certain occasion, took a strange fancy that she must, some how or other, get some of the food to eat of which the King of Benares partook day by day, or else that she would die. Her husband seeing how restless and excited his mate had become, inquired of her the reason. On this she told him the whole truth and assured him that she never could survive her trouble unless she had some of the food from the royal table of the Râja of

Benares. The king of the birds bemoaned her fate, but was hopeless as to the accomplishment of her wish. At this time a bird belonging to the company undertook to provide for the queen the food she wanted: taking his seat therefore on a tree near the open window of the royal palace, he watched his opportunity till the servant brought in the rice and other food for the king. Then flying into the chamber and alighting on the head of the dish-carrier, he laid hold of his nose, and bit it so hard, that he let go the dishes and scattered all the food on the floor. The bird then, having picked up as much as he wished, conveyed it to the disconsolate queen. [And so he does again and again.]

"Then Brahmahdatta, the King of Benares, being deprived of his food, began to think, 'I wonder what bird this is that comes here and dares to carry off my food in this way.'

"Accordingly, he ordered his fowler to catch the bird, and at last, being brought into his presence, he inquired what he meant by this conduct, on which the bird told the whole truth, and Brahmadatta, much pleased with his faithfulness, let him go, and told him he was always welcome to as much food as he desired from the royal table.

"Now, said Buddha, at that time I was King of the Birds, Udâyi was the faithful one who got the food, and Brahmadatta was Suddhôdana Râja."

[Kiouen LII contains 5,762 words, and cost 2.884 taels.]

CHAPTER LIII.

1 §. At this time, Suddhôdana Râja, surrounded by all the Sakyas of Kapilavastu, 99,000 in all, and accompanied by the four kinds of military escort, left the city in order to go to the spot where Bhagavat was sojourning. On perceiving him thus approaching, the world-honoured one thought thus with himself: "If I rise not to salute my father, men will say 'how comes it to pass that he who professes to teach others their duty, is neglectful of this first duty of all—respect to his father?' if I rise to salute him, then all my

followers must do the same; but this is not right;[1] if I alone rise, they will lose respect for me."

Thinking thus, and reflecting on the best course of action, Buddha forthwith, by the exercise of his spiritual power, ascended into space, and there manifested himself in various and wonderful transformations.

At this time, Suddhôdana, afar off, perceiving the spiritual transformations of Bhagavat, as he remained unsupported in the air, began to think thus with himself: "It is long since the Royal Prince Siddartha left his home, and he now has evidently attained to the spiritual power of a Rishi." Thinking thus, the Râja descended from his chariot, and approached the spot near which Bhagavat was. Buddha perceiving his Royal Father drawing near, descended from the air, and occupied the same spot as before.

Then the Râja beholding his son's appearance, that he wore no royal head dress, but was closed shaved, and clad in a poor Kashâya robe, was, for a moment transfixed to the earth; but recovering himself after a while, he found relief in tears and sad lamentations, in which all those 99,000 Sâkya people joined.

[After a long argument between the Râja and the Prince, the narrative continues thus]

Then the king observing Sariputra and the other Rahats, seated around their master, inquired of Buddha who these were, and whence they came! on which the world-honoured one, turning to his father, and at the same time pointing to each of his disciples in succession, mentioned their names one after the other. On this, Suddhodana was not pleased; for he thought it derogatory to his son, a Prince of the Royal Kshatriya line, to be surrounded by followers belonging to the Brahman caste. And so rising up, he departed and returned to his palace.

The History of Upali.

§ 2. At this time, there was a youth called Upali, who had come

[1] That is, according to Buddha's law, no priest should rise, even in the presence of a king.

among the first of the people to the spot where Buddha was seated. This youth being led by the hand of his mother, now approached the world-honoured one, and standing thus, his mother desired that Buddha would allow her child to shave his head. On this Buddha consented, and during four different operations the youth entered successively the four Dhyânas.

Then Suddhôdana having returned to his palace, convoked all the Sâkya princes to an assembly, and explained how his son had now become possessed of supreme wisdom, and had begun to turn the wheel of the Law (establish his kingdom), and how he was surrounded by a body of Brahmans instead of Kshâtriyas.

Then they replied, "and what would the king have us to do?" On this Suddhôdana Râja recommended that as many of the Sâkya princes as were so disposed should leave their homes, assume the robes and become followers of Buddha. Whereupon, proclamation having been made, five hundred of the Sâkyas agreed to become disciples. They then determined to consign all their goods to the care of Upali; but he knowing their purpose, hastened to Buddha, and requested permission to enter the priesthood first. This being granted, Suddhôdana Râja and the five hundred Sakyas approached, and, on making their request known, they also were permitted to become disciples on condition that they first bowed down at the feet of Upali. So the pride of these Sâkya princes was mortified. Buddha then related the previous history of Upali thus:

"I remember in days gone by there were two men living in Benares who were great friends, but they were both poor and looked down upon by the world. At a certain time it happened that they just had in their house one pint of millet, which had been consigned to them by a stranger who was leaving the city of Benares. At this time a certain Pratyeka Buddha, having entered the city on a begging excursion, proceeded from house to house, holding his alms-dish in his hand before each door. Whereupon, the two poor men resolved to bestow the grain in their charge on this begging priest, and at the same time beseech his pity. Having done so, the Pratyeka Buddha accepted it, and, forthwith mounting into the air, flew away."

[Kiouen LIII contains 6,158 words, and cost 3.079 taels.]

CHAPTER LIV.

THE two friends, seeing the mendicant fly away thus, were filled with joy, and, joining their hands in adoration, they bowed down and worshipped; and as they worshipped they prayed that they might always be privileged to be born within sound of the true doctrine, and thus escape the evil ways of birth; whilst one in particular prayed that he might be born as a Brahman, and gain perfect knowledge of the four Vedas and the six treatises on the mechanical arts.

So it came to pass after their deaths that one was born in Benares as a Kshatriya, of the royal race, and his name was Brahmadatta; the other was born as a Brahman, and his name was Upakamanava, so skilful in learning that he was able to explain all the Shasters with ease. Now this Upakamanava had a wife, whose name was Manavika, very fair to behold, and of incomparable grace, and in her love the whole of Upakamanava's happiness consisted. Now it so happened, for some reason or other, that Manavika withdrew herself from the company of her husband, and lived altogether apart, very much to his grief and distress. At length, after the four months of extreme summer heat had passed, the wife said to her spouse, "Go now, my dear, to the market, and buy me perfumes and flowers, for I wish to enjoy the pleasures (five pleasures) of life again, and be as I was before." Upaka hearing this, was overjoyed and beside himself for delight. "What in the world," he said, "has made my wife alter her mind and become good-tempered again?" Whereupon, taking out a gold piece he had hidden, he went forth at noon-day to buy the necessary articles for his wife's adornment. Now the sun at this time was scorching hot and the earth dried up like a sheet of red copper (as red as a cock's feather); nevertheless, as Upaka went along from his house to the village, so overjoyed was he that he did nought but sing and shout for very delight.

At this time, Brahmadatta Râja was reposing in the balcony of his palace, sleeping through the heat of the day, when suddenly in his slumbers he thought he heard the sound of some one shouting out the words of a love song. Having listened and heard the sounds, the king himself began to entertain similar thoughts; and so the Gâtha says—

"Whether from one's own foolish thoughts,
Or from thoughts raised up by others,
From either cause the pollution of love arises,
As mysteriously as the lily appears on the water."

Meantime, Brahmadatta, having listened to the burthen of the love ditty, suddenly roused himself and said, "Who can this fellow be that in the broiling sun at noontime goes along singing his love-song?" Having thought thus, he looked through his window, and there he saw Upaka strolling along on the parched and reddened ground, carelessly trolling his lay as he went. Then the king, calling to his attendant minister, commanded him to bring in the fellow to his presence, on which the minister went out and cried after him, "Young man! (Mânava) come hither! come hither! the king wants you." Then Upaka's heart began to fail him and the hairs of his body to stand on end through fear, and he thought thus: "What crime have I committed that the king orders me to his presence?" But the minister meantime conducted him into the palace and brought him to the king. Now, as soon as ever Brahmadatta saw him, a sort of affection sprung up in his heart for him, and he addressed him in the following Gâthas:

"How is it you are not irritated with the heat,
Instead of singing your songs and being so light-hearted
At this time of day, when the sun pours its rays
On the earth, parched as red as the plumes of the cock?
How is it," etc. [repeated.]

To which Upaka replied in the following Gâthas:

"Mahârâja! at present no heat would irritate me;
What care I if I be roasted by the sun.
It is only when a man has had bad luck
That he gets angry at such trifling matters as these.
Though the rays of the sun were as hot again,
This would give me the least of trouble just now.
It is only when a man is vexed about all sorts of things
That he is irritable and weighed down by care."

Then the king addressed Upaka, and said, "Manava! and pray

what were your thoughts just now as you went along in the heat singing your ditty?" Then Upaka explained to the king all about his private matters at home. Then Brahmadatta addressed him thus: "Manava! I pray you don't leave me, but stop here with me, and I will give you two golden pieces." Upaka, having received these two golden pieces, still hankered after his home, and so addressed the king and said, "Mahârâja! I will venture to ask you for one more piece, and then the three you have given me, with the one I already possess, will make four, and these will buy abundant luxuries for my wife at this time of her returning affection." The king having heard this, said, "Pray don't go; I will give you eight pieces." Mânava having received these, still begged one more [and so on to one hundred and twenty pieces]. The king then offered him the government of a village, a town, a district, and at last consented to give him half his kingdom. Then Upaka, remaining in the palace with Brahmadatta, thought thus with himself: "Why should I not possess the whole kingdom? I have only to slay the king as he sleeps, and all will be mine." On this he took a sword in his hand, and proceeded to the side of the sleeping monarch, and was about to put his plan in execution, when the thought of such ingratitude suddenly stopped him, and, raising a shout, he woke the king, who inquired the reason of his making such a noise. Having told him the truth, the king at first refused to believe him, but afterwards, on Upaka's repeated asseveration that it was so, was constrained to credit it; but yet, owing to his extreme affection for him, freely forgave him. On this Upaka, seeing to what a pass his covetousness had nearly brought him, resolved to become a recluse and to leave his home.

Upaka having joined himself to the company of a famous Rishi of Benares, soon acquired supernatural powers *(and was able to touch the sun and moon with his finger)*. On hearing this, Brahmadatta, highly gratified, recited a Gâtha in the presence of his chamberlain, to the effect that Upaka by his previous merit had obtained this great eminence as a Rishi.

At this time, Brahmadatta had a barber, called Gangapala, who managed to shave his Majesty's head whilst he was asleep, without waking him; whereupon the king, in gratitude and admiration, presented him with a village to rule over (*i. e.*, made him a magistrate). But finally, Gangapala followed Upaka's example, and became a Rishi. In consequence of this, Brahmadatta and five hundred of his chief ministers proceeding to the place where these Rishis dwelt, paid them worship.

"At that time," added Buddha, "I was Upaka; Upali was Gangapala, and Suddhôdana Râja was Brahmadatta; whilst his five hundred chief ministers were these five hundred Sâkya Princes, who have now become my disciples."

Buddha having declared that Upali was the chief of his followers in the exercise of moral discipline, proceeded further, in reply to the questions of the Bhikshus, to relate the following particulars respecting Upali's previous history.

"There was once in days gone by a barber living in this city (Benares?) whose wife bore to him a son. Shortly afterwards the barber sickened and died. On this his mother took the child to the house of his paternal uncle, and gave him into the charge of the man and his wife, desiring that he should be brought up to his father's trade. Now his uncle was barber to the royal household, and constantly went to the palace, where he was detained more or less all the day, and had no time to attend to any other business. It came to pass, shortly after the child had grown up to boyhood, that a certain Pratyeka Buddha came to the city, and begged the hairdresser, the boy's uncle, to shave his hair and face. The barber, being in a hurry, put the holy man off till the next morning. Again the Pratyeka Buddha came on the following morning and requested to be shaved. Once more the barber put him off till noontide and the evening. So matters continued for several days. At last the youth, the barber's nephew, seeing the holy man constantly coming to his uncle's house and going away again, inquired the reason, and, finding out the state of the case, himself volunteered to shave the head of the saint. On this the latter consented, assuring him it should be for his great benefit. After it was over the Pratyeka Buddha, by the exercise of his spiritual faculties, mounted into the air and flew away gracefully as the King of the Hansas. Then the youth, seeing this miracle, closing both his hands, bowed his head in adoration, and prayed that hereafter he might meet with this Pratyeka Buddha, and be taught by him, and that he might ever be saved from the evil ways of birth, and remain in the condition of a man fit to profit by the instruction of Holy Teachers.

"Now, it so happened that at this very time the Râja was in his council chamber, surrounded by his ministers, occupied with state business (counting out his money), when suddenly one of them saw this newly-shaved Pratyeka Buddha flying away through the air. On this, they cried out to the king, 'See yonder, oh Râja! goes a holy man fresh-shaved flying through space.' The king, looking up and seeing the sight, was rejoiced to think of the good fortune that should accrue to the neighbourhood from such a circumstance, and quickly asked who had been the fortunate man that had shaved the saint. On this his family barber came forward and said, 'Who but I, your majesty, should have done the matter?'

"The youth hearing that his uncle had boasted thus, boldly came forward into the king's presence and denounced it as a falsehood, and declared that he had been the barber on the occasion. On this the king laughed at him, and said, 'You! how could you have shaved him? Where is your razor and where your appliances?' On this the youth brought forth his instruments, and some of the hair of the Pratyeka Buddha, and repeated, 'I shaved the holy man, and no one else.' The king, at length convinced, addressed his household barber and said, 'Wretched man! how dare you utter such a lie in my very presence? Be gone for ever from my palace and my kingdom.' So he banished the uncle and adopted the youth as the royal barber and nail-cutter.

"And so it came to pass that this youth lived and died, and after death continued to be born either as a Deva or man until he was again born in Benares in a barber's family, a beautiful youth, and as he grew up, well acquainted with all the accomplishments and arts.

"At this time Kâsyapa appeared in the world as Buddha. During his career he came to Benares, and dwelt in the deer park with two myriads of men who had become his disciples. At this time, the father of the child just named went to the park to attend to the requirements of the Bhikshus, and took his little boy with him. It so happened that they were reciting the law in the assembly, and some part of it the child heard; but the other part of it, with respect to discipline, he was not allowed to hear. This having happened more than once, he inquired the reason, and was told that only the Bhikshus were allowed to hear the entire rules of the community. On this he inquired, 'Why may I not become a Samanera, and join the community?' On this he went to the superior (Sthavira) and desired permission to take on him the vows of a recluse, and to leave his home and follow the Lord Kâsyapa. And so he became a Bhikshu, and was distinguished for his knowledge of the rules of moral discipline (Vinaya).

"Now it came to pass that among Kâsyapa's followers was one called Prabhâpala. Respecting him Kâsyapa predicted that he should be born as a Buddha, his name should be Sâkya, and one of his principal followers should be this youth distinguished for his knowledge of the precepts. And so, oh Bhikshus, it has come to pass, for I was then Prabhâpala, and that youth is Upali, who is the chief of my disciples in respect of his acquaintance with the moral law."

[Kiouen LIV contains 6,664 words, and cost 3.332 taels.]

CHAPTER LV.

History of Rahûla.

Now at this time Suddhôdana Râja requested Buddha and the priests to accept of his hospitality on the morrow, and as the world-honoured one remained silent, the Râja understood he had accepted the invitation, and so rising up, he paid his homage, and having circumambulated the holy one three times, he returned with his followers to his palace, and made all necessary preparations for the entertainment.

On the morrow, therefore, the Râja sent his messengers to the place where Buddha was, to bid him and the Bhikshus come to the feast, for all things were ready. Accordingly, the world-honoured one, surrounded right and left by his disciples, himself leading the way, went forward to the palace of Suddhôdana Râja. Having entered the royal apartment, they took their seats in due order according to the law. Then the king himself personally waited upon his guests, and after the feast was over he provided water for cleansing the mouth and hands, and then taking a small seat he came and took his place in front of Buddha and thus began the discourse. "Oh! that the honoured of men would open his mouth in instruction, and teach us some of his own divine lessons!" On this Buddha opened his mouth, and taught his father and the rest the secrets of his law. After the discourse, he arose and returned to his own place. Then by the intervention of Sâriputra, Suddhôdana Râja obtained light and became a disciple.

Now at this time Rahûla began to be about six years of age, having been born six years after his father had left his home. His mother, therefore, seeing Buddha had returned to Kapilavastu, and in recollection of all the charges which had been made against her, resolved to set the matter clear, and to vindicate both her own and her son's character. So Yasôdharâ sent messengers to Buddha to ask him to an entertainment on the morrow. Accordingly, as the day dawned, Buddha and his 1,200 followers proceeded to the palace, and entering into the apartment appointed, they took their seats in due order. Then Yasôdharâ instructed Rahûla her son in this wise—"My child! the great Shaman who is now our guest is your father, go to him then and speak to him!" On this the child Rahûla proceeded to the side of the world-honoured and said to him, "How are you, Shaman! are you quite happy and well?" Then Suddhôdana Râja asked Buddha plainly, "Is it true or not that this is your son?" To which the world-honoured one replied, "Yasôdharâ is perfectly pure and innocent. This is my son." Then the Râja and all the company present were exceedingly glad, they rejoiced and exulted for joy at the news.

Then Suddhôdana requested some of the priests to ask Buddha to relate the previous history of Yasôdharâ and Rahûla, and how it was that the child was borne so long by his mother.

Then Buddha addressed all the Bhikshus and said—"I remember in years long gone by, there was a certain king of the Brahman caste whose name was Jin-tien;[1] this monarch had two sons born to him, the one was called Sûrya (Sun), the other (Moon) Chandra.[2] They both of them had a distaste for the world and its pleasures, and desired to become religious mendicants. Now not long after their minds were so directed, the king their father died. Then the two princes, Sûrya and Chandra, consulted together as to the succession. The elder said, 'You, my brother, ought to assume the reins of government, and rule the kingdom.' The other said, 'It is clearly your duty, as the elder, to do so.' To this the first replied, 'Not so, you must of necessity be king because I am going to give up the world and become a recluse.' The other answered, 'It is your duty to reign, I shall not consent to be your substitute.' Then Sûrya replied, 'What are the rules customary before accepting the royal authority?' The other answered, 'First of all you adopt the royal title.' 'And if,' said Surya, 'a man after this disobeys or disregards the authority which the king takes, what is done to him?' 'He is punished heavily,' said the other. 'Well then,' said Sûrya, 'I now take the title of king, and I order you to conduct the empire in my stead. I am about to become a recluse.' Thus Sûrya, having given the kingdom to his brother, went into the desert as a hermit, to practise religion, accompanied by many of his relations and friends. Then Sûrya, seeing all his followers around him, undertook to be their teacher, and he made a vow to the effect that henceforth he would rely only on their charitable offerings for his own support, and that he would have nothing, and take nothing himself unless freely given him, down even to a draught of water and a tooth-cleaner (twig of willow for cleaning the mouth and teeth). But after a time it came to pass that Sûrya forgot his vow, and being in want of some medicinal herbs and other things, in the absence of any one to offer them to him, he went and helped himself. And so also one evening when he was thirsty, and saw a certain person's pitcher (*kundika*) full of water, he went and helped himself and put the empty pitcher on one side. Then the owner of the pitcher coming and finding some one had taken the water that was in it said, 'What thief has stolen the

---

[1] Man-Heaven or Man-God (*Manushya-deva?*).
[2] Confer, Weber's Râmâyana, pp. 4, 5, *n*.

water out of my pitcher? It is no Rishi that dwells here, it is a thief and nothing else.' Then Sûrya acknowledged what he had done, and received the full pardon of the other. But his heart was weighed down and full of grief because of his broken vow. Then a youth, one of his followers, coming to him for some business or other bowed down at his feet, as he was accustomed when he came into his presence, but Sûrya Rishi forbad him and said, 'My son! no more bow down to me, for I am a thief!' To which the youth replied, 'Upâdhyaya! (master) how so!' Then he told the entire circumstances of his case, and demanded that they should punish him as a thief. But they declined to do anything in the matter, and so Sûrya Rishi resolved to give himself up to the king, to be treated as his crime deserved. Then his brother Chandra, hearing that Sûrya wished to come to his city, sent forth horses and elephants, etc., to conduct him there, and on his approach Chandra bowed down at his feet in reverence. But Sûrya forbad him and said, 'I am a thief, come here to be punished, do not pay me reverence!' Then Sûrya told the whole circumstances; on hearing them Chandra was very sorry, but all at once he bethought him of an expedient and said, 'I pass a law that all Rishis may take medicinal herbs and water when they need them.' To this Sûrya replied, 'Mahârâja! you make this a law now, but it was not so before!' but Chandra replied, 'It has been so from the day I ascended the throne, I have freely permitted all Shamans and Brahmans to take these things, so you have committed no robbery.' Sûrya was still dissatisfied, and at length, at the suggestion of his little cousin who was standing by, Chandra ordered the Rishi to go into his own royal garden, and consider himself as a prisoner. Now by a strange accident after this interview was over, Chandra entirely forgot about his brother being in the garden for six days; after this interval the recollection of the fact came back, and he hurriedly inquired of his ministers whether the Rishi had gone or not? Hearing that he had not gone, he immediately gave orders that all the culprits in his kingdom who were suffering imprisonment should be set at liberty, and all other creatures, birds and beasts, and then going to the garden, he offered to Sûrya every kind of charitable offering, in the way of meat and drink, and then gave him the option of leaving whenever he liked. On this Sûrya departed."

"Now," said Buddha, "at that time I was Sûrya, and Rahûla was Chandra, and because he allowed that Rishi to remain for six days in the garden, unattended to and without food, therefore he was himself for six years shut up in his mother's womb, unable to find deliverance."

"Again, I remember in years gone by there was a large herd of cows kept by a certain rich man. Every day the wife and daughter of the owner of the cows went to milk them. Once the mother took the girl with her, and made her carry the larger of the two milk pails; on returning home, the mother kept urging the girl to go faster as that part of the road was dangerous. But the girl only complained of the heavy weight of the pail of milk. At last, when her mother continued to urge her on, she got angry, and put down the pail and said, 'Here, mother! you carry my pail for a bit, whilst I step on one side for a purpose.' And so having got rid of the milk-pail, she let her mother carry it a distance of six krôsas, whilst she dawdled behind. Now this girl was afterwards born as Yasôdharâ, and because of her undutiful conduct to her mother in making her carry the heavy pail for six krôsas, she had to carry Rahûla for six years."

The world-honoured one having explained these matters, and further preached the law to Suddhôdana and his guests, rose up and departed.

Then Yasôdharâ sent Rahûla to the place where Buddha was, and told the child to ask his father for his kingdom (or authority over a district). On this the child came to where Buddha was, and going up to him said, "I want the Shaman to give me a kingdom. I want the Shaman to give me authority over a district." On this Buddha holding out his hand, Rahûla took it, and thus they went on together. Finally Buddha delivered Rahûla to the care of Sariputra, who instructed him in the rules of moral discipline, and finally he was admitted as a member of the community. And on this occasion Buddha bare record that, of all his disciples, Rahûla should be most remarkable for holding or keeping the precepts of the law (moral precepts). [*The foregoing is what the Mahasanghikas say. The Kasyapîyas say somewhat otherwise, as follows*]:—

Now, when Suddhôdana had prepared the feast for the world-honoured one, he gave strict orders through the palace that no one should tell Rahûla that Buddha was his father. Accordingly, the next morning Rahûla, surrounded by children of his own rank, proceeded to the grove where Buddha was, to tell him that all was ready. Then Buddha, surrounded by the Bhikshus, 1,200 in number, proceeded in order and with much decorum towards the king's palace. Rahûla, observing the decorous behaviour of the Bhikshus, and comparing it with the noisy conduct of the children, was very much impressed, and on reaching the palace, he watched the assembled priests take their seats with their accustomed gravity, and then went up to the balcony where Yasodharâ, his mother, was. She, too, had watched the world-honoured one and his followers approach, and on seeing her husband with his shaven crown and Kashâya robes, she burst into tears. And so the Gâtha says—

"The young wife of the Sâkya Prince
Was called Yasodharâ (Sudara),
When she saw for the first time the marks of a Recluse,
Her heart was grieved, and her tears flowed fast."

Rahûla, finding his mother thus giving vent to her grief, inquired of her why she wept, on which she said, "My child, yonder Shaman, whose skin is bright as gold, is your father." Then Rahûla replied, "Never since I was born have I heard better news," and quickly ran down, and going up to Buddha, sat down by his side, and covered himself over with the robe of his father. The Bhikshus wished to drive him away, but the world-honoured one forbad them and said, "Let him stay, and let him hide himself in my robes." Then the feast over, Suddhôdana having himself waited on the priests, and provided water, etc., for cleansing the mouth and fingers, the king occupying a small seat near the world-honoured one, listened to the exposition of the law. Then Buddha began his discourse[1]—

"Of all sacrifices (that by) Fire is the chief,
Of all exhausting passions Grief is the chief,
Of all men a King is the chief,
Of all waters the Sea is the chief,
Of all stars the Moon is the chief,
Of all lights the Sun is the chief;

---

1 The stanzas following are also to be found in the "Sela Sutta" (sects. 19, 20) of the "Sutta Nipáta." Translated by Sir M. Coomára Swámy (Trübner & Co.).

Above, below, and through the earth,
Amongst all creatures that have life,
Whether gods or men, Buddha is chief."

Having repeated these lines with a view to excite in Suddhôdana some desire or thought about religion, the world-honoured one arose and departed to his place.

Then Suddhôdana having to be occupied for some time in official duties, Rahûla took the opportunity of leaving the palace and going after Buddha. On this the world-honoured one took him by the hand, and went onwards with him to the Nyagrodha grove. Then, at his own request, Rahûla was admitted by Sâriputra into the community as a Samanera. [*The Bhikshus having reminded Buddha that the age for ordination was* 20, *the world-honoured made it a rule that at* 15 (*Rahûla's age*) *a youth may be received as a Samanera* (*novice*).]

Meantime, Suddhôdana having sent every necessary article of food for the use of Buddha and his followers, now sat down to meat himself, and desired to have Rahûla by his side; but on sending for him he was nowhere to be found. Then the king ordered messengers to go to the different resorts of the prince; first to tho Asoka grove, and see if he was in either of the palaces there. Not finding him, he sent to the Nyagrodha grove, and then the messengers came back with the news that Rahûla had entered the community. Then Suddhôdana was filled with grief, and rising up he went to the place where Buddha was. Arrived there the king explained how he had successively intended to leave his kingdom to Nanda, Ananda, Aniruddha, and Rahûla, but all these had become Ascetics, and now the king said, "I may as well resign my throne, for there is no one to succeed me." [*Then Buddha made the rule that no one should be admitted to the community, except he had the express sanction of his parents.*] Then for the sake of Suddhôdana, the world-honoured one entered on an explanation of the law, and so filled the king's heart with joy. After this the Râja returned home.

[*There are other teachers*[1] *who say that Rahûla was born two years before Buddha commenced his six years' penance, and that seven years after he had arrived at supreme wisdom, he went to Kapilavastu. This*

[1] Five teachers.

would make Rahûla exactly 15 *years old at the time of his becoming a Samanera.*]

Again the body of teachers (sthaviras ?) say that Mahâprajapati having through much weeping lost her sight, then twelve years afterwards when Buddha returned to Kapilavastu, she, with Rahûla and 99,000 of the Sâkyas, went forth to salute him. Then hearing of the wonderful miracles which he wrought, such as causing fire to proceed from one part of his person and water from another, she took some of the miraculous water, and washing her eyes with it was restored to sight.

Then all the Bhikshus astonished at this miracle, Buddha said this was not the first time such an occurrence had taken place in the history of Mahâprajâpati, and at the request of all the disciples, he related the following history.

[Kiouen LV contains 5833 words, and cost 2.917 taels.]

CHAPTER LVI.

"I REMEMBER, oh Bhikshus! in years gone by there was a mountain in the Kasi country, near Benares,[1] which was called Utsanga, on the southern face of which was a garden beautifully adorned with flowers, and water-tanks, and shady groves. Now in this mountain at a certain time there gathered a herd of elephants, amongst which was a certain female elephant that gave birth to a young one of a perfectly white colour except its head, which was of a dark rosy colour like the head of the Indragôpa[2] bird. Moreover, this elephant had six tusks (chhadanta), and its seven parts planted on the ground (four feet, two tusks, and trunk). Now, this young elephant, having grown up to its full size, was so piously endowed that it even fetched food and other necessaries for its parents, so that it would never touch anything to eat himself till they had first been supplied. And so it happened that on one occasion, having wandered rather far in search of food, this elephant was seen by a certain chief of hunters, who, having set eyes on him, thought thus :

---

[1] According to certain teachers.

[2] But this is generally regarded as a beetle, or cochineal.

'An elephant like this none ought to ride but King Brahmadatta himself.' Having thought thus, he went straight to Brahmadatta and said, 'Mahârâja! you must know that in such and such a place there is a certain beautiful elephant, its body perfectly white, etc., fit only for your majesty to ride. May it please you, therefore, to send proper persons to the spot to trap this elephant and bring it to your majesty.' Then the Râja summoned his elephant trappers to his presence, and told them just what the lord of the huntsmen had stated, and then ordered them to go at once and take the elephant and afterwards bring him to his presence. Then these trappers, taking with them cords and snares, went to the spot indicated, and, by means of certain charms (calls) they soon caused the young elephant to approach the spot. No sooner had he come near than the trappers enclosed him in their snare, and having safely bound him, they brought him at once to Brahmadatta Râja.

"Then the king, seeing the party approaching, went forth to meet them, and was so charmed with the beauty of the captive animal that he exclaimed, 'There never was such a beautiful creature, fit only for a king to ride.' Then the king himself proceeded to feed and provide for the animal, using every kind of endearing gesture and attention. Nevertheless, the elephant did nothing but sigh and moan and weep. King Brahmadatta, seeing this, and wondering at it, came and stood in front of the creature, and, clasping his hands together in token of respect, spoke to it thus: 'I have given you every kind of choice food, I have taken every care that your cords and housings do not hurt you, and I have treated you with the utmost gentleness, and yet I see that your heart is so sad that all my tenderness is lost. How is it that you are so sorrowful! What can be done for you to give you any pleasure. Tell me and it shall be done!' Then the young elephant addressed Brahmadatta and said, 'I could explain it all in a moment, if that would give your Majesty any pleasure.' Then the king reflected, 'How wonderful to hear this creature reply to me in human language!' Then the king bade him tell him all the case and explain the matter thoroughly. On this the young elephant told him how he had been accustomed to feed his father and mother, and how he was trapped in the very place where he was seeking food for them, and then he represented how broken-hearted his parents would be, and he said, 'Let me but go give them some food, and I promise your majesty I will return and partake of all you provide for me.' Then the king was astonished beyond measure at the singular piety of the elephant, and he thought, 'I would rather myself be condemned to hell than prevent this faithful creature from fulfilling his duty to his parents.' So he loosed him at once and let him go, and bade him be ever happy in attending to the wants of his parents, and so the Gâtha says:

"'Go and welcome, thou faithful elephant Nâga,
Nourish and cherish thy parents as in duty bound.
I would rather lose my life, and end it now,
Than cause thee and them the grief of separation.'

"So Brahmadatta having set the elephant at liberty, he gradually found his way back to his native mountain. But meantime his mother, from grief at losing her son, had wept herself blind, and so had wandered away from the place where she had dwelt before, nor could she find her way back to the spot she had left. And now the elephant cub, coming to the place, and not seeing his mother, set up a loud cry and wept for very sorrow. Then the mother, hearing the cry and knowing the voice of her offspring, at once replied with a lamentable and tearful cry. The son, guided by the sound, soon came to the spot where his mother was, and seeing her standing unmoved by the side of a water-tank, he ran forward, and, filled with joy, he took his trunk full of water and bathed his mother with the cooling stream. Then the mother, through the power of that refreshing stream, recovered her sight, and perceiving her offspring before her, she asked what had befallen him that he had been absent so long from her. Then he told her his adventure, and when she had heard it she exclaimed, as she rejoiced with exceeding joy, 'Oh! may that merciful Râja Brahmadatta partake with me in my happiness, and never want wife or child, servant or minister, to wait upon him and supply all his requirements.'

"Then Buddha explained that at that time he was the young elephant king—the elephant-mother was Mahâprajâpati Gotamî, and that she recovered her sight in the same way as the elephant dam had done."

The History of the conversion of Nanda.

§ 2. Now it came to pass that the world-honoured one, amidst all the followers whom he had converted, regretted most of all not to find Nanda, the Sâkya Prince. He had repeatedly urged him to leave his home and follow him, but Nanda had refused, saying he would gladly administer of his substance to the support of Buddha and the priests, but that he would not leave his home and become a disciple. All his invitations having been in vain, the world-honoured one, having finished his noon-day meal, taking with him one disciple, proceeded to the house of that Sâkya Prince, Nanda. Now just at this time Nanda was on the top of his house with his female companion (Sundarî), and, as they loitered up and down and looked about, or sat down, suddenly they saw the world-honoured one approaching. Then, through a feeling of reverence, Nanda got up, and, descending from the tower, went forth to meet Buddha, and bowed down at his feet. Having then stood on one side he spake thus: "Welcome, O Lord! Whence dost thou come? Oh, enter, I pray you, my unworthy mansion and rest awhile!" On this, the Lord entered the house of Nanda and took a seat. Having spoken a few complimentary words, he then sat silent. On this, Nanda began to speak, and asked the Lord if he would partake of either food or drink. But Buddha assured him he had already eaten and required nothing in addition. Then Nanda replied, "But may I not offer you a dish of broth (congee) provided at an irregular[1] hour?" Buddha replied to Nanda, "As you please." Then Nanda said, "Even so, my Lord!" and he took Buddha's patra, and, filling it up with congee, he offered it to him as a meal provided at an irregular hour. But Buddha hesitated to accept it, as did also the attendant he had brought with him, and then Buddha, with his follower, rose from his seat, and made as though he would return to his dwelling-place.

Then Nanda, the Sâkya Prince, taking the patra full of honey and rice, went out and followed Buddha. Meantime his sweetheart (Sundarî) at the top of the tower, seeing Nanda carrying a patra full of honey and rice out of the house, called out to him and said,

---

[1] "*Fi shi tseung,*" an extraordinary supply of food—*i. e.* exceptional or irregular as to time.

"Nanda, my Prince! (Arya) where are you going?" On this Nanda, pointing to the dish he held in his hands, said that he was going to offer the food therein contained to Tathâgata, and would immediately return home. Then Sundarî replied, "Oh, do come back soon, and don't let anything delay you."

Meantime, the world-honoured one, having left Nanda's house, began to walk here and there, and to stop in the different streets of the town, wishing everyone to see Nanda following him with the dish full of (unseasonable) food. So when the people saw it, they began to say, "Why Nanda has become a disciple, and is following his master!"

At length the Lord, having arrived at the Sañgharama, made a sign with his hand to one of the Bhikshus to take the dish full of food from the hand of Nanda. On this the Bhikshu, perceiving the intention of the Lord, went straightway up to Nanda and took the dish. Then Nanda, bowing his head in reverence, desired permission to return to his home; on which Buddha replied, "Nanda! return not to your house, abide here." But Nanda urged that he wished not to become a recluse, but rather to remain in a position to show hospitality and charity to the Lord and the priests.

Then Buddha replied, "In this vast continent of Jambudwîpa, which is seven thousand yojanas across, broad at the top, narrow at the bottom, like the tapering of a chariot from front to rear, there are a vast number of priests, numerous as the tender shoots which grow up in a bamboo plantation. Now, suppose there were a pious man or woman who carefully tended all these Rahats, and provided them with a sufficiency of all the articles of the four sorts they needed, and after their Nirvâna erected monuments over their ashes, and presented before these monuments every kind of religious offering—flowers, incense, lamps, etc.; tell me, Nanda! do you think that man or woman would acquire much merit or little?" Nanda replied, "very much merit, oh Lord!"

"Nevertheless," said Buddha, "the man who leaves his home to become my disciple, has much greater merit. Moveover, Nanda! you should be satisfied that the enjoyment of pleasure is momentary and passing, and is attended with much sorrow; for all the indulgences of sense are impermanent and perishing, full of evil and misery—regard them so, oh Nanda! and you will cease to hanker after them, and desire to escape from their power."

Nanda hearing this discourse about the misery of bodily indulgence, although he had no real desire to become a recluse, yet out of deference to Buddha, acquiesced and said, "I ought to become a disciple." On this, Buddha made a sign to one of the Bhikshus, and desired him to send for the hair-cutter at once, who having arrived, approached to Nanda as though to shave his head; on this Nanda addressed him and said: "What advantage will it be, if you do cut off my locks?" to whom Buddha replied, "Suffer it to be so; for thus you enter into my community, and by the very discipline, you cast away all sorrow, and put an end to all the sources of misery." Then Nanda permitted him to shave his head, and after seven days he assumed the Kashâya robes, and the alms-dish, and so completed the act of professed discipleship.

Now Nanda was a man of great personal beauty, his body straight and comely and of a golden hue, and just like that of Tathâgata. So he had a Kashâya garment made similar to his master's, and having received it, he put it on. Then all the Bhikshus, seeing him at a distance gradually approaching the assembly, thought that he was the lord himself, and so proceeded to rise from their places to salute him, and only when they discovered their mistake did they return. Then the Bhikshus expostulated with Nanda for having a garment precisely the shape and size of their lord's, and represented the case to Buddha himself; on which he asked Nanda if it were so, and when he said, "Yes! my Lord! it is as you say," then he forbad it, and said, "From this time forth, let no Bhikshu presume to wear a garment (sañghati) of the same size as mine! or if he does, let him be dealt with as the law (Pratimôksha) directs!" Then Nanda thought thus—"The master does not allow my garment to be of equal size with his, at any rate I may have a beautifully adorned and shining one (bespangled)!" And so he assumed one of this character, and with painted eyes, and luxurious slippers, his umbrella in his left hand and his alms-dish in his right, he proceeded to the spot where Buddha was and said, "Lord! I desire to go to the town and beg my food!" Then Buddha answered and said, "It is clearly out of the question, and impossible, oh youth! for surely you have accepted the vows and become a recluse, is it not so?" "True! my lord!" Nanda answered, "it is so." "Then if this be the case," said Buddha, "what means this bespangled garment, and your body so cared for, your eyes anointed with unguents, and your feet shod with delicate slippers, that umbrella in your hand, and the pâtra in the other as if you were going to beg? If, Nanda, you were living in a desert place (Arañyaka), and your garments were soiled and unpretentious, you might then be permitted to go a begging to get food enough to keep you alive; but not as the case is now." And then the world-honoured one added this Gâtha and said—

"When shall we see this Nanda,
Dwelling in a desert spot, go a-begging?
Contented with little; careless about the rest;
And rejoicing to have got rid of all anxious thought!"

Then the lord, moved by this circumstance, assembled the Bhikshus and said, "Brethren! from henceforth let none of my disciples wear a decorated robe, or use any unguents, or lightly hold his pâtra, and so go a-begging; whoever commits himself thus, let him be dealt with according to the law."

Nevertheless, Nanda, though obliged to give up his beautiful robe and the other personal adornments we have named, could not forget the joys of his royal home, and the delight afforded him by the company of Sundari, and so all day long in his retreat he did nothing but draw the figure of his sweetheart on a fragment of a tile, with a burnt piece of stick as a pencil, and delight himself with gazing at her from morning till night. Then Buddha, having been acquainted with the circumstance, assembled the Bhikshus, and solemnly warned them against any such misconduct as this, and forbad it under penalty of expulsion from the community. Then again, at a certain time Nanda was commissioned, according to his turn, to take charge of the Vihâra and guard it. On which he began to think thus—"Tathâgata is going to the town to beg his food, I will take the opportunity of escaping and returning to my home!" The lord, knowing his thoughts, said to him before he departed, "Nanda! if you should have occasion to leave the Vihâra, be sure before you go to close all the doors of the different apartments." The world-honoured one having said this, departed at once for the town, to beg his daily meal. Then Nanda thought thus—"Now is my opportunity for escape and to return home;" so going out of the Vihâra, he saw that the door of the lord's chamber was open, he went therefore and closed it; and as he did so, he thought, "I will just shut this one door and then hasten to my home." No sooner had he shut this door, than he saw the door of Sariputra's chamber wide open, then he ran to shut that door and thought, "Now then I will go back to my home," but just then he saw Mogalan's door standing open, and so he ran and shut it; no sooner had he done that, than he saw the door of Mahâkâsyapa's chamber open [and so on with [1] Mahâkâtyâyana's, Uravilva Kâsyapa's, Nadikâsyapa's, Gayakâsyapa's, Upasena's, Kuvira's[2] (?), Mahachunda's, Revata's, Upalivata's door]. Having thus gone from cell to cell shutting the doors, and seeing that he had no sooner shut one than another opened, and when he shut that, another—Nanda began to think thus with himself, "It is no use taking any more trouble, these Bhikshus will be sure to find fault with me, whether the doors are open or shut. I will hasten away and return home, for the master will be back soon." Having thought thus, he hurried through the Nyagrodha garden wishing to escape; but just then the world-honoured one, by his spiritual power perceiving what was taking place, immediately transported himself to the spot, and entered the Nyagrodha garden just as Nanda was hastening away from the Vihâra towards Râjagrîha. Suddenly catching sight of Buddha, Nanda sat down behind a tree to conceal himself. But the lord by his power caused the tree to rise straight up into the air, and so Nanda was discovered sitting in his place of concealment.

Buddha then addressed him—"Where are you going, Nanda?" to which he replied, "I was going back to my home, for I cannot reconcile myself to give up the pleasures of my palace and the society of Sundari, and I can find no comfort in the practice of the Brahma-chariya (continence), I therefore desire to give up the attempt and to return home." Then Buddha, on account of this confession, spake thus—

"Does the man who wishes to escape from the wood,
When escaped, return and enter it again?

---

[1] Kia-tchen-yen for Kia-to-yen-na.
[2] Kauchtila? or Mahakauchtila.

You, oh Vâgara! seeing these things,
From the net escaped, return you to the net."[1]

Then the lord, having recited this fragment of the law for the good of Nanda, further exhorted him in these words, "You should, oh [2]venerable Nanda, compose your mind to obey the directions of my law, and so entirely rid yourself of all disappointment and sorrow in the diligent practice of self denial and abstention." Thus the world-honoured one instructed Nanda; but notwithstanding all this, he could not forget the pleasures of his former life, and he still longed to give up his religious profession, and to return home to his palace and his mistress.

Now about this time, a certain nobleman asked Buddha to partake of hospitality at his house, on which occasion it happened to be Nanda's turn to take charge of the temple and guard it; at this time Nanda thought, "I will take this opportunity while the lord is away to return to my home." But Buddha, knowing his thoughts and his purpose, spoke to him before he went, "Remember, Nanda! that you must sweep and water the temple, and fill all the pitchers (kundikas) with water." On this the master went to the town. Meantime Nanda reflected thus—"What should prevent me returning home at once." Whilst thus planning his escape, he looked towards the cell of Buddha and saw it was full of dirt, on which he thought, "I will just sweep out the dirt from the cell of Buddha, then I will go." Resolving on this, he went in and fetched a broom and proceeded to carry out his purpose. But as soon as he had brushed the dirt away, a breeze seemed to spring up and blew it all back again, leaves and dust and dirt. Then Nanda thought, "I will just run and fill up the different pitchers (kundikas) of the priests, and then I will hurry home." Thinking thus, Nanda went to each cell, and taking the water-vessels filled them up in succession, but no sooner had he filled up one than it upset and all the water was wasted again. Then Nanda thought, "what is the use of trying to sweep up the dirt, or fill the water vessels—it is all in vain. Tathâgata will soon be here; I will hurry home as fast as I can."

---

[1] Fu-ka-lo. There seems to be a play on the word "Vâgurâ," a net. *Vide* also *Kai-yuen-shi-kian-mu-lu,* vol. i, fol. 20.

[2] Chang-lo, it may be "oh honourable."

Thinking thus, he hastened through the Nyagrodha wood, intending to return to his palace. Then the world-honoured, as he sat in the nobleman's house, by the exercise of the power of divine sight (samanta chakku), perceived how the case was with Nanda, and so, by his power of transformation, he passed unseen from the nobleman's house straight to the Nyagrodha wood, and there appeared right in front of Nanda, as he was hurrying onwards towards Râjagriha. Then Nanda, seeing Buddha, and wishing to hide himself from him, ran down a high bank into a hollow, and there crouching down, sat still. Then Buddha, by his spiritual power, caused that hollow place to become level as one's hand. Seeing Nanda there, he asked him whither he was going, and on what business? Then Nanda again told his master that he had no heart for the life of an ascetic, and he longed to go back to his palace and the arms of Sundarî his mistress.

Then Buddha began to discourse on the deceptive character of female beauty; he bade Nanda think that the body which he was so enamoured of was but a collection of bones and flesh—within it, what vileness and filth, what impurity and disgusting secretions, etc.; and then he added as an argument, the following verses again:

"Does the man," etc. [as before].

And then Buddha dwelt on the power of religion and self-control to secure peace and expel sorrow. But the teaching was all in vain, for Nanda still longed for a life of pleasure, and could not endure the restraint of discipleship.

And so it came to pass that he got six of the common (lewd) sort of priests to come to him, and from morning till night they did nothing but talk about worldly matters and forbidden pleasures. Then Buddha, perceiving the evil consequences of this conduct, determined to break off the intimacy between Nanda and these worthless priests, sent a message to him, and said, "Nanda! the Tathâgata wishes you to accompany him to Kâpilavastu." Nanda readily assented to this intimation, and so they went together. On entering the city, they gradually passed along till they came to the shop of a fishmonger. Then Tathâgata, seeing within the shop a mat of straw, on which a hundred and more dead and stinking fish were placed, he bade Nanda go inside and bring him a handful of the straw; having done this and held it in his hand a little while, Buddha told him to fling it away. After this, the Master bade him smell his hand, and asked him if he perceived anything disagreeable? On this, Nanda explained that the smell of the fish was most offensive and impure.

[Kiouen LVI contains 5784 words, and cost 2.892 taels].

CHAPTER LVII.

§ 1. Whereupon Buddha replied, "very true! very true, Nanda! and so it is if a man keep evil company; the influence of this society will always affect the life of such a person, and produce its evil consequences;" and then he recited this Gâtha:

"Just as a man living in a fisherman's hut,
Takes in his hand a single straw on which fish had been placed,
And so scents himself with the stink of the fish,
So is he who keeps bad company."

(And then Buddha enters a perfumer's shop, and taking a small quantity of scent, and placing it on Nanda's hand, he addresses him thus):

"As when upon the hand is poured a little scented water,
Or aromatic powder of any kind,
The power of the perfume destroys all other scent,
Such is the influence of a virtuous friend upon the life."

Then Buddha, having left Kâpilavastu and returned to his own place, being surrounded by his disciples, he addressed Nanda thus: "Nanda! if you desire the company of friends, choose not the bad, or the six Bhikshus with whom you have now made alliance, but consort with Mogalan, or Saripûtra, or Mahâkâsyapa, or Katyâyana, or Uravilvakâsyapa, etc., and then credit shall be given you. And then he recited these verses:—

"If a man makes friends of bad men,
He will lose his character, even in this world.
By the influence of such companions
A man hereafter goes to hell,

But if one choose the good and virtuous as friends,
And follow their example in the daily work of life,
Though he may not come to great advantage (in the present world),
Still he shall escape the cause of future pain."

Notwithstanding all the advice of the world-honoured one, Nanda still hankered after the enjoyments of worldly rank and sensual pleasures. Whereupon Buddha resolved to have recourse to some expedient to wean him from these fascinations. So by his spiritual power he transported him from the Nyagrodha plantation, to the top of the *hiang-tsui* (perfume-drunken) mount. Now it happened that, owing to a heavy storm of wind, two branches of a tree had, by friction, become ignited, and so a great fire had taken place on that mountain; in consequence of this fire many of the monkeys inhabiting the mountain had been seriously burnt—amongst the number, one in particular was dreadfully disfigured; Buddha showing this one to Nanda, asked him if he saw the sad state to which it was brought. Whereupon Nanda replied, "Yes! indeed, world-honoured one, I see it."

Then Buddha asked him if his sweetheart was as beautiful as the burned monkey; on which Nanda having professed that there could be no comparison between the two, Buddha transported him at once to the Trâyastrinshas heaven, and showed him Sâkra with five hundred Devîs attending him, and then asked Nanda if his sweetheart was as beautiful as one of those Devîs; on which Nanda confessed that no comparison could be made, and that the burned ape was not more inferior to his sweetheart in point of beauty, than she was to the Devîs. (The rest of the history of Nanda is identical with that found in the *Manual of Buddhism*, pp. 205-6).

Whereupon, Nanda having arrived at the condition of a Rahat, Buddha declared to all his disciples that he was the most eminent of all his followers in point of mastery over the senses; and then he related this story : "I remember more than ninety-one kalpas ago, there was a Buddha born in the world, called Vipasyi Tathâgata, he lived in a city called Pandumati, where reigned a king called Pandu. In this city there was a rich Brahman who constructed for Vipasyi and his followers a bath-house, and was gratified beyond measure to see the spotless forms of the Bhikshus as they came forth from the bath. After the death of this Buddha, the Brahman erected a stûpa for his ashes, and greatly venerated it. [The story then proceeds to relate that this Brahman was Nanda in a former birth].

The History of Bhadraka and others.

§ 2. Now at this time, Devadatta seeing the number of Sâkya youths, who had left their families to become followers of Buddha, thought thus with himself: "I too will go to the place where Buddha resides, with a view to become one of his followers." On this, going to his parents, he explained his intention, and having received their consent, he clad himself in a beautiful garment, and proceeded in a sumptuous chariot, drawn by elephants, to the place where Buddha dwelt. Having arrived there and made known his purpose, the world-honoured one, looking into the previous history of Devadatta, saw that he was not in a condition to become a disciple, and so bade him return home again, and bestow his wealth in charity, so as to fit himself for the condition of a Bhikshu.

Devadatta then goes to Sariputra, Mugalan, and Kâsyapa, with a view to induce them to admit him into the fraternity, but they each refuse on the ground of their master's previous decision.

[Kiouen LVII contains 5930 words and cost 2.96 taels].

CHAPTER LVIII.

The History of Ananda and other disciples.

Now it came to pass that Devadatta having been refused admission into the fraternity by all the chief disciples, he returned to Kapilavastu, riding upon his white elephant. At this very time, also, Ananda had sought his parents' permission to join the community, but in vain, on account of some jealous feeling his mother had encouraged in her breast, because of Buddha's exceeding beauty, when he was living at home. Ananda having thus been thwarted of his intention, retired into a desert place, and by silence and self-inflicted austerities, gained the reputation of being a Rishi. On this his parents relented, and gave him permission to join the company of the Sâkya youths who had entered the community.

At this time there were at Kapilavastu two brothers, the younger called Maniruddha (*formerly called Aniruddha, Ch. Ed.*), the elder called Mahanama; the former of these had become a special favourite with Bhadraka, who had been anointed king of the Sâkyas in succession to Suddhôdana. This Bhadraka was the son of a Sâkya princess called "the dark Gotamî." And now, having reigned twelve years, it came to pass that Maniruddha gained the permission of his parents to become a recluse, on condition that the king also resigned his throne; and so Maniruddha proceeding to the palace found the king in the Nâtaka Hall, listening to the music of his dancing women. After a time he entered, and proceeding to the king saluted him, and stood on one side. [After some discussion, the king agrees to become a recluse on the expiration of a week].

And so it came to pass, that Bhadraka, Maniruddha, and all the remaining Sâkya princes on a day agreed upon, advanced to the place where Buddha was residing, in a village called Anumegha, and having saluted him in the customary manner, requested to be admitted into his community; whereupon Buddha gave his consent, and admitted them all except Ananda and Devadatta. These two accordingly proceeded to the Himatâla Region, and joined themselves to the company of a Paribrâjaka, called Sangha. After remaining with him some time, Ananda desired to return to the place where Buddha was, and having obtained permission of his master (Upâdyâya) Sangha, he prepared to set out.

[Kiouen LVIII has 6244 words and cost 3.122 taels.]

CHAPTER LIX.

The History of Bhadraka and others—*continued.*

Now when Devadatta saw Ananda about to leave the place where their master resided, he asked him whither he was going. On being informed, he begged Ananda to wait until he also obtained permission to accompany him. And so they went both together, and having arrived at the place where Buddha was residing, they made their obeisance and stood on one side. Then Devadatta addressed Buddha as follows: "I formerly requested permission to enter your community, world-honoured! but you refused permission: do you object now to see me the disciple of another—for a recluse I have become." To whom the world-honoured replied, "Devadatta! and why have you done so? why have you thus turned against me?"

Then the other disciples seeing the constant enmity which Devadatta bore Tathâgata, requested to know the reason of it; on which the world-honoured related the following story.

The Story of the Bird with two heads.[1]

"I REMEMBER in years gone by, there was a two-headed bird re-

---

[1] This story is also found in the "Panchatantra" (translated by Lancereau), book v, fable 14, and also in the "Avadânas" (translated by Stas. Julien, cv). It seems likely that our own "swan with two necks" may be derived from it. Ensigns bearing this emblem may be derived from the same source. The moral of the tale is evidently the necessity of agreement between the members of the "body corporate," denoted by the two heads, *i. e.*, "king and people." [The fable found *supra*, p. 231, "the foolish dragon," is also in the "Panchatantra," book iv, fable 1, *Le singe et le crocodile*].

siding in the Himatâla Region; the name of the one head was Garuda, of the other Upagaruda. Now when this bird with two heads wished to sleep, the heads took it in turn which should watch; if Garuda slept, then Upagaruda watched (and *vice versâ*). Now it so happended, that once on a time whilst Garuda was watching, and Upagaruda asleep, that they were close to a Madhuka tree, which was in full bloom. And so, fanned by the breeze, a lovely blossom of the tree was wafted close to Garuda's beak. Whereupon the wakeful head began to reflect thus: 'Although I should eat this blossom by myself alone, yet when it enters our stomach, both of us will enjoy its exquisite flavour.' And so the head that was awake eat the flower unknown to the other.

"When therefore Upagaruda awoke, perceiving from his inward sensations that something delicious had been eaten during his rest, he said to his companion, 'Where did you get the scented blossom which I perceive, from my inward sensations and flavoured breath, you have eaten during my sleep?' The other replied, 'Whilst you were asleep, I saw a Madhuka blossom wafted by the air close to my beak, and as I thought you would benefit from it as well as myself, I ate it without naming it to you.' Then Upagaruda was very angry on this account, and vowed that he would eat what he liked when the other was asleep, and not say a word about it. And so they lived on, and time passed, till once they happened to alight near a certain poisonous tree, and Garuda went to sleep whilst the other watched. Then the head that was awake seeing a blossom of the poisonous tree near him, began to think thus, 'I will eat it even if it kills us both.' So snatching it up, he swallowed it. Then the other perceiving himself in pain awoke, and at once challenged his companion with having eaten something whilst he was on watch. 'Yes,' said the other, 'I have eaten a blossom of yonder poisonous tree, and we shall both die.' 'Alas! what a suicidal and wicked act,' said the other, 'why have you acted so?' And so the Gâtha says:

"'You in days gone by were once asleep,
And then I ate a luscious perfumed flower,
Borne on the gentle breeze close to my beak;
On this account you entertained an angry temper.
So every foolish man, bereft of faith and reason,
Plots against those with whom he lives,

And desiring to bring them to destruction,
Destroys himself and them together.'

Then Buddha said, "at that time I was Garuda, and Devadatta was Upagaruda. And so because I have acquired supreme wisdom and desire by benefitting myself to benefit others, he has contracted a spirit of hatred and revenge against me, and would gladly destroy me if he could."

And so it happened that the several Sâkya princes having entered the community, obtained the condition of Rahats, except Ananda, who only acquired the first step (Sowan).

Bhadraka, meantime, overwhelmed with joy, could do nothing but exclaim, "ah me! what delight! ah me! what delight!" and the other disciples hearing him thus constantly repeating these words, asked Buddha to explain why he did so. On this, the world-honoured one having sent for Bhadraka, asked him to explain why he repeated nothing else but the words, "ah me! what joy."

[On this Bhadraka relates his experiences when he was a king. How he feared death in a thousand shapes, although surrounded by troops and guards; and how he looked forward to the future with dread. But now, though alone in the forest, or in the solitude of the mountain, "I have no fear," he said, "and my mind is in perfect peace as to the future, and therefore I exclaim 'ah me! what joy!'"]

Buddha next explains how Bhadraka, in a former birth, was made "king of the beggars" of Benares, by Brahmadatta. Having given some food to a Pratyeka Buddha, he was born in consequence as a Sâkya prince, and became Râja of Kapilavastu, and finally a Rahat.

Now it so happened, that on one occasion Bhadraka, after becoming a Rahat, having received some food from a number of beggars who had come out from Sravasti, was observed by Pasena (Pasenajit), king of Kosala, who was riding on his white elephant, in company with Silabhadra, his chief minister. On inquiry, Pasena found out who the recluse was; whereupon he desired his minister to approach to Bhadraka, riding on his elephant. Being not far off, the Râja descended and approached the saint. He then inquired why he received such food as this at the hands of the beggars. To this Bhadraka replied, "Mahârâja! it is not because of my poverty that I receive food from these beggars; for indeed I possess seven precious kinds of wealth. But I would gladly make these poor people, and all living things as rich as myself, and so I take their food. Having my eyes opened, I would also recover them and all others from the blindness of ignorance, and open their eyes. Having escaped from the meshes of anger and passion, I would set them and all others at liberty also. Having crossed over the sea of sorrow and trouble, and arrived at the other shore, I would gladly rescue them also and others from the waters that engulf mankind. Having escaped from all chance of sickness or disease, I would gladly heal these and all others also, and therefore I accept their food." Then Pasena replied, "Holy one! (arya) I also am poor, and without the seven precious possessions of which you speak; would that you would pity me also, and come frequently to my house for food." Bhadraka having assured him that such a step was unnecessary, departed from the king.

[Kiouen LIX contains 6,124 words, and cost 3.062 taels.]

CHAPTER LX.

History of Maniruddha and others.

On a certain occasion Buddha, residing at Benares, in a place occupied by an old Rishi, in the Deer Park, requested Maniruddha to proceed to the city to gather alms for himself and the community. Maniruddha accordingly proceeded to beg from door to door, but with no success. Suddenly, in a miraculous manner, there appeared five hundred vessels full of food, which accompanied him back to the Deer Park, and so afforded sufficient food for the whole community.

On this, Maniruddha having returned to the preaching hall and sat down, exclaimed, "wonderful! wonderful indeed is the miraculous power of our teacher. This event that has just happened puts me in mind of what occurred in days long ago, when there was a dreadful famine in Benares, so fatal to the inhabitants, that all the neighbourhood was filled with the dead, and the fields covered with bleached bones and skeletons. Now there was a poor man in the city at that time, without any means of support, and his supply of food nearly all gone. Just then a Pratyeka Buddha having gone round from house to house a-begging, had got nothing, and was returning to his hermitage to sit in meditation. The poor man having perceived this, went after him, and invited him to share with him his two last handfuls of cockle seed, and took him back to his house for this purpose. After the repast, the Pratyeka Buddha having departed, the poor man went out into the neighbouring cemetery (Sitavana) to pick up a few sticks. Everywhere he was surrounded by skeletons. Suddenly one of these skeletons jumping up, sprang on to the back of the poor man, and twisting his legs round his neck, could not be got off. It was in vain he used his utmost force; he could not free himself from the skeleton on his back. At length, when the sun was just sinking in the west, and darkness coming on, the man tried to reach his home unobserved. But as he entered the city, some men perceiving him carrying this skeleton on his shoulders, cried out, 'Psha, man, what are you going to bring that skeleton into the town for?' On this he answered, 'Indeed, my good friends, I have exerted my utmost strength in vain, for I cannot get the thing off my shoulders. Do you all come and try to help me.' On this, the men came and all began to pull at the skeleton's legs and arms; but all for no purpose, for there he remained unmoved and unmovable. Hereupon the poor man gradually crept to his abode, and having opened the door and gone in, all of a sudden the white-boned skeleton changed itself into yellow gold and fell off his shoulders on to the ground. Then the man seeing this wonderful sight, said to himself, 'I will not keep all this treasure to myself; I will share it with others.' On this he went to king Brahmadatta, and said, 'Mahârâja, be it known to you I have discovered a treasure, and I wish it to be used for the good of the country.' On this, Brahmadatta calling his attendants, bade them accompany the man back to his house. Having reached the door and gone in, the man pointed to the gold on the floor and said, 'behold the treasure!' But to the attendants there appeared nothing but the bones of a skeleton; and so turning to the poor man, they said in a rage, 'How dare you, sirrah, mock us thus? We will return to the king and acquaint him with your impudence.' On this, going back to the palace, they explained what had happened. The poor man, however, nothing daunted, soon followed them to the king, and besought him to come and see for himself the treasure he had discovered. On this, Brahmadatta Râja set out in company with the citizen, and, arriving at his house, there saw a ghastly skeleton lying on the floor, whilst the man, pointing to it with exultation, exclaimed, 'There, Maharâja, lies the treasure of which I spoke.' On this, the king, turning to him, indignantly said, 'How dare you, fool that you are, presume to mock me thus! What makes you call this stinking skeleton a golden treasure?' On this, he replied, 'Indeed, Maharâja, it is pure gold, and nothing else.' And he thrice asseverated that it was no skeleton. At length, taking up some of the pieces in his hand, he uttered the following vow: "If this gold was conferred on me for some good deed done in times gone by, oh! let the king, let the king Brahmadatta also perceive that it is gold!' Having uttered this prayer, suddenly the Râja's eyes were opened, and he saw before him a heap of gold, and then said, 'Well done, my friend! What good deed of yours has brought this good fortune to your house? What spirit or deva have you entertained to give you such a treasure as this?' Then he related what he had done for the Pratyeka Buddha, much to the delight of the king.

"Now, at this time the Pratyeka Buddha was Tathâgata in a former birth, and the poor man was Maniruddha (the speaker)."

[The text then proceeds to relate in Gâthas to what wonderful consequences the gift of the handful of cockle seed led, through an indefinite series of births.]

The remainder of this chapter is filled with some trifling allusions to Ananda in his former births. The whole concludes with a story of Ananda when going to Sravasti to beg. On this occasion he came to a large tree midway between the Jetavana Monastery and the town. This tree, called Sisava, was the resort of numerous

Brahmans, who, as Ananda went along, challenged him to tell the number of leaves on the tree. Ananda answered with precision, "On the eastern branch there are so many hundreds and so many thousands; on the western branch so many hundreds and so many thousands." Having said this, he went on his way. Then the Brahmans, hoping to deceive him, gathered certain handfuls of leaves from the tree, and then, on Ananda's return, they inquired, "How many leaves did you say were on the tree?" Ananda, perceiving at once their intention, replied, "On the eastern branches are so many hundreds and thousands (deducting a certain number), and on the western branches so many hundreds and thousands (deducting a certain number)." On hearing this reply, the Brahmans were convinced of the superior wisdom of Ananda, and, embracing the tenets of Buddha, became Rahats.

CONCLUSION.

There are three other leading disciples, viz., Pûrnavasu, Kompira, and Nandaka, of whom nothing is known as to their previous births, but only that they became disciples.

It may be asked, "By what title is this Book to be called?" to which we reply, the Mahâsañghikas call it "Ta-sse" (*great thing.* Mahavasṭu).[1] The Sarvastavadas

---

[1] So I would restore *Ta-sse.* Wassilief (§ 114, *Bouddisme*) gives

call it "Ta-chong-yen" (*great magnificence.* Lalita Vistara).[1] The Kasyâpiyas call it "Fo-woug-yin-un" (*former history of Buddha*). The Dharmaguptas call it "Shi-kia-mu-ni-Fo-pen-hing" (*the different births of Sakya-Muni-Buddha*). [This was the first translated into Chinese, about A.D. 70.] The Mahisasakas call it "Pi-ni-tsong-kan" (*Foundation of the Vinaya Pitaka*).

[Kiouen LX contains 5,924 words, and cost 2.962 taels.]

---

us *da-cine* as the equivalent of the Chinese characters, but I think there must be an error of type here.

[1] So restored by Wassilief (§ 176, *cp. cit.*)

THE END.

ADDITIONS AND CORRECTIONS.

Title Page.—I use the compound "*Chinese-Sanscrit,*" in order to denote the mixed language in which Chinese Buddhist books are generally composed. It must be remembered that the greater number of these works were translated into Chinese by natives of India.

P. 1, n. 3.—The "Pure Heavens" are called in the Southern Records "Suddháwása Brahmaloka, from whence there is no return to the world." *Vid.* J. A. S. B., Sep. 1838.

P. 6.—Omit the "R" in J. R. A. S. B., and in all subsequent cases.

P. 9.—The "True Law" and "Law of Images," two important epochs in Buddhist development; the first extended over five hundred years after Buddha's death, the second over the succeeding thousand years.

P. 13, line 7.—For "*Bodhuatwa,*" read "*Bodhisatwa.*"

P. 26.—For § 2, read § 1.

P. 28.—For "*Vâjora,*" read "*Vâjra.*"

P. 33, line 7.—Compare the Southern account "for the purpose of redeeming the world." J. A. S. B., Sep. 1838, p. 799.

P. 33, line 35.—For "*Kama,*" read "*Karma.*"

P. 34, line 25.—After "*exalted standard,*" place "2."

P. 35, line 21.—Omit the full stop after "on every side," and substitute a comma; also substitute a small "a" for the capital "A" in the word "At."

P. 35, line 22.—The constellation *Kwei* is called *Uttrá salha* in the Southern Records. J. A. S. B., Sept. 1838, p. 800.

P. 37.—It must be understood that the parentheses printed in italic, which occur in the text, are translated from the Chinese. They are so introduced, to indicate that they are explanations of the previous subject matter.

P. 38, line 2.—For "*Brahmas*," read "*Brahmans*."

P. 41.—For remarkable agreements between the circumstances of Bôdhisatwa's birth, and the legendary (apocryphal) accounts of Christ's birth, *vid. Lord Lindsay*, "Christian Art," vol. i, p. 44, and *ss*.

P. 43, line 5.—The account in the Christian legend makes a date tree to bend to the Blessed Virgin. The "Koran" says that the Virgin brought forth her Son under a withered date tree. (Lord Lindsay, *op. cit.*, 47.)

P. 47, line 9.—Compare this account of the birth of Bôdhisatwa from the side of his mother, with the less pleasing Orvieto sculpture of the creation of Eve. (*Hist. of our Lord*, by Mrs. Jameson, vol. i, p. 96.)

P. 52, line 20, ss.—Compare the account of the idol in the temple of the city of Hermopolis coming down and bowing before the infant Saviour, when Joseph and Mary entered the hospice. (*Apoc. Gosp. of the Infancy of Jesus*, cap. x. *Codex Apoc. N. Test.* i, p. 75.)

P. 55, line 1, ss.—It is worth while to compare with this account of the peculiar marks of Buddha's person, the description of Christ given in the apocryphal letter of Publius Lentulus to the senate of Rome.

P. 56, line 20.—For "attained," read "attain."

P. 57, line 22, ss.—The accounts given in the text agree closely with the Southern Records. (Compare J. A. S. B., Sep. 1838, p. 802.)

P. 58, line 2.—Compare the account in the text and picture in Mrs. Speirs' book, from the Cave of Ajunta, with the illustration 108, in Mrs. Jameson's work (cited above) after Guido.

P. 61, line 28.—For "previous," read "precious."

P. 79, line 32.—For "Suddârtha," read "Siddârtha."

P. 96, § 3.—This, of course, describes the custom known as "Svayambara," *i. e.*, "choice for oneself," about which, *vide* Mrs. Speirs and Talboys Wheeler, *passim*.

P. 104, note.—For "Ass." read "As."

P. 105, line 18.—No doubt the Deva T'so Ping is the same as Ghatíkára.

P. 121, line 25.—With this custom of circumambulating a sacred object or person *three times*, compare the "decursio" of the Roman soldiers, and the lines

"Ter circum accensos cincti fulgentibus armis
Decurrêre rogos."

P. 129, line 25.—The first watch extended from 6 P.M. to 10 P.M.; the second from 10 P.M. to 2 A.M.; and the third from 2 A.M. to 6 A.M.

P. 136.—The flight of Bôdhisatwa on his horse Kantaka, is the subject of the illustration on the cover of this work, copied from pl. lix, *Tree and Serpent Worship.*

P. 142, line 25.—Omit "to" after "or."

P. 145, line 1.—For "Kashya," read "Kashâya," and in all subsequent cases.

P. 165, line 6.—For "eating," read "eaten."

P. 173, line 21.—Of course *Karma* will be understood to signify "the necessary consequence of works done during some previous existence."

P. 176, note.—For "tsen," read "tseu."

P. 192, line 22, ss.—This incident seems to be the origin of the term Ajapâla, applied to this Nuga or Nyagrodha Tree; although the Southern Records say that it is so called because "shepherds and goatherds used to seek shelter under it."

P. 199, line 1, ss.—This seems to be the subject of pl. xxiv, fig. 2, *Tree and Serpent Worship.*

P. 221.—Compare this account of the army of Mâra, with the translation from the Thibetan (*Lalit. Vist.*, p. 293), and also note three on the same page.

P. 227, § 2.—Compare this story with that translated by M. Julien (*Les Avadânas, l'homme et la perle*, T. ii, p. 30).

P. 231, § 5.—This story is found in the Panchatantra (translated by Lancereau), book iv, fable 1.

P. 232, line 26.—For "Udambara," read "Udumbara," and so throughout. The Udumbara is the *Ficus glomrata.*

P. 239, line 8.—"Tripusha" may also be read "Trapusha."

P. 240.—The offering of the two merchants seems to be the subject of the sculpture, pl. lviii, pillar 1, middle disc, *Tree and Serpent Worship.*

P. 244, note.—For "Childer's," read "Childers'."

P. 251, line 20.—For "neither tend," read "tend neither."

P. 261, line 16.—For "who lately inhabited this heaven," read "who lately descended from the Tusita heaven."

P. 261, line 17.—For "he *has* arrived," read "he *will* arrive."

P. 273, line 27.—This "chatta appearing by itself" may be useful in distinguishing the story of Yasada from that of Bôdhisatwa, which it resembles so much.

P. 276, line 37.—Instead of "Sâgara," read "Sankha," and so throughout.

P. 278, line 7.—The six "Abidjnâs" are the six supernatural talents which Bodhisatwa acquired on the night before his complete enlightenment.

P. 288, last line.—Supply "towards," after "hurried."

P. 290, line 8.—It seems likely that the scene in fig. 2, pl. xxxv, *Tree and Serpent Worship*, represents this very dalliance of Senapati. The village at any rate is Uravilva.

P. 315, line 19.—Omit "during the season of the rains."

P. 319, line 4.—Omit the comma after "was."

P. 320, line 13.—For "Bikshuni," read "Bhikshuni," and so throughout.

P. 349, line 1.—The story of Yasodharâ is told at full length in the text. Among other proofs of her innocence she causes a large stone to float on the surface of the water, and on this stone she places her child. This incident is also narrated in the *Lalita Vistara.* The error corrected in the translation of M. Foucaux (*Lalita Vistara*, p. 431), is strangely repeated in the "Glossary" to the "Life of Bouddha Sakya-mouni," by Mme. Summers, p. 198.

P. 373, line 22.—For "Râjagriha," read "Kapilavastu;" and so also on p. 375, line 8.

[*There are so many Glossaries of Buddhist terms already published, that I have not thought it necessary to produce another*].

INDEX.

D D